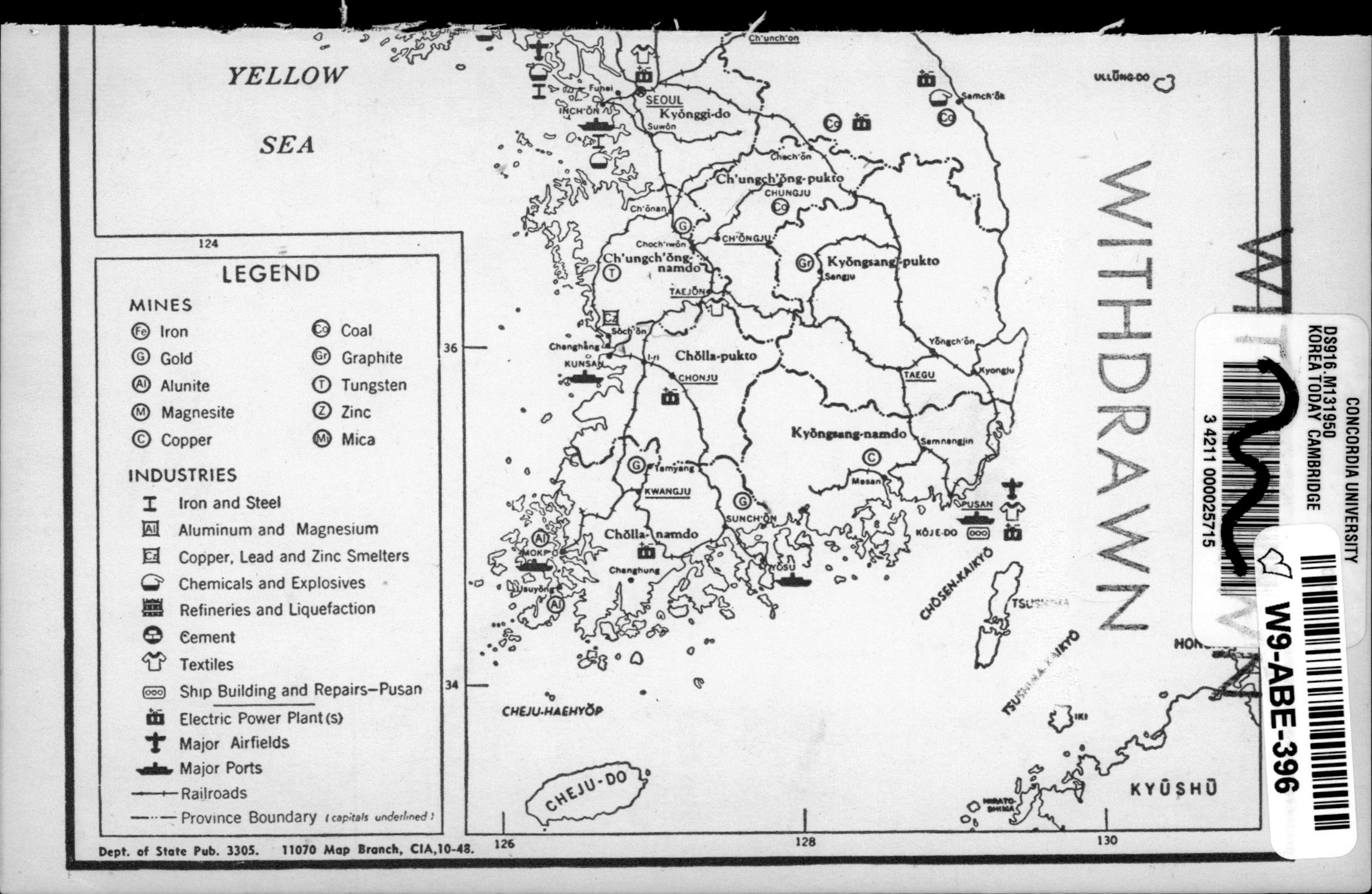
YELLOW
SEA
LEGEND
MINES
Iron
Gold
Alunite
Magnesite
Copper
Coal
Graphite
Tungsten
Zinc
Mica
INDUSTRIES
Iron and Steel
Aluminum and Magnesium
Copper, Lead and Zinc Smelters
Chemicals and Explosives
Refineries and Liquefaction
Cement
Textiles
Ship Building and Repairs—Pusan
Electric Power Plant(s)
Major Airfields
Major Ports
Railroads
Province Boundary (capitals underlined)
Ch'unch'on
SEOUL
Kyŏnggi-do
Suwŏn
Fusei
INCH'ŎN
Chech'ŏn
Ch'ungch'ŏng-pukto
CHUNGJU
Ch'ŏnan
Choch'iwŏn
CH'ŎNGJU
Ch'ungch'ŏng-namdo
TAEJŎN
Kyŏngsang-pukto
Sangju
Sŏch'ŏn
Changhang
KUNSAN
Chŏlla-pukto
CHONJU
Yŏngch'ŏn
Kyongju
TAEGU
Kyŏngsang-namdo
Samnangjin
Masan
Tamyang
KWANGJU
SUNCH'ŎN
PUSAN
KŎJE-DO
Chŏlla-namdo
Changhung
MOKPO
YŎSU
CHŎSEN-KAIKYŌ
TSUSHIMA-KAIKYŌ
IKI
HIRATO-SHIMA
KYŪSHŪ
CHEJU-HAEHYŎP
CHEJU-DO
ULLŬNG-DO
Samch'ŏk
124
126
128
130
36
34
Dept. of State Pub. 3305. 11070 Map Branch, CIA,10-48.

KOREA TODAY

THE INSTITUTE OF PACIFIC RELATIONS

The Institute of Pacific Relations is an unofficial and non-partisan organization, founded in 1925 to facilitate the scientific study of the peoples of the Pacific area. It is composed of autonomous National Councils in the principal countries having important interests in the Pacific area, together with an International Secretariat. It is privately financed by contributions from National Councils, corporations and foundations. It is governed by a Pacific Council composed of members appointed by each of the National Councils.

In addition to the independent activities of its National Councils, the Institute organizes private international conferences every two or three years. The Institute conducts an extensive program of research on the political, economic and social problems of the Pacific area and the Far East. It also publishes the proceedings of its conferences, a quarterly journal, *Pacific Affairs*, and a large number of scholarly books embodying the results of its studies.

Neither the International Secretariat nor the National Councils of the Institute advocate policies or express opinions on national or international affairs. Responsibility for statements of fact or opinion in Institute publications rests solely with the authors.

NATIONAL COUNCILS

American Institute of Pacific Relations, Inc.
Australian Institute of International Affairs
Canadian Institute of International Affairs
China Institute of Pacific Relations
Comite d'Etudes des Problemes du Pacifique
Indian Council of World Affairs
Japan Institute of Pacific Studies
New Zealand Institute of International Affairs
Pakistan Institute of International Affairs
Philippine Council, Institute of Pacific Relations
Royal Institute of International Affairs
U.S.S.R. Council, Institute of Pacific Relations

IPR INTERNATIONAL SECRETARIAT

1 East 54th St., New York 22, N.Y.

KOREA TODAY

BY

George M. McCune

WITH THE COLLABORATION OF

Arthur L. Grey, Jr.

ISSUED UNDER THE AUSPICES OF
THE INTERNATIONAL SECRETARIAT
INSTITUTE OF PACIFIC RELATIONS

HARVARD UNIVERSITY PRESS
Cambridge 1950

1 East 54th Street
New York 22, N.Y.

II

Printed in the United States of America
American Book–Stratford Press, Inc., New York

To

Robert J. Kerner

Foreword

THE present volume is the outgrowth of a research project initiated by the International Research Committee of the Institute of Pacific Relations in 1947. Because of his long personal knowledge of Korea and his work on Korean problems for the U.S. Government during the war, Professor George McCune was selected as the most qualified scholar to write this general survey of postwar Korea. A short preliminary report of the project was made available as a document at the Tenth Conference of the Institute in 1947 and plans were subsequently made to revise and expand this into the present book. Despite repeated interruptions due to illness, Professor McCune succeeded in completing about nine-tenths of the study before his death in 1948 deprived the world of a devoted scholar.

The manuscript was completed during 1949 and 1950 by his wife, Mrs. Evelyn McCune, and Mr. Arthur L. Grey, who have made some additions to bring the study up-to-date, especially in regard to economic developments in Korea. I wish to express my deepest thanks to them for their assistance in completing the manuscript and to Miss Mary F. Healy for taking charge of publication arrangements.

Readers may be interested to know that Professor McCune was working on another study for the Institute of Pacific Relations, namely, *A Short History of Korea*. Only about four chapters of this study had been completed in first draft at the time of his death but it is still hoped that arrangements can be made for Mrs. McCune to complete this book.

The present study serves in part to supplement the earlier Institute study, *Modern Korea* (1942) by Dr. A. J. Grajdanzev. It is to be followed by a companion volume, a *Geography of Korea*, by Professor Shannon McCune of Colgate University.

Although this study is issued under the auspices of the International Secretariat of the Institute of Pacific Relations, it should be noted that the authors are responsible for all statements of fact or opinion expressed in the book.

WILLIAM L. HOLLAND,
Secretary General

New York, May 1950

Author's Preface

FOR some two thousand years of recorded history and another two thousand of legendary background the Korean people have developed a national character with all the accomplishments of a common cultural heritage, language, and way of life. The past few decades of their history have included first the twenty-year effort to play a part as a modern independent nation, then a forty-year period of colonial rule by the hated Japanese neighbors, ending with the so-called liberation of the country in 1945. Since then the new nation has been struggling against great odds to assume its rightful place as one of the larger small-nations of the world and to overcome the disintegrating effects of past history and of international rivalries which have divided the country in military occupation, in ideology, and now even in autonomous government.

In examining the situation in the new Korea, the historian faces a formidable task in obtaining accurate information and unbiased interpretation. In many instances he has no access whatsoever to sources necessary for a true picture of even the major facts involved. Furthermore, the highly controversial nature of the contrasting ideologies and nationalisms in the two halves of the country makes extremely difficult an objective analysis of events. It is a perplexing task to give the Koreans their proper place in a drama which has been so dominated by the policies, personalities, and rivalries of the occupying authorities. Nevertheless, it has been my primary purpose in this volume to go beyond a mere description of the American and Soviet activities in Korea, and to present as clearly as possible the development of the Korean people during this period of transition.

The disparity between the amount of detailed material concerning the two areas will be immediately obvious to the reader. The southern zone occupied by the United States has naturally provided more information than the northern (Soviet) zone. However, as anyone who has used government reports is well aware, the information must be carefully used. This is also true of the opinions of the officials connected with the administration, as these men have been dealing with the highly explosive problem requiring considerable caution in reporting. The U.S. Military Government in Korea for a considerable period supplied monthly reports averaging over a hundred pages per issue, and later the South Korea Interim Government issued similar reports called the *SKIG Activities*. These reports form the most substantial body of source material, together with other official U.S. Army reports and subsequent reports issued by the U.S. Department of State.[1] Many journalists have visited the country and have written with varying degrees of bias on the ideological problem and on the American administration. Most of the reports for the northern zone have come either by way of Moscow or through refugees fleeing southward. Scattered published accounts concerning the administration and the various activities of the Soviet authorities and the subsequent Korean regime in the north have also been issued (mostly in Russian publications).

The book has been divided for convenience into two major sections on politics and economics and subdivided by presenting northern and southern zones in separate chapters. An ap-

[1] More recently, the Economic Cooperation Administration has provided fuller information on economic problems.—*Editor*.

pendix includes a selection of the major documents concerning international relations and economic statistics.

I am greatly indebted to many Korean and American friends who have supplied me with documentary material and with their own observations and opinions after service in Korea. Most of these friends I have been unable to cite in the following pages. A large proportion of Americans who have been associated with the American government in Korea are intensely concerned over the situation there and are deeply interested in the welfare of the Korean people.

I wish to make special acknowledgment of the help given me by Mr. Arthur Grey, a graduate economics student at the University of California who is named as my assistant in the preparation of this book. Mr. Grey entered Korea at the beginning of the occupation and saw much of the early economic developments in the transition from Japanese to "occupied" economy. He drafted in large measure the sections dealing with the economy of the country. However, the results and conclusions as presented herewith are entirely my responsibility, representing as they do my own opinions and point of view.

My wife has been of constant aid in all steps of writing this volume. It would have been impossible to complete it without her assistance. Because of my continued ill health during the preparation of this book, there have been many others who have provided material aid. I am particularly grateful for the friendly cooperation of my colleagues in the Department of History, particularly the Chairman, Professor John D. Hicks, and Professor Robert J. Kerner who arranged in various ways to provide me the time for this work as part of my University duties.

Though the study has been prepared for the International Secretariat of the Institute of Pacific Relations, at the request of its Secretary General, Mr. W. L. Holland, it should be noted that the Institute is not to be considered responsible for statements of fact or opinion in the book.

G. McCune

Note

THE reader who is unfamiliar with spoken Korean may be confused by the wide variations in the Romanized spellings of Korean words encountered in Western language materials. In general, the transliteration of Korean words and names occurring in the present study conforms to the McCune-Reischauer System for the Romanization of the Korean Language (as set forth in the *Transactions of the Royal Asiatic Society*, Korea Branch, Vol. XXIX, 1939) which resembles the Hepburn and Wade-Giles systems for the transliteration of Japanese and Chinese.

Pronunciation is according to the rule of sounding consonants as in English and vowels as in Italian. Since spoken Korean contains a wider array of vowel sounds than can be accommodated in the simple English alphabet, certain diacritical notations have been employed in transcribing. For present purposes, the reader need only take note of the sound ŏ which is pronounced like a in above. Certain other vowel sounds are: o as in moss, u as in full, ae as in bag, and oe as the German o. Aspirated sounds are indicated by ', such as n'. The plosives k, p, t, and ch should be pronounced without appreciable aspiration. When voiced, they are written g, b, d, or j.

Common usage makes it impossible to obtain complete uniformity in the transliteration of personal names. For example, the same Chinese character may be Romanized variously as Paik, Park or Pak, depending upon personal preference in evaluating the consonants and in reproducing the vowel sounds. Where the spelling employed in the text is at variance with the general phonetic rules (according to the McCune-Reischauer system), this deviation is to be explained by the fact that the person himself romanizes his name in that way (i.e., Rhee Syngman for Yi Syngman), or that the particular spelling is more familiar to Western readers (i.e., Kim Ilsung for Kim Ilsŏng). With the exception of the name Rhee Syngman which is frequently inverted in Western language sources to read Syngman Rhee, the surname always appears first in accordance with Korean usage. Korean personal names usually consist of three syllables (sometimes two, such as Kim Koo or Lee In) which represent a like number of Chinese characters. In the text the rule has been followed of representing the second and third syllable as a single word. Euphonic changes which arise in spoken Korean from the occurrence of certain sounds next to each other have been ignored.

Contents

Selected Documents Relating to Korean Foreign Relations

APPENDIX A

Tables

APPENDIX B

APPENDIX C

Introduction

BLACK List Forty was the code name for Korea to the U.S. combat troops which landed on Korean territory. It was an appropriate label as Korea soon became, during the three and a half years of occupation, the "end of the line" with respect to American military supplies and personnel as well as the principles and practice of American democratic ideals. U.S. responsibility for the present situation in Korea has been, and is, enormous. It is a responsibility shared, but not lessened, by the U.S.S.R. and by independence-hungry Korean leaders not yet prepared for full responsibility.

The Cairo declaration that "in due course Korea shall become free and independent," made by the chiefs of state of the United States, the United Kingdom and China on December 1, 1943, was reaffirmed at Potsdam on July 26, 1945, and subscribed to by the Soviet Union on August 8, 1945. Today Korea is divided by an artificial barrier, the 38th parallel; two governments claim sovereignty over all of Korea and operate in divergent patterns on each side of the line. Both governments are dependent upon outside forces and nations for aid and protection. Divided Korea today is far from being free and independent; it has made but few and faltering steps in that direction.

Officially the line was chosen to mark the separation between

Japanese forces which would surrender to the Russians and those that would surrender to the Americans. It was a hasty military decision, perhaps adequate for its limited military objective. But as time went on the line became one to separate two zones of occupation, two spheres in which contrasting methods of control were exercised, and finally two Korean governments which adapted the more divergent features of their sponsors. The North—the former Soviet Zone—has the larger area, roughly 48,300 square miles, but one-third the population, roughly 9,000,000. The South—the former American Zone—is roughly 37,000 square miles in area and now has over 20,000,000 inhabitants.

When the columns of the Soviet First Far Eastern Army marched into Korea from bases near Vladivostok in late August 1945, they were enthusiastically greeted by Koreans displaying pictures of Stalin and waving Korean and Allied flags. Troops of the U.S. Seventh Infantry Division, which landed at the west-coast port of Inchŏn on September 8, 1945, and then occupied positions in various parts of South Korea, enjoyed a similar popularity. Welcoming flags and banners were everywhere and American troops found themselves enthusiastically hailed by smiling Korean throngs. There could be no doubt of the genuineness of the expression of gratitude in these demonstrations, but if the American and Soviet forces took it for adulation, they were indeed mistaken.

The significance of the hurriedly-made Korean flags was lost on many of the foreign troops. They failed to realize that to most Koreans, the advent of foreign troops meant a liberation, a first step to freedom and independence. They were exultant over the liquidation of Japanese colonial rule to which they had been subjected for thirty-five years. However, they were also quick to suspect American and Russian intentions. As early as the second day of the occupation, Korean political leaders pressed U.S. Army officials for details on how the two occupying powers were going to cooperate in establishing a Korean government. They were not satisfied with the vague replies which their questions elicited.

The obvious signs of tension between the American and Russian areas of occupation could not be concealed behind assurances of cooperation. In South Korea, the hastily-made welcoming banners and flags quickly disappeared and with them faded the enthusiasm of the people toward the occupying forces as U.S.-Soviet disagreement became increasingly plain. If the festive atmosphere persisted in North Korea, it was because the Soviet Union and the puppet Korean regime were kept in the forefront of public attention by wholesale advertising of Communist slogans and symbols on literally every wall and in every shopwindow.

It was not surprising that the Korean people were quickly disillusioned with the occupation and gravely concerned over their country's future. Koreans were simply displaying their sense of political realism, acquired by long experience with the effects of foreign rivalry, when they read the intentions of the United States and the Soviet Union from the conspicuous absence of cooperation between the two powers and from the unofficial insinuations they made against each other, rather than from official high-sounding assurances of unanimity. In the following three years of occupation, the two powers demonstrated that their activities in Korean affairs were influenced by bitter disagreement in the tradition of earlier international rivalries which had been so largely responsible for the destruction of Korean independence.

The United States has a peculiar responsibility for Korea in spite of official efforts to ignore, deprecate, or side-step it. The U.S. was the first Western nation to break into Korea's medieval isolation by means of its 1882 treaty of amity and commerce. For twenty years after the signing of this document American representatives were favored at the Korean Court. They were considered influential agents of a friendly power during a period when Korea was subject to the pressures of a major rivalry between China and Japan and a minor one between England and Russia. China was eliminated as a possible ally in 1895, England in 1902, Russia in 1905. The two powers then left in the field were the United States and Japan. President Roosevelt saw no reason at that time for opposing Japanese expansion on the Asiatic continent and so, by the end of 1905, Japan had no competitor for Korea except the Koreans themselves and they were unable to stop the annexation which came in 1910. Fear of a possible re-enactment of invasion from a resurgent Japan is at present an obsession of Koreans, both north and south. They see in the present U.S. policy of the creation of a strong Japan, a terrifying resemblance to the events of 1902–1904, which resulted in a Russo-Japanese war and their own loss of statehood.

In South Korea the task of setting up a Korean government was nursed through many vicissitudes by the U.S. Army, Military Government and State Department. The Army Commander, Lt. General John R. Hodge, started out by rejecting the newly-organized Korean Republic which had been set up before American entry into the country. He solved the troubles attendant upon this move and that of an initial retention of Japanese officials by proclaiming that "Military Government is the only government" in South Korea. The U.S. Army Military Government in Korea was contracted to "USAMGIK," but its obvious dependence upon intermediaries led Koreans to call it "the interpreters' government."

The first attempts to provide a measure of Korean participation in the formulation of Military Government policies were unsuccessful. The Representative Democratic Council resembled the Japanese Central Advisory Council and was dominated by rightists. In December 1946 a more ambitious attempt to secure Korean participation was undertaken with the establishment of the South Korean Interim Government (SKIG) and the half-appointive, half-elective South Korean Interim Legislative Assembly (SKILA), which exercised limited powers within a framework of authority dominated by the military governor.

SKIG and SKILA managed to survive bitter internal crises, which, however, reduced them to impotence.

At Moscow, December 27, 1945, it was decided to establish a joint Soviet-American Commission which would work toward a unified provisional Korean government. However, the first session of the Joint Commission held in the spring of 1946 failed ostensibly over the question of the selection of Korean members. This was followed by top-level negotiation between Secretary of State Marshall and Foreign Minister Molotov where a compromise was reached allowing for the holding of a second conference. The second series held in the spring and summer of 1947 also failed. The United States then referred the whole problem of Korea to the United Nations for further action. The U.N. Temporary Commission on Korea (UNTCOK) supervised the holding of elections in South Korea in May 1948. The Assembly thus elected hastily set up its constitution, president, committees and cabinet under the direction of Syngman Rhee, in time for the formal investiture ceremony performed by General MacArthur August 15, 1948. Final action on the part of the United Nations Assembly, which had originally planned a coalition government, came in December and was, therefore, merely a benediction.

Developments in the northern zone of occupation followed a readier pattern, and the Soviet occupying forces speedily secured the establishment of a Korean regime which closely conformed with the Russian prototype within a very short time. Moreover, the Soviet Union was well acquainted with Korea and Koreans. The Imperial Russian government had been deeply involved in Korean affairs from 1896 until 1905, when Japan summarily ended its activity in the peninsula. During the period of Japanese control, thousands of Koreans took refuge in Outer Mongolia, Siberia, and the Russian Maritime Province. Koreans were active in the Communist International, and the Communist Party was in the vanguard of anti-Japanese activity in Korea.

It was a relatively simple matter, therefore, for the Soviet occupying forces to act effectively in Korea through local Communists and the cadre of Soviet Koreans who had come with the occupying forces. The directness of purpose of the Soviet forces and the existence of a body of highly-disciplined Korean Communists ready to carry out Soviet policy assured the speedy establishment of a typically Soviet regime. For this reason, there was, in reality, very little difference, in either organization or personnel, between the Soviet-sponsored People's Committee regime, established in the early weeks of the occupation, and the Democratic People's Republic of (northern) Korea, recognized by the Soviet Union as the sole legal Korean government in early September 1948.

Korea has a key position in contemporary Far Eastern politics, partially owing to the three-year American-Soviet occupation of the country. The establishment of two governments "in this small space of 85,000 square miles" has been catastrophic. The job ahead of Korean leaders in the construction of a modern state is a task whose magnitude might well appall them. They need time and capital, and they have neither. They need leadership and their leaders are unprepared. Owing to the despotism and inefficiency of Korean government under the old monarchy and the efficient but still despotic administration of the Japanese, leadership will be slow in developing from the common people.

Though the Korea of today is modernized in many essential respects the people are little better prepared for political responsibility in a modern world than they were in 1900. The Korean independence movement during the intervening years demonstrates this point in its lack of unified and directed action under the guidance of mature leaders. The only experience that Koreans have had in the exercise of democratic procedures has been in small village governments and in Christian institutions. Many Koreans are aware of their shortcomings and are exerting themselves in heroic ways to overcome their difficulties in time. They are aware that they must face the facts of their situation and that they must adopt a program of austerity if they are to succeed in launching their new state into a modern world. In the last analysis the problem is theirs. They are eager to accept their responsibilities, but if the 38th parallel cannot be abolished without a bloody civil war and if pressure from Russia cannot be alleviated and that from a renascent Japan be averted, their chance to retain their freedom has already ceased to exist.

CHAPTER ONE

The Historical Background

THE HISTORY OF AN OLD KINGDOM

KOREA has a long history. Located on a peninsula with admirable boundaries but with the disadvantage of being at a crossroads of civilization, and peopled by a race which many centuries ago became unified as a distinct group with its own physical and cultural characteristics, Korea has grown to a nation of twenty-nine million persons. Korea has also become one of the world's most acute trouble spots.[1]

The peninsula of Korea is roughly 150 miles wide and 600 miles long and has an area of 85,228 square miles. The country is mountainous with a coastline dotted with islands, a combination of scenic attractions which has given rise to a native poetical tradition in praise of the beauty of the land. On the north, the Yalu and Tumen rivers form the boundary which separates Korea from Manchuria. For a short distance of some eleven miles at the mouth of the Tumen River, Korea shares a boundary with Soviet Siberia. Famous Paektu (White Head) Mountain is the source of both rivers, with its highest peak rising to an elevation of over 9,000 feet.

Northern and eastern Korea is largely mountainous territory,

[1] There is no modern history of Korea written in the English language. An excellent short survey, drawing upon modern materials, may be found in an article by Sir Paul Butler, "A Korean Survey," *International Affairs*, July 1946, pp. 361-75.

whereas the southern and western sections are for the most part hill-and-valley country. The Diamond Mountains (called Kumgang-san by the Koreans), situated in central Korea next to the eastern coast, have long been a mecca for tourists from all parts of the Far East owing to the spectacular scenery found there.

Along much of the eastern coast the mountains rise abruptly from the seashore, a marked contrast with the western coast where the ground rises gradually from the shore. The western half of the country is therefore well suited to farming and as a result comprises most of the rich rice lands which support a large portion of the population. The eastern coast, on the other hand, has natural resources best suited to the production of hydro-electric power and to deep-sea fishing.

The origin of the Korean people, like that of other old nations, is obscure, but the traditions, folk-lore, customs and beliefs of the people studied in the light of finds discovered in recent years in the shell-mounds, grave-sites and monuments of various kinds afford some information as to the ancestors of the present inhabitants of the peninsula. Recorded history does not begin in Korea until about the time of Christ, but from then on the history of the Korean people is well documented.

Tradition places the founding of their society in the year 2333 B.C. by a mythical personage named Tan'gun. Another famous figure is that of Kija, a Chinese refugee, who is credited by Korean tradition with the founding of the first Korean kingdom, Chosŏn, in 1122 B.C. The archeological evidence so far uncovered in Korea does not substantiate either the Tan'gun or the Kija tradition, but it throws much light on prehistoric Korea. According to deductions made from such evidence, various clans and tribes inhabited the peninsula in the centuries before the Christian era. They possessed a neolithic culture from which they emerged during the first millennium before Christ, reaching the stage of a bronze and iron culture shortly before the opening of the Christian era. These tribes were a mixture of Tungusic and proto-Caucasian invaders, who had arrived in successive waves via the plains of Manchuria and the steppes of Mongolia and Central Asia.

Traces of the early neolithic settlements are found in all parts of Korea. In southern Korea these early inhabitants were called the Sam Han (Three Han). These Three Han achieved a considerable reputation for their tribal organization, certain unique customs, and their skill at handicraft. Accounts of the Three Han may be found in the Chinese records of the Han dynasty. In northern Korea the dominant early tribesmen were called the Yemaek (second cousins of the Sam Han), and they joined together to form the ancient kingdom of Chosŏn (founded according to tradition by Kija). Chosŏn finally gave way in 108 B.C. to a Chinese invasion. The Chinese then established several colonies in northern Korea, the most famous being that of Lolang (called Nangnang by the Koreans), with its capital at Pyŏngyang.

The tombs which the Chinese left behind, dating from the second century before Christ to the third century after Christ, have proved a treasure-house of information about the art and industries of Han China. Excellent examples of lacquer, bronze mirrors, pottery, jewelry, battle equipment, and so on, have been found in the few tombs, among hundreds in the area, which have been excavated up to the present time. A fertile field awaits the Korean archeologist in the further discovery and study of Lolang grave finds.

Recorded Korean history begins with the period known as the Three Kingdoms, 57 B.C. to 668 A.D. During this period the country was divided into three parts: the northern section occupied by the warlike kingdom of Koguryo, the southeastern by Silla, and the southwestern by Paekche. Koguryo, whose jurisdiction extended over the greater part of Manchuria as well as over the northern part of Korea, fought off invading barbarians in many campaigns and engaged in one great war with China, in 613, from which the Koreans came off victorious. Fifty years later, however, Koguryo came to an end before the combined attacks of the T'ang dynasty of China and those of Silla.

During the fourth century, when Koguryo strength and prestige were still at their height, Buddhism was introduced into the kingdom along with a flood of other cultural features of Chinese civilization. The southern kingdoms of Silla and Paekche, in their turn, assimilated Chinese culture through the introduction of Buddhism, with spectacular success, and in due course passed it on to Japan.

Allied with the newly established T'ang dynasty of China, Silla soon overthrew the two rival kingdoms and set up a hegemony over the entire peninsula in 668 A.D. The supremacy of Silla lasted for almost three hundred years, during which time the high quality of its culture earned for the period the term of Golden Age. The capital of Silla, Kyongju, was the center of a well-to-do, rather benevolent, civilization. Korea never had anything like it in the more sophisticated and turbulent ages that followed. Many Buddhist temples, monasteries and pagodas of great size and splendor were built and all the appurtenances to furnish them provided. Some pagodas, temples and bronze bells still remain as monuments of this age.

During the Koryo period (935–1392) which followed the Silla, the capital was located at Songdo in central Korea. It was during this period that the name Korea came to be applied to the country by Westerners. The last two centuries of this era were disturbed by the recurrent invasions of the Mongols which ended, finally, in Mongol domination of the country, the first time that the whole peninsula had come under foreign rule. The king accepted the overlordship of the Khan and married a Mongol princess. In 1275 the Koreans joined the Mongols in their unsuccessful invasion of Japan. The Koryo kingdom had also to wage constant warfare against Japanese piracy during most of the fourteenth century. Despite these troubles, Korea reached a high level of achievement culturally. Korean scholars made great progress in literature, Korean artisans perfected the well-known celadon pottery associated with the period, and Buddhist culture in all its aspects reached its zenith.

General Yi T'aejo in 1392 ended the dissolution of Koryo by

establishing his own dynasty in a new capital fifty miles south of Songdo at Hanyang, or as it was known from then on, Seoul. The dynasty remained in power until the Japanese annexation of Korea in 1910. During its 500-year rule the Yi dynasty passed through several brilliant periods of political and cultural development. The first, occurring immediately in the opening years of the fourteenth century, was probably the greatest. At that time an alphabet was invented which was admirably suited to the Korean language, movable metal type was developed (at least fifty years before Gutenberg), encyclopedias and histories were written, and good government established according to the strictest of Confucian principles.

Two hundred years after the establishment of the dynasty, the Japanese invasion of 1592 put an end to the prosperity of the country but seven years of conflict resulted in the withdrawal of Japanese troops and the abandonment of Hideyoshi's plan of conquest. One cause of the Japanese retreat was the brilliant naval victories of Admiral Yi Sunsin, who invented the iron-clad turtle ship which he directed with such superior strategy that he was able to break the strength of the Japanese navy. The austerities endured during this devastating war resulted in another renaissance in Korea, which was cut off in twenty years by the invasion of the Manchus.

In 1653 there occurred a small incident of interest to Westerners. A Dutch ship, the *Sparrow Hawk*, was wrecked on the island of Quelpart and the thirty-six survivors were brought to the capital for investigation. They were forbidden to leave the country and were turned loose to earn their living as best they could. Thirteen years later eight of these men contrived to escape to Japan in a junk, and from there returned to Holland by one of their own ships calling at the Dutch port of Deshima. On his return to Holland one of these men, Hendrik Hamel, wrote an account of his adventures which provides the Western world with the first authentic report on the hermit kingdom.

Not until 1882 did Korea break down the stubborn isolation which had been self-imposed during the Yi dynasty, to make a treaty with a Western power—and then only because Japanese pressure forced it. The first Western nation to conclude a treaty with Korea was, curiously enough, the United States. For many centuries Korea had maintained the so-called tributary status within the orbit of the Chinese Confucian system without restricting her own independence. Contact with China, therefore, had been relatively unhampered and extensive. There had also been a more or less constant contact between Korea and Japan from the year 1609 on, although these contacts were limited to one port, that of Pusan. Trade was carried on between the two countries through this port via the island of Tsushima. A modern treaty took the place of the old agreement, in 1876.

Korea was slow in adapting to the Western world, in contrast with Japan which adapted and adopted so fast. After two revolts, one in 1882 and one in 1884, the Korean court turned to the conservative Chinese government for support, which was forthcoming in the person of the Resident, the young Yuan Shih-k'ai. Chinese conservatism was opposed by Western liberalism coming from the missionary group, and also by a Japanese economic penetration that was gathering momentum rapidly. In 1894 the Tonghaks, a revolutionary group of cultists opposed to all foreign interference, Asiatic or Western, gained considerable ground among the Korean lower classes and in an attack upon the government caused confusion among their rulers, followed by the arrival on Korean soil of both Chinese and Japanese troops. At this moment Japan was prepared to act decisively to end Chinese influence in Korea and to enforce "reforms" upon the Korean court, and China, although unwilling to withdraw, was still in no position to force the issue. The Sino-Japanese War (1894–1895) was hardly a war. It lasted only a few months and ended with an easy victory for the Japanese. In the treaty which followed, Korea's tributary relationship with China was severed and her so-called independence was then guaranteed by Japan.

In the decade 1895–1905 Western diplomacy opened Korea

to much greater Western influence: railroads were built, mines opened, and commerce developed. At this time Russian interests in Korea, coupled with the expansion of Russian imperialism in Manchuria, came into conflict with Japanese imperial ambitions. The ultimate result of this clash was the Russo-Japanese War (1904–1905) which successfully eliminated the Russians from their position of rivals of the Japanese in Korea. At this time and immediately following the war Japan, furthermore, obtained the consent of the other powers to the absorption of Korea into the Japanese Empire, and step by step, in spite of the vigorous opposition of the Korean people, this was accomplished. Annexation was finally completed in 1910, at which time Korea became a colony of Japan.

The long historical continuity, during which Korean cultural and social patterns became firmly fixed, has left a unique heritage to the Koreans. They became a nation of one race, one language, one culture, and one proud past. The homogeneity of the Korean people is a significant factor in an evaluation of Korean political problems. Whatever disunity and diversity appear on the Korean political stage are not products of fundamental differences in race or culture within the Korean community, but are consequences of less substantial causes.

Factionalism, nonetheless, has long been a characteristic of Korean politics and was particularly vicious in the last years of the monarchy. Party warfare was an old story in the Korean court, and in the period from 1560 to 1725 the monarchy was greatly weakened by such strife. During part of that period, a struggle between two parties, the Nam-in (Men of the South) and Puk-in (Men of the North) was especially dominant and its traces are still evident today with the north-south division of the country. Party members even wore distinguishing colors and dress. In the latter part of the nineteenth century, party warfare centered in the controversy over Westernization, with a conservative clique opposing the progressive element.

Korea has had many periods of brilliant government and cultural achievement, but in the latter nineteenth century, while the country was attempting to adjust to the Western international system, the Korean monarchy fell into a state of disintegration. The Confucian principles which had been adopted by the Korean court long before had been pursued to such extreme ends that government was corrupt, inefficient and inflexible. Leadership could not arise from the people because of despotic rule, and the people, therefore, took no part in a government which was conducted by a bureaucracy that was reactionary and factional. Only in the small villages and within the social circle of the family could the people exercise democratic privileges.

Reform measures in the latter days of the monarchy made almost no headway. A few steps were taken in the direction of better educational methods, reorganization of government, improvement of the administration of justice, and the granting of a somewhat larger measure of popular representation. But the urgency of such reform to bring the nation abreast of the outside world was not grasped by either the government or the people. In the decade 1885 to 1895, immediately after Korea was opened to the West, the country slipped backward into conservatism in obedience to Chinese dictation. Then, in the next decade, when Chinese influence was eliminated, the country was subjected to the pressure of power politics in a way which completely thwarted any constructive effort at reform from within.

Soon after the opening of Korea in 1882 the struggle for power began in its modern phase. The first two protagonists were Japan and China. Other secondary tensions were reflected in Korean politics, however, such as the Anglo-Russian rivalry which resulted in the occupation of Port Hamilton by British forces in 1885. Chinese designs to convert the tributary status of Korea, which had no counterpart in Western international practice, into a protectorate were finally challenged by Japan in the Sino-Japanese War. The result for Korea was the loss of the once comfortable connection with China which was regarded as a protection in time of trouble. The new independent status was one of anarchy, for Korea had no opportunity to develop a foreign policy which had a reasonable chance of success. The futile efforts to obtain American support and the desperate tactic of playing off Russia against Japan culminated in the Russo-Japanese War and the end of Korean independence.

During the transition from traditional to modern times three important forces dominated Korean politics: (1) the strong historical and cultural ties which bound the Korean people together into a single unit and led them to resist almost fanatically foreign domination despite the weakness of their own government; (2) the extreme conservatism and factionalism which pervaded the social and political structure and hindered reform; (3) the ancient ties with China which were considered an essential safeguard for independence instead of a limitation upon sovereignty. These three forces—nationalism, conservatism, reliance upon an ally—emerged as dominating characteristics of Korean policy before annexation and they persisted throughout the Japanese era to re-emerge with the removal of Japanese power.

THE LAND AND ECONOMY OF OLD KOREA

Korea occupies a peninsula slightly larger in area than Minnesota, or the United Kingdom without Northern Ireland, about 85,000 square miles. The population, about 29,000,000, is just a little more than that of Spain, ranking eleventh among the nations of the world. Physiographically the country is singularly mountainous and does not lend itself readily to geomorphic classification.[2] "Actually each abrupt mountain which shelters the villages and each minute plain on which the paddy fields have been laid out has a unique character." [3] This rugged character of the Korean terrain has imposed severe restrictions upon the economy of the country. However, it has also made for one

[2] See Shannon McCune and Arthur Robinson, "Notes on a Physiographic Diagram of Tyosen," *The Geographical Review*, Vol. 31, October 1941, pp. 653-58. Here McCune and Robinson do divide Korea into geomorphic areas.

[3] *Ibid.*, p. 658.

of Korea's most valuable resources, its hydro-electric potential. Steep slopes make fast-flowing streams, though at the price of a dearth of navigable waterways.

The Korean peninsula has about 5,400 miles of coastline. Good harbors (except artificial ones) are few on the east coast, numerous on the south and west coasts. However, the advantages of those on the west coast are offset by the great tide differences. At Inchon, the principal west coast port, there is a maximum difference of twenty-nine feet between low and high tide, the second greatest tide movement in the world.

Korea, lying from north to south in the north temperate zone, has a variety of climate comparable to the Atlantic seaboard of the United States.[4] The northernmost latitude is about the same as Portsmouth, New Hampshire, and the southernmost about the same as Charleston, South Carolina. Seoul, the capital city in the middle of the peninsula, is at about the same latitude as Richmond, Virginia. The climate is somewhat of a mean between that of maritime Japan and continental China. Maximum temperatures are slightly higher than those of Japan, minimum temperatures considerably lower. The greater extremities of winter are more pronounced in the northern part of the country, while central Korea has a climate much more like that of Japan. The annual rainfall is generally similar to that on the eastern coast of the United States, and is a good deal less than that of Japan. The country is, however, prone to unevenly distributed rainfall, which, while having the advantage of occurring in the critical growing season, often has the undesirable characteristic of being concentrated within far too brief a period, causing disastrous floods. On the other hand, this uneven-

[4] Korean climatic conditions are summarized in, Andrew J. Grajdanzev, *Modern Korea*, John Day Co., for the Institute of Pacific Relations, New York, 1944, pp. 14-22. For more complete data, see Shannon McCune, *Climate of Korea: Climatic Elements*, Korean Research Associates, Ypsilanti, Michigan, 1941, and further publications in the same series; also by the same author, "Climatic Regions of Korea and Their Economy," *Geographical Review*, January 1941, pp. 95-99. A comprehensive volume on Korean geography has been published in Germany: Hermann Lautensach, *Korea*, Leipzig, 1945.

ness in precipitation is sometimes manifested in the other extreme of ruinous drought. "There is a saying in Korea that of every three harvests one is good, one is fair, and one is very poor." [5]

Korea has a considerable variety of mineral deposits, though in most instances not in great abundance nor in ores of very high grade. Though coal deposits are not large, Korea is better endowed with this resource than some Western industrial nations, notably Italy. The known deposits are almost entirely of anthracite, and a little lignite. Taken together with the water resources for electric-power generation, Korea is in a rather favorable position in respect to power potential.[6] Korea has considerable deposits of iron ore but is wholly lacking in petroleum. Korea is the world's fifth largest gold producer. Graphite, tungsten, and alunite (an aluminum-bearing ore) are found in considerable abundance. Zinc, lead, copper, baryites, magnesite, fluorspar, lithium, mercury, molybdenum, and silver ores are found in concentrations of varying quality. There are also deposits of mica and iron sulphides. In many instances Korea is far better supplied with minerals than is Japan. The great preponderance of these resources, as well as the bulk of the forested area, is in the north, while climatic conditions and terrain make for the concentration of agriculture in the south.

Almost nothing was known of Korea in the Western world until well into the latter half of the nineteenth century.[7] Well after treaty ports had been pried from China and even considerably after the opening of Japan, Korea remained closed to the Western powers. In fact, even to China, the semi-suzerain

[5] Andrew J. Grajdanzev, *op. cit.*, p. 18.

[6] *Ibid.*, pp. 131-32, and for the following information on mineral resources, pp. 140-47. For a statistical summary of Korean mineral production see Table 5, p. 58.

[7] The following commentary written in 1872 indicates how isolated Korea still was at that date: "It is not an exaggeration to say that geographers know more of central Africa and its mountain and river systems than they do of the interior of this mere promontory, interposed like a wedge between the seas of China and Japan." "Corea," *Edinburgh Review*, Vol. 136, October 1872, p. 300.

power in Korea, and to Japan, which had long engaged in trade with the country, not much was known of Korea. Europeans knew, through the Korean trade with Peking, something of the products of this mysterious country. The knowledge that Korea was rich in gold played its part eventually in the defiance of Korean seclusion by adventurous Europeans.

The disintegrated state of Korean society at the time of the opening of the country to Western trade was reflected in the backward state of the arts and industry. An earlier notable craftsmanship had suffered a long decline and the singular isolation of the country left technology sterile. The stagnated Korean economy was meager, much more so than even that of either Japan or China.[8] The country remained medieval.

Political corruption and decadence thwarted economic development. Wealth and the instruments of economic action were in the hands of the long-since impotent noble *yangban* class, or landed aristocracy. The bulk of the population remained tied in virtual serfdom to the land. The absolutism and caprice of the system with its oppressive taxes, venal exactions, and extreme insecurity of property successfully prevented the rise of a sizable and influential merchant class such as was associated with the evolution of European capitalism from the medieval economy.

The economy was almost wholly agricultural. Such little handicraft industry as prevailed afforded only the most scant standard of living. A little mining was carried on by crude methods and in the face of governmental bans. Europeans who visited the country in the late nineteenth century almost universally complained of the awkward primitive monetary system and the nonexistence of passable roads .

Western appraisals, at the time of the opening of Korea, placed only very moderate value upon the trade which would ensue with the country. Yet there was a scramble for economic

[8] W. R. Carles, a British diplomat, who was one of the first Europeans to travel in Korea, was impressed by the low level of living standards, even for the Orient. W. R. Carles, *Life in Corea*, Macmillan, New York, 1888.

concessions from the country, resembling, on a smaller scale, the rivalry of foreign powers for similar advantages in China. Russia, the United States, Great Britain, France, and even Belgium and Italy, became involved or sought involvement in the economic life of Korea.

For a time after Korea's opening, China was able to maintain her traditional influence and in a limited way encouraged the economic development of the country. Russia obtained significant trading rights but lacked the capital to secure her ends. For a time American capital played an important role. The first modern mines, the first electric lighting, the first modern office building, the first gas plant, the first street railroad, were all American. And the first railroad in the country, the line from Inchon to the capital, was commenced under concessions to Americans.[9]

However, both the international rivalry and the unique importance of American enterprise in Korea were short-lived. The emergence of Japan in an exclusive position in Korea after the Japanese defeat of Russia, 1904–1905, was foreshadowed by the much longer experience Japan had had in dealing with Korea. This experience and the military defeat of her rivals, their indifference or their financial ineptness, bestowed upon Japan the monopoly of Korea she sought.

Japan had had active commercial relations at Pusan on the southern coast, the foremost Korean port, by treaty since 1609.[10] This was during a period of Japanese seclusion following the defeat of Hideyoshi. With the opening of Japan and its attendant extroversion, a revision of relations was sought with Korea. Japan showed prowess in combining Oriental and West-

[9] The part played by Americans in this development of Korea is described in the biography of the United States Minister, Dr. Horace N. Allen, by Fred Harvey Harrington, *God, Mammon and the Japanese*, University of Wisconsin Press, Madison, 1944.

[10] George M. McCune, "The Exchange of Envoys between Korea and Japan during the Tokugawa Period," *Far Eastern Quarterly*, May 1946, p. 317.

ern methods[11] and exacted the first Western-style treaty from Korea in 1876. The Japanese, being on the ground first and knowing how best to exploit Korean trade, enjoyed a strong initial advantage.[12] As one by one Japan disposed of rivals, she approached her objective, until, with the establishment of the protectorate in 1905, she could put at an end any participation in the Korean economy other than her own or that having her sanction.

[11] M. Frederick Nelson, *Korea and the Old Orders in Eastern Asia*, Louisiana State University Press, Baton Rouge, 1946, p. 126.

[12] A commentary written in 1885 noted: "Nearly the whole of the trade of Chemulpo [Inchon] is in the hands of the Japanese. . . . Two other ports, Pusan or Fusan and Wonsan, have also been opened to foreign commerce, and there also the Japanese have succeeded to a great extent in anticipating other nations." "The Ports and Trade of Corea," *Edinburgh Review*, Vol. 162, July 1885, pp. 273-74.

CHAPTER TWO

Korea as a Japanese Colony

POLITICAL DEVELOPMENTS

The Japanese Administration

THE TREATY of Portsmouth (1905), which terminated the Russo-Japanese War, and the acquiescence of Great Britain (by renewal of the Anglo-Japanese Alliance in 1905) and of the United States (by the policy of Theodore Roosevelt) gave Japan a free hand in the peninsula. Within the next five years Japan successively assumed control of Korea's foreign relations, established a Resident-General in Seoul (1905), forced the abdication of the recalcitrant Korean Emperor in favor of his feebleminded son (1907), and in 1910 formally annexed the peninsula.

In the first few years of subjection the Koreans offered considerable armed resistance and the populace at large put up a stubborn opposition to Japanese domination. Armed resistance was stamped out and the independence movement went underground. Korea was then ruled as a subject nation by the Japanese Government-General and every effort was made to assimilate the country culturally, politically and economically.

Colonial control in Korea passed through several stages of development, each of which was significant in establishing certain institutions and procedures. In the first decade, 1910–1920, the Japanese created the administrative machinery of control and set the pattern of colonial exploitation; in the second decade, 1920–1930, they established a special form of social and economic domination by building an alliance between themselves and Korean aristocratic and middle-class groups; and in the third decade, 1930–1940, the Japanese overlords built up their colony to feed their growing war machine by accelerating the rate of economic exploitation and of political suppression. During the war years Korea became an armed camp and as such operated as part of the Japanese total-war effort.

During the thirty-five years of Japanese domination, Korea underwent great changes. In 1945 Korea bore but slight resemblance to the nation that had fallen apart only a generation before; it was obvious that there could be no reversion to the Korea of the nineteenth century, but that a re-created Korea would have to be built upon the remains of the structure inherited from the Japanese. It is pertinent, therefore, to examine in some detail the framework and operation of the Japanese colonial administration—the Chosen Government-General.[1]

Until November 1942, Korea was a Japanese colony administratively under the supervision of the Overseas Ministry. In 1942 Korea became an integral part of Japan, coming under the supervision of the Home Ministry. At the apex of Korea's pyramid of power stood the Governor-General, whose imperial appointment was recommended by the Japanese Premier on the advice of the Home Minister. The Governor-General exercised wide powers over administration, justice, and public safety; he appointed provincial governors and municipal mayors as well as all officers of the Government-General. Although he was governed in general by the laws of Japan, he issued decrees

[1] The following studies are useful: Hugh Borton, "Korea: Internal Political Structure," *Department of State Bulletin,* November 12, 1944, pp. 578-83; Andrew J. Grajdanzev, *Modern Korea,* New York, 1944; George M. McCune, "Korea: A Study in Japanese Imperialism," *World Affairs Interpreter,* Spring 1940, pp. 77-85; Harold J. Noble, "Recent Administration in Korea," *Amerasia,* April 1941, pp. 84-90; Nym Wales, "Rebel Korea," *Pacific Affairs,* March 1942, pp. 25-43; Oswald White, "Japanese Administration of Korea and Manchuria," *Journal of the Royal Central Asian Society,* 1943, pp. 19-36. Some of the statistical data presented here are taken from *Chosen Sotokufu Tokei Nempo 1936* (Chosen Government General Statistical Abstract, 1936), Seoul, 1938.

on a wide variety of Korean matters and imposed fines or prison sentences outside the provisions of the regular laws.

The Civil Administrator, appointed by the Premier, was the chief administrative assistant of the Governor. He was assisted by a secretariat, and supervised the government bureaus. In October 1943 the bureaus were reorganized, with the result that some changes were made in the previous structure. The seven new bureaus included three unchanged units, Justice, Education and Police, and four enlarged bureaus, Finance (enlarged by addition of the Monopoly Bureau), Agriculture and Commerce (enlarged from the previous Agriculture and Forestry Bureau), Mining and Industry (reorganized from the Industrial Bureau), Communications (enlarged by addition of the Railway Bureau).

A Central Advisory Council, an all-Korean body, nominally represented Korean interests in advising the Governor. Its 65 councilors were appointed by the Governor from the wealthy aristocracy and business class and served for a three-year term. The Council could offer advice only at the request of the Governor and then upon a specific subject. It was obviously a powerless puppet group which did not represent the Korean people.

Local government in Korea was graded down from the province to the village: there were 13 provinces (*do*), about 20 municipalities (*fu*), 200 counties (*gun*), 100 towns (*yu*), 2,000 townships (*men*), and more than 50,000 villages (*ri*). The local organization in many respects paralleled the set-up at the national level; the heads of provinces, municipalities, and counties were all appointed by the Governor-General. In each of the levels of local government there were advisory councils, elected in part by qualified voters, i.e., taxpayers.

Japanese personnel dominated the government from top to bottom although a number of Koreans who were willing to collaborate were given minor posts. In 1945 almost one-half of all government employees were Koreans, but the percentage of Koreans as against Japanese was less and less at each stage upward. Generally speaking, Japanese colonial policy called for a virtual monopoly by Japanese of administrative positions on the higher levels. Koreans were appointed to clerical and minor posts only. In 1936 there were a total of 87,552 officials and employees in the various bureaus of the Government-General and in the provincial, municipal and educational offices. Of these, 35,282 were Koreans and 52,270 were Japanese. More than 80 per cent of the highest ranking officials (*Chokunin* and *Sonin*), 60 per cent of the intermediary rank (*Hannin*), and about 50 per cent of the clerks, secretaries and minor employees were Japanese.

Not only were Koreans excluded from important government positions, but the Korean people as a whole did not take part in government affairs despite the inauguration of a system of elective and semi-elective councils in 1919 after the outbreak of the independence movement. At that time, various reforms were promulgated, including the institution of advisory councils which were to be partially elected by local communities. The functions of these councils were extended in 1931 and 1933. The Koreans as a whole, however, paid almost no heed to council elections because of the restrictions on voting and the obvious puppet character of the councils themselves. (In 1936, out of a municipal population of 1,700,000, only 56,687 persons were registered voters.) The councils, however, served the purposes of the Japanese administration by allying many wealthy Koreans with the Japanese officialdom.

In the final analysis Japanese control of Korea rested upon force. Force was exercised by a police power which penetrated into the life of the entire community and was supplemented by the military power of the army. The executive authority of the Governor-General included his right to call upon the commander of the armed forces in Korea for troops whenever he deemed an emergency to exist. Japanese army posts were strategically located throughout the peninsula where they were an ever-present reminder of the power of Japan.

Police control in Korea, carried out by both civil and military police, was not limited to the maintenance of civil order and the prevention and detection of crime but extended into the field of politics, economic activity, education, religion, morals, health, public welfare, and fire control. In the 1943 reorganization, the Police Bureau (civil police), which was directly under the Governor-General, contained six sections: Police Affairs, Defense (including fire control), Economic Policy (price-control and rationing), Peace Preservation ("thought" control), Publication (censorship), and Sanitation.

According to official sources, the civil police numbered 21,782 in 1938 (one policeman to every 1,150 people), of whom 40 per cent were Koreans. In 1941 the total number of civilian and military police in Korea was estimated at 60,000 (one to every 400 persons).

The police in Korea had the power to exercise summary jurisdiction and it was estimated that more than 100,000 cases were tried in police courts each year. In 1921, for example, 73,262 cases were decided by police; 71,802 of these ended in conviction. The chief of police had the authority to inflict a penalty of three months' penal servitude or a fine of not more than 100 yen. The Korean population was not protected by the writ of habeas corpus or other safeguards against arbitrary action, and police methods included third-degree interrogations, torture, searches without authorization and the use of informers. It was not difficult to conclude, therefore, that the Korean people were hostile toward police control and viewed it with apprehension. Because of these methods, however, the police were generally successful in forestalling overt action on the part of the Korean public.

The net effect for the Korean people of the Japanese administration was a thirty-five-year intermission in political responsibility and administrative experience at a time when the Korean people needed education, training and practice in modern techniques of democratic government if they were ever to become self-governing in a modern world. The old Korean monarchy had made no more than a gesture toward creating a modern Korean state. Korea in 1945, therefore, was politically immature according to Western standards, and the Korean people were inexperienced in exercising the normal activities of Western democracy such as free press, free speech, suffrage, and representative government.

Despite Japanese repression in Korea, the Korean people made some significant advances during the period. For example, in the field of literacy and education, the Korean people at the end of Japanese occupation possessed the prerequisites for building a sound democracy and were far in advance of their status in 1910. More than fifty per cent of the adult population could read the Korean native script notwithstanding Japanese efforts to replace the Korean language with the Japanese. The Japanese educational system failed completely in its express purpose of making the Koreans loyal Japanese subjects and of obliterating all vestiges of Korean identity. Inadvertently, however, the educational system helped to mitigate the deleterious effects of Japanese policy in other fields.

Other measures which the Japanese administration inaugurated for the purpose of destroying Korean nationalism were equally ineffective. In fact it may be said that the desire for independence was increased, rather than diminished, by the increased level of popular education, the experience of efficient though superimposed administration, and the industrial development which Japanese rule brought in its train, but in whose benefits the Koreans had only a limited participation.

Korean Nationalism

The independence movement began on the day that Korea lost its independence and never ceased to exist both as an organized movement and as a dominant spiritual force in the life of the Korean people. The armed resistance of the remnants of the Korean national army was suppressed and gave place in 1919 to the passive resistance movement of the self-styled Korean Provisional Government and later to guerrilla activity and partisan warfare. In 1935 and thereafter, a militant group of

Communists was active in northeastern Korea.[2] Periodically breaking into the open, the Korean independence movement never lost its hold upon the common man in Korea. A reservoir of patriotism was built up under Japanese rule and was consequently ready to be tapped at the moment of liberation.

Outside Korea there were many organized groups within the independence movement. Most of them supported the Korean Provisional Government (located in China), at least nominally, since its inception in 1919. The left-wing faction intermittently broke off from the coalition and there was constant difficulty in achieving solidarity within the movement. Inside Korea, the underground character of the movement precluded the existence of unity, although several organizations maintained nationwide contacts. In Korea, too, there was a cleavage between the intellectual middle-class patriots, associated in such organizations as the Young Korea Academy, and the radical Communist patriots, who operated within student, labor, and farmer groups.

Under these circumstances the Korean independence movement lacked leadership, unity, and a coherent program. It, too, seemed to reflect the political immaturity of the Korean people as a whole. Japanese rule did not succeed in destroying the national spirit of the Korean people, but it did succeed in suppressing Korean leadership and in weakening the latent capacities of the Koreans for assuming responsibility in governing their country.

The overlay of Japanese influence, superimposed upon the social and political life of the people, did not alter radically the basic heritage of ancient Korea. Korean nationalism was probably strengthened as well as modernized by the ordeal of overlordship. The tendency toward factionalism was allowed to continue uninhibited under the Japanese, who used the divide-and-rule technique and therefore added considerably to

[2] The activities of these Koreans were almost unknown abroad, but an extensive account in Russian appeared in an article, "Guerrilla Movement in the Northern Korea Regions," *Tikhii Okean*, 2 (12), 1937.

the lack of unity among Koreans. The conservatism of the Koreans was perforce altered by the impact of Western civilization, but there was no substantial political progress among the Koreans themselves. The Korean people after thirty-five years of Japanese rule were not much better off in terms of democratic experience than they had been under the Korean monarchy.

The Japanese Government-General was a house built on sand which collapsed at once with the withdrawal of Japanese force. The Korean administrators who had been employed by the Japanese possessed only limited experience and almost no responsibility, and were, of course, inevitably tarred with the brush of collaborationism. Removal of Japanese control was destined to result in chaos and confusion. Still, after doing things for thirty-five years in the Japanese manner, the Koreans were inclined to retain many elements of the Japanese administrative system and to build their new government on the heritage of the immediate past.

JAPANESE ECONOMY IN KOREA

Colonial Character

It was natural enough that Japan, which showed such proficiency in the ways of Western international behavior, should have officially publicized its colonial role in Korea as primarily that of a teacher and civilizer motivated only by the deepest concern for the welfare of the Korean people. When Japan gained a free hand in Korea in 1905, it was complaisantly accepted in Western countries that the Japanese were performing yeoman's service to the rationalized ideals of Western imperialism, and that Japan by her precociousness had demonstrated that she could be deputized to carry part of the white man's burden in the Far East.

The continued currency of this view when a large body of opinion in Western countries had become skeptical of the beneficence of colonialism is probably to be accounted for by the scant foreign interest in Korean affairs during the period of Japanese rule. The Western literature on Korea that appeared during this period for the most part generously praised the Japanese administration and said little more of actual conditions in Korea than did the effusive official Japanese reports.

Grajdanzev has demonstrated how exaggerated, and in many respects superficial, the supposed progress of Korea as a Japanese colony actually was.[3] In reality Japanese domination of Korea was no more beneficial for the Koreans, and possibly less so, than were other colonial regimes for their subjects. Exploitation was the keynote and virtually every development was undertaken with the objective of maximizing the benefits which would accrue either directly or indirectly to Japan. It has been observed of Korea under Japanese rule that "there are few countries in the world, even among the colonies, where such a large portion of the goods is taken out of the country." [4]

Japan came into practically full possession of the Korean economy in the years after 1905. By 1939 exports to "yen bloc," Japanese-dominated Asia accounted for 96.9 per cent of the Korean total. What other trade there was existed only at the suffrance of Japan and because of Japanese inability to supply certain goods which were required in the exploitation of Korean resources.

To take maximum advantage of their colonial position in Korea the Japanese built a railway system second only to that of Japan itself in the Far East.[5] Highways were built, an extensive postal system and telecommunications developed. Heavy and light manufacturing industry came into increasingly conspicuous evidence. The hydro-electric resources were harnessed. Municipal services were introduced. The crude and cumber-

[3] Grajdanzev, *op. cit., passim.* The major thesis of Grajdanzev's analysis is that Korea was systematically exploited to the detriment of the Koreans themselves.

[4] *Ibid.*, p. 236.

[5] Korean railways were in one respect possibly superior to those of Japan in that all the principal lines were of standard gauge.

some monetary system was supplanted by a currency system integrated with that of Japan. A financial and banking structure appropriate to the needs of a modern colonial power was erected. The population jumped as Western medical methods lessened the perils of epidemic diseases and a broader distributive system mitigated the parochial hardships of famine.[6]

Basically, however, the country remained unchanged, affirming how divorced the Japanese economy in Korea remained from the well-being of the Korean population. In terms of the percentage of the aggregate gross value of production represented by mining and industry as shown in the following table,[7] Korea appeared to have made great strides toward industrialization.

TABLE 1

DISTRIBUTION OF AGGREGATE GROSS VALUE OF PRODUCTION BY ECONOMIC ACTIVITY, 1938

	Percentage
Agriculture	46.4
Forestry	5.5
Fishing	4.8
Mining	5.5
Industry	37.8
	100.0

But the distribution of the population occupationally reveals a quite different picture: [8]

[6] Irene B. Taeuber, "The Population Potential of Postwar Korea," *Far Eastern Quarterly*, Vol. V, May 1946, pp. 289-307. For a discussion of the pre-modern Malthusian restrictions on population growth, see especially pp. 290-91.

[7] Grajdanzev, *op. cit.*, p. 84.

[8] *Japan-Manchukuo Yearbook*, 1941, p. 511.

TABLE 2
DISTRIBUTION OF THE POPULATION OF KOREA BY OCCUPATION, 1938

	Percentage
Agriculture	73.6
Fisheries	1.5
Industry	3.1
Mining	1.2
Commerce	7.0
Transportation	1.0
Public Service and Professions	3.9
Others	8.7
	100.0

This discrepancy between the percentage of the aggregate gross value of production attributable to agriculture and the percentage of the population engaged in agriculture indicates that a disproportionately small share of the national product was being received by those engaged in agriculture. Agricultural prices were depressed vis-à-vis those in other sectors of the economy and the great mass of the Korean people were engaged in agriculture. The further breakdown of the above figure of 73.6 per cent of the total population engaged in agriculture shows how decidedly this was the case: 75.6 per cent of the Korean population were occupied in agriculture in 1938, while only 5.4 per cent of the Japanese residents were so occupied.[9] Moreover, the Japanese had usurped the farmland that would yield the greatest return for themselves; a very large share of them were landlords or held the more lucrative managerial positions, as in the Oriental Development Company.

Economic Discrimination Against Koreans

Undoubtedly, the Japanese engaged in agriculture took a share of the national agricultural income disproportionately

[9] *Ibid.*

large for their numbers. Thus the economic status of the Korean people as contrasted with that of the Japanese in Korea points out the fundamental nature of the Japanese exploitation of Korea. In advancing their own interests in Korea the Japanese in essence were expanding the Japanese economy, not replacing the medieval agrarian economy of Korea. The old economy was pushed back where necessary to accommodate the new, but not supplanted. The age-old way of getting a living, the primitive agriculture under a feudalistic landlordism, persisted as the economy of most Koreans, but with the important difference of vassalage to Japanese economic interests.

Japan made large expenditures for capital development in Korea but this was only to further the exploitation of the country. Any advantages the Koreans realized from being brought into this vassal economic relationship with Japan were only peripheral and incidental. They were by and large disenfranchised from the Japanese economy, from the benefits and opportunities which a modern economy can confer. In fact, very possibly the position of the Korean people regressed. Significantly, for years before the war the Japanese Government-General in Korea had not published statistics on Japanese holdings in Korea.[10] The process of expropriation of the Korean peasantry could not be garnished into palatable form for foreign consumption. The Korean people were being confined within a narrowing circle of resources.

Few Koreans attained positions of responsibility or wealth. Nor was any substantial effort made to prepare them for technical or managerial positions. The result was that no sizable skilled industrial force was recruited from among the Korean people. In fact, household industry remained the only Korean industry. And as Japanese industry came to require the raw materials of this activity and to monopolize them, the Japanese authorities came to regard household industry as undesirable.

[10] Grajdanzev, *op. cit.*, p. 106; on this subject see also Hoon K. Lee, *Land Utilization and Rural Economy in Korea*, Kelly and Walsh, Shanghai, and University of Chicago Press, Chicago, 1936, p. 144.

Then law and the police power were increasingly employed to prevent raw materials from being so used.

Koreans suffered discrimination on every hand. They had to pay as a rule 25 per cent higher interest rates than did Japanese. Public finance had a highly regressive incidence, providing low taxes and even subsidies to desired Japanese industries and inflicting a heavy burden upon the less affluent Korean population.

Over-Utilization of Resources

The hegemony of Japanese self-interest was always manifest in economic policy. Not only were the benefits of the Japanese economy in Korea largely siphoned off to Japan, but such seeming technical advances as were made were sometimes of a sort that actually threatened certain replenishable resources with exhaustion, despite pretensions of conservation, or directed their allocation into uses which were detrimental to Korean welfare. While assessing the part played by the Japanese in the country, it is to be recognized that the Japanese regarded their position as highly permanent. Hence they made the capital expenditure necessary to bring the high potential capacity of backward Korea up to the point where it would complement the Japanese economy. However, the pressure of the requirements of the Japanese home economy, and later, the preparation for war and the subsequent actual waging of war led to many essentially short-run maximizations of the sort mentioned above.

While Japan made much of its afforestation of Korea, this program apparently failed, at least in the latter period of Japanese rule, to keep pace with deforestation. The tonnage for the fishing catch was pushed successively upward, but possibly at the expense of forcing the fishing resources of Korean waters beyond economic limits. The later levels of output of minerals and manufactured products were also sometimes achieved only by passing beyond the limits of economically sound production.

Distortion of Agricultural Production

Korea's primary resource, its agriculture, was more and more distorted by fostering the increased production of rice to the exclusion of a balanced agriculture. Despite the greater susceptibility of rice to droughts than certain other cereals, this one-sidedness was pressed because the Japanese were primarily interested in rice exports from Korea to Japan.

The fate of rice culture during the thirty-five years of Japanese rule illustrates how dependent the utilization of Korean resources and thus Korean welfare was upon the economic objectives of Japan. After rice riots in Japan in 1919, plans were laid for getting a great deal more rice for domestic Japanese use out of Korea. While this policy was conceived of as being an extensive program of agricultural expansion and improvement in Korea entailing substantial efforts in the direction of reclamation, in practice it amounted in large part to the more ruthless squeezing of existing production at the expense of Korean consumption. Subsequent policy was an oscillating one, at one time yielding to the complaints of Japanese farmers of overproduction and the competition of Korean rice, and at another re-emphasizing a need for greater output.

The level of exports of rice was little related to the needs within Korea during this period. The amount available for Korean consumption remained fairly constant, despite the fact that the population increased by 60 to 65 per cent during the thirty years after annexation. That Korea exported far more of her number-one crop than was desirable is reflected in the fact that even in a good year the "spring hunger" reduced Koreans to eating the bark and roots of trees. The inadequacy of the Korean food supply was further evidenced by the "fire field" system of cropping which in 1936 accounted for over one million acres. "Fire fields" refers to land burned over and planted by a host of the destitute who lead a nomadic existence in the mountainous regions of Korea.

Conclusive evidence of the deterioration of the Korean diet

can be given: per-capita domestic consumption in the five-year period 1931–1935 was 45 per cent lower than that in the years 1916–1920. Yet in the same period the percentage of the rice crop exported to Japan had increased from 14 per cent to 48 per cent.

Exploitation for Military Expediency

The ascendancy of the militarists in Japan after 1930 was followed by increased attention to achieving economic autarky. The establishment of the puppet state Manchukuo emphasized Korea's role as a link between the home islands and continental exploitation, and its consequently inferior status. Nevertheless, Korea took on new importance in the Japanese Empire in the 1930's.[11] Large outlays were made to develop its war potential between 1934 and 1939. Tax exemptions and direct money subsidies were generously dispensed to encourage the production of certain minerals in Korea. The production of light metals—aluminum and magnesium—was especially encouraged.

Gold production was given particular emphasis in this immediate prewar period, because it was a source of foreign exchange with which iron, oil, copper and other strategic materials could be acquired in the United States. Gold mining was de-emphasized in Korea in 1941 when Japanese warfare passed into that phase when gold no longer could move in commerce to the United States. Later, gold mines in many instances were stripped bare of machinery that could be better used for the purposes of the war which hungrily demanded every resource. What happened to gold mining was in general the fate of resources throughout the Japanese economy in Korea. As the war progressed the sources of consumer goods virtually dried up. After mid-1944 scrapping became commonplace as the Japanese tried to cannibalize the economy they had built and fed everything

[11] A brief résumé of Japan's prewar industrialization of Korea is to be found in Jerome B. Cohen, *Japan's Economy in War and Reconstruction*, University of Minnesota Press, Minneapolis, 1949, p. 33 ff.

that could possibly be sacrificed into war needs. In the wake of this policy, deterioration struck everywhere.

In summary it may be said that the development which took place during the period of Japanese rule in Korea hardly constituted a Korean economy. Koreans appreciably shared neither in the direction of this development nor in its benefits. The Korean economy was Japanese-owned and Japanese-directed and in no sense an entity in and of itself, but rather the geographical location of a portion of the wider configuration of the economy of Japan.

CHAPTER THREE

Korea in 1945

JAPAN'S ECONOMIC LEGACY

DURING the last stages of the war the Japanese economy in Korea suffered from a widespread breakdown in morale, which laid a paralyzing hand upon economic activity and control. Once hostilities had ended, the war-goods production which was so paramount in industrial output became, of course, purposeless. The political uncertainty that arose out of Japanese resignation to defeat and the impossibility of enforcing the discipline which had been exercised over Koreans quickly permeated the economic structure.

The Japanese in Korea became preoccupied with their possible fate. They made contracts for the disposition of property to Koreans and aggravated the deterioration of incentives to work by greatly inflating the currency through the wholesale granting of bonuses and otherwise monetizing their bank deposits. A great deal more money was in circulation than ever before while available consumer goods were in particularly short supply. At the same time, Koreans believed the economic millennium to be at hand, being greatly impressed by surpluses which would result from the release of Japanese stock piles of goods and the termination of the diversion of large portions of the rice crop to Japan. All of these factors made for certain collapse of the rigid system of rationing and price control and an inevitable rise in prices.

The Koreans expected immediate termination of all Japanese domination. Liberation was understood to mean the removal of Japanese from managerial and other positions of authority and a complete end of all Japanese influence in Korean economic affairs. Under the Japanese regime, Koreans had not been technically trained in large numbers and had had little experience in occupying positions of authority. Moreover, the Japanese economic organization in Korea was not coterminous with Korean boundaries but oriented to and integrated with the operations of establishments in Japan.

Further, though Korea suffered from neither aerial bombardment nor invasion,[1] its material assets had suffered crucially in the war. A large percentage of railway equipment had become inefficient and finally altogether inoperative; motor and street railway transport disintegrated; factories became less and less able to sustain output as a lack of replacement parts disabled their machinery; and a general shoddiness by war's end was the obvious indication of the deeper scars of attrition. A resumption of production would require extensive repair and replacement, but Korea was dependent upon Japan as a source of parts and equipment because of its integration with the Japanese economy. Moreover, to get the Korean economy back into operation required not simply resumption of production, but redirection from Japanese military to Korean peacetime objectives. It would not be a Korean economy but rather the vestigial remains of a segment of the Japanese economy until such a redirection could be accomplished.

Not only was the economic life of Korea Japanese-dominated, but the operation of certain organizations and institutions presented peculiar problems to the objectives of Korean independence because of their size and their orientation to the furtherance of Japanese exploitation. There were the vast and diverse operations of the Zaibatsu organizations and also the newer interests, such as Noguchi, which were better attuned to

[1] Excepting for limited Russian operations in extreme northeastern Korea.

the military program of continental expansion.[2] There was the huge exploiting arm, the Oriental Development Co., which was intended to encourage the settlement of Japanese colonists in Korea and was far and away the foremost landlord of the peninsula. Its ramified interests also took in lumbering, mining and manufacturing enterprises. The central bank, the Bank of Chosen, was privately subscribed by Japanese companies and had among its purposes the furtherance of Japanese penetration of the hinterland of northeastern Asia. Its interests spread well beyond the borders of Korea. An example of a more material dedication to Japanese self-interest was the railways. These were in large part conceived as a means of transshipment of Japanese goods into Manchuria, and a number of them had been built solely for military reasons.[3]

These then were the conditions prevailing in Korea at war's end. Production had collapsed; the currency was greatly inflated; economic controls had broken down. Korean liberation would necessitate sweeping out Japanese technicians and administrators, yet trained and experienced Koreans were few. The economy would require more than the fact of political independence to give it an independent existence. The physical plant was badly depreciated. The economy was oriented toward Japan and Japanese war purposes and was in large part Japanese-owned. Such was the legacy Japan bequeathed to Korea.

[2] Kate L. Mitchell, *Japan's Industrial Strength,* I. P. R., 1942, pp. 80, 82.

[3] In 1936 the Japanese Director of the Government-General Railway Bureau made a telling statement on the role of Korea and its transportation system in Japanese affairs: "With the advent of Manchoukuo as the turning point, there has taken place . . . an almost phenomenal economic development, naturally followed by the spectacular growth of general transportation means. Thus the mighty trio of Government railway lines, private lines and motorcar routes, coupled with the Japan Sea routes . . . have elevated the peninsula to a position more valuable as a land-bridge connecting Japan with the continents of Asia and Europe. Inasmuch as Chosen constitutes Japan's barricade and life-and-death line of vital importance from a view-point of national defense, it is all the more significant to complete the network of transportation in the peninsula." Koh Yoshida, "Overland Transportation in Chosen," *Japan and Manchoukuo,* 1935–36, Japan Publishing Co., Tokyo, 1936, p. 79.

WAR DIPLOMACY

Prior to the Japanese attack on Pearl Harbor, Korea's international position was unequivocally established: Korea was a colony of Japan and the legality of that tenure was unquestioned by any foreign state. There was a slight breach, however, in the attitude of the Chinese government after 1937. The self-styled Korean Provisional Government since 1919 had maintained its precarious existence in the international settlement in Shanghai, but in 1937 this organization made arrangements with the Chinese government to remove itself to Nanking and later to Chungking, where it received sanctuary and eventually considerable support. The Chinese government never granted official recognition of any sort to the Korean Provisional Government, but by indirect means the Korean group was aided financially and given other means of encouragement.

Immediately after the outset of the Pacific War, exiled Koreans hopefully applied for recognition of the Korean Provisional Government or at least for an official declaration looking toward the independence of Korea. In Chungking and Washington the Koreans were particularly active. In March 1942, a Liberty Conference was held in Washington for the purpose of gaining diplomatic action on behalf of Korea, but the Korean efforts did not elicit more than expressions of sympathy and encouragement from the various officials. The question of making a statement concerning the future independence of Korea and of granting some sort of recognition to the Korean Provisional Government was informally discussed in Washington in early 1942 by members of the Pacific War Council, who decided to postpone any such action until it might be more useful for arousing Korean opposition to Japan, or until some declaration might be included in the context of a statement of general aims in the Pacific. As for recognition of the Provisional Government, there was complete agreement that action would be premature and unwise. The reasons for that view were expressed a number of times by the United States government in response to inquiries, and were summed up as follows by Acting Secretary of State Grew on June 8, 1945, in reference to Korean participation in the United Nations Conference:

> . . . The United Nations which are represented at the United Nations Conference on International Organization all have legally constituted governing authorities whereas the 'Korean Provisional Government' and other Korean organizations do not possess at the present time the qualifications requisite for obtaining recognition by the United States as a governing authority. The 'Korean Provisional Government' has never exercised administrative authority over any part of Korea, nor can it be regarded as representative of the Korean people of today. Due to geographical and other factors its following even among exiled Koreans is inevitably limited. It is the policy of this Government in dealing with groups such as the 'Korean Provisional Government' to avoid taking action which might, when the victory of the United Nations is achieved, tend to compromise the right of the Korean people to choose the ultimate form and personnel of the government which they may wish to establish. . . .[4]

The first genuine commitment concerning Korea was made at the Cairo Conference by President Roosevelt, Prime Minister Churchill, and Generalissimo Chiang Kai-shek. In their joint declaration, released December 1, 1943, the Allies in the Pacific War stated: "The aforesaid three great powers, mindful of the enslavement of the people of Korea, are determined that in due course Korea shall become free and independent." The qualifying phrase "in due course" gave cause for considerable concern to the Koreans, who were looking forward to immediate independence. As the war progressed and plans for postwar settlement were being formulated, there was more and more discussion among those interested in the future of Korea, including the officials of the various governments, concerning the probability that a period of trusteeship would provide the best means of assuring an orderly transition from Japanese control to complete independence.

[4] *Statement by Acting Secretary of State Joseph C. Grew*, press release, Washington, D.C., June 8, 1945.

The powers signatory to the Cairo Declaration were in agreement in principle that Korea was to become independent "in due course," but there was still a question as to the attitude of the Soviet government. In 1945, before the entry of the Soviet Union into the Pacific War and before the capitulation of Japan, Russia also made known, secretly, its acceptance of the position of the other three powers. The first step was taken at Yalta in February 1945, where an oblique reference had been made in the context of a suggestion that Korea might appropriately be considered an area falling within one of the categories of trusteeship envisaged in the proposed United Nations Charter. The United States presented the view that Korea should become a multi-power trusteeship, if such plans materialized. Russia concurred. No commitments were, however, made at that time.

After the San Francisco meeting of the United Nations and the death of President Roosevelt, the indefinite understanding at Yalta concerning Korea was clarified by negotiation. The Soviet Union and the United States agreed through an exchange of views that a short-term, four-power (American, Russian, British, Chinese) trusteeship would best provide Korea with a fair start as an independent state and serve to guarantee its future independence.

The Soviet agreement on these points was, of course, kept secret in view of the fact that Russia had not yet taken up arms against Japan. When Soviet Russia declared war against Japan on August 8, 1945, it announced its adherence to the Potsdam Declaration (which included reference to the Cairo Declaration). Thus Russia also, before the surrender of Japan, publicly came out in support of Korean independence "in due course."

Before the plans for Korean independence could be implemented, however, military occupation of Korea in two separate zones had already become an accomplished fact, with the entry of Russian combat troops into North Korea on August 10 and of American troops into South Korea on September 8. As expressed by Secretary of State Byrnes, "For purposes of military operations the occupation of Korea was divided north and south of latitude 38 into Soviet and American areas." [5]

Pursuant to a Potsdam decision it was decided that Soviet troops would accept the Japanese surrender north of the 38th parallel and that American troops would accept the surrender south of it. "In no sense was this agreement more than a military expedient between two friendly powers," General John H. Hilldring, Assistant Secretary of State, declared in March 1947. "The line of demarcation was intended to be temporary and only to fix responsibility between the U.S. and the U.S.S.R. for carrying out the Japanese surrender. Nevertheless, now, nearly eighteen months later, this artificial and 'temporary' line still stands like a stone wall against the unification of Korea." [6]

CONFUSION IN TRANSITION

When Japan surrendered on August 14, 1945, Russian forces had already landed in northeast Korea and were rapidly moving southward. By agreement with the United States, however, the Soviet Union consented to the terms of surrender, which called for a division of Korea at the 38th parallel for the purpose of accepting the surrender of Japanese forces in Korea. On September 8, American forces landed in Korea. By that time, Soviet forces had already spread over most of their northern zone.

Throughout Korea the situation was in many respects much the same. However, the arrival of the Russian forces in the north almost a month before the disembarkation of American troops in the south made for some marked differences in the subsequent developments in the two zones. The Russians had overrun much of northern Korea by force of arms.[7] The Japa-

[5] *Department of State Bulletin*, December 30, 1945, p. 1035.

[6] In an address delivered before the Economic Club of Detroit, March 10, 1947. *Ibid.*, March 23, 1947, p. 545.

[7] Actual military operations between Soviet and Japanese forces continued for some days after the issuance of the Japanese imperial rescript accepting the Allied armistice terms.

nese sabotaged mines and factories in the path of the approaching enemy. They fled to the south in large numbers, much preferring to await the arrival of the forces of their military foe of the past four years to living in the shadow of the stern authority of a traditional enemy for two generations. The atmosphere between the Japanese and the occupying forces in the north was one of enmity.[8] In the south the Japanese assumed an attitude of guileless cooperation toward the occupying authorities.

Despite obvious advantages, the Americans were in some respects handicapped by their possession of the Japanese governmental machinery at Seoul. The Soviets had no Japanese administration at the national level to deal with, and the Japanese at the lower levels were in open flight or soon divested by local Korean groups of any organized authority. The Russians welcomed Korean revolutionaries constituting themselves the governing authorities. By careful retreat to a position of inauspicious but firm authority, the Soviet command early was able to place reliance in the local peoples' committees. Thus much of the American difficulty of attempting to administer directly in the face of a difficult language barrier and little orientation was obviated.

The primary duty of the occupying forces was to demobilize the Japanese military forces in Korea and to liquidate the Japanese administration. The former turned out to be almost a routine task, but the latter was a different matter since it carried with it the necessity of substituting another regime to replace the Japanese machine. In both the American and Russian zones a policy of expediency seemed to dictate the course of action in assuming responsibility in the vacuum left by the ousting of the Japanese. The Koreans in each zone sought to estab-

[8] For example, note the alarm with which the Japanese government viewed rumors that Soviet troops might participate in the occupation of Japan. In a message to General MacArthur on August 24, the Japanese government stated that such action would be "greatly regretted" in Japan. Message No. 34 from the Japanese government to General MacArthur, *New York Times*, August 25, 1945, p. 2.

lish themselves or to aid the occupying forces but they were under the severe handicap of a divided occupation and a confused policy. A large part of the confusion stemmed from the "temporary" character of the occupation, particularly during the first four months, from September until December 1945. The Moscow Agreement was reached in December and at that time it was hoped that the situation would become more stabilized as soon as the Russian and American commands could agree on methods for unifying the country under a provisional Korean government. After the breakdown of the Joint Commission meetings in May 1946, occupation policy in both zones shifted somewhat from that of expediency to a more constructive or permanent course of action.

At the outset, the occupying forces were faced with a complex political situation with which they were ill-equipped to deal. This situation was a natural consequence of the pent-up nationalism of the Koreans who had promptly set about taking over authority from the Japanese after the surrender. During the interval between surrender (August 14) and American landings (September 8), many prominent Korean leaders joined together in setting up a People's Republic in the capital, Seoul, with connections throughout the country, including the Russian zone. The Japanese authorities, fearful of the powder keg on which they were sitting, did not impede the formation of the Republic, but on the contrary granted its leaders special facilities in exchange for assistance in maintaining law and order.

The Korean leaders, headed by Lyuh Woonhyung, and including a large number of patriots released from Japanese prison cells after the surrender, called upon the Korean people for moderation. They organized local committees to preserve order and they convened a national congress in Seoul, attended by representatives from all parts of Korea, which on September 6 proclaimed the People's Republic. In northern Korea these local committees were being formed with the sanction of the

Russian occupying forces. The revolutionary character of the people's committees was obviously in keeping with Soviet policy.

The American Zone

When American forces arrived in South Korea on September 8, the People's Republic offered its services to the American command, but was given a cold shoulder. There was apprehension in American minds as to the maintenance of law and order.[9] The "Republic" had obviously been quickly and recently formed and there was no way of knowing anything of its pretensions until the local situation could be studied. Furthermore, the American commander was not in a position to support any Korean group claiming to be a government, although he was empowered to work with any Korean political parties or individuals to achieve the objectives of occupation. American policy called for caution in reorganizing the administration in the hope that more capable Koreans could be chosen for administering the country if they were not hastily recruited. One American participant later wrote: "General Hodge announced that the existing Japanese administration would continue in office temporarily to facilitate the occupation. . . . The plan was promptly dropped." [10]

The retention of Japanese in government posts, even under American command, created intense dissatisfaction. General Hodge immediately removed the high Japanese officials although he reported that the situation among the Koreans was

[9] One cause of apprehension was the insistent appeals from the Japanese who feared Korean uprisings. The following is an excerpt from a message from the Japanese government to the Supreme Commander for the Allied Powers, August 28, 1945: "Local Japanese authorities eagerly wait for an early arrival of the Allied forces which are to take over the maintenance of peace and order from the Japanese forces in southern Korea and urgently desire that the Allied forces will fully take into consideration the actual conditions on the spot before proceeding with the disarmament of Japanese forces and the transfer of administrative organs from Japanese hands."

[10] Bertram D. Sarafan, "Military Government: Korea," *Far Eastern Survey*, November 1946, p. 350.

"chaotic, with no central theme except a desire for immediate independence." President Truman on September 18, in a statement congratulating the Korean people on their liberation, stated: "Such Japanese as may be temporarily retained are being utilized as servants of the Korean people and of our occupying forces only because they are deemed essential by reason of their technical qualifications. . . ." [11] The change-over from Japanese to Korean personnel and American Military Government was rapidly accelerated until by the end of January 1946 only sixty Japanese remained of the 70,000 who had held government positions at the beginning of occupation five months before.

Relations between the American command and Korean political organizations during the early period of occupation were not maintained with ease or mutual satisfaction. In view of the character of the American directive on the subject of these relations—namely, that no group should be recognized as having governmental authority and that all parties were to be impartially treated—it was inevitable that there would result considerable confusion in Korean political circles. The newly-acquired freedom of political expression led to irresponsibility and intense rivalry. There were literally dozens of new parties which continued to spring up all over the country, but it soon became apparent that in the American zone only two groups would dominate the political scene, the People's Republic on the left and the Korean Provisional Government on the right. The latter did not have an organized following in Korea at the time of occupation. But soon after the return to Korea of Dr. Syngman Rhee, Korean Provisional Government leader, from the United States, the rightist elements consolidated their position behind the exile Provisional Government.

The American command nominally kept its neutral position, but, as one observer put it, "it was no secret that it favored the right and was anxious for the parties of the right to acquire

[11] White House press release, September 18, 1945.

strong popular support."[12] The People's Republic laid itself open to suppression by American Military Government because of its refusal to abandon its claim to be a "government." The Korean Provisional Government made certain gestures of reorganizing as a political party in order to conform to the American regulations, but its officers continued to allude to its official character.[13]

In October 1945, General Hodge made it plain that there could be no compromise on the issue by stating: "Military Government is the only government in southern Korea."[14] The People's Republic, however, continued to function as a government in outlying areas. Finally, the issue was squarely met early in December 1945, after a "Congress" of the People's Republic, which met November 20, refused to dissolve itself. General Hodge issued the following statement:[15]

> Before the arrival of my forces in Korea there was set up here an organization known as the Chosen In Min Kong Wha Kook (Korean People's Republic). The name connoted, and its actions indicated, that this organization was set up to be a government rather than as a political party and its leaders spread the word to the Korean people that it was their new government.
>
> They [the leaders] failed to keep their promise to me that the situation would be completely clarified [at the November 20 congress]. . . . I feel it necessary to the public understanding to announce that, regardless of what it calls itself, the Korean People's Republic is not in any sense a 'government.' . . .
>
> . . . I have today directed my occupation forces and the Military Government of Korea that the activities of any political organiza-

[12] Sarafan, *loc. cit.*, p. 350.

[13] A feature article concerning Kim Koo, including his picture and a lengthy statement extracted from a radio address, appeared in the official publication of American Military Government, *Chukan Digest*, No. 8, December 8, 1945. Mr. Kim called upon the Koreans for unity and made the following remark: "My cabinet members and I are here only as plain citizens but we will try to do our best with you for accomplishing our independence."

[14] *Ibid.*, No. 2, October 25, 1945.

[15] *Ibid.*, No. 11, December 29, 1945.

tion in any attempted operations as a government are to be treated as unlawful activities. . . .

The Korean Provisional Government group was the nominal victor in the opening struggle, and in late December 1945 took occasion to show its strength. On December 28 the results of the Moscow three-power conference were announced and the news reached Korea that a five-year trusteeship was to be imposed upon the country. Without waiting for clarification of the reports, the Provisional Government organized a general work stoppage and mass demonstration in the city of Seoul. It attempted to take over the police force and the judicial system and it whipped up public hysteria in opposition to the Moscow decision. The strength of the group was impressive, and its following among Korean employees of Military Government gave it especial power. However, the leftist factions continued to rally about the remnants of the People's Republic.

The New York Times correspondent reported on January 5 that the conservative elements had "fallen far behind liberal as well as radical factions" and that the People's Republic "continues to gain strength in rural areas." The *Christian Science Monitor's* representative reported on January 3 that "the so-called People's Republic, composed of Socialist and Communist elements, enjoys far more popular support than any other single political grouping." [16]

In order to obtain Korean support for Military Government at a time when a low ebb had been reached in its popularity, the Representative Democratic Council was formed on February 14, 1946. It was an all-Korean body appointed to act in an advisory capacity to the Commanding General; Dr. Rhee was made chairman of the group. Since the appointees were almost all right-wing conservatives, the leading liberals refused to participate, with the result that the whole scheme was abortive.

[16] These two quotations, together with other pertinent data, are to be found in, McCune, "Occupation Politics in Korea," *Far Eastern Survey*, February 13, 1945, p. 36.

Critics of the Council likened it to the Central Advisory Council of the Japanese regime. A few weeks later Military Government analysts reported that an all-time low had been reached in American popularity.[17]

The Soviet Zone

At the outset of occupation the Russians encouraged a sweeping overthrow of the previous regime—its organization as well as its personnel. The activities of the Korean committees of law and order, functioning under the leadership of the People's Republic, fitted into the Soviet pattern. On August 25, 1945, more than two weeks before American troops landed in South Korea, the Soviet Command ordered what it called "The Executive Committee of the Korean People" to take over the administrative powers of the Chosen Government-General, thus installing the Korean revolutionists in nominal control. The Committee thereupon immediately expropriated and nationalized Japanese property.[18]

A hierarchy of "People's Committees" composed of Korean laborers, farmers and political organizers was soon set up with top control exercised by the Russian command. On February 9, 1946, a Provisional People's Committee for North Korea was established in place of the Executive Committee as the central governing organ, and the various political parties (Communist, Democratic, and Independence) were united in a single New People's Party.[19] An all-Korean "cabinet" was formed, headed by Kim Ilsung, a famous Korean Communist and revolutionist who had been operating in Manchuria for a number of years. No military government administration as such was

[17] USAMGIK, *Opinion Trends*, No. 6, April 7, 1946. The Council finally lost its official status on December 18, 1946.

[18] Information contained in message from Japanese government to Supreme Commander for the Allied Powers, August 29, 1945.

[19] For further details, see John N. Washburn, "Russia Looks at Northern Korea," *Pacific Affairs*, June 1947, pp. 152-60, which quotes extensively from Russian radio and newspaper reports concerning the early steps in occupation.

established by the Russians, although the Soviet command and the political officers attached to it maintained a close watch over their Korean protégés.

The Russian pattern of control gradually emerged during the early period of occupation, namely, the establishment of a strong all-Korean Communist regime which would work closely with the Soviets. Extreme care was taken by the Russians to keep themselves in the background as far as government was concerned, although there was no hesitation in loudly proclaiming Russian virtues. The picture of Stalin was displayed and the claim that Russia won the war against Japan as well as against Germany was widely disseminated. This policy contrasted sharply with American policy epitomized by the Hodge statement: "Military Government is the only government in southern Korea." The Russians avoided much criticism by hiding behind the Korean regime even though Russian control was only thinly veiled. But there was also considerable evidence to indicate that the Russians actually did permit the Koreans of their choice to exercise real authority, whereas in the American zone, the Korean employees of Military Government were allowed little power and no authority.

THE SIGNIFICANCE OF ZONAL DIVISION

The division of Korea into two occupation zones had been ostensibly a purely military decision of only momentary importance, and the choice of the 38° north latitude line as the boundary of those zones a purely arbitrary one.[20] However, from virtually the beginning of occupation, this demarcation was a far more effective dividing boundary than most national frontiers. As time went on the zonal division hardened all phases of Korean life into two separate patterns. As the Korean problem became linked with the dismal course of U.S.-Soviet relations, Korea was alienated against itself despite the fundamental homogeneity of the Korean people. This division came to be

[20] See pp. 43-44 for further details as to reasons for deciding upon a zonal occupation, marked by the 38th parallel.

the dominant force in Korean political and economic affairs.

Korea had been ruled thirty-five years by a foreign power which had tried to destroy the feeling of independent identity of the Korean people. Nonetheless, despite these efforts and the long deprivation of statehood, the country emerged from this rule in 1945 a distinct national group. Korean nationalism had remained a strong undercurrent which the Japanese could not control. Koreans unanimously welcomed the Japanese surrender as heralding the beginning of an independent existence for their country among the family of nations. The failure of the two occupying powers to agree and the persisting division of Korea was a profoundly disillusioning answer to the country's long struggle for independence.

The simple physical facts comparing the two zones can be briefly summarized, but the disruption which this division produced in economic, social and political terms was of considerably more significance. The American zone comprised 37,055 sq. mi. with a Korean population in May 1944 of 15,944,000 (430 per sq. mi.), whereas the Russian zone was 48,191 sq. mi. in size with 9,170,000 Koreans (190 per sq. mi.).[21] The cultivated acreage in each zone was almost equal, but the southern zone had three times as many acres of irrigated rice land as the northern.[22]

Cultivated Area by Acres

	Paddy	*Dry Field*	*Total*
Southern Zone	3,072,300	2,695,000	5,767,300
Northern Zone	1,097,600	5,343,450	6,441,050

While it has been emphasized that the Japanese economic development in Korea was in no sense aimed at making the

[21] See tables, Appendix B, for additional population statistics. It should be noted, however, that soon after occupation the southern zone rapidly increased its population because of the influx of repatriation from Japan and refugees from North Korea. In September 1947, the American zone was estimated to have increased its density to 548 persons per sq. mi. whereas the Soviet zone had decreased slightly in population.

[22] A. Grajdanzev, "Korea Divided," *Far Eastern Survey*, October 10, 1945, p. 282. (Converted from *cho* to acres.)

peninsula an integral whole, the resources of the area were such that it could be assumed to be potentially able to develop the economic basis for a firmly independent Korea. In many instances, the rationalization of industry carried out in Korea during the latter years of Japanese rule had given an excellent start to future Korean economic development. However, a strange freak of nature had dispersed these resources in unequal proportions between north and south, making the resources of one region complementary to those of the other.

Divided in two at the 38th parallel, neither part could by itself demonstrate convincing potentialities for economic independence. Since the 38° line was not only without any topographic basis, but also without any foundation in previous political and economic fact as well, the division amounted in reality to the vivisection of Korea. The line cut across provinces, counties, even towns.[23] One dramatic effect of the economic division of Korea caused by this boundary was the bisection of the Haeju industrial area on the Ongjin peninsula. The utility of this new Japanese development for either zone was largely negated when the survey revealed that port facilities were located in one zone and factories in the other. This was only a conspicuous manifestation of the much broader meaning of division to Korea.

The greater part of the country's mineral wealth was in the north, as was the heavy industry. The lighter consumer goods and processing industries were concentrated in the south along with a larger share of the agriculture. But the mineral resources and the heavy industries of North Korea were almost valueless to the North Koreans because there was no means of converting the raw materials into consumer goods, nor were there export markets where they could be traded. Furthermore, most of the heavy industries were dependent upon certain imported

[23] A detailed account of the way the 38th parallel cuts across Korea and the consequences of this division is given by Shannon McCune, "Physical Basis for Korean Boundaries," *Far Eastern Quarterly*, May 1946, pp. 272-88.

raw materials which were no longer available. For example, the aluminum production utilized bauxite from the South Pacific and alunite from South Korea, iron and steel smelting required coking coal from North China or Manchuria, some synthetic fertilizers needed imported phosphates, other chemicals depended upon salt importations. These industries, therefore, immediately withered on the vine. Even if they had continued in production, there were no manufacturing plants in North Korea to use the raw pig iron, the steel, aluminum, magnesium, copper, lead and zinc ingots, or the tons of acids, carbide, glycerine, absolute alcohol or rayon pulp which had previously been produced and exported to Japan or sent to South Korea for processing.

In South Korea, on the other hand, there were many manufacturing plants but most of them needed the raw materials from North Korea, among other urgent requirements. The rice fields needed synthetic fertilizer and the railways needed coal. The blockade at the 38th parallel denied these commodities to South Korea. Only electric power crossed the line (except for the thousands of refugees). In food supply, also, the dividing line caused real hardship. South Korea, the rice-producing area, withheld its rice crop from North Korea, leaving North Korea with less than its limited supply under Japanese dominion whereas South Korea possessed more than double its previous supply.[24] On the other hand, the South Koreans were deprived of their normal supply of fish, beans, millet, corn and wheat from the north.

In most characterizations of the two zones, for purposes of comparison, South Korea is termed an agricultural area and North Korea an industrial zone. Although these generalizations have some validity, they are misleading. Tables 3, 4 and 5, which follow, show that North Korea was much richer than South Korea in many agricultural products and was by no means deficient agriculturally except in rice and barley production. Industrial production also shows an almost equal distribution,

[24] See Chapters VII and XI following for details.

based upon the value of output, for both zones, although South Korea virtually monopolized the manufacturing output of the country (74 per cent), while North Korea produced almost all of the heavy industry (86 per cent). In mining, Table 5 shows that North Korea held a commanding lead, but even here South Korea was the major producing area for some of the major minerals. The inescapable conclusion from a review of these facts is that North and South Korea complemented one another and were each highly dependent upon the other for the satisfactory operation of their mutual economies. The diversity of Korean economic development made the uniting of the country of utmost importance to the rational recovery of Korean agriculture and industry and the ultimate attainment of a normal living standard for the Korean people.[25]

TABLE 3

MAJOR FOOD CROPS, NORTH AND SOUTH KOREA, 1944 PRODUCTION

	Production in koku (5.12 bu.)			*Percentage*	
	Total	*South*	*North*	*South*	*North*
Rice	16,051,879	10,259,927	5,791,952	64	36
Other Grains, listed	20,020,989	12,702,435	7,318,554	63	37
Barley	7,672,285	6,975,098	697,187	91	9
Naked Barley	3,130,847	3,128,301	2,546	99	1
Wheat	1,909,180	790,736	1,118,444	42	58
Rye	247,986	189,325	58,661	77	23
Millet	3,916,849	1,121,139	2,795,710	29	71
Barnyard Millet	413,326	40,695	372,631	10	90
German Millet	46,549	16,313	30,236	34	66
Oats	197,925	4,972	192,953	2	98
Buckwheat	642,287	262,420	379,867	41	59
Sorghum	699,449	77,386	622,063	11	89
Corn	1,144,306	96,050	1,048,256	9	91
Soy Beans	2,695,529	941,750	1,753,779	35	65
Red Soy Beans	605,566	94,505	511,061	16	84
Green Beans	53,864	7,885	45,979	15	85
Peanuts	6,892	4,613	2,279	31	69
Kidney Beans	32,741	2,601	30,140	8	92
Peas	8,242	1,404	6,838	17	83

[25] For further details see George M. McCune, "Essential Unity of Korean Economy," *Korea Economic Digest*, January 1946, pp. 3-8.

TABLE 4

VALUE OF INDUSTRIAL PRODUCTION, NORTH AND SOUTH KOREA, 1937 AND 1940

	Korean Production in Yen 1000		*Percentage 1937*		*Percentage 1940 (est.*)*	
	1937	*1940*	*South*	*North*	*South*	*North*
Heavy Industries	420,862	950,765	17	83	14	86
Chemicals	304,948	699,442	16	84	12	88
Metals	50,766	129,669	15	85	15	85
Ceramics (incl. Cement)	25,072	61,654	38	62	30	70
Gas & Electric	40,076	60,000 †	16	84	15	85
Light Industries	538,246	922,869	75	25	74	26
Textiles	141,154	232,178	88	12	86	14
Machines	16,565	76,665	71	29	70	30
Lumber	11,737	35,028	68	32	70	30
Food	238,033	373,404	67	33	65	35
Printing	16,304	19,071	90	10	90	10
Miscellaneous	114,653	186,523 †	77	23	76	24
TOTAL	959,308	1,873,634	50	50	46	54

* Based on McCune, "Essential Unity of Korean Economy," *loc. cit.*, p. 7.

† The miscellaneous total was given as 246,523 in 1940, but the Gas and Electrical category was censored. For the purposes of computation here, it is estimated that Gas and Electric accounted for approximately 25 per cent of the Miscellaneous total.

Sources: For 1937, *Chosen Nenkan 1941*, pp. 452-83; for 1940 *The Japan Yearbook 1943–44*, p. 912. (The latter source does not give the regional distribution.)

The damaging consequences to the economic development of the country of splitting Korea in two is easily demonstrated. It is less easy to show the social and political effects of this division. Obviously, however, the implantation of hostile ideologies in each half of the country would bring about conflict. Unfortunately, there was already an historical background of antagonism between North and South Korea of many centuries standing. That hostility may have begun in prehistoric Korea, when the tribal groupings of the north and south could be differentiated, or in the Three Kingdom Period (57 B.C. to 668 A.D.), when North Korea was under the domination of one kingdom

TABLE 5

SELECTED MINERALS, NORTH AND SOUTH KOREA, 1944 PRODUCTION

	Production (metric tons)			*Percentage*	
	Korea Total	*South*	*North*	*South*	*North*
Alunite	12,000	12,000	——	100	—
Apatite (Phosphate Rock)	37,692	——	37,692	—	100
Asbestos, Chrysotile	4,337	4,117	220	95	5
Asbestos, Mountain Leather	378	283	95	75	25
Barite	5,079	——	5,079	—	100
Coal	7,618,866	1,556,458	6,062,408	21	79
Anthracite	4,767,262	1,526,513	3,240,749	32	68
Lignite	2,851,604	29,945	2,821,659	1	99
Cobalt	6	6	——	100	—
Copper	4,197	2,302	1,895	55	45
Fluorite	130,000	61,000	69,000	47	53
Gold	20	7	13	37	63
Graphite	102,994	45,598	57,396	44	56
Ilmenite (Titanium)	248	13	235	5	95
Iron Ore *	3,331,814	110,757	3,221,057	3	97
Lead	19,663	8,386	11,277	43	57
Limestone	837,276	15,128	822,148	2	98
Lithium Ore	764	730	34	96	4
Magnesite	388,187	——	388,187	—	100
Manganese	32,377	32,377	——	100	—
Mica (Phlogopite)	445	44	405	10	90
Molybdenite	605	521	84	86	14
Nickel	621	181	440	29	71
Pyrite	246,002	——	246,002	—	100
Pyrophyllite (Talc)	41,211	40,011	1,200	97	3
Tungsten	11,509	6,217	5,292	54	46
Zinc	15,114	3,788	11,326	25	75

* These figures include only the iron ore destined for exportation and do not include the ore mined and smelted in Korea, if the usual Japanese computing methods were employed.

and South Korea under two others. Later in Korean history there grew up strong political parties, the North and the South parties, which carried on a bitter struggle for supremacy. It is a commonplace in Korea for a "southerner" to characterize the northern Korean as uncouth, uneducated, and a troublemaker.

The "northerner," on the other hand, is often contemptuous of his southern neighbor whom he believes to be lazy, effete, lacking in ambition and a scheming rascal. The northern area has a revolutionary reputation, also. Under the old Korean monarchy frequent revolts originated in the north, and during Japanese rule, North Korea was much less tractable than South Korea.

Likewise, social differences between North and South Korea were of striking significance.[26] Basically the contrast stemmed from the difference in land utilization: South Korea was primarily a rice-culture area and North Korea a dry-field area. In consequence South Korea developed an agricultural economy of small farms with a high tenancy rate whereas North Korean agriculture was characterized by larger farms and more owner-farmers.[27]

Percentage Distribution of Farms by Size, 1938

	South Korea	*North Korea*	*Total*
Smallest Farms, less than 2.45 acres	77.4	34.9	63.3
Small Farms, 2.45 to 7.35 acres	21.0	50.0	30.6
Middle-sized Farms, 7.35 to 12.25 acres	1.3	11.6	4.7
Large Farms, more than 12.25 acres	0.3	3.5	1.4
	100.0	100.0	100.0

Source: Grajdanzev, *loc. cit.*, and *Modern Korea*, p. 113.

Farm Households by Kind, 1943

				Percentages		
	South Korea	*North Korea*	*Total*	*South*	*North*	*Total*
Owner-Operator	284,837	251,345	536,182	14	26	18
Part-Owner Part-Tenant	675,271	309,083	984,354	33	31	32
Full Tenant	1,044,490	437,014	1,481,504	51	42	49
Laborers, etc.	35,816	8,145	43,961	2	1	1
Total	2,040,414	1,005,587	3,046,001	100	100	100

Source: U.S. Department of State Economic Mission, "Land Reform in Korea," Seoul, Sept. 13, 1947 (mimeographed), Enclosure A.

[26] Grajdanzev, "Korea Divided," *loc. cit.*, made these social contrasts the central theme of his article.

[27] Statistical data on this contrast is clearly presented in two tables, one on the size of farms, the other on tenancy conditions.

The landlord in North Korea was less powerful than in South Korea, and agrarian reform, though less needed, was easier to put into effect without disrupting the economic and social system. From the standpoint of the social character of the two zones of Korea, it appeared that revolutionary Soviet policies of confiscation and socialization might meet little resistance in North Korea, and that American policies of conservatism and moderate reform might be acceptable in South Korea for a short time at least. But it was also obvious that the contrast in social conditions and reform policies between the two zones would ultimately bring about critical difficulties.

CHAPTER FOUR

Korea in International Affairs since 1945

THE MOSCOW PLAN

IN ORDER to overcome the highly damaging consequences of the continued division of the country and to specify definite plans for the future of Korea, the Foreign Ministers of the United States, the Soviet Union and the United Kingdom, in their meeting at Moscow in December 1945, concluded an agreement in which they were later joined by China. This agreement came to be accepted as the basic document governing the future development of an independent Korean state.[1] It provided for the convening of a Joint American-Soviet Commission, representing the two commands in Korea, whose primary duty was to assist in the formation of a provisional Korean democratic government through consultation with "Korean democratic parties and social organizations" as the first step in assuring the establishment of an independent and sovereign Korean nation. By the terms of the Moscow agreement (Article 3), furthermore, the Joint Commission was charged with the responsibility of framing proposals "following consultation with the provisional Korean Government, for the joint consideration of the Governments of the United States, Union of Soviet Socialist Republics, United Kingdom and China for the working out of an agreement concerning a four-power trusteeship of Korea for a period up to five years."

[1] See Appendix A for complete text of Moscow Agreement on Korea.

The First Joint Commission

A preliminary conference was held in January and February 1946 between the two commands for the purpose of arranging for coordination of administrative-economic matters between the two zones, but the conference was unsuccessful. On March 20 the full-dress Joint Conference opened, but after a number of sessions it adjourned *sine die* on May 8 without having reached any conclusion. The American command charged that the Soviet delegation was exclusively responsible for the breakdown of discussions. According to the Americans, "Russian delegates insisted that any Korean party representatives who had ever expressed criticism of trusteeship should be ineligible for consultation in forming the proposed Korean provisional government. The American position was that such an interpretation would deny the rights of free speech." [2]

The Russian command, on the other hand, charged that the Americans were taking a stand contradictory to the Moscow agreement pertaining to Korea. Secretary Molotov wrote: "The American delegation precluded the participation of a series of major democratic organizations of southern Korea and insisted that invitations to consultation be sent to groups which were opposing the Moscow agreement. . . ." [3]

The underlying reason for the failure of negotiations was the clash of opposing powers: the United States was determined to create a Korean government favorable to its interests; the Soviet Union was equally determined to provide for a Soviet-oriented Korean nation. The clash was personified in the disagreement on the eligibility for discussions of conservative anti-Soviet Koreans, notably Syngman Rhee, a repatriate from the United States, and Kim Koo, from China, both leaders in the defunct Korean Provisional Government of Chungking. The American command

[2] *U.S. Army Military Government in Korea, Summation of Activities,* August 1946, p. 101. (Hereafter referred to as *USAMGIK Summation.*)

[3] Appendix A, Molotov letter, April 19, 1947.

refused to have them barred; the Russians refused to consult with them on any terms.

After the breakdown of negotiations, the American and Russian commands moved farther and farther apart. The 38th parallel became an impassable barrier. The American government asked for the right to establish consular representation in Pyŏngyang, the Soviet capital of the north, but was refused. In retaliation, the Russian consular staff was forced by the Americans to withdraw from Seoul in June 1946, marking a low ebb in relations between the two powers. Despite this impasse, Lieutenant General John R. Hodge, American commander, addressed to the Russian commander several proposals for reconvening the Joint Commission, but no formula for solving the disagreement seemed acceptable.[4] Recourse to Washington and Moscow appeared to be the only way of breaking the deadlock. Major General Archibald V. Arnold, chief American delegate on the Commission, stated in Washington on October 10, 1946, that there "was no hope of accomplishing it [reconciliation] on the occupational level in Korea. . . . If anything is done, it must be on a higher level." [5]

Marshall and Molotov Notes

Ultimately, the subject of Korea was taken up in an exchange of communications between Secretary of State George C. Marshall and Foreign Minister V. M. Molotov during the Moscow Foreign Ministers' Conference of 1947. Secretary Marshall wrote Molotov on April 8, reviewing the Korean situation and requesting that the Joint Commission be reconvened "as soon as possible" and that it be charged with "expediting its work under the terms of the Moscow Agreement on a basis of respect for

[4] The correspondence between the two commands in Korea, and also the communications between Washington and Moscow, have been published almost in their entirety in the *Department of State Bulletin*. A compilation of these documents was also issued in October 1947 by the Department of State in a pamphlet entitled *Korea's Independence*.

[5] *New York Times*, October 11, 1946.

the democratic rights of freedom of opinion." He further suggested that a date in the summer of 1947 be chosen "for a review by the two Governments of the progress made to that date by the Joint Commission."

Foreign Minister Molotov in his reply of April 19 summarized the Russian position vis-à-vis Korea and suggested that the Commission reconvene on May 20 and report in July–August 1947. He was not explicit, however, as to the formula for choosing Korean organizations for consultation. In a further exchange of communications this question was considerably clarified by a compromise in which Marshall indicated that "freedom of opinion" would not be interpreted to include sanction to attack the work of the Commission, and Molotov accepted the American insistence on consulting many Korean groups which the Russians had previously barred by agreeing to the formula already proposed by General Hodge in his letters to the Russian commander.

THE FAILURE OF U.S.-SOVIET NEGOTIATIONS

The Consultation Problem

The second session of the Joint Commission opened in Seoul on May 22, 1947. The first important decision which had to be reached was the means by which Korean consultees would be chosen, the issue which had wrecked previous consultations and eventually proved the breaking-point of this session as well. In the preliminary negotiations each side had modified its stand somewhat, the Americans giving way to the Russian insistence that Koreans who actively opposed the Moscow decision should not be consulted, even though such a restriction might be interpreted as a limitation upon "freedom of opinion." The Russians, on the other hand, were now willing to accept for consultation many Korean groups which had previously opposed the Moscow decision provided they would declare their support and would cease fomenting opposition.

On June 12 a joint communiqué was issued outlining the agreed method of consultation. Groups of Koreans were invited to submit applications for participation in Seoul or Pyŏngyang by June 23, and also to submit their views concerning the proposed provisional government by filling out a questionnaire by July 1. Meetings of applicants were to be held in Seoul on June 25 and in Pyŏngyang on June 30, but oral consultation would not commence until July 5.[6] Applications were accepted as planned in both zones and the preliminary meetings were held on the dates scheduled.[7]

Applicants for consultation were numerous and the problem of carrying out the oral stage of negotiations was certain to be difficult. In the American zone 425 groups, claiming a total cumulative membership of 52,000,000 persons, submitted applications; in the Soviet zone, 38 groups, claiming 13,300,000 total members, applied. This membership showed much overlapping (one person belonging to several groups) and probably considerable exaggeration as well. (The adult population of South Korea was approximately 9,500,000, of North Korea, 4,-500,000.) In the American zone there were 39 political parties and 386 social organizations (civic, business and professional groups, labor and farmers' unions, etc.); in the Soviet zone there were three political parties and 35 social organizations.[8] In the south, the rightists claimed 25,000,000 members, the moderates and leftists each claimed 13,500,000. In the northern zone, the only applicants were members of the Democratic Front, hence leftists. Under the circumstances, therefore, leftist applicants were numerically stronger than rightists in Korea as a whole. Furthermore, the leftist groups were well disciplined to follow

[6] Department of State, *Korea's Independence*, Annex IX, pp. 41-45.

[7] At each of these sessions a joint statement was read to the public assembly. In Seoul the statement was read by Colonel General Shtikov, chief Soviet delegate, and in Pyŏngyang it was read by Major General Albert E. Brown, chief American delegate. Statement is published in *ibid.*, Annex X, pp. 45-49.

[8] Press release of Major General Brown, Seoul, July 12, 1947 (mimeographed).

the Soviet line, whereas the rightists were notoriously intransigent.

Even before the Soviet delegates arrived in Seoul, there were many indications that the Korean rightist politicians would not cooperate in good faith with the Joint Commission. The Anti-Trusteeship Committee which had been originally formed in December 1945 by rightist party leaders was resurrected for the purpose of blocking the work of the Joint Commission. (The Committee hypocritically claimed to be innocent of instigating opposition but its subversive activities were well known to both delegations.[9]) The Anti-Trusteeship Committee was an embarrassment to the American delegation, which was caught in a dilemma. If the rightists were repudiated because of their bad faith, the American delegation would have eliminated the largest group of anti-Communists in South Korea. On the other hand, if the Americans supported the Korean reactionaries, it was almost inevitable that the Joint Commission would collapse. At first the American command attempted to force the rightists into line, but the efforts proved unsuccessful.[10]

Breakdown of Negotiations

Disagreement began to develop in the Joint Commission early in July over the question of oral consultations. On July 10 the Russian delegation proposed a drastic cut in the number of groups to be consulted in South Korea—118 instead of 425—omitting most of the rightists who had shown little disposition to cooperate with the Joint Commission and had continued to

[9] The Committee's letter claiming innocence, dated July 28, 1947, may be found in, Department of State, *Korea's Independence*, Annex XI, p. 49.

[10] Several steps were taken to discredit the extreme conservatives: April 22, the Young Men's Association, rightist terrorists, were ordered dissolved; May 13, General Lerch declared illegal a rightist attempt to reinstate the "Korean Provisional Government"; May 18, orders were issued against mass demonstrations during Joint Commission meetings; May 25, General Hodge rebuked rightist Syngman Rhee publicly for making unfounded claims of American backing. Despite these efforts, the rightists continued to agitate against the Joint Commission and to "blackmail" the American command.

support the Anti-Trusteeship Committee. By July 15 the break had become serious and Major General Brown issued a unilateral press release publicly revealing the points of disagreement.[11] The Soviet delegation, he charged, wished to eliminate many of the groups submitting questionnaires either on grounds that they were not genuine social organizations or that they did not support the Moscow decision. The American delegation believed that the Soviet delegation was attempting to exercise veto power and that its position was contrary to the Moscow agreement and the Marshall-Molotov letters.

The Commission continued in session but progress ceased and the chief delegates began a battle of recriminations and accusations which rendered further negotiation futile. The American command had already withdrawn its ban on mass demonstrations against the Moscow decision and in effect invited the reactionary elements to attack the Soviets openly. Lyuh Woon-hyung, leading compromise candidate for leadership in a provisional government and famous head of the 1945 People's Republic, was assassinated on July 19; assailants attacked Soviet delegates on July 26. A leftist revolt believed scheduled for August 3 (the date of a memorial service for Lyuh) did not materialize, but a campaign against leftist leaders in South Korea was vigorously pursued during August.[12] This anti-Communist campaign was soon made the subject of sharp exchanges between Delegate Shtikov and Delegate Brown, the former accusing the Americans of instigating pogroms "aimed at disrupting the work of the commission," while the latter charged that the Soviets were abusing their "guest status" by trying to interfere in the internal affairs of the American zone.

In the meantime an American proposal of July 25 for a new method of reviewing the list of consultees was summarily re-

[11] "U.S.-Soviet Views on Consultative Groups," *Department of State Bulletin*, August 10, 1947, pp. 294-96.

[12] For further details see section on Suppression of Communism, Chapter V.

jected by the Soviet negotiators on July 29.[13] Another effort was made on August 12 by the American delegation, which recommended that there be no oral consultations, but that the Commission proceed with setting up a provisional government on the basis of the written questionnaires. These plans would call for a free election of a national legislature. The Soviet delegation at this point offered a counter-proposal which accepted the omission of oral consultations, but advocated a provisional assembly composed of equal representation north and south of only those parties that "fully support the Moscow agreement." This plan was rejected by the American delegation for obvious reasons.[14]

On August 11 Secretary of State Marshall proposed to the Soviet government that the Commission be instructed to report by August 21 "the status of deliberations."[15] In reply, Foreign Minister Molotov wrote, on August 23, that the Soviet government had no objection to asking the Commission to report, but that it could not consent to consultation with Korean groups active in the Anti-Trusteeship Committee, and that it considered the arrest of leftist leaders in South Korea "inadmissible."

THE UNITED NATIONS TEMPORARY COMMISSION

The communication of Foreign Minister Molotov of August 23 brought forth a lengthy reply from Acting Secretary Robert A. Lovett under the date of August 26, 1947. This letter proposed a new course of action to replace the seemingly hopeless Moscow plan, although Lovett stated that the new proposal

[13] *Department of State Bulletin*, August 10, 1947, pp. 296-97. The U.S. delegation proposed that each delegation consult parties in its own zone only. On August 1, the U.S. suggested that its delegation would consult, for the whole Commission, the parties which the Soviets wished ruled out, but this idea was also rejected. Department of State, *Korea's Independence*, p. 8.

[14] Department of State, *Korea's Independence*, pp. 8-9.

[15] See Appendix A for this and succeeding communications.

was "designed to achieve the aims of the Moscow agreement." The United States asked that the four powers originally slated to become trustees of Korea (the United States, the Soviet Union, the United Kingdom and China) attend a conference in Washington on September 8 to discuss the Korean problem. Secretary Lovett, furthermore, set forth a substitute for the Moscow plan, the chief feature of which was the holding of elections in Korea under the guidance of the United Nations for the formation of a provisional legislature and government. A seven-point program covering procedure was enclosed in the letter.

After receiving Foreign Minister Molotov's refusal to accept the new plan, the State Department on September 17 stated that the Korean case would be submitted to the United Nations General Assembly. The Soviets, however, put forth a plan of their own. In late August, Delegate Shtikov in Seoul had suggested that the Commission appoint a national assembly from consultative groups, and then on September 26 he proposed that both American and Soviet troops withdraw from Korea by January 1, 1948, to let the Koreans conduct their own elections.[16] The American government rejected both of these proposals in view of the fact that the State Department had already decided to carry through its plan of presenting the problem to the United Nations General Assembly.

In his address before the General Assembly on September 17, Secretary Marshall introduced the subject of Korea and notified the Assembly of the intention of the United States government to present the problem at the session.[17] On September 23 the American resolution was placed on the agenda; on October 17 a formal presentation was made by Ambassador Warren R. Austin; on November 5 the Political and Security Committee voted

[16] These proposals by the chief Soviet delegate in Seoul were repeated in letters of Foreign Minister Molotov to Secretary Marshall, the first proposal in his letter of September 4, 1947, and the second proposal in his communication of October 9, 1947. See Appendix A for these documents.

[17] Excerpt relating to Korea may be found in, Department of State, *Korea's Independence*, Annex I, pp. 15-16.

46 to 0 for the creation of a United Nations Temporary Commission on Korea to expedite the moves toward independence; and on November 14 the General Assembly adopted the resolution by a vote of 43 to 0.

In the deliberations of the United Nations, the Soviet Union and its satellites objected vigorously to the American plan, first on grounds that elections in "occupied" Korea would not be a true reflection of the Korean will, and next that Korean delegates should be heard first by the United Nations before the plan was adopted. Finally, the Soviets declared that the Korean problem was not an appropriate question to come before the United Nations and that the Soviet Union could not accept the decision reached. The Soviet bloc then boycotted the voting.

The United Nations Resolution [18] as finally passed called for the creation of a Temporary Commission consisting of representatives of Australia, Canada, China, El Salvador, France, India, the Philippines, Syria, and the Ukrainian Soviet Socialist Republic. The last-named state refused to participate. The resolution further "recommended" that an election be held in Korea not later than March 31, 1948, for membership in a national assembly, which, in turn, would form a national government. The United Nations Commission, having "facilitated and expedited" progress thus far, was then to consult with the newly formed government concerning the steps to be taken for transferring to it, as the Korean provisional government, final authority from the occupants and for the withdrawal of foreign armed forces.

Underlying the United Nations resolution was an emphasis upon the creation of a united Korea—the forming of a national government. But the attainment of such an objective seemed remote as long as the Soviet Union refused to participate in the plan. The upshot of the effort, therefore, appeared to be either an early abandonment of the project, or the continuation of a modified arrangement which would apply to South Korea only. The ultimate disposition of the Korean problem on the inter-

[18] See Appendix A for text.

national level was still far from solution when the United Nations Temporary Commission opened its sessions in Seoul early in January 1948.[19]

[19] For a discussion of later developments, see Chapter XII. Those developments include the activities of the Temporary Commission in connection with the May 10 elections, and the establishment of the southern Republic of Korea.

CHAPTER FIVE

The American Interim Regime

AFTER the Joint American-Russian Commission adjourned in May 1946, hope faded for an early abolition of the 38th parallel dividing line. This meant that in each zone constructive steps had to be taken at once to improve the unsatisfactory temporary administration. In a sense, therefore, May 8, 1946 (the date of adjournment of the Commission), was a turning point in the activities of the two occupying powers. The Soviet regime intensified its policy of communizing North Korea and of building up a strong native government. The Americans, likewise, turned attention to the encouragement of democratization, took up a campaign against Communism, and sought to establish an effective representative Korean administration under Military Government.

In the American zone, occupation policy tended to develop directly along three lines: (1) progressive relinquishment of more and more administrative responsibility to the Korean bureaucracy; (2) establishment of a semi-legislative assembly which could reflect Korean wishes and share the burden of policy formation; and (3) suppression of Communist agitation which threatened to weaken the development of democratic institutions.

USE OF KOREAN PERSONNEL

In South Korea, under the sponsorship of Military Government, Korean personnel was given more and more responsibility. On August 31, 1946, General Hodge requested the Military Governor, Major General Archer L. Lerch, to turn over operation of the various government departments to Koreans, leaving American military personnel to remain in advisory capacities only.[1]

Early in 1947, the capitol building was turned over to Koreans entirely and American advisers moved to other quarters. In February 1947, a Korean, Mr. Ahn Chaihong, was sworn in as Civil Administrator. Mr. Kim Yongmu, Chief Justice of the Korean Supreme Court and Head of the Judiciary, officiated at the ceremony, while Dr. Kimm Kiusic, Chairman of the Korean Interim Legislative Assembly, made the principal congratulatory address.[2] A further step was taken on May 17, 1947, when the Korean elements of Military Government were officially named the South Korean Interim Government (SKIG).[3]

The structure of USAMGIK and SKIG was similar to the Japanese administration which it replaced with the notable exception of the Legislative Assembly. The Judicial Branch, including the judiciary and courts, was little changed except in personnel. The Civil Administrator directed the activities of the various departments and offices of the central government as well as the provincial administration. As of September 30, 1946,

[1] *USAMGIK Summation*, August 1946, p. 99.

[2] Letter of General Archer L. Lerch to Mr. Kim, President of Korean Affairs Institute, *Voice of Korea*, March 1, 1947.

[3] The new name was adopted less than a week before the reconvening of the Joint American-Soviet Commission. The name USAMGIK was not dropped since it was still applied to the American staff which acted in an advisory capacity, and to the top control. However, all releases and publications of the various agencies of government soon bore the new heading. Eventually the monthly *USAMGIK Summation* was issued as *South Korean Interim Government Activities*, with SKIG first assuming full responsibility for the September 1947 issue.

the bureau divisions, renamed but otherwise unchanged, were as follows: 13 Departments: public information, internal security, police, transportation, labor, communications, finance, education, justice, health and welfare, commerce, public works, agriculture; 4 Offices: administration, property custody, Korean civil service, foreign affairs; 10 Provinces including the city of Seoul.[4] Directly under the Military Governor were a number of special agencies such as the National Economic Board, National Price Administrator, and National Food Administrator.

Despite the creation of a Korean bureaucracy which exercised considerable independent authority, the American command and the Military Governor exerted more than advisory power. The Military Governor still retained his authority to appoint key personnel, to promulgate ordinances, and to determine policy. A hierarchy of American Military Government officials, who were nominally advisers of Korean department and bureau chiefs but were more often the final authority on important issues, was established in adjacent offices. The American advisers held a tight grip on the operation of each department, particularly in the selection of personnel and in financial matters. Control was exercised mainly by requiring that all important directives be countersigned by the American advisers. In August 1947, 3,231 Americans, of whom 2,594 were military and 637 civilian personnel, were engaged in civil government activities.[5]

The Koreans expressed some dissatisfaction with the limitations placed upon them. "The matters of finance are essential to running a government," explained Brigadier General Charles G. Helmick, Acting Military Governor, on January 3, 1947, "and

[4] See *USAMGIK Summation*, September 1946, p. ii, for a complete chart, giving the subdivisions under each bureau. This listing may also be found in an article by the author, "Post-War Government and Politics of Korea," *The Journal of Politics*, November 1947, pp. 614-15. A reorganization was approved in May 1947 but was not put into effect during 1947. The bureaus were to remain much the same but changes were to be made in the subdivisions to make them conform more nearly to American practice.

[5] Department of State, Office of Public Affairs, *Background Summary on Korea*, 44-page pamphlet, August 1947, p. 7.

while Koreans are given more and more authority, the policy of finance is so closely tied up with responsibility of government that transfer has not yet been made. . . . One particular reason for the Americans' keeping close control is that a great deal of money from the U.S. is being used to further the civilian goods program, the import of fertilizer, and the import of grains. A very close contact exists and a control of finances must be maintained." [6]

On the policy-making level, the American command also sought to transfer greater responsibility to the Koreans. The chief deterrent was the overwhelming Korean dislike of accepting the supreme authority of the American command and of agreeing with the Moscow decision. Instead of cooperation, the Koreans were inclined to be antagonistic. This was especially true of the first advisory organization set up by the American command, the Democratic Council, which came into being in February 1946. The Democratic Council, headed by Syngman Rhee, and dominated by former Provisional Government members and extreme conservatives, proved to be a boomerang to the Americans by becoming the center of opposition to Military Government. It was of almost no value whatsoever in assisting in the framing of policy. Furthermore, the Council aroused intense antagonism to the Moscow decision and to the Russian delegation during the first sessions of the Joint American-Soviet Commission, when, as an instrument of Military Government, it should have been exerting its influence toward a satisfactory settlement of the question of the division of the country.

THE KOREAN INTERIM LEGISLATIVE ASSEMBLY

In the summer of 1946, the American command decided to establish an Interim Legislative Assembly, which would supersede the Democratic Council and would provide the Koreans with a more representative voice in policy matters. An ordinance of August 24, 1946, set forth the details of the organiza-

[6] Press conference, Seoul, January 3, 1947. *Voice of Korea*, February 15, 1947.

tion, functions and procedure of selecting the membership of the proposed Assembly.[7]

Half of the 90-man group was to be elected and half appointed. Indirect elections—passing in four stages from village to province—were set for October and November, and the Assembly was to meet for its first session on November 4.[8]

Almost immediately after the decision was reached for the creation of an Assembly, a tremendous struggle for power began in Korean political circles. The rightist groups took the American move as an indication that an "independent" South Korea might eventuate and they began to agitate for the setting up of a separate state. Their candidates were pledged to oppose the Moscow decision and to demand immediate independence. The leftists, on the other hand, opposed the election plans and accused Military Government of carrying out a policy of further separating the two halves of Korea.

Coalition Committee

In order to bring together dissident Korean groups, a Coalition Committee (sometimes called the Unification Committee) was formed early in October 1946, under the joint chairmanship of Dr. Kimm Kiusic, a moderate leader of the rightists (one-time vice-president of the Korean Provisional Government in Chungking), and Lyuh Woonhyung, moderate leftist (one-time head of the People's Republic).

In a declaration of principles, October 7, 1946, the Coalition Committee voiced adherence to the Moscow decision, called for an early reconvening of the Joint Commission, approved plans for free distribution of farmland, called for punishment of pro-Japanese and for release of political prisoners arrested under Military Government, and declared its support of freedom of speech, assembly, and organization. The Committee furthermore recommended to General Hodge that it be empowered to

[7] Ordinance No. 118, *Voice of Korea*, November 16, 1946.

[8] Order of the Military Governor, October 15. *New York Times*, October 16, 1946.

nominate the one-half membership of the Legislative Assembly appointed by him, and also that the Committee be empowered to supervise provincial elections for the Assembly.[9]

Coincident with the meetings of the Coalition Committee, a wave of violence, including strikes, riots and many other demonstrations of open rebellion, swept South Korea. In the city of Taegu alone fifty-three members of the police force were killed by enraged mobs, who counted their dead by the dozens also.[10] The American command announced that the uprising was the result of Communist agitation, while the Communists charged that it was the inevitable consequence of suppression and misrule. Whatever the cause, it was obvious that constructive measures had to be taken at once to re-establish authority and to meet the ever-increasing opposition to Military Government.

Joint Korean-American Conference

A Joint Korean-American Conference was therefore called to discuss the disturbances in South Korea. Meeting first on October 23, 1946, those attending included members of the Coalition Committee and of Military Government, the chief delegate of the United States on the Joint American-Soviet Commission, and the State Department adviser to General Hodge.[11] The extreme left-wing groups, who had not joined with the Coalition Committee, but who had appealed for permission to investigate the Taegu disorders in the name of the Committee of Nine Political Parties, were asked to send three delegates to the conference sessions.[12]

The Joint Korean-American Conference was moderately successful in fulfilling its purpose. Many of the complaints of the Koreans were aired and seriously considered by the Americans, who, in turn, had an opportunity to present their complaints as

[9] *USAMGIK Summation*, October 1946, pp. 16-18.

[10] *Ibid.*, October 1946, for details. See also *New Korea* and *Korean Independence* for additional news coverage, including reprints of dispatches from the American press.

[11] *USAMGIK Summation*, November 1946.

[12] *Ibid.*, October 1946, p. 18.

well, on a give-and-take level. In a series of statements issued early in November, the Conference announced that it had discussed the complaints concerning police, the presence of former Japanese collaborators in Military Government, the use of interpreters, and the widespread corruption. On the subject of the police, there was recognition of just cause for complaint. (The disorders in Taegu were not blamed exclusively on Communist agitation.) As to collaborators, the Conference concluded that "eventual solution is one largely to be determined by Koreans themselves. In a nation forty years in bondage, a certain measure of collaboration was in general the necessary price of continued existence." The difference between voluntary and forced collaboration was noted. Interpreters, it was agreed, "were a necessary evil," and corruption was to be more vigorously prosecuted. (The Americans announced that two American officers had recently been court-martialed and sentenced to long terms for violation of regulations in this regard.) [13]

Composition of Interim Legislative Assembly

The results of the elections for the Interim Legislative Assembly were announced early in November, but the opening session was postponed by order of General Hodge until such a time as investigations could be made as to reported irregularities in the election procedure. Dr. Kimm Kiusic, Chairman of the Coalition Committee, wrote to General Hodge "requesting that the results of the elections to the Legislature be invalidated. Dr. Kimm expressed the belief that Leftist candidates were handicapped by current police investigations." [14] Elections were annulled in Seoul and in one province, but a revote did not alter the situation. The elections had given an overwhelming victory to the extreme conservatives: 15 seats to members of the Korean Democratic Party, 14 seats to the Society for the Rapid Realization of Independence, and 2 to the Independence Party, all right-wing parties. Of the remaining 14 seats, only 2 went to

[13] *Ibid.*, November 1946.
[14] *Ibid.*

the left wing (from Cheju Island), and the other 12, although undesignated as party members, were claimed by the right wing.

On December 10, the commanding general announced the names of the 45 men he had appointed to the Assembly which was to convene for the first session on December 12. "Selections were made," he stated, "after nominations by the Coalition Committee and consultations with many of the leaders of political and professional thought. . . ." [15] Six members of the Coalition Committee itself were selected, three of the right and three of the left. Dr. Kimm Kiusic (who became Chairman of the Assembly), Lyuh Woonhyung, and Ahn Chaihong (who later became Civil Administrator in Military Government) were the leading trio. Four women were also appointed. No member of the Communist Party was included, but about 20 members of other leftist parties were appointed. Rightist party members were also included in General Hodge's list as well as a number of professional men without party affiliation.[16]

In September 1947, after almost a year of sessions, the roster of the Assembly showed a total membership of 85 with a distribution as follows: [17]

	Elected	*Appointed*	*Total*
Right	38	17	55
Moderate	1	15	16
Left	2	12	14
Total	41	44	85

By his appointments General Hodge was able to give better representation to the real wishes of the Korean people, because it was quite obvious to all observers that the election was undemocratic and superficial. In most areas there was literally no election at all—the village headman simply acted as spokesman

[15] *Ibid.*, December 1946, p. 13.

[16] For list of appointees and their party affiliations, see *New Korea*, January 2, 1947.

[17] Compiled from the roster of names and affiliations published in *SKIG Activities*, September 1947, pp. 115-16.

for his constituents. In other areas, the election rules were the same as those which had been used by the Japanese administration—only taxpayers and landholders voted. American Military Government had foreseen this situation and had provided for the half-elected, half-appointed Assembly, and had not attempted to institute a democratic election. On February 3 General Lerch, in a message to the Assembly, pointed out the need for suffrage legislation and stated: "The primary purpose of setting up the Korean Interim Legislative Assembly . . . was to provide the means by which the Korean people themselves could enact an ordinance providing for universal suffrage and a legislative assembly to succeed the temporary assembly. . . . It is my hope that the universal suffrage law and the provision for a Legislature completely elective in nature can be enacted sufficiently early to provide for the actual seating of the members of the new legislative body not later than June 30." [18]

Assembly Activity

With considerable fanfare the Interim Legislative Assembly opened its sessions on December 12, 1946, but a discordant note was struck when 38 members of the right wing boycotted the first session in protest to the appointment of liberal and left-wing members by General Hodge. The intransigent members finally took up their seats on December 23, but almost immediately began a campaign to embarrass Military Government.[19] In December 1946, Dr. Rhee, the titular head of the rightist coalition, had left Korea and had gone to the United States where he was engaged in a vigorous effort to secure support for the creation of an independent South Korea. In Korea his party carried on a parallel campaign and in effect blocked all constructive work of the Legislative Assembly. The Assembly recessed on December 30, and reconvened on January 6.

General Hodge found it expedient on January 4, 1947, to

[18] *Voice of Korea*, March 1, 1947.
[19] *USAMGIK Summation*, December 1946, p. 14.

issue a lengthy statement concerning the question of separate statehood for South Korea, which had aroused such bitter controversy between right and left and threatened to embroil the United States in further difficulty. Calling upon the Koreans for more unified action, he said:

> Either through lack of knowledge of fact or through malicious intent to deceive the Korean people, certain elements are creating the impression that the United States now favors and is actively working toward a separate government in southern Korea; and that the Korean Interim Legislative Assembly is a completely independent body designed as a forerunner of that government. Both of the above assumptions are incorrect and dangerous conclusions, entirely without justification, and are contrary to the announced basic policies of the United States and the other great Allied Power who liberated Korea from the Japanese.[20]

The conservatives increased their attack early in January when the Assembly reconvened, especially after the announcement of a further exchange of communications between the American and Russian commands looking toward the reconvening of the Joint Commission. A long appeal to the Assembly by the Acting Military Governor on January 9 for action on a number of pressing problems, mainly economic, which demanded the attention of the Koreans, was virtually ignored. On January 20, a resolution which had been brought forward by the conservatives in condemnation of the steps taken by General Hodge with regard to the trusteeship issue was finally brought to a vote. Efforts to amend the resolution and to postpone action failed. A large number of delegates absented themselves from the final session. The vote was: 44 for; 1 against; 9 abstentions. One part of the resolution stated: "That regardless of the fact that Koreans strongly object to the provision for trusteeship of Korea in the Moscow Agreement, General Hodge understands that signing the 5th Communiqué of the Joint Commission means supporting the Moscow Agreement in full. This is a distortion of the general will of the people. We, hereby, point

[20] *Ibid.*, January 1947, p. 12.

out the unreasonableness of his contention and oppose it strongly." The resolution went on to criticize General Hodge for forbidding freedom of speech.[21]

On January 25, General Hodge briefly pointed out that there were a number of erroneous statements in the resolution and suggested that the discussion in the Assembly on the trusteeship issue was in itself a demonstration of the freedom of expression guaranteed to the Koreans.

The American command continued to prod the Assembly to take constructive action on more appropriate issues. General Lerch, on February 5, 1947, in a letter to Chairman Kimm Kiusic, wrote: "I regard as both wasteful and useless the discussion of problems whose solution is beyond the power of the Legislature."[22] But in another communication, General Lerch optimistically wrote: "But with the new spirit of political collaboration and harmony which is being demonstrated, the prospects are bright for early solution to many of Korea's knotty problems."[23]

Not until August 12, 1947, did the Interim Legislative Assembly enact a franchise law acceptable to the Military Governor. First passed June 27, the law was returned to the Assembly for revision because of certain undemocratic features which it contained. On September 3 the Deputy Military Governor signed the revised act which was entitled "Law for the Election of Members of the Interim Legislative Assembly."[24] According to the terms of the act, the elections could not take place until at least eighty days after the selection of a Central Election Committee. The Military Governor announced that appointment to the committee would be made from a list of nominees

[21] *Ibid.*, pp. 22-23.

[22] *Voice of Korea*, March 1, 1947.

[23] *Ibid.*

[24] *SKIG Activities*, September 1947, p. 114. The law is not reproduced in the summation, but was mimeographed as a special release by SKIG. Further changes were made in the election law, upon the recommendation of the United Nations Temporary Commission, before it was used for the May 10, 1948, elections.

submitted by the executive, legislative and judicial branches of SKIG. The committee was appointed in late 1947 but plans for an election were held in abeyance pending the arrival of the United Nations Temporary Commission.[25]

Although the most restrictive features of the first franchise law were modified in revision, the document continued to possess certain weaknesses. Suffrage was limited to those twenty-three years of age or older; some 150 electoral districts were to elect about 200 members to the Assembly; no residence requirements were established for either candidates or voters; an elaborate and confusing method of appointing election committees for and timing the various steps in registration, nomination and election were set forth; voters were required to write the name of the candidate on the ballot (it was believed that this restriction might disenfranchise a large group of illiterates); and finally the act specified that the term of office "shall continue until such time as the Provisional Government of united Korea is established," which appeared highly unrealistic.

The second most important piece of legislation which was considered by the Legislative Assembly was a land reform law.[26] Late in 1947 a draft law had been drawn up, but no

[25] See Chapter XII, p. 222 ff., for an account of developments in 1948, including the May 10 elections.

[26] The actual enactments of the Interim Legislative Assembly during its year and a half of activity did not constitute an auspiciously important array of legislation. The eleven laws passed by this body were as follows:

(1) Amendment of an ordinance on the establishment of Seoul National University.
(2) "Collection of Summer Grains."
(3) "Elevation of the Town of Iri to City Status."
(4) Child Labor Law.
(5) Law for the Election of Members to the Korean Interim Legislative Assembly.
(6) Collection of Rice.
(7) "Abolishment of the Public Prostitution Law."
(8) "Act to Prohibit Aiding American Personnel to Violate Military Directives."
(9) Public Act No. 7, Amended.
(10) "Arbor Day as a National Holiday (April 5)."
(11) "Temporary Provisions Concerning the Law on Nationality."

action was taken. Throughout the debates, it was evident that the conservative majority in the Assembly would not submit to a liberal law and that the much-needed reform was likely to be blocked by the landholding classes. Ironically enough, the party platforms of the right wing contained sweeping promises, but they were unfulfilled. The draft act as ultimately prepared was vigorously attacked by the left wing, which was able to arouse considerable support from the tenant-farmers.[27]

The Korean Interim Legislative Assembly was by no means a success, but it had helped to give the Koreans a voice in their own government and it had been of value in helping them to take the next step in self-government. Viewed in retrospect, the activities of the Assembly showed a capacity for constructive cooperative action on the part of a liberal group of able Korean patriots. Their efforts were so often overshadowed by the malicious, self-aggrandizing propaganda and criticism of the extreme right and extreme left that their achievements were not easy to see. The work of the Coalition Committee and the Joint Korean-American Conference seemed to have been useful and constructive. The group of elected members of the Legislative Assembly, on the other hand, appears to have been the least promising element in the Korean political set-up, a fact which did not speak well for the future of Korean politics unless drastic changes were made in elective procedures and unless the Korean electorate could show more maturity. The November elections in the American zone could scarcely be used as a basis of judgment, although they indicated the probability that Western electoral processes could be adopted only with difficulty in Korea at an early date.[28]

Summary

SUPPRESSION OF COMMUNISM

The situation in South Korea was not conducive to a simple solution of the right-versus-left controversy. Even if Korea had

[27] See Chapter VII for further discussion of this problem.

[28] See Chapter XII, p. 222 ff., for discussion of May 1948 elections of the Korean National Assembly and the establishment of the Republic of Korea.

not been divided in two at the 38th parallel and occupied by the foremost exponents of contrasting political ideologies, the conflict between right and left would have arisen. The divided occupation made inevitable a test of power. The Soviet regime took up the challenge early in the occupation. The extent of infiltration and of direct assistance from north to south was open to question, but it was no secret that the American command believed that the Soviets had trained and sent to South Korea a strong underground group which controlled almost completely all Communist activity.[29]

One of the major objectives of South Korean Communists was to discredit Military Government and to arouse opposition to the Americans. In order to counteract the Communist influence the American command strengthened the rightist elements and in many instances this resulted in the support of anti-democratic Korean reactionaries who had been associated with Japanese colonial oppression. The second method used by the American command was outright suppression of Communist activity whenever it reached proportions threatening the maintenance of peace and order. The Korean police, many of whom were still influenced by the methods which they had used under the Japanese, carried out the suppression of Communists with unusual alacrity. The Taegu slaughter of October 1946, in which about fifty police and fifty civilians were killed in rioting, was partially a consequence of the anti-Communist campaign.

Communist leaders were arrested and thrown in jail in great numbers during the October riots. "As the result of activities prejudicial to law and order," stated American Military Government, "the arrest of Pak Heunyŏng, Lee Kangkook and Lee Chuhu, the three ranking members of the Communist Party of South Korea, was ordered."[30] Altogether there were some

[29] See Harold J. Noble, "Our Most Dangerous Boundary," *Saturday Evening Post*, August 31, 1946.

[30] Order issued September 6, 1946, for violation of Proclamation No. 2. *USAMGIK Summation*, September 1946, p. 15. See also *ibid.*, January 1947, p. 14, where it is reported that Pak was still wanted by the police.

1,500 persons prosecuted in connection with the uprisings, of whom 500 had been convicted by the end of the year. The case of sixteen of these men who were sentenced to death became a *cause célèbre* in Korea. On March 10, 1947, it was announced that nine of the death sentences had been commuted to life imprisonment and that one man had been released by order of the Supreme Reviewing Authority of the United States Army Forces in the Far East.[31]

In September and October 1946, Military Government suspended publication of all extreme left-wing newspapers and other publications in view of their persistent violation of ordinances regarding the inciting of revolt. Four newspapers were thus shut down and the extreme left was then unable so easily to dispense inflammatory propaganda.

On March 22, 1947, the leftists decided to demonstrate in a "flash strike" and in the resultant rioting further arrests were made. A total of 2,718 persons were arrested in South Korea; "almost 100 per cent of these were leftists," according to the statement of General Lerch.[32]

[31] Summary of the case is contained in a letter from the State Department to Mr. Choon Ho Penn, of Los Angeles, California, April 16, 1947, printed in *Korean Independence*, April 30, 1947:

"Eighteen ringleaders in these disturbances which resulted in the killing of fifty-three members of the National Police were tried by a United States Army Military Commission according to the highest procedures and principles of justice. They were found guilty of violating Proclamation No. 2 to the People of Korea of the Commander-in-Chief, United States Army Forces in the Pacific. . . . Sentence of death was imposed by the Military Commission and was upheld by the Commanding General of the United States Army Forces in Korea in referring the case to the Supreme Commander of the Allied Forces in the Pacific for final action.

"On March 10, 1947, the office of the Commanding General, United States Army Forces in Korea, announced the latest decision in the case involving persons connected with the October disturbances. It was stated that the Supreme Reviewing Authority of the United States Army Forces in the Far East had commuted to life imprisonment the death sentences imposed on nine Korean civilians in connection with their crimes at Taegu last October and that a tenth man, sentenced to hang, had been totally released."

[32] Press conference of General Lerch, April 3, 1947, press release, Department of Public Information, American Military Government.

A third general round-up of Communists took place in August 1947, while the Joint Commission was still in session, but after it had reached its impasse. Prior to the convening of the Commission, rightist elements had been circumscribed in their anti-Soviet activities, as has been pointed out above, but on July 10, 1947, the ban forbidding mass demonstrations against the Moscow agreement was removed. Violence flared into the open almost immediately. Terrorist bands of the right, with the apparent collusion of the Korean police, immediately began an anti-Communist campaign. Lyuh Woonhyung, former head of the People's Republic, was the first victim of the reign of terror. He was assassinated on July 19 on a Seoul street in broad daylight and in sight of a police box. He had been mentioned as a possible compromise candidate to head the proposed provisional Korean government.[33]

A leftist revolt thought to have been plotted for August 3, the date of the memorial service for Lyuh Woonhyung, did not materialize. A second plot, believed scheduled for August 15, the anniversary of the Japanese surrender, was more seriously considered and mass arrests took place on that date and during the following week in Seoul and in the provinces. On August 22, General Hodge disclosed that one hundred ringleaders of activity of a "revolutionary nature" had been arrested in Seoul and many more outside the city had also been apprehended on charges of rioting and interfering with the government's rice-collection program.[34]

[33] *Voice of Korea*, August 15 and September 15, 1947. For a report on the Korean National Youth Movement fostered by the reactionary groups and financially aided by Military Government, see *Time*, June 30, 1947, pp. 25-26. See also picture of the YMCA building in Seoul, damaged by rightist hoodlums on July 7, during a demonstration which was not prevented by the police, in *Voice of Korea*, August 15, 1947.

[34] This series of arrests resulted in a violent exchange of recriminations between the chief Russian delegate on the Joint Commission, General Shtikov, and the American command. General Shtikov said that the arrests were aimed at "disrupting the work of the joint commission," while General Hodge replied: "It is surprising to me that the Soviet delegation should make a statement that we are interfering with the commission when the

The campaign against the left which began on August 15 continued during September with more and more cases of Korean police brutality being reported. According to one estimate, at least two thousand Communists were in jail as political prisoners in early October.[35] Despite the injustices committed by the Korean police, American Military Government did little to intervene in the conflict though outspoken against terrorism. On December 1, 1947, however, Military Governor General Dean served notice to the extreme right that the Americans would not tolerate blatant miscarriages of justice when he decided to transfer a terrorism case from the Korean courts to a military court.[36]

The policy of suppression of leftist agitation was understandable and in many respects necessary under the circumstances, but the lack of a more vigorous constructive policy to encourage democracy served to weaken the position of the democratic and liberal elements. The preoccupation of the Korean police and of certain segments of the American command with the ever-present Communist threat tended to obscure some of the democratic issues at stake. Roger N. Baldwin, Director of the American Civil Liberties Union, on his return from a visit to Korea during the summer of 1947, wrote a severe indictment of the Korean policy.[37] Among other things, he said, "We have offered no constructive demonstration of democracy for its own sake as a counter-lure to communism; . . . by nurturing the police state we drive moderates into the communist camp. . . ."

---

people we arrest have been interfering with the South Korean Government." Associated Press dispatch, Seoul, August 22. General Hodge's statement was issued as a press release, August 22, 1947.

[35] *Chicago Daily News* dispatch, Seoul, October 12, 1947. Also dispatch of October 26, 1947, which tells of rightist "goon squads" having "the moral—and frequently physical—support of the 30,000 rightist-minded police."

[36] The Korean courts had pronounced a maximum penalty of seven years' imprisonment on one member of a group of rightists who had beaten two political opponents to death. *Voice of Korea*, December 31, 1947.

[37] "Blunder in Korea," *The Nation*, August 2, 1947, pp. 119-21.

KOREAN PARTY POLITICS

Political activity of the various Korean parties continued hectic and unstable.[38] The rightist parties were strongly organized and held predominant power despite their lack of a democratic base. The three major parties of the right, the Korean (Han'guk) Democratic Party, the Society for the Rapid Realization of Independence, and the Korean Independence Party, were talking of merging in January 1947, but the plans did not materialize. The dispute between pro- and anti-Joint Commission elements in each of these rightist parties caused considerable division in the ranks in May 1947, and the fight continued over the question of cooperation with the American command in regard to elections and the United Nations Commission. On December 2, 1947, Chang Duksoo, leader of the cooperation faction in the Korean Democratic Party, was assassinated by a rightist police officer under circumstances which involved the Kim Koo-Syngman Rhee opposition.[39] The right wing, therefore, was showing various signs of internal weakness at the end of 1947.

The leftist parties were more difficult to analyze because they were constantly changing in name and personnel, shifting from the extreme left to moderate liberalism. The extreme left, or the Communist Party, continued to maintain its organization intact but was forced to operate underground. The Southern Korea Labor Party, organized in November 1946, became the party of the Communists, and thus also stood on the extreme left. The more moderate leftist groups, which at times associated with the two extreme leftist parties, included the Laboring

[38] An analytical chart, "History of Political Parties, 1919–June 1947," prepared by the Historical Section of USAFIK, illustrates the confused character of Korean politics. About 20 primary groups are traced in this chart. In *SKIG Activities*, September 1947, pp. 118-19, 32 "leading political parties of South Korea, as of 30 September 1947" are listed according to the classification rightist, leftist or neutral. There are 15 rightist, 10 leftist and 7 neutral parties in that list.

[39] *New York Times*, December 5, 1947.

People's Party, the Revolutionary Party, the Labor Mass Party, and the Korean People's Party.

After February 1946 the leftist front operated under the name of the Korean National Democratic Front which re-elected the following central committee chairmen on January 29, 1947: Kim Wonbong, Revolutionary Party; Hŏ Hun, Southern Korea Labor Party; Pak Heunyŏng, Communist Party; Lyuh Woonhyung, Korean People's Party.[40] Those four men were the outstanding leaders of the left. The first two had been rounded up in October 1946 and had been beaten by police but eventually were released. Pak Heunyŏng was still wanted by the police, having escaped to North Korea after the order of September 6, 1946, for his arrest. Lyuh Woonhyung, who had been appointed to the Interim Legislative Assembly but had declined to participate, went into political "retirement" during 1947. In July he was assassinated during the period of the anti-Communist purge discussed above.

It was difficult to assess the relative strength of the left and right in South Korean politics. In general it may be said that the right was in a much more powerful position because of its wealth, political control, and the conservative tendency within Korean society. The right also traded heavily on its platform of demanding immediate independence. The left, however, had a strong popular following because of its revolutionary agrarian and industrial platform. The left, furthermore, was aided in its campaign by the support of the Soviet regime. The rank-and-file following of the leftists was drawn chiefly from the farm population, which not only was dismayed by the lack of a land distribution plan but was bitterly opposed to the rice collection program of Military Government. The farmer was forced to sell rice at the government ceiling price but had to buy other commodities on the black market. The factory workers, though small in number, were also discontented because of the fact that their factories had been turned over to Korean "profiteers" instead of to the workers.

[40] *USAMGIK Summation*, January 1947, p. 14.

The March 1, 1947, independence day demonstrations were the occasion for an estimate of the relative popular strength of the right and left. Riots throughout South Korea caused at least eight deaths in clashes between rival leftist and rightist groups attempting to outdo each other in demonstrating. In several provinces the leftist crowds had been twice as large as the rightist. The turnout which the leftists had marshaled was impressive even though it had been preceded by an intensive propaganda campaign. There was no doubt that the left possessed a substantial following. The "flash strike" of March 22, three weeks later, engineered by the leftists as a further demonstration of strength, was less conclusive. The direct communist character of the strike did not arouse the enthusiastic acceptance that the leaders anticipated, and in some quarters the results were interpreted as a sign of essential weakness, at least in the extreme left.

Repeated but ineffective efforts were made under American initiative to build up a middle-of-the-road or coalition group. The Coalition Committee mentioned above was only partially successful. Certain Korean leaders with American support continued to work for the formation of a genuinely democratic party until finally, in October 1947, the Democratic Independence Party was organized. The leaders were such men as Kimm Kiusic (Speaker of the Interim Legislative Assembly) and Ahn Chaihong (Civil Administrator).[41] This party was virtually a "government" party and as such received American backing even though there was some criticism of its close association with the occupying forces.[42] Some observers believed that the political situation in South Korea possessed the basis for the

[41] *SKIG Activities*, September 1947, p. 117.

[42] In the appointments for membership in the Central Election Committee made by General Dean in December 1947, two members of the Democratic Independence Party were included among a group of otherwise non-political appointees. *Voice of Korea*, December 31, 1947. In 1948, many of the moderate leaders alienated the American support by opposing separate elections for South Korea and by participating in conferences with North Korean leaders. See concluding Chapter, pp. 262-64.

development of a successful moderate political movement, but under the circumstances of divided occupation the struggle between the two extremes would no doubt continue to dominate the situation for some time to come.[43]

[43] Occasionally "national" issues brought together even the extreme right and left, as on November 1, 1947, when a "Joint Provisional Committee," composed of representatives from 12 major parties, including the Korean Democratic Party on the far right and the People's Republic Party on the far left, was formed to work for the immediate withdrawal of occupation troops and the establishment of a United National Government. *Korean Independence*, December 31, 1947, quoting the *Central Daily News* of Seoul.

CHAPTER SIX

American Economic Policies

LIQUIDATION OF JAPANESE INTERESTS

Technical Personnel and Training

THE REMOVAL of Japanese technicians and managers was regarded as an urgent political necessity, in spite of the fact that their departure would create a serious problem. Within five months practically all of the Japanese had been removed. This sudden change, of course, caused a good deal of confusion. It was made much more serious by the extreme scarcity of Koreans who were qualified either by training or experience to succeed the Japanese. The Japanese at no time encouraged the development of adequate schools for the training of the scientists, engineers, and administrators, nor even of the skilled workers, required to operate the economic establishment in Korea. The public schools themselves, even at the elementary level, suffered from lack of trained personnel, which is not surprising when possibly 90 per cent of the adult population had had no formal schooling. At the technical level there was a critical shortage of qualified instructors, and in the shops learning on the job was handicapped by the shortage of skilled workers.

The problem was psychologically complicated by the traditional Confucian attitude which exalted scholarship but disdained the manual arts. This attitude was a barrier to the inclusion of vocational training in the school curricula. School officials, influenced by the low social status of the manual laborer and the craftsman, regarded such training as degrading to the prestige of their institutions. In addition, the general deterioration of physical equipment and the difficulty of replacing it seriously hindered expansion of technical education.

The reconstruction of the educational system in South Korea was one of the most noteworthy achievements of the American occupation authorities, thus maintaining the tradition set by the earlier American missionaries who had introduced modern schools to Korea, championed the principle of mass education, and gave many promising students the opportunity to study abroad. From the very beginning of the occupation, Korean educators were given an active responsibility in the institution of reforms. Curricula were revised along democratic lines and textbooks were rewritten. Military Government distributed fifteen million textbooks written in the native *Ŏnmun* alphabet for use in the elementary schools. This was a spectacular achievement, since the Chinese characters, which were infinitely more difficult to master, had a persistent popularity among the influential educated class. This accomplishment was implemented by the transcribing of Chinese classics, which constitute an important share of Korea's literary heritage, into the *Ŏnmun* and the preparation of a dictionary to standardize the *Ŏnmun* spelling.[1]

Military Government gave increased attention to scientific and technical training and sponsored in-service training programs and short-term extension and refresher courses. In October 1947, funds were allocated to a technical training board for disbursement to suitable schools for training workers in urgently required skills. However, the deficiencies in Korea's capacity to train students in the scientific and other fields of higher educa-

[1] For a year-by-year summary of cultural and educational developments in Korea during the occupation period, see the articles by Evelyn B. McCune "Korean Literature, Arts, and Crafts," in the *New International Yearbook*, 1947–49.

tion were particularly hard to remedy. Equipment and textbooks for middle school and college instruction were not easily obtained, and a qualified teaching staff sufficiently large to meet existing needs probably would not be available for years. Some small progress was made in this direction through voluntary contributions by members of the American occupation forces and private organizations in the United States which enabled a very limited number of students to attend American schools. The terms of the initial financial and property settlement negotiated between the United States and the southern Republic of Korea provided that a twenty-five million dollar U.S. Foreign Liquidation Commission loan to Korea should be used, among other things, for creating an education fund to assist Korean students who wish to study in American educational institutions in Korea, China, and the Philippines.[2] In addition the U.S. Economic Cooperation Administration planned to spend almost four million dollars during the fiscal year 1949–50 for the technical training of Koreans in the United States and Korea.

In general, however, the fulfillment of Korea's educational needs was a long-run task, and during the occupation the most that could be hoped for was that the groundwork was being laid for the satisfaction of future educational requirements. As stated by an Army report, "the solution . . . of Korea's educational difficulties reasonably may be expected to be inordinately consumptive of both time and money and Korea is hardly in a position to be lavish with either." [3]

[2] The places where Koreans would be permitted to study under the terms of the settlement are not specified in the agreement itself, though they are noted in a State Department publication, *Korea, 1945 to 1948* (Far Eastern Series 28), p. 39. The obvious absence of any mention of the United States as a possible place of study is not explained.

[3] J. T. Suagee and Nels W. Stalheim, *The Impact of the War and Japanese Imperialism upon the Economic and Political Rehabilitation of Korea*, Civil Affairs Division, War Department, Washington, D.C., January 1947 (mimeographed) p. 10.

Japanese Property

Along with the removal of all Japanese from the positions they held in Korea went the problem of divesting them of their ownership of Korean property. This posed many legal and administrative problems. The premise governing the disposition of Japanese property was that the wealth owned by Japanese individuals, corporations, and the state alike represented expropriation and exploitation of the Korean people and that inordinately high profits had adequately recompensed them for their investments.

Consequently, Ordinance Number 2, promulgated by the Military Governor on September 2, 1945, did not fix upon Military Government, or any Korean government which might succeed it, any responsibility for compensating Japanese owners divested of their property by the Ordinance.[4] The Ordinance provided that property belonging to enemy governments, their nationals, and in the custody of banks, individuals, and corporations or deposited with trustees on or after August 9, 1945, could be disposed of only in accordance with its terms. In general, property of the Japanese government could not be disposed of, while the property of private individuals might be sold providing (1) that such transactions were made for the benefit of Koreans or the United Nations or their nationals; (2) that adequate consideration was paid as would subsequently be determined by the government of Korea; and (3) that the owner selling such property reported the transaction to Military Government and that the proceeds of sale were delivered to Chosun Bank or its agents for deposit to the credit of the government of Korea. The Ordinance declared void any transactions already made since August 9, 1945, but provided for their validation upon application to Military Government.

The Ordinance created considerable confusion, some of its terms being apparently conflicting. The normal machinery for

[4] Individual Japanese were presumed to have recourse only to their own government for losses sustained in Korea.

recording property titles was inoperative, a fact which made compliance with the law difficult, and no provision was made for the parties to a transaction to secure official advice as to whether or not the contemplated sale was a valid one. The principal difficulty, however, was that Military Government lacked sufficient information about the actual property situation at the time of the promulgation of the Ordinance to carry out its provisions. Subsequently it was necessary to retract the policies laid down by the Ordinance. Ordinance Number 33,[5] promulgated early in December, vested title to all property owned by Japanese on or after August 9, 1945, in Military Government. This made the status of Japanese property unequivocally clear. As agencies of Military Government became aware of the nature of Japanese assets, they began to devise means of controlling them. The initial step was the creation of the office of the Property Custodian, entrusted with general responsibility for the care and administration of enemy property.

In November 1945 the Materials Control Corporation, the converted Japanese Critical Materials Company organization, was given charge of all surrendered or abandoned Japanese movable and tangible property subject to market operations.[6] This included Japanese army supplies and equipment, warehouse stocks of foodstuffs, building supplies, consumer goods and bundles of clothing and household items taken from Japanese about to be repatriated, in excess of quantities they were allowed to take out of the country.[7] The Oriental Development Company became the New Korea Company and an arm of the Department of Agriculture, and continued to operate not only its own varied interests but, in December 1945, was designated

[5] Ordinance No. 33, December 6, 1945, OMG (Office of the Military Governor), Seoul.

[6] Ordinance No. 24, November 5, 1945, OMG, Seoul.

[7] Japanese repatriates at first were authorized to take with them such household goods as they could carry on their persons and 1,000 yen (won), then given the arbitrarily fixed value of fifteen yen to one dollar. Later repatriates were also authorized to take bedding.

as the manager of all former Japanese farm lands. It thereby became a responsible agent of the Property Custodian for the conservation, utilization, and accounting of such property. The Department of Finance became the responsible agent for the administration of Japanese bank and insurance company property. The Department of Commerce, then the Bureau of Mining and Industry, assumed jurisdiction over former Japanese extractive and manufacturing establishments. Private railroads were placed under the authority of the Department of Transportation. In general the authority of the Property Custodian was thus delegated to the regular branches of government.

It was not until May 1946 that decentralization of property custody functions was undertaken.[8] Local property custodians were enabled to make short-term arrangements for the occupancy or use of vested property and to dispose of property whose value would otherwise deteriorate. Finally, local property officials were empowered to take over Japanese property in their areas. However, more than two years of occupation passed before Military Government undertook to make a comprehensive survey of these assets.[9]

During the first year and a half of occupation, policy regarding the disposition of assets confiscated from the Japanese remained undefined.[10] There were distinct difficulties involved in taking either of the two principal courses open. On the one hand, disposition of the property into private hands would have meant handing over certain resources to interests which had little or nothing to do with their development. It also would have disrupted controls over the economy which seemed neces-

[8] Ordinance No. 73, April 23, 1946, OMG, Seoul.

[9] See U.S. Army Forces in Korea, *South Korea Interim Government Activities*, December 1947, p. 11 (hereafter cited as *SKIG Activities*).

[10] To justify its inaction on the property question, Military Government indicated that the ultimate decision on such problems should be made by a Korean government rather than by the Americans. Furthermore, it was claimed, premature action might stand in the way of the reunification of the country. Critics, however, attributed this cautious policy to the characteristic indecision of Military Government.

sary in a period of acute scarcity. On the other hand, nationalization for even the larger enterprises might have risked the double danger of attack from conservative interests in the United States and the possible inability of a Korean state to manage such enterprises efficiently.

In March 1947 Military Government finally committed itself to a definite course. At this time it was declared that vested property should be sold as soon as responsible and efficient purchasers could be found.[11] There proved to be a dearth of qualified investors, however, principally because Military Government could not give any assurances as to the future. The great political uncertainties which faced the country, and "the ultimate probabilities regarding nationalization,"[12] strongly discouraged investment. Uncertainty as to the eventual influence the Soviet Union was to exercise throughout the Korean peninsula was also a major deterrent to private investment.

The program of disposal therefore remained unsettled. In August 1947 it was decided that certain types of holdings would be disposed of through sale as physical assets, rather than as business organizations. It was announced that certain mining rights and mining properties classified as "small businesses" were to be sold by the Property Custodian "to prevent the dissipation of unprotectable assets and to promote utilization by Korean capital."[13]

In September 1947, the National Office of Property Custody was authorized to conduct a more or less experimental program of corporate reorganization for vested enterprises. A few companies having main offices in Seoul were selected to serve as pilot models for a program which was to encompass virtually all vested concerns in which at least 90 per cent of the stock had formerly been in Japanese hands. The reorganization of an

[11] *SKIG Activities*, December 1947, p. 13. Property formerly held by the Japanese government in Korea was, of course, to be retained intact for a successor Korean government.

[12] *Ibid.*

[13] *Ibid.*, October 1947, p. 7.

enterprise was intended either to prepare it for disposition into private hands or to facilitate its control by a responsible agency of Military Government. In some instances business leases for vested property were negotiated where satisfactory sales could not be made.[14]

The Military Government procedure, almost from the beginning of occupation, was to appoint managers, often former employees of the firms, to act in behalf of the administering Military Government agencies and responsible to them. Any profits earned by these enterprises were to be banked by the administering agency to the credit of the Property Custodian. According to some observers, such arrangements were not satisfactory in practice. To quote one Military Government report, "the inability of SKIG to supervise its vested operations effectively has resulted in the diversion of goods to unauthorized channels for sale at open market prices. While the extent of these diversions are not quantitatively ascertainable, they do represent one source of supply for the black market in government-controlled commodities." [15] Instances of misappropriation, one may suppose, were much more common than the official record indicated. There was also an important problem as to the efficiency of enterprises ostensibly not operated for the direct profit of their managers [16] but at the same time held only very loosely responsible to the Property Custodian. Cases where numbers of employees greatly exceeded reasonable need were noted in a number of enterprises under government operation. For example, the lowered efficiency of the Department of Communications was indicated by the fact that it had more employees than before the war to handle 40 per cent less business. Likewise, railway employment was considerably greater than before the war, although traffic was much less. Perceptible decreases in railway employment, which did not appear until the

[14] *Ibid.*, February 1948, p. 13.

[15] National Economic Board, *Price Developments in South Korea*, Hq. USAMGIK, Seoul, September 1947, p. 6.

[16] *Ibid.*, p. 9.

latter part of 1947, were by no means commensurate with the reductions in operations.[17]

In part, increases in the working force reflected the generally reduced efficiency of equipment. But it seemed probable that employment practices also concealed potential unemployment. The Western practice of hiring or dismissing labor in accordance with changes in output was not strictly followed, since in Korea labor was the cheapest production factor. This, and the fact that the management of a "vested" enterprise may not have felt any particular incentive to maximize profits, may have made management indifferent to achieving the most efficient level of employment. Moreover, the alternative to these practices would probably have meant widespread unemployment.

The seemingly inadequate control of vested property through managers finally prompted Military Government to dispose of these assets to private owners. Even so, Military Government avoided a clear-cut statement on the ultimate character of the economy. Although the area of private ownership was enlarged, no vested enterprises were to be sold. Military Government had already decided to keep a number of highly important industries under government control,[18] and it also reserved the right to decide at the time of reorganization whether or not any enterprise should be retained by the government. The firms thus retained would in effect become public corporations. If carried out, these policies might give South Korea an economy of a mixed character rather than one predominantly privately controlled. However, by 1948 impending changes in the political administration threatened to change the entire picture.

To carry out the program of corporate reorganization, a survey of the nature and assets of the 3,800 companies or jurid-

[17] *SKIG Activities*, March 1948, Table 8, Employment, p. 104; Table 3, Passenger Traffic, p. 100; Table 4, Freight Car Loadings, p. 101.

[18] Military Government, however, in most ways became further committed to the development of a private enterprise economy. See *SKIG Activities*, May 1948, p. 15.

ical persons believed to have main offices in Seoul was undertaken late in 1947. The work of the first few months, covering but a fraction of these firms, revealed how poorly informed the Office of the Property Custodian was concerning the property under its nominal control.[19] A complete survey promised to extend over a considerable period of time and the disposition of the vast block of former Japanese industrial, commercial and mineral assets was still a long way from realization. By the end of March, reorganization meetings had been called for only nine companies.[20] The sale of the former Japanese agricultural land entrusted to the New Korea Company was finally commenced in March 1948.[21] However, most other former Japanese property, representing about 90 per cent of all modern industry in Korea, remained under government control. The Republic of Korea established in 1948 appeared to favor a permanent continuation of such control.

MONEY, PRICES AND DISTRIBUTION

Developments Prior to Occupation

The volume of money in circulation in June 1939 was 300 million yen but by June 1944 had risen to 1,800 million yen. The immediate post-surrender tidal wave of Japanese currency issues raised the amount to 8,000 million yen on August 31, 1945. During the war government spending at first showed a gradual rise, but after 1943 it was sharply accelerated by the in-

[19] Of 409 companies examined by March 1, 169 were tentatively approved and further plans for reorganization were mapped out, 38 companies were not located, 22 were found to be dissolved, 26 had offices in North Korea, 41 had head offices in other provinces, 13 were found to be associations or educational institutions, 4 had head offices in Manchuria, 38 were branches of Japanese corporations, 30 had individual owners (not corporations), 23 were partnerships of Koreans with Japanese, 3 were partnerships with foreign nationals holding an interest, 2 were wholly owned by Koreans. *SKIG Activities*, February 1948, p. 14.

[20] *Ibid.*, March 1948, p. 14.

[21] See Chapter VII for discussion of land distribution.

creased diversion of the economy to military purposes.[22] The problem of a scarcity of goods in terms of money became critical by late 1944, and large raises in price ceilings followed.[23] These increases proved inadequate to offset the effects of the acute shortage of raw materials and consumer goods, and official prices were superseded as the measure of value by those of a black market, which handled 15 to 25 per cent of all goods at prices up to thirty times the official prices. The following table indicates the vast discrepancies which existed between official prices and black market prices immediately before the end of the war in July 1945.[24]

TABLE 6

COMPARATIVE OFFICIAL AND BLACK-MARKET PRICES, July 1945

Commodity	*Official Wholesale Price (won)**	*Black (open) Market Wholesale Price (won)*
First-class Cleaned Rice, per *suk* (5.1 bu.)	49.22	2,100
Cleaned Barley, per *suk*	20.50	600
Wheat, per *suk*	39.71	800
Sheeting Cotton, per 40 yards	27.15	250
Charcoal, per 22.5 kg.	4.68	30

* Although the Japanese yen was still the standard of currency at this time, the equivalent Korean term, won, has been used here for uniformity with subsequent material.

[22] An analysis of the inflationary impact of conditions similar in many ways to those in Korea is to be found in *Survey of Current Inflationary and Deflationary Tendencies*, 1947, Pt. III, "Inflation in Undeveloped Countries: India," pp. 63-75, Department of Economic Affairs, United Nations. See also ECAFE Survey, 1948.

[23] *Price Developments in South Korea, op. cit.*, p. 2. Increases were about 100 per cent above the 1937 level.

[24] *Ibid.*

The flood of currency issued during August 1945 did not produce an immediate rise in prices. In fact, in certain major grain commodities there was at first an appreciable decline,[25] and other prices remained stable or rose only slightly. But this comparatively stable situation was of short duration, and by December the inflationary effects of speculation by brokers and hoarders, the flood of currency, and the general shut-down of production following the repatriation of Japanese managers and technicians were rampant.[26]

Military Government Price and Rationing Policies

Proclamation No. 1 issued by General MacArthur on September 7, 1945, continued controls existing under the Japanese, but the price and rationing provisions had already broken down. In view of the psychological reaction of the Korean people to liberation and the lack of American personnel qualified to enforce such controls, their continuation seem undesirable and the decision was made to institute a "free-market economy." During October all commodities[27] were decontrolled. When the free market in rice was established on October 5, Military Government announced a policy of open-market trading whereby it contracted to buy rice at 32 won per bag.[28] One of the uses of rice so accumulated was to provide a reserve which could be dumped on the market to depress prices. By early November the price of rice in Seoul was 70 won a bag; on November 23 it was 100 won per bag, and the following week it reached 160 won per bag.

Once started, the price rise was rapidly accelerated when speculators, seizing upon opportunities for quick profits, bought up stocks of goods in short supply. In this situation the farmers were also prone to hoard, and prices rose still higher. In Decem-

[25] *Ibid.*

[26] *Ibid.*

[27] Commodities produced or sold under government monopoly (salt, tobacco, opium, ginseng, sugar, and medical items) were kept under control.

[28] This was a 54 kg. straw bag, called a large *mal* by the Koreans, approximately two-fifths the capacity of a *koku* (5.1 bushels).

ber Military Government took cognizance of this situation by raising its open-market purchase price for unhulled rice from the October offer of 32 won per 54 kilogram straw bag to 175 won in an effort to ensure a supply of food for distribution to the urban population.

An incentive goods program was inaugurated as an inducement to farmers to cooperate with the food collection program. This program "failed as a result of inadequate supplies of incentive goods, transportation difficulties, and a poorly disseminated information program which did not reach many farmers until after the incentive goods were gone." [29] Then from February to April 1946 the collection program was conducted on a compulsory basis. The rice so collected was sufficient to provide only about one-third of the daily caloric intake. Many could not pay the inflated prices prevailing on the open market to obtain additional food, and food riots occurred.

In May 1946 a summer grain collection program was announced embracing barley, naked barley, wheat, and rye. This program was intended to ensure the food supply of non-farmers for the four-month period between the summer and fall grain harvests. Food was to be collected from farmers on a quota basis and rationed to consumers. The program was hampered by the worst floods in twenty-five years which destroyed 20 per cent of the crops. Only 16 per cent of the crop, or 49 per cent of the quotas, was collected.[30]

The next step was taken in August 1946 when the National Food Administration announced its plan for the collection of rice "in order to provide for the food needs of Koreans during the eight-month period between December 1, 1946, and August 1, 1947." [31] This program was more successful than the previous cereal collection efforts. At the termination of the first phase of the program in March 1947, 84.2 per cent of the quota, or

[29] National Economic Board, *Survey of Grain in South Korea,* USAMGIK, Seoul, April 1, 1947 (mimeographed), p. 2.
[30] *Ibid.*
[31] *Ibid.,* p. 5.

about 30 per cent of the total rice crop, had been collected.[32] The rice thus acquired, the summer grains subsequently collected, and the importation of substantial quantities of cereals, particularly American wheat, enabled the South Korean Interim Government to maintain a ration which supplied 68 per cent of the daily caloric consumption during the period December 1, 1946, to July 1, 1947.[33] On the latter date, the continued influx of refugees from the north made necessary a 20 per cent reduction in the ration.

Despite the fact that the summer grain collection quota in 1947 was only one-third of the 1946 quota, the collection program was far from being a complete success. The crop was poor, afflicted by an early spring drought and damaged by prolonged rains at harvest time. Further, a USAMGIK report stated that "there has been propaganda against the collection and there are no teeth in the law." [34] The rice program for 1947–48, however, continued to have mandatory provisions [35] and it was much more successful.

The National Economic Board termed the cereal ration "the most substantial stabilizing factor in the economy of South Korea." [36] After October 1946, official price calculations for commodities other than rice were based upon multiples of rice prices. The so-called "rice formula," then devised, incorporated the principle of the first Military Government price declaration which decided upon fifty times the prices of a previous year as the most satisfactory norm. Intermediate policy had set prices averaging ninety times the 1937 level for certain goods in short supply being produced in Military Government vested factories.

The rice formula itself was first applied in the pricing of

[32] *Ibid.*

[33] *SKIG Activities*, August 1947, p. 15.

[34] *Ibid.*, p. 16.

[35] National Food Regulation No. 6, dated August 18, 1947, *ibid.*, pp. 21-27.

[36] *Price Developments in South Korea*, *op. cit.*, p. 5.

seed cotton purchased from farmers. It was based upon the price then being paid the farmer for his rice which equaled fifty-six times the average price of rice for the years 1937, 1939, 1943, and 1945. While this formula was given wide application and remained the goal in pricing determinations of the government, exceptions were made at many points. The extent of these exceptions is indicated in Table 7. As prices continued to

TABLE 7

VARIATIONS IN APPLICATION OF RICE FORMULA

Number of Times by which September 1947 Price Exceeded Base Period (1937, 1939, 1943, 1945) Average	
Polished Rice, retail	55
Railroad Passenger Fares	40
Marine Coastal Freight Rates	24
Truck Freight Rates	11
Passenger Bus Rates	20
Retail and Wholesale Electric Power Rates	13
Gasoline Prices	35
Kerosene Prices	42

Source: USAMGIK, *Price Developments in South Korea*, p. 5.

rise, it became evident that there was no likelihood of confining the price level to fifty times the 1937 prices. By February 1948, a rice formula of eighty times the 1937 price was under consideration.[37]

The proportion of the consumer goods supply affected by price controls was not known accurately. The government was unable to apply price controls to privately-produced commodities and on June 30, 1947, an open market was declared on all commodities produced by private facilities with raw materials from non-governmental sources.[38]

[37] *SKIG Activities*, February 1948, p. 122.
[38] *Price Developments in South Korea*, op. cit., p. 5.

Currency and Public Finance

The cereal collection and distribution program was carried on with heavy subsidies through the fall of 1946 and into the spring of 1947. These subsidies, while intended to alleviate the effects of inflation upon the urban consumer, were themselves exerting a serious inflationary effect upon the economy, but in view of the important contribution cereal price stabilization made to general economic stability, they were thought worthwhile. The tremendous increase in notes authorized by the Japanese in August 1945 multiplied the amount of currency in circulation threefold. Thereafter this amount was more than doubled. In the first ten months of occupation, the value of notes in circulation rose by approximately 1,000 million won. By September 1946 the rate of increase in the value of notes in circulation was nearly 1,000 million won a month. During December the increase was at a rate of over 100 million won a day. By the end of 1946 total note issue stood at 18,000 million won as against 9,400 million won six months earlier.[39] One year later it amounted to nearly 33,400 million won.[40]

Military Government's efforts to control prices were actually accentuating the conditions it sought to combat. Whereas Military Government had been offering 175 won per bag (54 kg.) for unhulled rice in December 1945, the government price on the 1946 crop was 580 won. Official retail prices which had been 750 won per *suk* of polished rice in the spring of 1946 were 1,700 won a year later.[41] The government was spending over 3,000 million won annually in subsidies to cover the differential between the purchase price to the farmer, plus the costs of milling and distribution, and consumer prices.[42] In the

[39] James Shoemaker, *Notes on Korea's Post War Economic Problems*, Institute of Pacific Relations, New York, April 1947 (mimeographed), p. 12.

[40] *SKIG Activities*, February 1948, p. 132, Table 2.

[41] The Japanese unit, the *koku*, is called the *suk* in Korean. One *suk* of cleaned rice is equal to 3.7 large *mal* of unhulled rice.

[42] *Price Developments in South Korea*, *op. cit.*, p. 4.

absence of adequate government revenues, these subsidies were largely financed by the issuance of currency originating in government overdrafts on the central bank.[43] The tremendous size of these subsidies, from 15 to 20 per cent of the national budget, and the perilous state of the public revenues led to a discontinuance of the subsidy in June 1947.

However, the elimination of subsidies was far from being sufficient to enable the Korean government to achieve a balanced budget. The optimistic expectations in the April 1, 1947, to March 30, 1948, budget that revenues would cover 40 per cent of the anticipated expenditures were not realized. The budget proved to impose no limit on expenditures and supplemental appropriations were approved by the Military Governor for several departments.[44] The wide gap between income and expenditure led to a further increase in note issue.[45] By August 1948, when the American occupation ended, the total note issue had receded to 30,000 million won as compared with over 33,000 million won at the first of the year. In the last months of the year, however, the usual seasonal trend of the harvest period was again sharply apparent and the volume of currency in circulation reached the new high of 43,400 million won in December.[46]

In the long run Korea will probably require a drastic overhauling of its tax system. Under the Japanese administration the government normally derived only 25 per cent of its income from taxation.[47] The bulk of its revenue was obtained from the operations of government-owned public utilities and the profits of government monopolies. In many instances the public util-

[43] The assumption made in justifying these overdrafts was that American aid tended to compensate for the inflationary implications of these increases in the currency. The government incurred an obligation of 3 per cent interest to the Chosun Bank on these funds.

[44] *SKIG Activities*, August 1947, p. 115.

[45] *Ibid.*, October 1947, p. 103.

[46] *Republic of Korea Statistical Summation*, No. 5, May 1949 (mimeographed), p. 56.

[47] Shoemaker, *op. cit.*, p. 13.

ities in 1947 were operating with losses, and the tobacco and salt monopolies had become much less profitable. However, it seems undesirable that public utilities should be used as a lucrative source of public funds. One of the principal shortcomings of the public utilities operated by the Japanese in Korea had been that their services were priced too high to permit their use by the great mass of Koreans. Since one objective of Korean operation of these utilities was to encourage the expansion of service, and thus advance the national standard of living, these enterprises were expected to do little more than pay their own way.

Tax administration collapsed with the end of the Japanese regime and could not be satisfactorily restored.[48] Although all sources of governmental revenue greatly declined,[49] taxes fell disproportionately far. In 1946 only 15.4 per cent of the collected revenues came from taxes. Most notably poor was the collection of income taxes which were to have accounted for 42 per cent of the 1946–47 tax revenues. Actually only 61 per cent of this assessment was collected.[50] In the case of easily collected excise taxes and transfer taxes, where the latter were collected through or from financial institutions, collections were generally good, but business, land, inheritance, and excess profits taxes, like income taxes, had a poor record. Low tax receipts were often blamed on the reluctance of Korean tax officials to take the matter of collections very seriously.

Perhaps somewhat anomalously, the railroads, which were for the Japanese a relatively poor source of revenue among

[48] One tax reform proposal had been made which had the probable advantage of being difficult to evade even under poor tax enforcement. It called for a 5 per cent agricultural production tax to be collected in kind in conjunction with the cereal collection programs. Receipts from the sale through rationed channels of the commodities so collected were to go into the government tax revenue fund.

[49] The decline was relative to prices and the costs of government, of course. In the meaningless terms of absolute numbers, collections in 1946 were nearly nine times as great as in 1938.

[50] *SKIG Activities*, September 1947, p. 98.

public enterprises,[51] became an important source of public funds. Tobacco and salt revenues had fallen largely because the Monopoly Bureau prices had not been kept at a parity with the rising level of other prices. In the first half of the 1947–48 fiscal year, nonetheless, monopoly revenues were the greatest single source of income of the government, as shown in Table 8. Railroad profits had become an important second source of income, while taxes were a poor third.

TABLE 8

COMPARISON OF MONTHLY AVERAGE OF PROJECTED AND MONTHLY COLLECTION, FISCAL YEAR 1947–48

(In thousands of won)

Department	*Monthly Average of Projected Revenue*		*Average Monthly Collection, April-Aug. 1947*		*% of Projected Revenue Collected*
	Amount	*% of Total*	*Amount*	*% of Total*	
Dep't. of Finance					
Monopoly Bureau	654,167	50.9	401,400	44.2	61
Taxes	312,500	24.3	158,153	17.4	51
Department of Communications	25,000	1.9	23,022	2.5	92
Department of Transportation	225,000	17.5	276,586	30.5	122
Other Departments	69,571	5.4	49,200	5.4	71
TOTAL	1,286,238	100.0	908,361	100.0	70

Source: Adapted from Table 5, *SKIG Activities*, Sept. 1947, p. 97.

Despite efforts to economize and to eliminate overlapping of government agencies, governmental activity continued to demand a prodigious share of Korea's very limited resources. In September 1947 overdrafts made on the Chosun Bank during the occupation totaled well over three times the revenues for that period,[52] and the National Economic Board became concerned about the supplemental appropriations which permitted

[51] According to Grajdanzev, the railways had yielded a relatively low return for Korean conditions, less than 5 per cent in 1938, which "confirms the view that the railways were built primarily for military purposes, rather than for immediate profits." *Modern Korea, op. cit.*, pp. 215-16.

[52] For details, see Table 2, Appendix B.

government departments to ignore budget limits.[53] There was a strong tendency for governmental functions to be carried on in keeping with the more ample American standards, rather than upon a supportable Korean scale.[54]

Widespread scarcities and the expansion of the currency supply to cover governmental budgetary deficits created a rampant inflation which had not yet abated more than four years after the end of the war. The urban wage earners and salaried workers whose productivity was most seriously impaired by the collapse of the Japanese controlled economy in 1945 suffered most from the subsequent rise in prices. This group was afforded modest but important relief by the Military Government policy of distributing grain to non-self-suppliers at controlled prices. As agricultural production recovered during 1947 and 1948, it became possible to expand the grain rations of city dwellers. In 1948 3.0 *hop* (450 grams) of grain per person was being supplied to more than seven million people.[55] However, the National Assembly of the Republic of Korea refused to re-authorize the compulsory collection of grain from farmers during the 1948–49 crop season, allegedly because of the abusive manner in which the police enforced the collection of quotas. As a consequence of this the subsequent rice collection program was conspicuously unsuccessful with only 51.9 per cent of the goal being collected.[56] Government stocks of grains on hand for rationing purposes in January 1949 were only 60 per cent as large as those of a year earlier, and it became neces-

[53] *SKIG Activities*, September 1947, pp. 94-95, and October 1947, p. 107.

[54] A Military Government explanation was that the period was exceptional and necessitated unusually large expenditures. These outlays, it was pointed out, should not be chargeable against any single year because they represent costs attributable to conditions generated in a past period and with implications for the future. See, Suagee and Stalheim, *op. cit.*, p. 28.

[55] *Joint ECA-State Department Semi-Annual Economic Report, January-June 1949*, Seoul, American Mission in Korea, September 7, 1949 (mimeographed), p. 5.

[56] *Republic of Korea Statistical Summation*, Number 5, May 1949 (mimeographed), p. 5.

sary to reduce the daily grain ration to 1.5 *hop* (225 grams) per person and to remove four million persons from the ration rolls by June 1949.[57] The government prepared to buy grain on open market for urban distribution.[58]

The immediate effect, at least, was a serious worsening in the economic position of the non-farming population. The precipitous drop in the number of persons on the ration rolls and in the size of the rations was accompanied by a sharp rise in the price of grains during the summer of 1949. Open market prices for rice and barley averaged 597 won and 225 won, respectively, per small *mal* in the cities. By June 1949 the price of rice had risen to 881 won per small *mal* and that of barley to 597 won.[59] The effects of the abandonment of compulsory grain collection upon prices were aggravated by poor rice crop prospects during the summer of 1949 and continued government deficit financing.[60]

There was very little possibility that the government would be able to balance its budget in the near future. There was every danger that government open-market purchases of rice for distribution at controlled prices would make a powerful contribution to continued inflation as had the very similar Military Government program of grain subsidies that was abandoned in June 1947. Moreover, the land reform program enacted in 1949 was of such a nature that it would require a good deal of government financial support for several years. With the establishment of the Republic of Korea to succeed American authority in the south, the time had arrived for government fiscal policy to be based on something more than temporary expedients. Unfortunately the new Korean government lacked the courage to follow the politically difficult course of drastically raising taxes and sharply reducing government expenditures which was necessary for financial stability.

[57] *Joint ECA-State Department Semi-Annual Economic Report, January-June 1949, loc. cit.*

[58] *Ibid.*, p. 4.

[59] *Ibid.*, p. 6.

[60] *Ibid.*

CHAPTER SEVEN

Agriculture in South Korea

AGRICULTURAL PRODUCTION

During 1945 and 1946 practically all South Korean crops were smaller than in preceding years.[1] Chemical fertilizers which were necessary for the effective utilization of Korea's depleted soils were completely unavailable in these years with the result that farmers were discouraged from planting as large areas as formerly. The effects of the diversion of nitrates and sulphates from fertilizer production by the Japanese during the war years were evident as early as the 1944 harvest. In South Korea, which was totally lacking in commercial fertilizer production facilities, there was no way of immediately remedying this situation. Thus while the average yield per hectare planted in rice had been 2.04 metric tons in 1941, it was only 1.67 metric tons in 1946.[2]

With the arrival of large quantities of ammonium nitrate, potassium sulphate, ammonium sulphate, and superphosphate from the United States in time to prepare the fields for the 1947 crops, a turning point was reached. The subsequent rice harvest was about 15 per cent larger than in 1946 and exceeded the crop average for the period 1940–44. Continued fertilizer imports under U.S. sponsorship made it possible to

[1] Out of all crops, only fruits, which constituted but 4 per cent of the total food production, showed a net increase in 1946 over the 1940–44 base.

[2] *SKIG Activities*, August 1947, p. 48.

sustain this recovery, and the 1948 crop was, in fact, one of the largest in history. Unseasonal summer droughts in Kyonggi province surrounding the capital city of Seoul and in adjoining provinces caused severe crop failures in some localities during 1949 and made the resulting harvest somewhat smaller than had earlier been expected. Nonetheless, it was expected that South Korea would be virtually self-sufficient in foods in 1950.[3] A statistical summary of South Korea's cereal crop production is given in the following table. The relief and recovery expenditures which the U.S. Economic Cooperation Administration planned to make during 1950 would sustain fertilizer imports

TABLE 9

ESTIMATED PRODUCTION OF CEREALS—SOUTH KOREA

(In thousands of *suk*—1.119 bushels)

Period	*Brown Rice*	*Summer Grains*	*Other*	*Total*
1930–34–36*	13,587	8,583	1,442	23,612
1940–44*	13,718	9,450	1,241	24,409
1945*	12,854	3,414	894	17,162
1946*	12,047	5,810	948	18,805
1947†	13,850	5,274	722	19,846
1948‡	18,000	5,000	1,000	24,000
1949‡	14,700	6,500	1,000	22,200

* USAMGIK, *Present Agricultural Position of South Korea*, Seoul, 1947, p. 10.

† *Republic of Korea Statistical Summation*, August 1939, p. 9.

‡ Estimates reported in the *Joint ECA-State Department Semi-Annual Economic Report on Korea, January-June 1949*, Seoul, American Mission in Korea, September 7, 1949 (mimeographed), p. 2.

at a high level.[4] About 30 per cent of the total $150 million ECA allocation for Korea during the fiscal year 1950 would be

[3] See the *Joint ECA-State Department Semi-Annual Report on Korea, January-June 1949*, pp. 2-3, and p. 125 ff. below.

[4] For a general discussion of the ECA program see p. 251 ff. below.

for financing fertilizer imports.[5] In addition, one purpose of the planned expansion of coal and electricity production during 1950 would be to provide the electric power necessary for the establishment of Korean fertilizer factories in the near future.[6]

Table 9 shows that the recovery of production in other cereal crops was not commensurate with that which occurred in rice. In part, these declines were deliberate. As early as September 1946 the Military Government had developed a two-fold plan which was intended to, first, make the country as nearly as possible self-sufficient in foodstuffs, and second, to alter the composition of Korean agricultural production.[7] Realization of the second objective was essential to the achievement of the first to some extent; it was hoped that the existing preponderance of cereals and legumes in the Korean diet would be offset by an emphasis upon other crops and an increased supply of meat.

The production of rye and buckwheat, both "poor land" crops, was to be greatly curtailed and the land planted in more profitable crops. The shortage of fertilizer during the war had encouraged the heavy planting of rye; from an average of 14,322 *suk* in the period 1930–34–36, the rye crop had jumped to 137,758 *suk* in 1945.[8] By 1948 rye production was commencing

[5] Fertilizer imports totaling $45,400,000, including ocean freight charges, were planned for 1950. This figure includes a proposed expenditure of nearly a million dollars on fungicides and insecticides. See *South Korea Economic Guides*, prepared by the Division of Korea Program, Economic Cooperation Administration, May 1949, unnumbered graph entitled "Proposed Budget Fiscal 1950." Net of freight figures are given in *Economic Aid to the Republic of Korea*, prepared by the ECA and the Department of State, June 1949, pp. 30-31.

[6] *Ibid.*

[7] The long- and short-term objectives of this plan are set forth in the USAMGIK publication, *Agricultural Production Goals for 1947*, Seoul, March 1947, 24 pp. This study was prepared by the National Economic Board and the Department of Agriculture and Forestry, USAMGIK. At this time Dr. Hoon K. Lee, an American-trained agricultural economist and an authority on Korean land utilization, was the Director of the Department of Agriculture and Forestry.

[8] *Republic of Korea Statistical Summation*, May 1949, p. 8.

to decline. The 1947 buckwheat harvest was only half of that in 1946.[9] Increases in the production of other summer grains and cereals were expected ultimately to bring the cereal crops other than rice up to the level of production of the long-run average of the caloric value of these crops. The 1946 USAMGIK plan also called for increases in the potato and vegetable crops. The potato crops increased significantly over their long-run averages and the vegetable harvests in 1948 were 70 per cent greater than the 1930–34–36 average.[10]

It was planned that in the long-run the fruit production would show substantial increases, and the livestock population would be expanded to provide more farm motive power as well as a larger consumption of meat. The production of poultry and other early-maturing livestock such as rabbits and hogs would be especially encouraged. While shortages of root-stock precluded any great increase in the relative importance of fruit crops, the long-run increase in the production of these crops continued after 1945.[11] The production of leguminous crops declined markedly from their long-run averages, principally because of a decline in soy bean production which accounted for nearly 90 per cent of the total legume production in the 1930–34–36 period.[12] Certain industrial crops—tobacco, silk, and cotton—have been encouraged to increase up to their long-term averages. Cotton and tobacco production figures were approaching these levels by 1949, but sericulture will require considerably longer to recover, owing to the heavy destruction of cocoons during the war.

During 1949, 118 irrigation and reclamation projects were brought to completion, under construction, or being planned. The Economic Cooperation Administration estimated that, when and if these projects were all completed, they will make

[9] *Ibid.*

[10] *Ibid.*

[11] In 1948 fruit production was about 168 million pounds as compared with the 1930–34–36 production of 90 million pounds. *Republic of Korea Statistical Summation*, August 1949, p. 9.

[12] *Ibid.*

possible an estimated increase of 415,929 *suk* in the average annual production of brown rice.[13] The ECA budget included $1,950,000 for irrigation and reclamation projects and the Republic of Korea appropriated 1,678 million won in its 1949–50 budget for this purpose.[14] In the spring of 1949, 217,000,000 trees were planted on 217,000 acres in South Korea, twice the number planted in 1948. Because of the shortage of fuel, however, wood was being cut twice as fast as it could be replaced by new growth.[15] For this reason it was necessary to import 30 million board feet of lumber under the ECA program. The fuel shortage in South Korea since the war thus made it impossible to develop the timber resources the area required and at the same time gravely undermined attempted soil erosion control measures. The ECA reported concerning its plans to increase coal production that "indirectly these projects should benefit the forestry situation as much, if not more, than the direct efforts at reforestation also being undertaken with the ECA aid." [16]

A number of other measures undertaken since 1945 have had salutary effects on agriculture. Among these were the encouragement of agricultural experimentation, the encouragement of new crops, and the importation of superior varieties and breeds of plants and livestock. Other measures such as storing rice and other grains each year for use in sowing "catch crops" in case of untimely flood or drought damage were also effected.[17] Basically, however, the continued recovery of Korean agriculture will depend upon the availability of commercial fertilizers. In 1948, 85,000 metric tons of fertilizer compounds were imported under American auspices and in 1949 165,000 metric tons. The latter quantity was more than had been applied to Korean soils in any previous year [18] and 61 per cent more than the

[13] *ECA-State Department Semi-Annual Report, January-June 1949*, p. 7.
[14] *Ibid.*
[15] *Ibid.*, p. 8.
[16] *Ibid.*
[17] *SKIG Activities*, September 1947, p. 32.
[18] Economic Cooperation Administration, *The Economy of South Korea, Basic Survey*, Washington, May 1949, p. 5.

average annual application during the period 1936–40.[19] Yet even this greatly increased supply would not permit the maximum economic use of Korea's land resources. In Japan the customary application of commercial fertilizer per unit of planted area is nearly twice that in Korea with Japanese agricultural yields almost 50 per cent higher.[20]

TABLE 10

PRODUCTION, FOREIGN TRADE, AND DOMESTIC CONSUMPTION OF BROWN RICE IN KOREA, 1915–1949 RICE YEARS[a]

Period	*Average Annual Production*	*Net Exports*	*Net Imports*	*Available Supplies*	*Population (millions)*	*Per Capita Disappearance (pounds)*
	(*In million lbs.*)					
1915–19[b]	4,546	626	0	3,920	17.1	229
1920–24[b]	4,675	1,138	0	3,537	18.6	190
1925–29[b]	5,094	1,614	0	3,480	20.4	170
1930–34[b]	5,482	2,698	0	2,784	22.1	126
1935–39[b]	5,694	2,294[c]	0	3,400	23.8	143
1940–44	6,246[d]	2,596[e]	0	3,650	25.1	145
1945	4,138[d]	0	0	4,138	19.0[f]	217
1946	3,884[d]	0	85[d]	3,969	19.9[f]	199
1947	4,365[d]	0	199[d]	4,564	20.3[f]	225
1948	5,803[g]	0	0	5,803	20.7[f]	280
1949	4,739[h]	209[i]	0	4,530	21.1[f]	215

[a] Rice year: December 1 of specified year to November 30 of following year. Figures for 1945–1949 refer to South Korea only.

[b] From *Civil Affairs Handbook, Korea Section 7: Agriculture*, Army Service Forces, 1944, p. 63; Grajdanzev, *Modern Korea*, p. 118 presents a similar table (1915–1938) but indicates a further drop in the last period.

[c] Five-year average from data in *SKIG Activities*, August 1947, p. 28.

[d] USAMGIK and SKIG monthly activity reports.

[e] Estimate; actual export figures not available. Source: *Present Agricultural Position of South Korea*, p. 3.

[f] Estimated populations are for middle of rice years. Preliminary tabulation of the May 1949 census indicated that population may have been overestimated by several hundred thousand in 1948 and 1949.

[g] ECA estimate.

[h] Pre-harvest estimate by ECA.

[i] Planned.

[19] *Ibid.*, p. 6.

[20] *Ibid.*, p. 5.

The Korean Food Supply

It is possible to get a somewhat more precise idea of the comparative dietary position of the Korean people in recent years than is reflected in the varying volumes of agricultural production. The preceding table showing the estimated per capita disappearance of brown rice in Korea over a period of years indicates the operation of other factors, such as the extent of exports to Japan, population changes, etc.

In spite of increases in total production in each successive period between 1915 and 1944, per capita disappearance of rice within Korea actually declined. Although the population increased rapidly during this period, the drain of exports of rice to Japan further decreased the amount available for domestic consumption. With the termination of exports after the Japanese surrender, domestic consumption was free to advance. Probably the contrast between 1944 and 1945 rice consumption is much greater than the 1940–44 average indicates, for production declined considerably in 1944. If exports are assumed to have remained at the level of the estimated 1940–44 average, actual domestic per capita consumption may have been as low as 102 pounds.[21]

The comparison of probable per capita consumption of the principal items constituting the over-all Korean diet for the period 1932–36 and the year May 1946 to April 1947, as shown in Table 11, however, indicates a serious deterioration of the diet from the prewar period. The year May 1946–April 1947 is taken as representing somewhat of a probable mean of the food position of the average Korean during the first and second postwar years.

While the average per capita disappearance of rice soared in the immediate post-liberation period, it showed little conformity with the general pattern of consumption. Furthermore, the breakdown of the distribution system—the termination of

[21] 1944 production was 5,175 million pounds, as compared with the 1940–44 average of 6,246 million pounds.

TABLE II

COMPARISON OF PER-CAPITA CALORIC INTAKE
OF PRINCIPAL FOOD ITEMS*
1932–36 Average and May 1946–April 1947]

Commodity	*Calories per pound*	*Net Annual Consumption per capita 1932–36 (pounds)*	*Total Annual Calories 1932–36*	*Net Consumption per capita May 1946–April 1947 (pounds)*	*Total Calories May 1946–April 1947*
**Rice	1,590	123	195,570	189	300,510
**Wheat	1,615	23	37,145	32	51,680
**Barley	1,650	87	143,550	47	77,550
Millet	1,680	84	141,120	9	15,120
Other grains	1,680	24	40,320	6	10,080
Soybeans	1,590	38	60,420	9	12,720
Other legumes	1,590	14	22,260	1	1,590
Potatoes:					
Irish	325	53	17,225	18	5,850
Sweet	490	17	8,330	22	10,780
Vegetables	140	143	20,020	72	10,080
Fruit	300	11	3,300	7	2,100
**Sugar	1,805	4	7,220	Neg.	Neg.
Candy	1,785	—	—	.5	892
Fish	816	47	38,352	33	26,928
Meat	1,242	6	7,453	6†	7,453
Eggs (number)	79	10	790	5	395
**Canned goods	1,274	—	—	1	1,274
Oil (Sesame)	2,765	.4	1,106	.3	830
Totals:		684.4	744,181	457.8	535,832
Average Daily Caloric Intake			2,039		1,468

* 1932–36 average is for all Korea; May 1946–April 1947 figures are for South Korea only.

** Commodities of which quantities were imported.

† No figures available for actual meat consumption. It is assumed to have remained at the same level, despite reduced livestock population, because of increased slaughtering.

Sources: 1932–36 Average, *Civil Affairs Handbook, Korea*, p. 93. May 1946–April 1947 figures computed from various USAMGIK reports.

rationing and the subsequent hoarding, the skyrocketing of prices and the difficulty of getting rice from production to consumption areas—in the early months of liberation, created great inequalities in diet among the population. To the general political and economic confusion was added the disturbance caused by the mass exodus of Japanese and the immigration of Koreans. Departing Japanese sold household goods which they were forbidden to take with them and spent a large part of the proceeds in an extravagant consumption of foodstuffs. Freed from regulation, farmers indulged in making rice wine and candy, which the Japanese had prohibited, and consequently marketed less of their crops. Landlords held back their shares awaiting further price rises. The wealthy who could pay the high prices were able to command an ample food supply and the agricultural population in general was better fed than it had been in years, but the urban working population suffered increasingly as prices rose.

Large imports of American wheat became necessary "to prevent disease and unrest." The augmentation to the domestic food supply afforded by these imports is included in the diet given in Table 11. Although an effective rationing system (supplying the larger part of the diet of over eight million non-self-suppliers) eventually curtailed the previous dissipation of foodstuffs and although the production of cereals improved, crops in 1946, aside from rice, fell short of supplying the dietary level of 1932–36. In fact, as indicated in Table 11, the per capita daily caloric intake in the year May 1946–April 1947 was less than 75 per cent of that in the given prewar period. It was estimated [22] that during the 1932–36 period Koreans consumed 14,000 calories annually, or 38 calories per day, of unclassifiable foods, presumably such items as edible weeds, roots and bark, the diet of the sufferers from "spring hunger." Thus not only by Western standards, but from the standpoint of the actual minimal food requirements of the vast majority of the Korean people as well, even the prewar diet was very meager.

Since nothing like equality existed among individual diets in the prewar period, consumption being largely determined by income, the great mass of the very poor subsisted upon fewer

[22] *Civil Affairs Handbook, Korea*, p. 93.

calories and a less desirable diet than the per capita average shows. Meat, eggs, fruits, and sugar were found almost exclusively in the diets of the higher-income groups. In the occupation period, the diet of the farm population may have improved qualitatively somewhat, but the average urban Korean family was worse off than before. Rice was the only food that was more available.

The glaring deficiency in the prewar diet of foods of animal origin was even more pronounced in the occupation period. There could be no optimism concerning any notable immediate improvement in the supply of meat. The livestock population throughout the occupation period contrasted very unfavorably with the prewar position.[23] Evidently livestock breeding was being discouraged even before the war, either expressly, or implicitly through a constricted food supply. Also, heavy slaughtering apparently occurred during the war, particularly of hogs. The single available figure for 1944, 886,842 head of work or beef cattle, when compared with the 1946 figure of 556,220 head, appears to confirm the heavy destruction of draft animals which reportedly occurred late in the war and during the early months of occupation. Even the low 1932–36 meat consumption could only have been sustained at the expense of further destruction in the May 1946–April 1947 period.

Much more serious than the meat deficiency was the 14 pound, or 30 per cent, decline in the per capita consumption of fish.[24] The May 1946–April 1947 figure represented some improvement over the situation in the late stages of the war and the very early occupation period. Like virtually all other economic activities in South Korea, the fishing industry was thrown into chaos by the breakdown of Japanese authority. Under the supervision of Military Government officials these difficulties were rapidly overcome and marine landings increased by 50 per cent

[23] See Table 9, Appendix C, for details.

[24] Both as a source of food and as a vocation, fishing is vitally important, the fishing industry being second only to agriculture in the economy of the country.

over the preceding year to a total of 309,253 metric tons.[25] The progressive deterioration of the physical facilities of the South Korean fishing fleet made it impossible to sustain this figure, however, and in 1947 marine landings declined to 302,231 metric tons. In 1948 the total catch declined still further to 285,269 metric tons, and for the first seven months of 1949 the total fell below that for the corresponding period of the preceding year by more than three per cent.[26]

The Japanese had made offshore fishing a big industry by the introduction of power launches and other modern equipment. However, the Korean fishing fleet was not kept in repair during the war, and many of the better vessels were removed by the Japanese before the occupation began. Those vessels which remained in Korea underwent rapid deterioration in common with most of the country's industrial resources. Consequently fishing was concentrated in inshore waters to the point of threatening depletion, while offshore grounds remained abundantly stocked.[27] Military Government imported nets and other expendable equipment but did not have the financial resources at its disposal to undertake the extensive rehabilitation required. Moreover, the complete dependence in some respects upon external sources of supply caused some seemingly minor shortages to assume vexing importance.[28] The Economic Cooperation Administration viewed with concern the deterioration of this vital Korean industry and planned to spend $6,080,000 for

[25] See Table 10, Appendix C for marine landings figures during the period 1931–48.

[26] Reported in *Republic of Korea Economic Summation*, May 1949, p. 14, and August 1949, p. 10.

[27] USAMGIK, *Present Agricultural Position of South Korea*, Seoul, April 1947, p. 16.

[28] For example, with the termination of all trade with North Korea, South Korean fishermen were cut off from their principal source of carbide which was essential for illumination on important after-dark voyages. Economic Cooperation Administration and the Department of State, *Economic Aid to the Republic of Korea*, ECA Recovery Program for Fiscal Year 1950, Washington, June 1950, p. 34.

the procurement and construction of fishing vessels during the U.S. fiscal year 1950.[29]

Before the war Korea was a large food exporter. As much as 40 per cent of the rice crop and 60 per cent of the fishing catch left the country in some years. No doubt these exports were excessive in relation to the domestic diet, but after the war with no food exports, the country's food position was still unsatisfactory. In fact, Korea became a food deficit country, so that about 12 per cent of the May 1946–April 1947 consumption was derived from imports, largely from the United States. Production which was generally below prewar levels was required to meet the needs of a population that had increased roughly 25 per cent between 1935 and 1948.

Modest improvement was made in the food production situation through 1947, although crops did not attain a level which permitted the discontinuance of food imports. In April 1947 one economist who had been in Korea and studied the country's economic position since the war stated that it did not then seem probable that improvements could "be carried forward rapidly enough to make South Korea self-sufficient in food within the next three years but if the present program can be carried forward continuously . . . and if present plans in respect to the fishing industry are carried out, within less than a decade South Korea can become not only self-sufficient in food but may even be able to develop a modest food export industry. . . ."[30]

By 1949 South Korea was self-sufficient in foodstuffs and the export of 100,000 metric tons of rice to Japan was being planned for 1950. The fact that the 1949 rice crop was not as large as had been anticipated earlier might necessitate some revision of these plans, although the South Korean government still hoped to export the projected quantity of rice, importing wheat or

[29] *Ibid.*

[30] James Shoemaker, *Notes on Korea's Post War Economic Problems*, *op. cit.*, p. 14.

barley to meet minimum food needs. Such a transaction would provide several million dollars net foreign exchange income, owing to the price differential between rice and the other grains. Food imports under the ECA program during the U.S. fiscal year would be limited to vegetable oils and salt and would have a value under $800,000.[31]

South Korea's food export industry will necessarily be modest, because of the increased domestic requirements occasioned by a greatly enlarged population. A long-term food export rate of about 20 per cent of the prewar volume seems reasonable. Yet exports of foodstuffs on even this moderate scale would be critically important in Korea's future foreign trade. Rice exports probably will continue to be for many years a strategic item in Korea's trade balance.

AGRARIAN PROBLEMS IN KOREA

In 1936 the average acreage per Korean farm household was only about 3.6 acres.[32] This average, however, did not indicate the holding of the typical farm family, as actually 63 per cent of all farm households in 1938 cultivated less than 2.4 acres each, and half of them cultivated areas smaller than 1.2 acres.[33] It is obvious that the amount of land cultivated by most farmers was not large enough to provide the bare necessities of life.

Apologists for Japanese expansion frequently pointed to the depressed agricultural conditions in Japan as reasons for the Japanese acquisition of areas such as Korea. In reality the problems of agricultural overpopulation were more acute in Korea than in Japan.[34] With a considerably larger area in a warmer,

[31] *ECA-State Department Joint Semi-Annual Report, January-June 1949, op. cit.*, p. 3. Salt imports were necessary because of the absence of mineral salt deposits in Korea and the inadequate facilities for the production of salt by solar evaporation. Vegetable oils would be used for the manufacture of industrial oils and soap.

[32] *Civil Affairs Handbook, Korea*, p. 19.

[33] *Ibid.*, p. 20.

[34] See Irene B. Taeuber, "The Population Potential of Postwar Korea," *loc. cit.*, p. 289.

more productive climate, a more developed irrigation system, and its advanced industrial development, Japan had a number of advantages. While the average of 3.6 acres per farm household was about an acre greater than in Japan, conditions of soil productivity and the lack of subsidiary occupations made the position of the Korean farm family worse than that of its Japanese counterpart. In addition, the average acreage cultivated by families in Japan had remained constant in the twenty-year period before World War II. Yet, in Korea, the absence of any substantial land reclamation or opportunities for an alternative vocation, in the face of a rapidly growing population, caused an appreciable decline in the area operated per farm household.[35] Other conditions resulting from the colonial subservience to Japan have already been discussed. "The fact is that before the war even Japan, with its 2.5 times the number of people per cultivated acre, as compared to Korea, enjoyed a far greater measure of economic well-being than Korea. This applies not only to Japan as a whole but to the Japanese farmers as well despite their low economic status." [36]

The prices of agricultural commodities were ordinarily depressed.[37] This was attributable not only to the cheap rice policy of Japan. In 1938 the net value of production per worker in Korean industry was nearly 14 times that of workers in agriculture, a ratio so disparate for agriculture as to represent something more than the normal depression of this sector of the economy. It reflected the low productivity of Korean agriculture per worker or, in other words, the manifestly inefficient man-land ratio in agriculture. As expressed by Grajdanzev, it was not Korea but Korean agriculture which was overpopulated.[38]

Another factor which exerted a depressing effect upon Korean

[35] *Civil Affairs Handbook, Korea, op. cit.*, p. 20.

[36] *Ibid.*, p. 20.

[37] See Hoon K. Lee, *Land Utilization and Rural Economy in Korea, op. cit.*, pp. 265-66.

[38] Grajdanzev, *op. cit.*, p. 85.

agriculture was the system of farm tenancy. Tenancy was centuries old in Korea, and the relationship between landlord and tenant derived from strong feudal antecedents. A Japanese agricultural expert observed that in Korea "small tenants worked like servants under landlords and lived under feudalistic restraints, a system which had almost disappeared in Japan Proper." [39]

The principal hardship for the tenants was the high rent, generally 50 per cent of the crop, although one writer surmised that it may have averaged as high as 60 per cent.[40] Despite Japanese laws to the contrary, the tenant was often obliged to continue to pay taxes and imposts under the force of the old custom. This practice was especially prevalent in southern Korea. In addition the tenant paid for water and delivered to the landlord his share of the crops (which entailed no small expense if the landlord lived in the city). Since most landlords were absentee owners, tenants were obliged to deal with agents, who often compelled them to bring presents and to work for them, who ordered harvesting at a time convenient to themselves, increased rents to their own advantage, and burdened the tenants in other ways. In practice, a tenant's contractual rights were negligible. In 1930 a survey showed that only 27 per cent of rent contracts were in written form and 81 per cent were for no fixed term; i.e., the tenant could be evicted at will.[41]

Perhaps the most distressing thing about tenancy under Japanese rule was its uninterrupted growth. In the twenty years after 1918, the number of non-farming landlord families had doubled, the number of farmer-owner and owner-tenant families had declined materially, and the number of tenant families had increased by 45 per cent. A change in the methods of com-

[39] Shiroshi Nasu, *Aspects of Japanese Agriculture*, Institute of Pacific Relations, New York, 1941 (mimeographed), p. 55.

[40] Grajdanzev, *op. cit.*, p. 114. State Department Economic Mission sources have accepted the 60 per cent figure as more representative.

[41] Grajdanzev, *ibid.* See also H. K. Lee, *Land Utilization and Rural Economy in Korea*, *op. cit.*, pp. 162-67.

piling this data after 1932 makes impossible a direct comparison of circumstances in succeeding years. However, information for the period between 1932 and 1936 indicates continued decline in farmer-owner and owner-tenant categories and the appearance of two new growing classes at the bottom of the agricultural ladder, itinerant fire-field cultivators and agricultural laborers.[42]

The Japanese found that landlordism was a convenient device for furthering their own principal interests in Korean agriculture, which no doubt accounts, in part at least, for the lack of interest in reform. Landlordism was useful for pumping rice out of Korea to Japan. Korean tenants, after paying rent and taxes, were left with only a small share of the rice which they produced, while the system put into the hands of the landlords large surpluses to be marketed in Japan.

Reform Measures During the Occupation

Very early in the occupation, Military Government announced that henceforth maximum rents were to be 33⅓ per cent of the annual crop instead of the former average of 50 per cent.[43] This gave some reason to expect that a general land reform program would soon be announced by Military Government. However, proposals were made but no action was taken. The disposition to tenants of the 500,000 acres of paddy lands and 150,000 acres of dry fields of former Japanese-owned property was discussed as the first phase in an over-all land reform program. Eventually, this program envisaged the redistribution of land owned by Korean absentee landlords also.[44]

An ordinance to be called "The Homestead Act" was proposed in February 1946, which would have permitted the tenants to homestead the land they occupied. Upon fulfilling the terms of the homestead, including the payment of a sum 3.75 times

[42] Absolute figures on tenure groups may be found in *Civil Affairs Handbook, Korea*, pp. 25-28. Percentage figures may be found in Grajdanzev, *op. cit.* pp. 108-09.

[43] Ordinance No. 9, October 5, 1945.

[44] U.S. Department of State Economic Mission, *Land Reform in Korea*, Seoul, Sept. 13, 1947 (mimeographed), p. 1.

the value of the annual production, that is, 25 per cent of the crop for 15 years, the tenants would be given title to the land in fee simple.[45] As it turned out, the reform was not put into effect until a full two years later. Military Government explained that, "Although the program had wide support, its execution was postponed in 1946 because Military Government authorities decided that, on the basis of several opinion polls, the Koreans preferred to wait for the establishment of a Provisional Government before proceeding with land reform." [46] Among Koreans the issue was highly charged with politics and was a major issue in the cleavage between left and right. The Korean Interim Legislative Assembly, which was organized in December 1946, was preponderantly representative of landlords and thus understandably reluctant to initiate programs which might jeopardize the position of the propertied class. Even a measure to distribute the former Japanese holdings among the tenants would endanger their position.[47]

Such rightist proposals as were made upheld the principle of compensation, while leftists insisted upon outright confiscation. And although Military Government placed the matter in Korean hands, it attached a proviso which meant an explicit taking of sides on the issue. According to Brig. Gen. Charles G. Helmick, then Acting Military Governor, Military Government would "not confiscate farmland owned by Koreans for redistribution. If a land reform law is enacted by a Korean legislative assembly while Military Government is in power, land owners will receive adequate compensation." [48] Advocates of farmland confiscation from absentee landlords justified their position on the grounds that Korean landlords were a generally

[45] *Ibid.*, Enclosure C, "Proposed Ordinance for Sale of Japanese Agricultural Property South of 38° North Latitude."

[46] *Ibid.*, p. 1.

[47] Formerly Japanese-held agricultural property comprised about 12.5 per cent of the cultivated land in Korea. It included a large part of the most desirable agricultural land in the country.

[48] *Chukan Digest*, Department of Public Information, Seoul, No. 60, December 14, 1946.

parasitic class, and that, during the Japanese occupation, many of them had willingly collaborated with the Japanese administration.[49] This attack did not answer, however, the non-political arguments of certain observers who believed that landlords should be compensated in order to create a class with sufficient liquid assets to undertake the financing of Korean industrial development.[50]

By late 1947 Military Government grew impatient with the slow processes of the Korean legislators and the Military Governor urged the Interim Assembly to enact a law embodying the principles already approved by the Land Reform Committee.[51] A National Land Reform Administration (NLRA) was to be established as an agency of the state to acquire by compulsion privately-owned land at a "standard price" of three times the value of the annual crop, less any encumbrances against the property. Land so acquired, plus land confiscated from the Japanese, would be sold at the "standard rate" to tenants and others in accordance with priorities assumed to reflect the relative fitness of various types of families to take over its operation. Purchasers would be freed of all obligations other than the mortgage to NLRA.

Persons entitled to compensation under the law would be paid in registered negotiable bonds issued by the Farm Loan Bank and liquidated in annual installments extending over a

[49] In criticizing the compensation terms of proposed legislation Yong-jeung Kim, President of the Korean Affairs Institute, Washington, D.C., stated, "With a few exceptions they [landlords] acquired their possession by usury or by other fraudulent means." *Voice of Korea*, January 17, 1948.

[50] This idea was first advanced by Dr. Arthur C. Bunce in an article, "The Future of Korea," *Far Eastern Survey*, May 17, 1944, p. 86. Dr. Bunce was at this time a professor of agricultural economics at Iowa State College. In January 1946 Dr. Bunce headed a U.S. Department of State Economic Mission to Korea. He and his staff worked assiduously on means of remedying the land tenure problem and drafted the land reform ordinances promulgated by the Military Governor in March 1948. Dr. Bunce later became the head of the Economic Cooperation Administration to Korea.

[51] See the *Legislative Land Reform Law*, Draft, December 4, 1947 (mimeographed).

period of fifteen years. According to the proposal, "the face value of the bonds shall be expressed in rice or other agricultural products, as the case may be. . . ." The holder of a bond would be paid annually in won, at the current price for one-fifteenth of the agricultural products indicated on the bond.[52] Thus former owners would stand fully protected against the "invisible" confiscation of inflation.

The NLRA was to have a monopoly of the purchase and disposition of all land subject to the law. It would thus act as a buffer between landlord and tenant so that much of the intimidation and arbitrary action which might arise from direct dealing would be avoided.

Despite the moderate character of the proposed legislation, the Interim Legislative Assembly showed little disposition to approve of it. The South Korea Labor Party (Communist) attacked the scheme charging (1) that the sale of land to tenants under the proposed terms of 20 per cent of the value of the crop for fifteen years, coupled with their obligation to assume the payment of taxes and all costs of upkeep, would place upon them a burden heavier than that of the 30 per cent rent exacted by landlords, and (2) that to eliminate the feudal system, expedite industrial development, and alleviate the low living standards of the people, the land should be distributed to landless farmers free.[53]

By the spring of 1948 it was apparent to Military Government that the Interim Assembly was unlikely to pass any meaningful land reform program. Undoubtedly Military Government was not insensitive to the criticism it received for its failure to do something about the land problem, and no amount of reiteration that a decision must be left to the Koreans themselves could quiet the objections of Korean and American observers alike. Finally, on March 22, six weeks before the elections, the Military Governor, Maj. Gen. William F. Dean, promulgated two ordinances which created the National Land Administra-

[52] *Ibid.*, Section 8.

[53] "Land Bill Called Feudal," *Korean Independence*, December 24, 1947, p. 1.

tion and transferred the landholdings of the New Korea Company to the new organization for sale to Korean farmers.[54] These decrees were intended to accomplish, by direction, the reforms which the Military Governor had urged the Interim Assembly to enact. In all important respects these ordinances were the same as the proposed land distribution plan recommended to the Assembly in December 1947.

Although it applied to former Japanese holdings only, the reform was a step forward against the distressing tenancy conditions which beset Korean agriculture.[55] The program would place in the hands of 587,974 tenant families, 686,965 acres (280,394 *chungbo*) of land. The 3,318,115 persons living on that land comprised 24.1 per cent of South Korea's farm population. The decree assured a widespread and equitable distribution of the land within this group. It expressly limited tenants in their purchase of land to the extent that a single buyer would not have his total holdings increased to more than two *chungbo* (about 4.9 acres).

The Communists and certain other left-wing groups sought to pursuade tenants to boycott the land sales, but, judging by the enthusiastic response to the land reform even in rural areas that were considered "radical," these efforts had no effect. When American control of South Korea ended on August 15, 1948, less than five months after the beginning of the program, 85 per cent of more than 1,400,000 separate plots of land involved had been sold and shortly thereafter the distribution was virtually complete.

Land Reform after 1949

The obvious popularity of land reform made it politic for office-seekers participating in the May 10, 1948, National As-

[54] Ordinances 173 and 174, dated March 22, 1948.

[55] Also see Shannon McCune, "Land Redistribution in Korea," *Far Eastern Survey*, January 28, 1948, and June 2, 1948; and C. Clyde Mitchell, "Korean Farm Tenant Purchase Program," *Land Economics*, November 1948, pp. 402-05, and "Land Reform in South Korea," *Pacific Affairs*, June 1949, pp. 144-54.

sembly elections to go on record as favoring the distribution of privately-owned lands as well. The new constitution of the Republic of Korea subsequently passed by the National Assembly stated that, "farmland shall be distributed to self-tilling farmers. The method of distribution, the extent of possession, and the nature and restrictions of ownership shall be determined by law" (Article 86). Despite these assurances, almost a year went by before any such law was passed, and even then it was very uncertain that the law would ever actually be enforced. Meanwhile landlords, in the expectation that some sort of land distribution law would eventually be enacted, were compelling their tenants to buy land on very unfavorable terms or be evicted.[56]

The second regular session of the National Assembly convened on December 20, 1948, and, according to law, would adjourn three months later. When the date for adjournment approached and the Assembly had not yet acted on the budget for the coming fiscal year as required by the constitution, it became necessary to prolong the session. Although conservatives blocked the efforts of more liberal members to extend the session to allow time to act on the land reform bill,[57] then still pending in committee, the bill was subsequently brought up for discussion and passed before adjournment.

On May 2 the National Assembly adjourned and at its final session President Rhee praised the bill as satisfactory.[58] Nonetheless, the "government," or administration, announced that it wished to amend the bill and because the Assembly was not

[56] Some indication of the hardship these forced purchases were producing is given in an account by Chin Kook Kang, the chief of the Farm Land Bureau of the Ministry of Agriculture and Forestry, of his visit into the farming areas during January 1949: "What I regretted most during my tour was that landowners were compelling their tenants to buy their land and therefore the latter was obliged to meet the former's request by selling their cows and farming tools. It is therefore anticipated that the farmers will be confronted with great difficulties in the coming cultivation season." (Seoul) *Union Democrat,* February 6, 1949, p. 4.

[57] (Seoul) *Union Democrat,* April 3, 1949, p. 1.

[58] *Seoul Times,* May 19, 1949, p. 1.

in session to consider these amendments, the bill was necessarily abrogated.[59]

The government, which was very responsive to the wishes of the landowning group, was known to be cool to the passage of any liberal land reform measure. The draft of a land reform bill which was generally regarded as very favorable to the farmers had been placed before the cabinet shortly after the establishment of the Republic of Korea by Minister of Agriculture and Forestry, Cho Pongam. Cho's vigorous advocacy of strong measures for agrarian change incurred the enmity of the President and other government leaders and he was finally dismissed on February 22, 1949. The cabinet rejected his bill and subsequently submitted a very conservative draft measure to the Assembly committee on industry and economy for passage by the Assembly. This bill was attacked by certain young "radical" assemblymen when it was reported out of committee and a number of its provisions were modified along the lines of the bill originally submitted by the Ministry of Agriculture and Forestry.[60] It was this modified bill that passed the Assembly.

The abrogation of this bill was one of the high points in a conflict which raged on several legislative fronts between the National Assembly and the government during the spring of 1949. The Assembly was antagonized by this and other actions which it regarded as high-handed and threatening to its prerogatives. Therefore, the Assembly reconvened in special session and on June 15 returned the bill to the President by a vote of 97 to 19 out of 153. Although this was not quite a two-thirds vote as required by the constitution, no further question was raised by the government and the law was promulgated on June 22, 1949.

The law provided in general for government purchase of all holdings not farmed by the owner and of all holdings of more

[59] *Loc. cit.*, May 20, 1949, p. 1.

[60] For discussions of the various land reform proposals see *Seoul Times*, February 9 and May 19, 1949; *Union Democrat*, February 27 and March 27, 1949.

than three *chungbo* (7.5 acres), irrespective of whether they were cultivated by the owner or not.[61] Land planted in certain special crops such as orchards, sapling gardens, and mulberry trees managed by the owner, farmlands cultivated directly by religious or educational institutions, and certain partially reclaimed lands or tidal flats might be exempted where their area exceeded three *chungbo* at the discretion of the government (Article 6).

The Ministry of Agriculture and Forestry was charged with the administration of the law. To assist in its enforcement Land Committees were to be established in the capital, and in each province, county, island, city, town, and township (Article 4). This administrative organization and the provisions of the Land Reform Act were to replace the National Land Administration and the provisions under which it operated.[62]

As under the reforms proposed by the Military Government, the government was to acquire ownership of the land by purchase from its present owners and then sell it to tenants or other qualified persons. For the purpose of determining the appropriate compensation in each district, the government, on the recommendation of the local Land Committee would select representative farms of every description and fix a common rate of compensation on the basis of 150 per cent of the average production of the main crop of this farmland. The amount of compensation on every farmland in the district would be determined in accordance with this common rate.[63] The principle of progressive diminution—the greater the land holding, the less

[61] Article 5 (2) and 6 (1) in a mimeographed English text of the bill entitled "Land Reform Bill, Drafted by the Committee on Industry and now being considered by the National Assembly." This is the version of the bill passed by the Assembly.

[62] Article 28 rescinded South Korean Interim Government Ordinance Number 173, which established the National Land Administration and enumerated its functions.

[63] Article 7 (1). Compensation for special crop lands such as orchards, sapling gardens, or mulberry fields, which were to be purchased by the government for distribution, was to be based upon current market values. Article 7 (3), (4).

paid—would be applied in fixing the compensation actually to be paid.[64]

This law also resembled the earlier land reform proposals and the Military Government land reform ordinance in its protection of the compensation to the owner against impairment by price inflation. Article 8 stated that compensation shall be made by "negotiable government guaranteed bonds issued by the government. The face value of the bond shall indicate the number of units of the main crop of the land for the current year . . . The bonds shall be redeemed by yearly installments spread over five years; paying one-fifth of the face value each year in cash (won) *calculated at the legal* [*current*] *price of the agricultural product*." [Italics ours.]

Qualified farmers or farm families [65] were eligible to purchase up to three *chungbo* of land and no more irrespective of the kind or grade of that land (Article 12). Ownership would be inherited but sale, donation, or transfer of ownership was to be prohibited until the farmer had fully paid for the land.[66]

The Land Reform Law in effect provided for government subsidization of land distribution. The government would buy the land for 150 per cent of the value of the annual crop and distribute it to farmers for 125 per cent [67] of the same base. Under the Military Government ordinance both the compensation paid to landlords by the government and the purchase price to be paid by tenants was 300 per cent of the annual

[64] Article 7 (5).

[65] Article 11 provided that farmers or farm families were eligible to purchase lands in the following order:

"(1) Farmers who are cultivating the farmlands at present;
(2) Farmers who cultivate farmlands too small compared with their farming potentiality;
(3) The bereaved families of those who have died for this country, if they have experience in the management of a farm;
(4) Farm employees who have experience in farming;
(5) Farm families repatriated from foreign countries."

[66] Articles 15 and 16 (1). It would also be unlawful to mortgage or create other superficies on the land (Article 16 (2)).

[67] Article 13 (1).

value of the crop. Purchasers could now liquidate their indebtedness by the payment of ten annual installments[68] of 12.5 per cent as compared with fifteen annual payments of 20 per cent each under the earlier law. The Land Reform Law further provided that 30 per cent of the purchase price would be subsidized by the government to "poor farmers who receive land allocation."[69] Small landlords who sold land to the government also would receive 30 per cent additional compensation.[70]

Although the government promulgated the Land Reform Law, there was little conclusive evidence that the law would be vigorously administered. In fact, as late as October 1949 it was reportedly not yet being enforced at all. Meanwhile, landlords were able to continue making sales to their tenants on their own terms.

Some of the government's arguments against the Land Reform Act seemed plausible but certain other factors raised doubts about their validity. For example, in abrogating the bill on May 16, 1949, the government stated that the compensation bonds to be issued to former landowners should not be freely negotiable government guaranteed instruments as provided in the bill, but negotiable only for securing industrial investments.[71] The government also criticized certain of the subsidy provisions of the bill on the ground that these provisions would impose a severe financial burden upon the country.[72] However, the government at the same time had a bill pending before the Assembly which provided for government retention of ownership and active control over the vested former Japanese enterprises which comprised the overwhelming bulk of Korean industry, despite the fact that these enterprises were notoriously inefficient and unstable financially under over-centralized government control. In theory, at least, the funds the landlords

[68] Article 13 (2).
[69] Article 7 (5).
[70] *Loc. cit.*
[71] *Seoul Times*, May 19, 1949, p. 2.
[72] *Ibid.*

derived from the sale of their farmlands could be siphoned off into purchases of these industrial undertakings and the inflationary capabilities of these funds thereby largely neutralized. Government retention of the vested enterprises appeared virtually to ensure that all available capital would continue to flow into luxury consumption and speculative transactions in scarce commodities, rather than into productive investment channels.[73]

It was true that the subsidy provisions of the Land Reform Act would impose an added inflationary burden upon public finances; yet at the same time the government showed singularly little inclination to abate the tide of deficit spending elsewhere. The ECA mission noted in its semi-annual report for the period January–June 1949 that, "the actual deficit on ordinary account has already reached 17.2 billion for the first four months (April–July) of the fiscal year 1949–50, or about three-fourths of the estimated regular deficit of 24 billion for the whole year. For the same period of 1948, the deficit was only 4.0 billion won. Thus the present budgetary trend is away from rather than toward financial stabilization. . . ." [74] In these critical circumstances the government was anomalously planning tax reductions.[75]

Land reform was assuredly no economic panacea; the permanent relief of Korean agriculture can come only from increasing industrialization which will gradually reduce the pressure upon the land. However, no other reform at the moment could make such a great contribution to political stability and to the eventual raising of the rural standard of living.

[73] The concentration of capital in speculative channels was a serious problem. For example, one of the reasons advanced by the Bank of Korea for the sharp rise in rice prices during the spring of 1949 was that "rich persons" were buying and hoarding rice. *Seoul Times*, April 26, 1949, p. 4.

[74] *ECA-State Department Semi-Annual Report, January–June 1949*, p. 26.

[75] *Ibid.*, p. 29.

CHAPTER EIGHT

Industry and Labor in South Korea

MINING, MANUFACTURING, AND TRANSPORTATION

General Industrial Conditions

As ALREADY pointed out, industry in Korea was such an integral part of the economy of Greater Japan that most of the industrial plant existing in Korea at the end of the war was incapable of independent existence. For capital goods Korea relied almost wholly upon Japan, and certain important stages in the production of consumer goods also depended on Japanese parts or supplies. For example, light bulbs were fabricated in Korea, but the tungsten filaments used in these bulbs were manufactured in Japan, even though Korea was a large producer of tungsten ores. The ore was shipped to Japan to be refined and manufactured into wire, which was then shipped back to Korea for use in the production of light bulbs.

The outward evidences of industrialization in Korea in 1945 were not unimpressive. Because of inadequate maintenance during the war, however, many factories were reduced to a fraction of their former production and others were mere shells, either never finished or stripped of much of their equipment to meet the more urgent requirements of the Japanese war economy. Moreover, a good deal of heavy industry had been constructed to produce military supplies and was thus largely useless for the purposes of a peacetime economy or had been dismantled as war potential by American ordnance teams. The industrial capacity was further impaired by the accelerated pace of deterioration after the Japanese surrender. The collapse of Japanese management meant the virtual abandonment of numerous plants. In the absence of responsible custodianship, the properties fell into further disrepair and were exposed to vandalism and pilferage. The situation in many plants throughout South Korea is illustrated by the Chungyang tungsten ore mine which suspended production on August 13, 1945. Two years later when the mine was visited by representatives of the Bureau of Mining, "the condition of the property indicated it had been systematically looted" and it "was in very poor condition." Residents of the surrounding area were processing waste piles and picking some ore from the veins in the underground workings.[1]

The collapse of production occurring in large sectors of industry, together with the serious impairment of the capacity of many other plants to produce, greatly reduced the volume of industrial output. There was a 43.7 per cent decline in the number of factories operating at the time of the Industrial Labor Force and Wage Survey in November 1946 as compared with 1944.[2] Because of the lack of trained supervisory and operating personnel and the uncertainty which discouraged the opening of many plants, 30 to 40 per cent of the industrial establishment built up during Japanese rule was in danger of being lost. Military Government estimated in late 1946 that production was not averaging more than 20 per cent of capacity. While some improvement took place during 1947, the disruptive factors already mentioned, and certain others which will be discussed subsequently, continued to keep output at very low levels. In fact, it was not until 1949 that industrial conditions commenced to show general signs of improvement.

[1] *SKIG Activities*, September 1947, pp. 43-44.

[2] Table 5, "Number of Industrial Establishments in South Korea by Province, June 1944 and November 1946," in *Selected Economics Statistics for South Korea*, USAMGIK, Seoul, April 1947 (mimeographed).

Coal

As in so many other countries, one of the principal problems in Korea at the end of the war was a critical coal shortage; and during the next three years this continued to be one of the most serious factors retarding the country's economic recovery. In the first days of the occupation Military Government worked frantically to find Koreans who could bring order out of the chaos that prevailed in the coal industry after the collapse of Japanese organization. As an emergency measure one large Korean coal operator was given practically unlimited authority to direct the coal industry but this was soon revoked when he was found to have a record of criminal collaboration. Military Government officers then for a time worked directly in the mining areas upon problems of organization.

Although production was at a virtual standstill, the coal problem was even more a matter of transportation than of production in the early weeks of the occupation. Large stockpiles of coal were available above ground at the Samchŏk mine. This mine was the largest coal producer in South Korea but it was located on the east coast without rail connection to other points in South Korea. It was only after a period of very anxious attention by the Military Government Bureau of Mining and Industry, that the distribution system was made to function again. Several small (LST-type) U.S. Navy cargo vessels joined Korean vessels in hauling coal out of the Samchŏk area to the southern port of Pusan. From this point distribution to the other urban centers was accomplished mainly by rail, which also presented problems because of the deplorable condition of the railroads at that time. Final distribution of the coal to users was accomplished by the Chosen Coal Company, the former Japanese coal distributing monopoly, which was placed under the direction of Military Government officers.

The usual post-liberation shortages of trained personnel and usable equipment prevented an immediate return to previous high levels of output. However, the coal industry was generally better supplied with technicians and experienced miners than other types of mining. This factor and the emphasis placed upon a resumption of coal mining by Military Government explain why coal production showed a greater proportionate recovery than most other types of mineral output. Summary figures of the South Korean coal supply in the years 1946–48 are given below.

TABLE 12

COAL SUPPLY OF SOUTH KOREA, 1946–1948
(Metric tons)

	1946	*1947*	*1948*
Domestic Anthracite	270,000	463,153	799,385
Domestic Lignite	25,976	37,055	68,040
Imported Bituminous	617,033	690,104	967,903
TOTAL	913,009	1,190,312	1,835,328

Source: Republic of Korea Statistical Summation, May 1949, p. 17, and August 1949, pp. 25-29. The figure for 1946 anthracite production is an estimate.[3]

Although coal production rose sharply in 1947, it still failed to meet domestic needs. Stockpiles were exhausted during 1946, and the revival of manufacturing created a demand which far outstripped the increases in coal production. For the maintenance of even the very modest level of economic activity car-

[3] Anthracite production in privately operated mines for 1946 is not known; however, the level of private production in the two subsequent years makes it unlikely that 1946 production exceeded 20,000 metric tons. Production in government (former Japanese) mines was 251,156 metric tons. Summary figures of government production reported in the ECA study, *The Economy of South Korea, Basic Survey*, Washington, May 1949, p. 14, differ greatly from those given in the sources reported above. Since these sources are very detailed in their reporting and in the nature of primary materials, they have been accepted and the unexplained much higher figures in the *Basic Survey* disregarded.

ried on during the occupation period South Korea was highly dependent upon bituminous coal imports from Japan, which in each year were greater than the quantity of coal mined in South Korea. The distribution of coal supplies in 1947 shows how restricted this activity was. One-half of the coal, including most of the imports from Japan, was required to keep the railroads operating at even a minimum level. Fifteen per cent was required for United States military installations. Only 35 per cent of the coal supply was available for domestic and industrial use.[4]

As shown by the figures in Table 12, Korean coal production in 1948 was 40 per cent greater than in 1947. In the first six months of 1949, 527,719 metric tons of anthracite coal were mined, as compared with 421,238 tons mined during the same period of 1948.[5] In view of this rate of expansion it was very probable that the all-time production high of 1,526,513 metric tons of anthracite coal mined in 1944[6] would be reattained in 1950. Continued expansion beyond 1950 also seemed likely. The discovery of important new coal deposits since 1945 indicated that South Korea's coal resources had by no means been fully utilized,[7] and the U.S. Economic Cooperation Administration intended to finance intensive surveys to locate additional deposits. The instruction of Korean mining technicians and miners in American coal-mining methods had proved very successful and ECA assistance to South Korea in acquiring mining machinery would make it possible for greater use to be made of known coal deposits and of improved know-how.

[4] *SKIG Activities*, September 1847, p. 61. The acute shortage of coal for household use since 1945 encouraged the increased use of peat fuel, which is widely available.

[5] *Republic of Korea Statistical Summation*, May 1949, p. 17, and August 1949, pp. 25-26.

[6] See Table 5, p. 58.

[7] For example, during the occupation it was found that the potentialities of the Yŏngwŏl mine were much greater than was indicated by the extent of the existing workings. It was estimated that within two to three years the output could be raised to 100,000 tons per month. In order to accomplish this, however, the construction of 24 miles of railroad with the necessary sidings and loading stations in addition to an extensive enlargement of the workings was reported to be required. *SKIG Activities*, October 1947, p. 40.

Unless more effective ways were found of utilizing South Korea's coal resources in the future than were known in the past, however, the area would continue to be unable to meet its coal requirements without bituminous imports, irrespective of how much domestic production might be expanded.[8] Korean anthracite is of very inferior quality. Owing to the friable and graphitic nature of this coal, it readily disintegrates into powder during the course of mining, stockpiling, and shipping, a fact which makes it difficult to use and expensive for industrial purposes. The low content of volatile matter in this coal requires that at least 50 per cent of it be formed into briquettes with 10 per cent bituminous coal and 2 per cent pitch as inflammable additions. South Korean lignite coal is also of poor quality and is generally unsuitable for industrial use. Shortly after the occupation began it was frequently stated that the blockade of shipments of coal from North to South Korea was having a very paralyzing effect upon South Korean industry. Actually at this time the elimination of the frontier at the 38th parallel would have had almost no effect upon the coal situation in South Korea, for North Korean coal production was also very depressed and the area was similarly dependent upon outside sources for bituminous coal.[9]

[8] Before 1945 some factories had furnaces which used Korean anthracite but they were relatively inefficient and expensive. One of the important fields of investigation for future Korean industry is the better utilization of this anthracite. The Japanese were making some experiments along this line, even though their own bituminous resources were adequate. One large Osaka thermal power plant installed specially-built furnaces to use Korean coal. The American ECA mission to Korea has been interested in the possibility of increasing the usefulness of Korean anthracite through liquefaction processes, and the use of anthracite in locomotives.

[9] See Chapter 10 for a further discussion of the North Korean coal situation. North Korea had two advantages over South Korea in its coal position: (1) larger and more accessible resources of anthracite coal; (2) a superior grade of lignite, in larger quantity. Neither of these advantages, however, would have contributed substantially to the solution of the immediate problem in South Korea, at least during 1946 and 1947, even if the blockade had been removed.

Electricity

Before World War II the Japanese had developed an electric power system in Korea which was generally adequate to supply the country's prewar needs. The preponderant share of this electricity was generated by water power at dams located along the waterways of northern Korea. This source of electric power assumed even more than normal importance after the war because of the coal shortages in South Korea which prevented local thermal power plants from generating as much electricity as they had in the past, and far less than the 132,500 capacity of these plants.[10] The most important steam power electric plant was located at Yŏngwŏl in an interior region without rail connections.[11] This plant had a name plate capacity of 100,000 kilowatts, but it could not be put into operation until the adjoining coal mines were rehabilitated.

Despite other difficulties between North and South Korea, the transmission of electricity across the 38th parellel continued without interruption until May 14, 1948. During the period from August 16, 1945, to May 31, 1947, South Korea received 837,678,737 kilowatt hours of electricity from North Korea. An agreement reached at the end of this period provided for the continued delivery of a maximum of 80,000 kilowatts.[12] South Korea was generating only an additional 25,000 kilowatts, making a total supply in the area of about 105,000 kilowatts.[13]

Electric consumption mounted steadily after January 1946,[14] due to the increased demand for power accompanying the re-

[10] South Korean hydro-electric plants had a rated capacity of 67,400 kilowatts, making a total generating capacity of 197,200 kilowatts in South Korea.

[11] See p. 144 n.

[12] *Voice of Korea*, July 31, 1947. This agreement also provided for an increase in deliveries to a total of 100,000 kilowatts following the receipt of equipment from the American zone and the rehabilitation of North Korea power facilities therewith.

[13] *SKIG Activities*, November 1947, p. 115.

[14] See Table, *ibid.*

vival of industry, the improvements in the supply of light bulbs, and the expanded use of electricity for heating in South Korea. As winter approached, the electricity demand increased beyond the limit set in the agreement. On November 10, 1947, South Korea was using 135,000 kilowatts of North Korean power. On November 24 notification was received from North Korea that consumption would have to be kept within the 80,000 kilowatt limit. Immediate cutbacks were made but "there was no coordinated plan for saving power which resulted in many lines being cut out from time to time." [15]

Because of these difficulties Military Government gave more attention to the rehabilitation of the Yŏngwŏl plant and other thermal-electric plants and considered plans for increased utilization of the limited hydro-electric resources of South Korea. An Emergency Electric Power Committee was created to coordinate electric power distribution and consumption.[16]

The electric power service from North Korea had weathered the vicissitudes of Soviet-American relations for two and a half years, when on May 14, 1948, just four days after the general elections in South Korea and fourteen days after the adoption of a "national" constitution in North Korea, this last vestige of economic relations between the two areas terminated. Broadcasts from Pyŏngyang had stated earlier that unless representatives were sent from South Korea to discuss the terms of payment with the regime of North Korea, the service would be suspended at noon on May 14. The American authorities in the south believed that the principal purpose of this ultimatum was to secure *de facto* recognition of the North Korean regime, and therefore refused to deal with any but Russian authority. The broadcasts were ignored and when the deadline came, power ceased to cross the 38th parallel.

The agreement which had been signed between representatives of the American and Soviet commands on June 17, 1947,

[15] *Ibid.*
[16] *SKIG Activities*, December 1947, p. 116.

concerning the terms of payment for power supplied from North Korean sources to the American zone between the time of surrender and May 31, 1947, had fixed the total cost of this service at 16,334,735 yen ($3,828,862). Payment was to be made in specified equipment and materials to be delivered by the American command within six months of receipt of specifications.[17] If it became impossible to keep commitments for the delivery of particular materials by specified dates, new terms of delivery, or the substitution of other materials, were to be determined by mutual agreement. The June 17, 1947, agreement also specified that arrangements governing payment for power used subsequent to May 31, 1947, were to be agreed upon within one month.[18] No new agreement was made, however.

According to General Hodge, 35 per cent of the promised goods had been delivered to North Korea by the time power was cut off, and 40 per cent more was either in Seoul or en route to Korea. As for the remaining 25 per cent, the previous offer to settle in American dollars still stood, General Hodge said.[19] In a note addressed to the Soviet commander, however, he declared that "as a prelude to any future deliveries of goods in payment or to negotiations for future payments, I must request that the flow of power be resumed at once. . . . Since you as Soviet Commander in control of North Korea are responsible for acts in your zone, it is my duty to protest against this high-handed action." [20]

Hodge was also outspoken in charging that the power shut-off was to be attributed to Soviet opposition to the South Korean

[17] Both the cost of power and the price of goods to be delivered in payment were to be valued at 1941 prices. The price of power was fixed at 0.0195 yen per kilowatt hour and the rate of exchange was fixed at $23.44 per 100 yen.

[18] The substance of this agreement was reported in a U.S. note to the Soviet Ministry of Foreign Affairs delivered June 26, 1948, concerning the distribution of electric power in Korea. *Department of State Bulletin,* July 11, 1948, p. 50.

[19] *New York Times,* May 14, 1948, p. 1.

[20] *Ibid.,* May 22, 1948, p. 5.

elections.[21] In a note addressed to Hodge, the Soviet commander emphatically denied this charge, stating that the People's Committee had "for the past three months repeatedly warned the American command of the necessity to pay its indebtedness for electric current and to draw up an agreement for the future delivery of current.[22]

Actually the supply of power had been continued for months beyond the period specified for the completion of the payments. An agreement covering power used since May 31, 1947, which was to have been signed by July 17, 1947, had never even reached the negotiation stage. Plainly such remonstrances as those made by General Hodge had little chance of effecting a restoration of service, since American good faith also was impaired by the failure to meet the obligations stipulated in the agreement. Moreover, the Soviet command, or the People's Committee, was in a position to act as the final arbiter by virtue of its control over the disputed power.

In early July 1948, the Soviet commander stated, in reply to American diplomatic representations in Moscow,[23] that service would be resumed as soon as payments for power received up

[21] Hodge spoke caustically of a promise made to South Korean leaders, Kim Koo and Kimm Kiusic, by North Koreans at a conference held in Pyŏngyang in early May that the power would not be cut off, saying, "Whose promise was this? Apparently it was the usual type of communist false promise made in an effort to keep South Koreans from expressing themselves in a free and democratic election—and like all such promises, was made to be broken when it became politically expedient." *Seoul Times*, May 18, 1948, p. 1.

[22] This note declared further that the People's Committee had warned that unless this were done it "should be forced to cut the flow of electric current in South Korea." The letter also noted "that the Soviet command could not fulfill the functions of an intermediary between the American command and the People's Committee." Hodge was requested to negotiate with the People's Committee "to whom belongs authority in North Korea and under whose administration in particular are nationalized industries, including electric power stations." Dispatch from Seoul, *New York Times*, June 18, 1948, p. 17. In this connection, American authorities claimed that the statements broadcast by Pyŏngyang radio had not constituted notification and that they had awaited a formal communication from the north. *Seoul Times*, May 18, 1948, p. 4.

[23] *Department of State Bulletin*, July 11, 1948, p. 50.

to May 31, 1947, were made. Payments, however, would have to be made to the North Korea People's Committee.[24] The Soviet commander, by speaking on behalf of the Committee, thus retreated somewhat from his earlier position. On July 22, General Hodge informed the Soviet commander that the Americans would deal with the Korean regime if the Soviet command chose "to designate certain Koreans to act as its authorized representatives to participate in any further negotiations regarding electric power." Thus Hodge made a small concession to the Soviet demands. He also said that the Koreans designated by the Soviets could take delivery of all commodities then in Seoul intended as payment in kind for the electric bill owed by the southern zone.[25]

The compromise offered by General Hodge was apparently considered inadequate by the Soviet command, because no further action resulted. It may be noted that while General Hodge was persistently refusing to deal with the People's Committee of North Korea, terming it a puppet regime, his disdain was by no means wholly shared by responsible Koreans. Cho Chungsoo, the Director of the Department of Commerce of the South Korea Interim Government, was reported as having informed Lee Moonhan, the power director of the North Korea People's Committee, of his willingness to journey north to discuss the problem. He declared that he could not do this of his own accord, however, since sovereignty in South Korea resided in the American command, which refused to negotiate with the People's Committee.[26]

In the absence of any agreement between the two commands, South Korea was obliged to limp along on such power facilities as it could muster. A report made by the Emergency Electric Power Board in March 1948 stated that South Korea might well sustain a production of about 75,000 kilowatts during the

[24] *Korean Independence,* July 7, 1948, p. 1.
[25] *Ibid.,* July 28, 1948, p. 1.
[26] *Seoul Times,* May 19, 1948, p. 1.

first four-month period from May to August 1948.[27] No such level of output was achieved and average production for the seven months June to December 1948 was only 56,100 kilowatts.[28] The curtailment of the electric power supply seriously impeded industrial activity. Many manufacturing plants which had only recently resumed operations were forced to shut down. The Seoul *Union Democrat* reported that in Inchon, the coastal port near Seoul, industry had "literally died out" as a result of the power shortage.[29]

The production of electric power within South Korea during the first six months of 1949 was 65 per cent greater than in the corresponding period of 1948 as a result of a more effective use of existing facilities and some improvements in them and because of the installation of U.S. emergency power barges at Pusan and Inchon having a total rated capacity of 42,000 kilowatts. The total power supply was still 19 per cent below that of the corresponding period in 1948.[30]

The ECA reported in May 1949 that a supply of 130,000 kilowatts represented the minimum power requirements of South Korea during the winter months and that a supply of 220,000 could be utilized. Yet the probable supply for the winter months was only about 60,000 kilowatts.[31] Not only were existing power generating facilities inadequate but, furthermore, the ECA stated, "should all plants in South Korea be able to furnish capacity output on a continuous basis, South Korea would be embarrassed by power failures in a very short time. Lack of proper maintenance and shortage of materials and of supervisory personnel make capacity operation without major breakdowns virtually impossible at present." [32]

[27] *SKIG Activities*, March 1948, p. 118.

[28] *Republic of Korea Statistical Summation*, May 1949, p. 16.

[29] *Union Democrat*, February 6, 1949, p. 2.

[30] *Joint ECA-State Department Semi-Annual Economic Report on Korea, January–June 1949*, p. 10.

[31] Economic Cooperation Administration, *The Economy of South Korea, Basic Survey*, p. 22.

[32] *Ibid.*, p. 23.

The expansion of coal production was prerequisite to an expansion of the supply of electric power.[33] The ECA planned to import conveyor belting, locomotives, and other equipment essential to the expansion of coal production during the U.S. fiscal year 1950. About two million dollars of aid funds would be used in opening up four new mines in the Yongwol area. Another three million dollars would be expended in making Yongwol accessible by rail. Nearly six million dollars was to be spent for rehabilitating existing electricity generating facilities and for a moderate expansion in capacity. The main projects provided for the doubling of the installed capacity of the Sumgin Gong power plant to a total of 28,800 kilowatts and the construction of a 15,000 to 20,000 kilowatt thermal electric plant to serve the Samchok industrial region. Preproject planning for another thermal electric plant at Samchŏk would also be commenced.

Industrial Raw Materials

South Korea's mineral resources are in some critical respects completely inadequate for even modest industrialization. Such basic metals as iron, copper, and aluminum ores are much less extensively available and there are no known deposits of certain other critical industrial minerals which are found in some abundance in the north. South Korea has abundant resources of gold, tungsten, and graphite, and is also modestly supplied with zinc, lead, copper, silver, molybdenum, fluorite, mica, asbestos, talc, and manganese. During World War II many deposits were worked almost to exhaustion or beyond the point where they could be economically worked after the war.

Tungsten and graphite mines were put back into operation early in the occupation. While the production of these two minerals accounted for a large share of the mining operations in South Korea after the Japanese surrender and were especially

[33] The ECA coal and electric power projects are outlined in the ECA-State Department report, *Economic Aid to the Republic of Korea*, pp. 32-34.

important in creating such export credits as the South Korean Interim Government was able to build up in the United States, it was only a small fraction of the output of the war and prewar years. Tungsten production (tungstic oxide, WO_3) in 1946 was 424 metric tons, 714 metric tons in 1947, and 1,179 metric tons in 1948. Output in 1944 was 6,217 metric tons.[34] Graphite mines were not opened until August 1946, but produced 536 metric tons in 1947 and 566 metric tons in 1948. Japanese output of both amorphous and crystalline graphite in 1944 was 45,598 metric tons, of which probably about 5,000 metric tons were crystalline.[35]

Monthly gold production was very erratic during the occupation. Many mines had been dismantled by the Japanese and others were in disrepair. Government restrictions also delayed the recovery of gold mining. A considerable amount of small-scale bootleg mining was carried on. Official production figures were therefore incomplete. There is no record of postwar gold production for the period before May 1947. Reported gold production in 1948 was 3,466 fine ounces. In 1944, South Korea produced approximately 225,000 fine ounces.[36]

Silver is commonly found as a compound with gold or copper. Silver production in 1948 was 38,500 fine ounces, or less than two per cent of the amount mined in 1940.[37] Copper and

[34] Postwar mineral production figures cited here and below may be found in *SKIG Activities*, September 1947, pp. 43-44; *Republic of Korea Statistical Summation*, May 1949, pp. 22-23; *Voice of Korea*, June 14, 1947. Figures for 1944 production are given in Table 5, p. 58 above.

[35] Crystalline graphite is superior in utility and value to amorphous graphite which may be substituted by synthetic graphite. Although the largest amorphous graphite mines in Korea were located in South Korea, the major crystalline mines were in North Korea. Before the war, Korea was the world's largest producer and exporter of graphite, a strategic mineral which the United States does not possess in adequate quantity to meet its needs.

[36] Production in 1944 had already been cut by more than half from the peak output in 1941. For a complete survey of Korean gold resources and production, see George M. McCune, "Gold Mining in Korea," *Voice of Korea*, November 30, 1946.

[37] Military Government Mining Bureau sources. 1944 figures are not available.

lead deposits are only economically workable in conjunction with gold or silver mining. Domestic deposits of both of these minerals were insufficient to supply local requirements even in the prewar years. Copper production in 1948 totaled 1,125 metric tons as compared with 2,302 metric tons in 1944. Lead ore production in 1948 was 497 metric tons and 8,386 metric tons in 1944. Zinc deposits are somewhat larger and it is possible that with a thorough rehabilitation of zinc mining it may be possible for Korea to again become an exporter of this metal. Zinc ore production in 1948 was 423 metric tons as compared with 3,788 metric tons in 1948. Gold and tungsten were expected to be the principal exportable minerals in the future, and the ECA planned to concentrate upon expanding their production in its 1950 program. As with coal, other mining in Korea was severely restricted by the lack of facilities to maintain existing mines and mining and metallurgical technology suffered critically. There was, for instance, a serious decline in the yields from scheelite (tungsten) ores because of a lowered efficiency in refining practices.[38]

Facilities in South Korea for processing minerals were very limited. There were no integrated plants for iron and steel production. Copper milling and basic manufacturing facilities were apparently adequate relative to the domestic supplies of ore. Some aluminum-processing plants existed, and there were limited means for smelting, refining, reducing, and dressing other minerals. The processes were frequently hampered by mechanical breakdowns, inadequate supplies of processing materials, and transportation difficulties. The ECA expected to assist in installing a new tungsten mill at the Sangdong mine and to rehabilitate the Samwha iron works at Samchŏk. Improvements would also be made in South Korea's small steel industry which would reduce the area's dependence upon imports for needed steel shapes and forms.

There were some shortages due to inadequate imports of essential supplies and deficiencies of domestic production and,

[38] *SKIG Activities*, October 1947, p. 43.

on the other hand, some minerals were produced in excess of domestic demand but lacked export outlets. Talc production, for example, had to be suspended in the middle of 1947 for lack of markets.[39] Formerly Japan had absorbed much of the production of this mineral and greater domestic consumption had provided a market for the remainder.

Similarly the supply of construction materials was only partially satisfactory. The forest resources of South Korea were small and the supply of lumber was far from adequate. Estimated log production in 1946 was capable of supplying only about 18 per cent of requirements.[40] As mentioned earlier, the ECA planned to import lumber to meet basic requirements. Korean houses customarily required little wood in their construction, but industrial building was seriously hampered by the shortage of construction materials. The fuel shortage and transportation difficulties impaired the operation of the only cement plant, the former Chosen Onoda establishment at Samchok. In 1948 South Korea's cement requirements were estimated to be 500,000 metric tons. Only a fraction of this amount could be produced locally. The ECA was planning the construction of another plant at a cost of $3,950,000 which would enable South Korea to supply over half of its requirements.[41] Brick and tile production was more satisfactory, especially because brick manufacturing is largely a household industry.

Manufacturing

Since Japan regarded herself as the economic nucleus of her empire, Korea was considered, especially before 1936, to be primarily a source of raw materials, first as a supplier of foodstuffs, and then increasingly of fibers, industrial crops, and certain minerals. Such industry as existed was generally confined to light consumer goods and mainly carried on in small establishments. Under these conditions, food processing remained

[39] *Ibid.*, August 1947, p. 73.
[40] See Table 12, Appendix C, for details of production and requirements.
[41] ECA, *Economic Aid to the Republic of Korea*, *op. cit.*, p. 35.

the most important single industry in Korea, with textiles holding a poor second place. This development was more general in the south where the Japanese had first settled and were more numerous. Beginning about 1933, and especially after 1936, Japan relaxed the restrictions upon new businesses in Korea and turned increasingly toward exploiting Korean resources, particularly in the north where the major mineral and power resources were located.

While South Korea was more important for its light consumer manufactures than for heavy industrial production, it was by no means adequately equipped to meet its own modest consumption needs.

TABLE 13

MANUFACTURING ESTABLISHMENTS IN SOUTH KOREA BY PRODUCTS, NOVEMBER 1946

Product	*Number of Factories*	*Percentage of Factories Operating*	*Number of Workers Employed*	*Percentage of Workers Employed*
Metallic	499	9.5	8,966	7.3
Machines & Tools	878	16.6	17,394	14.2
Chemicals	574	10.9	19,171	15.7
Electric, Gas, Water	78	1.5	2,711	2.2
Ceramics & Cement	731	13.9	9,693	7.9
Textiles	615	11.7	36,269	29.8
Lumber & Woodworking	584	11.1	6,502	5.3
Food Processing	726	13.8	8,383	6.9
Printing & Binding	233	4.4	4,540	3.7
Engineering & Construction	175	3.3	5,598	4.6
Others	156	3.3	2,932	2.4
TOTAL	5,249	100.0	122,159	100.0

Source: USAMGIK Industrial Labor Force and Wage Survey, November 1946.

The textile industry which, as shown in Table 13, accounted for the largest share of total factory employment in 1946, was by no means able to supply minimum needs. Ten years earlier, even with a much larger production, the industry had been able to provide only 41 per cent of the textiles consumed in Korea. Some expansion subsequently took place, but textile factories were in poor condition in 1946 and domestic sources, particularly of cotton, could supply only a small part of the needed raw materials. Military Government, considering the textile situation to be of immediate importance to Korean welfare, undertook to restore factory capacity and to arrange for imports of raw cotton from the United States. Satisfactory progress was made in reorganizing and rehabilitating the factories, but cotton imports were slow and uncertain and production was thereby greatly restricted.[42] Military Government continued its efforts and in late 1947 took further steps to expand textile production. An ambitious goal of ten yards of cloth per capita was set for realization in the near future.[43] However, although yarn production increased, cotton cloth production did not and in both 1947 and 1948 not as much cloth was produced as in 1946.

The textile situation was relatively favorable. The production of most other consumption goods was much less satisfactory, although by the fall of 1948 much had been accomplished in the rehabilitation of key industries. Facilities had been set up for the production of certain important commodities, such as the manufacture of bicycles, ball bearings, tin cans, nail-making machines, rope and cable, shoes, and tires. Scores of small plants for the production of kitchen utensils and hardware were operating.[44] Household manufactures, which had been encouraged by Military Government, also were making an important contribution to the supply of consumption goods. Fortunately, Korean living standards in rural areas had remained simple and largely unaffected by the Japanese modernization. The agrarian poverty which had necessitated self-sufficiency had kept many of the native handicraft arts intact despite Japanese restrictions and these were thus able to provide a substantial share of the needs of the people.

By late 1948, two small steel-rolling mills, two wire-drawing mills, facilities for the reconstruction of fishing boats, one

[42] *SKIG Activities*, August 1947, p. 77.
[43] *Ibid.*, October 1947, p. 10.
[44] ECA, *The Economy of South Korea, Basic Survey, op. cit.*, pp. 16-17.

pump manufacturing plant, two mining equipment establishments, factories for the manufacture of textile repair parts, two locomotive works, establishments for the manufacture of agricultural implements, and 19 transportation and parts manufacturing plants were back in operation.[45] However, the position of heavy industry in South Korea was especially bad. Although the country's heavy industrial requirements were in some respects less than they had been for the Japanese war economy, no general economic revival such as was now needed could succeed if the region had to stand alone economically. Northern Korea probably produced 75 per cent of the total industrial output of Korea by value before 1945 and most of the heavy industrial goods. Even if the country were now operating as a single economic unit, it would still need outside assistance to maintain the economy at its previous level of activity. Under the circumstances of division, the political stability of South Korea demanded a large measure of external economic support. Thus the ECA reported, "Stress has been laid . . . on developing the economic potentialities of South Korea in order that it may have economic sinews of its own on which to rely rather than face the constant danger of economic and political domination by the more highly developed northern part of the country." [46] The continuing demands upon the United States to supply or finance the procurement of certain consumption goods, raw materials, industrial replacement parts, fertilizer, and petroleum and petroleum products would use up nearly 80 per cent of the ECA budget for 1950 of 150 million dollars.[47] The magnitude of these expenditures left only a little over 20 per cent for additions to the existing production capacity of the South Korean industrial establishment and prevented the ECA from planning for the elimination of a deficit in South Korea's balance of payments by the time of the conclusion of the anticipated three-year ECA project period.

[45] *Ibid.*
[46] ECA, *Economic Aid to the Republic of Korea, op. cit.*, p. 24.
[47] *Ibid.*, p. 5, and *passim.*

Transportation

At the end of the war Korea had two principal means of transportation, railroads and animal power. Automobile transport was very limited in Korea before the war, and used mainly by the Japanese military forces. By 1945 the number of operable motor vehicles was fewer than ever and modern coastal ships were almost nonexistent.

The railroads, which were in bad shape at the end of the war, deteriorated further in carrying thousands of persons in the process of repatriation. As a result of long neglect, the small repair shops were overcrowded with "bad-order" cars and locomotives. Once the supply of replacement parts was exhausted, it was difficult to keep more than 55 to 60 per cent of the locomotives in operation.[48] The streetcar systems, which were a vital means of passenger transportation in Seoul and Pusan, were in a deplorable state. In Seoul the deterioration of equipment of the Seoul Electric Company had reached the point where only 30 out of 257 streetcars were operating.[49]

The most important factor in the rehabilitation of transportation was the receipt of 101 locomotives from the United States, which comprised nearly 40 per cent of the locomotives in operation on September 1, 1947. Eventually other supplies also became available from the United States. A large number of army vehicles were turned over to Korean use and streetcar parts were also provided. Over 200,000 railway ties were imported in the summer of 1947.[50] In July 1946, the Korean-built ten-car streamlined train, the "Korean Liberator," was placed in operation. During 1947 considerable work was done on the Korean National Highway project, the largest engineering undertaking in South Korea since the liberation up to that time. By February 1948, the Bureau of Transportation was able to inaugurate scheduled intercoastal freight and passenger service.[51]

[48] *SKIG Activities*, September 1947, p. 126.
[49] *Ibid.*, August 1947, p. 75.
[50] *Ibid.*, p. 78.
[51] *SKIG Activities*, March 1948, p. 97.

Yet these improvements were small in comparison with the generally unfavorable condition of transportation during the occupation period. The limited objectives of Military Government economic assistance did not permit full-scale rehabilitation. No regular supply channels could be established for obtaining needed replacement parts and these could only be secured in very urgent cases.[52] The equipment to be repaired would be out of service indefinitely while the needed items were being obtained through the circuitous line of authority that extended through Tokyo to Washington. Although bituminous coal imports from Japan were resumed early in the occupation, this supply was for a long period subject to pronounced variations, thus further impairing railroad operations.[53]

The greater leeway of the ECA in financing imports permitted a more consistent attack upon transportation problems, including the establishment of a regularized supply of items not manufactured within South Korea. By 1949 the main railway repair shops were again functioning efficiently and 7,000 out of a total of 9,000 freight cars were in operation, permitting a five-fold expansion of tonnage carried over 1946.[54] In April 1949 construction began on three railroad lines into the coal fields of eastern Kangwŏn province. Track maintenance was being facilitated by the manufacture of certain necessary accessories in the railroad shops. Freight handled by ship had increased and the ECA planned to spend three million dollars for the construction of five coal-carrying ships in Japan.[55]

In 1949 the electrical communications services—including telephone, telegraph, and radio facilities—were generally ade-

[52] The difficulty of procuring certain raw materials also created bottlenecks in the supply of some parts. One of the most common requirements for streetcar maintenance was mercury for rectifiers (*SKIG Activities*, December 1947, p. 121). Mercury was not produced commercially in South Korea.

[53] For example, low bituminous imports during the month were in large part responsible for keeping 62 per cent of all locomotives idle in December 1947. *SKIG Activities*, January 1948, p. 112.

[54] *Joint ECA-State Department Semi-Annual Economic Report on Korea, January–June 1949*, *op. cit.*, p. 2.

[55] *Ibid.*, p. 16.

quate to meet existing needs if fully rehabilitated, although these facilities were very small and in many respects obsolete by American standards. Years of undermaintenance would make necessary the replacement of a large part of the equipment within the next few years. About 80 per cent of the underground and aerial telephone and telegraph cables were more than 35 years old and badly damaged by age, weather, and ground electrolysis.[56] With the purchase of RCA international radiotelegraph and radiotelephone communications facilities by the Republic of Korea on December 28, 1948, all communication services were brought under government ownership.

LABOR AND WAGES

Political Conditions and Organization

The suppression of trade unionism in Korea was one of the many ways by which Japan succeeded in retarding the political and social development of the Korean people. The consequent discouragement to the development of a sense of responsibility and of the capacity to organize effectively for the expression of democratic self-interest had an obvious significance for the postwar period.

Like the political activity which accompanied liberation, trade unionism was unstable, volatile, and confused in the early occupation period. While labor unions were going through the formative period from inception to consolidation and political orientation, Military Government endeavored to institute some reforms in working conditions and to encourage the labor movement to take shape along American lines. The resolution of problems around the conference table was emphasized, and national and provincial labor mediation boards were established.[57]

Labor-management relations became more clearly marked by friction as prices continued to rise and labor unions assumed more definitive forms. The tension was accentuated as labor

[56] *Ibid.*, p. 18.
[57] Ordinance Number 34, December 8, 1945.

organizations became instruments in the wider political struggle between right and left. In fact, the major labor organizations in 1947 were the Taehan No Chung ("Korean Federation of Labor Unions"), which Military Government described as an "extreme rightist" organization, and the Chun Pyung ("All-Korea Labor Council"), an "extreme leftist" organization.

In many respects, the Taehan No Chung was an obvious "company" union. According to a Military Government report, the board of trustees of the Taehan No Chung labor college in Inchon was composed entirely of managers of industrial plants, and all students, after entering the school, had to join the Taehan union.[58] Its leaders was Chun Chinhan, a rightist political opportunist who unhesitatingly used the movement for the furtherance of his personal ambitions. The Chun Pyung was closely associated with the Communist South Korean Labor Party and provided the latter with one of its most important sources of strength. Military Government observed that the Chun Pyung failed to cooperate with the Department of Labor and the National Mediation Board, but that the Taehan No Chung manifested "an interest in learning healthy labor union practices." [59]

While purporting to inculcate the principles of American trade unionism, Military Government at the same time sometimes deprived Korean workers of many legitimate and fundamental rights exercised by American labor. It was prone to take a conservative or oppressive stand in the increasing labor difficulties generated by the inflation and the very troubled waters of Korean politics. The views and tactics of rightist Koreans became increasingly predominant in labor relations. The rightist-controlled police and rightist private organizations [60] engaged in open terrorism of striking workers. By 1947 such tactics had succeeded in the almost complete suppression of

[58] *SKIG Activities,* October 1947, p. 75.
[59] *Ibid.,* August 1947, p. 103.
[60] The largest of the rightist organizations was the Korean National Youth

Chun Pyung activity. Two members of a delegation of the World Federation of Trade Unions (at that time admittedly leftist in sympathies but still supported by many non-communist labor organizations) who visited Korea in April 1947 declared that workers were being subjected to conditions which "are incredible in this twentieth century of civilization." [61]

On December 1, 1948, the National Security Law outlawing the Communist Party was promulgated. The South Korean Labor Party itself went underground and its affiliate and front organizations, which continued to operate more or less openly, led a very precarious existence. The government recognized only labor organizations belonging to the Taehan No Chung and over this latter body it exercised a close control.

During early 1949 it appeared that previous Military Government encouragement to the Taehan No Chung to develop as a responsible non-communist working class body might at last be bearing fruit. An insurgent movement which represented a "growing realization of the real function of the federation as a champion of labor's legitimate interests" reached its climax in March and April.[62] This faction under the leadership of Yu Kit'ae was in undisputed control of the organization's 118,000 members until the disaffected chairman, Chun Chinhan, got

headed by General Lee Bumsuk from 1945 to 1948, which was superseded by the Korean Youth Association with President Rhee as honorary leader. In April 1949 it became the Students National Guard. All three were officially sponsored bodies. See especially Richard Wilson, "Korean National Youth, Inc.," *School and Society*, July 30, 1949, pp. 65-67; *Time*, June 30, 1947, pp. 25-26. General Lee told Correspondent Mark Gayn (*Japan Diary*, Sloane, New York, 1948, p. 437) that the youth leadership schools he was establishing in 1946 would teach "methods of combating strikes."

[61] United Press dispatch from Chicago dated April 28, 1947, quoting Willard S. Townsend, president of the C. I. O. United Transport Workers, and Ernest Bell, international secretary of the British Trade Union Congress. Tass in a Tokyo dispatch quoted Mr. Bell at greater length on his experiences in South Korea. *Trud*, April 8, 1947, translated in *Soviet Press Translations*, Far Eastern Institute, University of Washington, Seattle, June 14, p. 37.

[62] *ECA-State Department Joint Semi-Annual Economic Report on Korea, January–June 1949, op. cit.*, p. 19.

President Rhee to intercede, with the result that Yu had to give up his chairmanship and share his authority with Chun on a "supreme committee" over the organization. Chun represented Korean labor at the organizational meeting in London during December 1949 of the anti-communist International Confederation of Trade Unions.

The South Korean government, by putting pressure on the Taehan No Chung to the point where it was little more than a semi-official labor front, left little hope for the establishment of a genuine trade union movement in Korea. Part of the responsibility for these dangerous developments rested upon the U.S. Military Government because of the precedents of governmental control over unions which were established during the occupation, as well as upon the previous repressive Japanese labor policy in Korea. Harried by the dividing activities of communists or supposed communists, Military Government had exercised a strongly paternalistic control over labor unions. In October 1945 it had instituted what in effect was compulsory arbitration of labor disputes and banned strikes in "essential" industries.

There was not only the danger that the government's interference with the legitimate trade unions might drive many leaders of such unions into silence, as it seemed to wish, but that this policy would also undermine the government's own position by strengthening that of the communists. There could be no doubt that the Korean communist underground movement of the 1920's and 30's created an important class of self-appointed working-class leaders schooled in revolutionary Marxism and capable of heading dissident movements. The ECA mission in Korea has reported that the Taehan No Chung "has paid little attention to backing individual unions in their specific disputes. For example, miners in South Cholla province went unpaid and the Federation did not attempt to aid them; the Korea Electric Power Company union had a bitter dispute with the company management, without Federation support." [63]

[63] *Ibid.*, p. 20.

The apparent impossibility of labor's securing redress of the grave injustices which have arisen under unstable and inflationary economic conditions by lawful means certainly encouraged the labor movement to develop along extremist lines.

Wages [64]

Under Japanese rule there was much room for improvement in the conditions of the Korean working population. Large Japanese enterprises had consistently made extraordinarily high profits,[65] and the standard of living of Korean workers was very low. However, in the unstabilizing circumstances of the liberation, including the collapse of industrial production and the great inflation of the currency, the economic position of the urban wage-earning and salaried classes became much worse. As the following table indicates, prices rose far more rapidly than wages following the Japanese surrender and in the early months of the occupation.

TABLE 14

INDEX OF WAGES AND PRICES,
JULY 1945–MARCH 1946
(Essential commodities, June 1937=100)

		Prices	*Wages*
July	1945	200	200
August	"	3,000	800
September	"	4,200	1,000
October	"	6,500	1,500
November	"	8,000	2,000
December	"	11,500	2,300
January	1946	13,200	3,200
February	"	14,200	3,200
March	"	19,000	3,500

Source: *USAMGIK Summation*, November 1946, p. 50.

[64] Also see J. L. Kaukinen, "The South Korean Wage Earner Since Liberation," (U.S. Bureau of Labor Statistics) *Monthly Labor Review*, April 1949, pp. 401-06.

[65] Grajdanzev, *op. cit.*, p. 182 n.

Economic conditions in South Korea were so radically altered after the occupation that in many respects economic data compiled on the basis of the old relationships no longer gave a valid picture of the actual situation. The collapse of the Japanese organizational structure and the repatriation of Japanese personnel destroyed many of the institutional channels through which the government had gathered information. It became impossible to obtain with any regularity even the most rudimentary wage data.[66] Military Government pointed out the pitfalls which any extended analysis would encounter under these conditions: "The absence of any data on expenditure patterns for farm and urban populations, the lack of reliable production statistics on controlled commodities produced in vested and private factories and the unavailability of data indicating, on a per capita basis, those goods received as incentive and general distribution goods by the rural and urban groups are among the reasons why definite conclusions cannot be reached." [67]

The principal sources of information seem to have been periodic specialized studies, of which the industrial wage survey of November 1946 was the first. In addition the Chosun Bank continued to compile indexes of wages and prices, but discontinued the computation of a real wage index in view of the questionable value of such an interpretative measure, as pointed out by the Military Government in the statement above. These indexes of wages and prices for 1945–47 are given in Table 15.

In March 1948 Military Government conducted an income

[66] Although the compulsory mediation and arbitration laws appeared to place the government in a position where it would be informed on changes in wage rates, these facilities had very little use. The Chun Pyung openly refused to cooperate with the government and the Taehan No Chung, which was organized somewhat later, was almost wholly occupied with its activities against the communist and leftist organizations. Only the Seoul Electric Company local of the Taehan organization seems to have pursued primarily trade union objectives in 1947.

[67] *Price Developments in South Korea*, p. 7; also *SKIG Activities*, November 1947, p. 28.

TABLE 15

INDEXES OF WAGES AND PRICES IN SEOUL BY MONTHS, 1945–47
(1936=100)

	1945		*1946*		*1947*	
	Prices	*Wages*	*Prices*	*Wages*	*Prices*	*Wages*
January	238	246	10,913	3,386	45,912	12,589
February	238	247	11,785	4,083	51,355	12,761
March	242	253	16,007	4,512	54,087	13,419
April	249	275	17,516	5,343	50,640	14,777
May	254	277	18,143	7,027	49,622	15,166
June	259	282	19,876	7,251	51,121	15,812
July	—	293	20,453	7,439	51,112	16,730
August	4,323	—	20,058	7,826	54,183	17,010
September	4,942	—	25,102	10,125	56,567	17,835
October	6,384	—	28,114	10,837	58,937	17,742
November	7,531	—	31,258	12,093	66,667	18,215
December	9,605	2,564	37,201	11,936	76,998	17,704

Source: Chosun Bank, *Monthly Statistical Review,* January 1948, II-24.

and expenditure study [68] for the purpose of determining what changes should be made in wage rates to bring them into closer conformity with the greatly increased prices. This study showed that on an average the main occupation of a household head in wage earning and salaried employment provided only 28.1 per cent of the monthly household expenditures. The study showed further that these families were obtaining an almost equal amount of income from loans, or 27.3 per cent, and that the greatest single source of family income was the sale of possessions, which amounted to 31.3 per cent of the total. It seems unlikely that working class families could sustain such deficits in income through borrowing and the sale of possessions month after month. National Economic Board observations of practices in government-controlled factories suggested that the items of loans and sale of possessions often concealed illegal bonuses in kind and profits from black-market operations in controlled commodities. Thus it was impossible to determine the actual income positon of working class families as a group

[68] Wage Stabilization Committee, National Economic Board, USAMGIK, *Income and Expenditure Study,* March 1948.

with any accuracy, although it was apparent that wage payments were far too low and that this encouraged resorting to undesirable means of supplementing legal wages. There could be no doubt that working class income was much lower and more uncertain than before the war.

The fact that many consumer goods were sold at controlled prices as well as on the open market made it very difficult to estimate the cost of living. In many important instances the goods produced in the government-controlled factories were sold at prices as low as 20 per cent of the prices on the open market. The great discrepancies in the two sets of prices made it clear that the controlled production was supplying only a fraction of the total demand.[69] In October 1947, the purchase of a number of commodities ordinarily consumed by working class families [70] would have required at open-market prices an expenditure of about three and one-half times the estimated wage of the household head, whereas in 1936 the cost of these commodities was less than 60 per cent of the estimated average wage. If the family had been able to purchase exclusively at controlled prices those commodities which were so distributed,[71] its expenditure would have amounted to slightly under 85 per cent of the estimated average wage. Controlled prices were particularly important insofar as supplies of cereals and

[69] Military Government found another significance in the discrepancy in prices in the case of foodstuffs which it did not produce but bought for distribution to rationed users. An increase in the open-market price in such an instance was interpreted as indicating the extent to which the available supply had been acquired by the government for allocation at controlled prices. Open-market price rises in such commodities, it was stated, reflected the diminished supply available to meet the demand of higher-income groups which regularly consumed quantities in excess of the amount rationed. *SKIG Activities*, November 1947, p. 27.

[70] The commodities covered were selected from the Military Government list of 26 essential commodities used in family living. They were cleaned rice, soy beans, dried myungtai (a fish), pork, cotton sheeting, cotton shirting, matches, and laundry soap. Rice constituted about ⅔ of the total expenditure in 1936, and somewhat less under both the open-market and controlled sets of 1947 prices.

[71] Of the above commodities only the supplies of dried myungtai and pork were sold only at open-market prices.

beans were regularly rationed to urban users.

Partly as a result of the income and expenditure study of March 1948 mentioned above, it became possible to compile a weighted index of family living costs. The index number for March 1948, using the 1947 average as a base, was 152. According to the income and expenditure study, wages in the occupations covered [72] averaged 4,850 won at this time. In May 1949 the weighted index number of family living costs was 199, a 31 per cent gain over March 1948, while a Ministry of Social Affairs report indicated that the average monthly wage had advanced to 9,520 won,[73] or a gain of 94 per cent. Probably this upward adjustment of wages in terms of prices was at least partially attributable to the recommendations of the National Economic Board committee conducting the income and expenditure study to the effect that a more equitable wage pattern should be adopted. The ECA mission reported that during the early months of 1949 the economic condition of the working class was better than at any previous time since liberation. However, living standards were still considerably below those of the prewar period.[74] When the voluntary program for collecting the 1948–49 rice crop failed, forcing a 50 per cent reduction in the ration rolls, the living costs of tens of thousands of urban families took an abrupt turn upward. In April 1949 a family of five which had paid 5,900 won for its rice in previous months, would, as a result of the greatly reduced rationed supply, have to pay 10,000 won for the same amount.

Labor Legislation

Aside from the ordinance establishing the National Labor Mediation Boards, which has already been mentioned, a num-

[72] Wages of clerical, skilled, and unskilled workers in public utility, transportation, construction, and mining employment.

[73] *Republic of Korea Statistical Summation*, May 1949, p. 4. The occupational categories represented by this figure were somewhat different than those given above, being construction, mining, machine and tool, and textile.

[74] *ECA-State Department Joint Semi-Annual Economic Report on Korea, January–June 1949*, p. 19.

ber of other labor measures were put into effect by Military Government. The earliest of these were ordinances intended to control inflation by placing a ceiling upon wages. These controls were notably ineffective, partly because Military Government was operating on only one axis of the inflationary problem. They were further weakened because application of these wage controls was limited to wages paid by Military Government and its controlled enterprises and U.S. military units. In other employment, wages were free to rise and, of course, did. After several upward revisions of these ceilings, this attempt at wage control was abandoned. In the inflationary situation prevailing in South Korea, minimum-wage legislation was considered to be impractical and unnecessary.

Two other measures instituted by Military Government were the passage of a maximum hours law and a child labor law. The maximum hours law provided that all employment in industries covered by the law should be limited to 60 hours per week, with overtime rates affecting all work in excess of 40 hours. The passage of Public Act Number 4, the child labor law, in June 1947, was one of the most important measures enacted by the Interim Legislative Assembly. The child labor law prohibited the employment in industry of children under 14 years of age. It was followed by an order of the Department of Labor which implemented its provisions concerning the hours and conditions of work of minors under 18 years of age. The order prohibited night work, provided for rest and meal hours, and required employers to make certain provisions for the education and recreation of children in their employ.

The child labor law was notable since approximately 40 per cent of the population was below the age of 14.[75] (In the United States, by comparison, only about 25 per cent of the

[75] This figure is from a census survey of February 1947 in Kyŏnggi and South Chungchŏng provinces. In urban areas the percentage in this age group was found to be even slightly higher. *SKIG Activities*, October 1947, p. 6. Figures have been corrected in recognition of the Korean custom of regarding a person as being already one year old at birth.

population is 14 years old or younger.) [76] However, despite undoubtedly low productivity per worker, industrial and commercial activity was evidently too depressed in 1947 to make this regulation a burden. According to one report, over 70,000 persons were unemployed in the city of Seoul alone.[77] Unemployment continued to be serious. The May 1949 census reported 889,169 unemployed persons in South Korea.[78] Informed official sources believed the actual number of unemployed might be nearly double this figure.

The most important law affecting the labor field enacted after the establishment of the Republic of Korea was the sweeping Law on Public Officials. This law, which excluded only "simple manual laborers" from its provisions, forbade collective movements not connected with official duties among the employees of the railroad, communications, and the salt, tobacco and ginseng monopolies, as well as among workers in the regular government departments. This law was rendered even more serious to the trade unions by the impending legislation to nationalize most of the formerly Japanese enterprises. The logical extension of the Law on Public Officials to these enterprises would completely destroy legal trade unionism in South Korea. Some groups, including both the Chun and Yu factions of the Taehan No Chung, felt that the Law on Public Officials was clearly in violation of Article 18 of the national constitution, which provided that, "freedom of association, collective bargaining and collective action of laborers shall be guaranteed within the limits of the law."

[76] *Sixteenth Decennial Census of the United States, Population,* Volume II, Part 1, p. 26.

[77] *Chong Ang Ilbo,* Seoul, November 21, 1947, quoted in *Korean Independence,* Los Angeles, Calif., December 31, 1947.

[78] *Republic of Korea Statistical Summation,* May 1949, p. 4.

CHAPTER NINE

The Soviet Political Regime

POLITICAL ORGANIZATION

SUFFICIENT materials to make a thorough study of the development of the interim regime in North Korea are not available. The major steps taken by the Russian command and the framework of the structure that was erected are deducible from a variety of reports, some emanating from North Korea via Moscow and others from the southern zone of Korea.[1]

As has been briefly indicated in a previous chapter, the Soviet command set up a Provisional People's Committee for North Korea early in the occupation and then proceeded to fill in the structure with Korean personnel who were sympathetic with

[1] As might be expected, many of the available reports on North Korea are highly colored either in favor of, or opposed to, the Communist regime. The most useful source available was a Korean-language book, published by the Information Bureau of the North Korea People's Committee, *Inmin Winŏn-hoe Taehoe Chungyo Munhŏnjip* (Important Acts of the Assembly of the People's Committee of North Korea), Pyŏngyang, Korea, April 5, 1947, 239 pp. Contents of the volume include the texts of the important legislation enacted by the Interim People's Committee prior to the meeting of the convention (land reform, labor legislation, nationalization of industry, women's rights, private property and business, elections), a lengthy report on economic developments in North Korea, the economic plan for the following year, regulations concerning the establishment of the People's Assembly and of the permanent People's Committee, Presidium and Supreme Court. The book also contains data on the personnel elected to the various People's Committees. This work is referred to hereafter as *Report of People's Committee*.

Russian policy. The regime set up by the Russians gave the impression, whether erroneous or not, that Korean leaders possessed more than nominal authority in the government of North Korea. The Russians followed the policy of placing trustworthy Korean protégés in positions of power and of allowing them to exercise control, a policy which was in contrast with the American one of exercising the control directly and of selecting (in as democratic a fashion as possible) Korean personnel to fill in below.

The interim governmental organization followed the pattern of the Soviet Union, the last step being taken in February 1947, with the selection and the first convening of the People's Assembly of North Korea in Pyŏngyang, the northern capital. It is perhaps significant to note that from February 22, 1947, onward, the term "interim" was dropped from all organizational designations in North Korea.

At the time of the breakdown of American-Soviet negotiations in May 1946, the regime in North Korea was headed by the People's Interim Committee which was implemented by a graded series of People's Committees at each of the lower levels of government. Party activity was circumscribed within the bounds of the New People's Front composed of the Communist, Democratic, and Independence Parties.

During the summer of 1946, in preparation for an election which was to take place in November, the groundwork was laid for the establishment of a completely "democratic" government on the Soviet pattern. The New People's Front was transformed into the Korean National Democratic Front which was composed of the Labor Party (formerly the Communist Party), the Democratic Party, the Chŏndo-kyo Friends Party and four semi-social organizations, the North Korea Workers' Alliance, North Korea Farmers' Alliance, North Korea Democratic Young Men's Alliance and North Korea Democratic Women's Alliance. The Democratic Front was represented in the central government by a Central Committee. Elections were held on November 3, 1946 (declared a national holiday) for membership in the People's Committees of North Korea.[2] These elections called for the selection of deputies to compose the Provincial Committees, Municipal Committees and County Committees. Provincial Committees were selected on the basis of one member for each 30,000 population, and Municipal and County Committees represented 3,000 persons per member.[3]

The elections brought out 4,501,813 persons, or 99.6 per cent of the total number of registered voters. (The total population of North Korea was a little over 9,000,000, and since about half of the Korean population is under 21 years of age, the above figure would mean an almost 100 per cent turnout.) The Korean National Democratic Front gained a sweeping endorsement, receiving 97 per cent of all ballots cast. A total of 3,459 deputies, including 453 women, were elected for Provincial, Municipal and County People's Committees. Party distribution was as follows: Labor Party, 1,102; Democratic Party, 351; Chŏndo-kyo Friends Party, 253; no party, 1,753. Occupational distribution by percentages was: laborers, 14.5; farmers, 36.4; businessmen, 30.6; traders, 4.3; artisans and manufacturers, 2.1; professional men, 9; churchmen, 2.7.

The next step in establishing a North Korean regime was the convening of a sort of constituent assembly, representing the People's Committees elected in November 1946. Such an assembly, named the Convention of People's Committees, met in February 1947. Its membership was chosen by the Provincial,

[2] Election rules were presented in *Report of People's Committee*, pp. 35-72, but there was little information on the elections themselves, except on p. 188. See the following concerning elections: P. Ivanov, "Elections in Northern Korea," *Pravda*, November 2, 1946; "Election Results for the People's Committees of Northern Korea," *Izvestia*, November 16, 1946; V. Smolensky, "The Situation in Korea," *Pravda*, November 16, 1946. Translated in *Soviet Press Translations*, December 14, 1946, and March 15, 1947, Far Eastern Institute, University of Washington, Seattle.

[3] The six Provincial Committees ranged in size from 30 to 65 members; the 90 or so County Committees averaged about 30 members each; and the nine Municipal Committees varied in size from 20 to 45 members. Municipal representation differed for large and small cities, from one per 2,000 to one per 8,000 of population. See *Report of People's Committee*, pp. 39-40.

Municipal and County Committees, which selected one-fifth of their number to represent them. The makeup of the Convention, therefore, reflected the general character of the People's Committees themselves. Total membership numbered 1,159; 147 represented the Provinces, 88 the Municipalities, and 889 the Counties. An additional 35 members represented the seven parties and social groups.[4] There were 158 women delegates. The parties were represented on a different ratio than the committees themselves—the Labor Party outnumbering all others whereas in the committees non-party members were in the majority. In the Convention the Labor Party had 579 delegates; Democratic Party, 137; Chŏndo-kyo Friends Party, 122; and no party, 321.

The occupational distribution of the group was as follows:

Farmers	318	Churchmen	34
Laborers	329	Authors	3
Businessmen	330	Traders	8
Teachers	45	Manufacturers	11
Doctors	23	Artisans	6
Scholars	39	Others	13

The age distribution showed a preponderance of young people at the Convention: 20-26, 92 members; 27-35, 325; 36-45, 448; 46-55, 208; 56-65, 78; over 66, 8. One interesting background factor was included, namely, the years that members had served in Japanese jails because of independence activity: the figures revealed that 79 members had served more than five years in jail, 28 had served more than 10 years and 7 had been in jail for more than 15 years.

The Convention of People's Committees was held in Pyŏngyang, the northern capital, from February 17 through February 20, 1947. It voted and approved unanimously, article by article, all of the legislation enacted by the People's Interim Committee since its inception a year before, including "laws on land re-

[4] Personnel data on the Convention was derived from the *Report of the People's Committee*, pp. 4-10.

form, on the work of laborers and employees, on the nationalization of industry, transportation, means of communication and banks which belonged to Japanese and to traitors among the Korean people, laws on equal rights for women, on safeguarding private property, on measures to encourage private initiative in industry and trade, and also a law concerning the election of People's Committees in the provinces, districts, cities, counties and villages." [5]

The Convention also adopted a national economic plan proposed by Kim Ilsung, Chairman of the People's Interim Committee, and also decided to establish the People's Assembly of North Korea. As its concluding act, the Convention "adopted a petition to the governments of the U.S.S.R. and the United States, requesting the speedy resumption of the work of the Joint Soviet-American Commission with regard to the formation of the United Interim Democratic Korean Government in accordance with the decision of the Three-Power Moscow Conference of Ministers of Foreign Affairs." [6] All of these acts were accomplished in a period of four days. The Convention was obviously acting as a rubber stamp in approval of the policy decided by higher authority.

The People's Assembly of North Korea was created by the Convention as a "permanent" body, a national legislature, which would meet every two years unless called in special session. It was one-third the size of the Convention but represented the Provincial, Municipal and County Committees at the same ratio. The 237 members of the Assembly were each given a biographical sketch in the *Report of the People's Committee*, providing considerable data on the background of the leadership which emerged after liberation in North Korea.[7] Some of the pertinent data is summarized here.

[5] *Izvestia*, March 5, 1947, Tass dispatch from Pyŏngyang, Korea, February 24. Translated in *Soviet Press Translations*, May 15, 1947, Far Eastern Institute, University of Washington, Seattle. (The text of these laws was reproduced in *Report of People's Committee*, pp. 17-71.)

[6] *Ibid.*

[7] *Report of the People's Committee*, pp. 138-67.

Of the 237 members, 35 were women. The Labor Party contributed 88 members, the Democratic Party and the Chŏndo-kyo Friends Party each 30 members, while the unaffiliated numbered 89. Businessmen and manufacturers were the largest group, numbering 85; farmers, 57; laborers, 51; the so-called "intelligentsia" numbered 32; churchmen totaled 12. Three of the churchmen were Methodist ministers, one a Buddhist priest, and several were Chŏndo-kyo churchmen. About 15 were listed as university or college graduates, and an additional 12 had attended a university. Over 30 had completed middle school (similar to American high school). The average age was under 40 years. Many of the members listed records of revolutionary activity and jail sentences. Almost all had been active in organizing People's Committees and party organization after liberation.

The People's Assembly met briefly, February 21 and 22 only. It elected a Presidium of eleven persons, chaired by Kim Tubong, head of the Labor Party; it also elected a Supreme Court of North Korea and confirmed legislation concerning the judiciary. A new People's Committee of North Korea (the "interim" was dropped) was also confirmed after the policy of the preceding committee had been approved.

The People's Committee of North Korea was in effect a 22-man executive cabinet. It was headed by Kim Ilsung, the chairman, and included two vice-chairmen, a secretary, 14 department heads and 4 bureau chiefs. Of these, 16 were Labor Party members, two each were from the Democratic Party and Chŏndo-kyo Friends Party, and two were members of no party. Most of them were graduates of Japanese universities, such as Kyushu and Keijo Imperial Universities and Waseda, Meiji, Nippon and Kansai. The Kansai graduate was the only woman in the Committee, Hŏ Chŏngsook, 39-year-old Propaganda Minister. One of the vice-chairmen was a 54-year-old Christian minister, Hong Kiju, Democratic Party leader. The Education Minister was Han Sŏlya, a prominent novelist and literary figure in Korea. Average age of the group was forty-four years.[8]

The fourteen departments of the Committee were the following: Planning, Industry, Interior, Foreign Affairs, Agriculture and Forestry, Finance, Transportation, Communications, Commerce, Public Health, Education, Labor, Justice and Public Censorship; the four bureaus were listed as follows: General Affairs, Secretariat, Rationing and Propaganda.

The political structure organized by the Soviets in North Korea has been aptly analyzed as a three-cornered system: first, the People's Committees, second, the political parties, and third, the people's militia.[9] As has been shown above, the People's Committees had become a well-established part of the system as a consequence of the elections of November 1946. They were the actual organs of administration at each level of government: local, provincial and national.

The political parties had also become tailored to fit the scheme of things, all of the parties belonging to the Korean National Democratic Front. From time to time there appeared to be rumblings of discontent from among members of the minority parties, the Democratic Party and the Chŏndo-kyo Friends Party, but these independent moves were either the occasion for a purge or were quickly diverted. Meanwhile the dominant Labor Party exercised almost complete control of the political scene, guided with care by Soviet advisers.

The third element in the structure of control was the Korean people's militia. Early in the occupation the Soviet forces had recruited young Koreans, armed them with confiscated Japanese military equipment, and trained them for military service. Ostensibly the objective was to render "assistance to Soviet troops in driving out the Japanese imperialists and in restoring normal life in the country." [10] But the militia soon came to have a position of primary political importance. Numbering at least 150,-

[8] Factual data on the People's Committee was derived from *ibid.*, pp. 204-06.

[9] See Washburn, *loc. cit.*; also McCune, "The Occupation of Korea," pp. 191-92.

[10] Washburn, *loc. cit.*, p. 153, quoting a Russian source.

000 men (estimates ran as high as 500,000),[11] this well-indoctrinated and experienced militia provided a native Korean force for the sustenance of the communist People's Committees, so that if the Soviet armies withdrew, the regime which they had set up would not collapse for lack of military strength.

THE CHARACTER OF RUSSIAN CONTROL

The Soviet contentions as to their political accomplishments in North Korea were summarized by Foreign Minister Molotov as follows:[12]

> As regards northern Korea, considerable progress has been achieved in the field of democratization as well as in restoring the national economy and culture since Japan's surrender. Broad democratic reforms assuring political liberties and raising the living standard of the population have been carried through. I am referring primarily to the inauguration of general suffrage; the law on equal rights of women; the establishment of local bodies of power and of the People's Committee of northern Korea on the basis of free democratic elections; the land reform, as a result of which 725,000 landless farmers and small holders were given more than 1,000,000 hectares of land free of charge which had previously been the property of Japanese colonizers and their accomplices in Korea; the nationalization of former Japanese industry; the law on the eight-hour working day, safety of labor and social insurance; the reform of national education, as a result of which the Korean language has been reinstated in the schools, the school network extended and the enrollment of students enlarged, etc.

The apparent ease by which the Soviets seemed to be governing North Korea was misleading. The censorship of news placed a fairly effective blockade on public information as to the course of events in the north. It was quite obvious even from the Russian reports themselves that freedom of expression

[11] General Hodge estimated the strength at 120,000 to 150,000 in a closed session of the House Appropriations Committee, Washington, on March 26, 1947. The document from North Korea (*Report of the People's Committee*) makes no mention whatever of military affairs. Also see p. 266 below.

[12] Letter to Secretary Marshall, April 19, 1947, see Appendix A.

and freedom of political activity were denied to the Korean people. It could also be assumed that a certain degree of terrorism was practiced to keep the opposition in line. Most reports reaching the American zone characterized North Korea as a "police state." The Democratic Front effectively eliminated anyone not subscribing to the accepted party line through a series of purging elections within the party. The ration system was manipulated in many instances to keep political obstructionism at a minimum. Another device for political control was the threat of revoking the deeds to land distributed under the land reform of March 1946, if the new owner did not support the party or do his part in supplying the government with produce.[13]

As to the role which was played by the Russians themselves in the administration, there seems to be no doubt that strong control was exercised. However, the Soviet civil administration kept well in the background and gave the Koreans maximum experience in self-government. The Soviets made a determined effort to see to it that the rank and file of the Korean administration as well as the mass of the people believed that they were responsible for their own government. Control was effected by Russian political officers in the capital and in each province, who rarely appeared before the People's Committes but who exerted control through the ranking members of the Labor Party. Thus, while important decisions in policy were made by the Soviets, the Korean party members appeared to initiate and support such decisions, so that the impression was created that they were Korean in origin and implementation.

Most observers agreed that the Soviet system quite readily

[13] For a thorough criticism of the Russian occupation policy, see Harold J. Noble, "North Korean Democracy: Russian Style," *The New Leader*, May 31, 1947. Another account of some value which is critical but journalistic is, Henry Chung, *The Russians Came to Korea*, Washington, 1947. At the opposite extreme is an account written by Anna Louise Strong, who wrote a glowing but incredible description of conditions in the north after a visit there, "First Report from North Korea," *Soviet Russia Today*, October 1947, pp. 8-9 *et seq.*; November 1947, pp. 20-21 *et seq.*

adapted itself to the Korean scene, or at least that it was much more easily adopted by the Koreans than was the Western democratic system sponsored by the American command. This was particularly true because of the thirty-five years of Japanese domination which had further accustomed the Korean people to expect dictation from above. The course of events in the American zone seemed to indicate that the Korean as an individualist was inclined to be irresponsible and that he did not assume a mature or stable outlook when suddenly presented with almost unlimited freedom of opinion, expression, and organization. The mass of the Korean people in the north reacted favorably toward the Russian regime especially when it was accompanied by many of the revolutionary benefits of a socialist society. In South Korea, on the other hand, the so-called fundamental freedoms of democratic society were not much appreciated by the Korean people in view of the lack of social reform and because of the irregularity with which democracy was applied.[14]

[14] Further political developments in North Korea are discussed in Chapter XII.

CHAPTER TEN

Economic Policy in the Soviet Zone

ECONOMIC PLANNING

ECONOMIC conditions throughout Korea, it has been noted, were generally the same in both zones at the time of occupation. The extensive parochialism found in old China never prevailed in Korea, and, under the Japanese, institutional uniformity and conformity were raised to a high degree by centralization. However, with the coming of occupation, the Japanese economy of exploitative colonialism was rapidly modified into two divergent institutional patterns in the north and in the south.

In the south, as already noted, the Americans had failed to give the economy any specific orientation. In North Korea developments took a radically different course. The overthrow of the Japanese regime was used as an opportunity to make broad modifications in the character of the whole economy. During the first year after liberation reform programs were inaugurated over a wide area: nationalization of large industry, land reform, measures of financial and monetary change, social security and labor legislation. These changes laid the groundwork for a program of broadly conceived economic plans announced in early 1947.[1] In comprehensiveness and approach, the plans fol-

[1] "Report Concerning the Development of the North Korean People's Economy," reproduced in *Inmin Winŏn-hoe Taehoe Chungyo Munhŏnjip* (Important Acts of the Assembly of the People's Committees of North Korea), *op. cit.*

lowed the Soviet Union for their model, though they did not necessarily imply the establishment of a socialist state.

The advent of economic planning in North Korea was keynoted in an address by Kim Ilsung to the Assembly of People's Committees of North Korea in February, 1947.[2] The general objectives of the plan, Kim stated, were (1) to double the volume of production over that in 1946; (2) increase the productivity of labor by 48 per cent; (3) place greater emphasis upon the mining of coal so essential to the operation of transportation and industry; (4) improve the condition of the railroads; (5) expand agricultural production, including expansion of the agricultural area, sufficiently to meet the food requirements of the laboring and urban populations; and (6) encouragement of household industries and production of consumer goods.

In Kim's speech and in a report of the Assembly of People's Committees some of the details as to production goals were developed. Quite evidently 1946 was not a very satisfactory year for either agricultural or industrial production. The general ferment and uncertainty which had attended liberation and the consequences of division were felt in the north as well as in the south. Moreover, the reform programs no doubt had significant disruptive effects, at least in the short run, until adjustments to them could be made.

It has been mentioned that the Soviet command had certain advantages over the Americans for carrying out an economic program. However, the favoring factors were only relative. The personnel shortage in industry possibly was even more acute in the north than in the south. It is doubtful that the Russian zone, even though retaining Japanese technicians and bringing others from the U.S.S.R., contrasted very favorably with the south in this respect in 1946. Some technical personnel was lost in the exodus south and probably a sizable portion of possible managerial personnel was deemed unusable by the standards of political purity which excluded collaborationists from positions of responsibility. Yet, by all reports, a vigorous educational pro-

[2] *Ibid.*, pp. 72-74.

gram, much more ambitious than any such undertaking in South Korea, was launched quite early in the north. Among the measures to encourage industrial education was the sending of Russian instructors to Korea to teach technical subjects. In 1946, 500 experts and 3,000 skilled laborers were reported to have been trained, and in January 1947 alone 1,500 experts and 20,000 skilled laborers completed training.[3] If in any measure accurate, these figures would indicate a very substantial enlargement of the trained labor force. To a great extent the basis for the large expansion in production which was contemplated for 1947 lay in this expansion of the supply of trained workers.

The objective of doubling production in 1947 was not the unreasonable goal it might seem to have been, since in many industries production was at a virtual standstill during 1946. For example, pig iron production was planned to increase 23 times in 1947. However, 1946 production had been but 1,000 tons and the 1947 target was only a small fraction of the production in 1944.

The appearance of a second plan in 1948 for the year 1948–49 [4] indicated that the 1947 plan was probably only the first and most elementary of many economic plans for Korea which would succeed each other at least as long as the Soviet Union played host to a government in the country. Successive plans might be expected to demonstrate greater refinements of detail and to cover periods of time greater than one year.

Capital development normally accounts for an appreciable share of an industrial nation's resources. In the United States, for example, capital expenditures accounted for an average of approximately 19 per cent of the gross national product in the years 1919 to 1935.[5] One important motive for planning in the postwar period has been to survey the means for maximiz-

[3] *Ibid.*, p. 79.

[4] *Korean Independence*, July 14, 1948, p. 1.

[5] Simon Kuznets, *National Income and Capital Formation, 1919–1935*, p. 59.

ing the expenditures of scarce resources upon programs of capital investment for reconstruction. In Great Britain, France, and the Soviet Union in the year 1948 gross capital investments of approximately 18 to 20 per cent of the respective gross national products were being planned.[6]

Such a level of investment carries clear implications of planning having necessarily to deal with long-term needs and probabilities. Postwar Korea desperately needed capital development on a large scale. The U.S.S.R., the inspirational example of North Korean planning, was a stern illustration of a high rate of capital formation despite the consequences of a very low production of consumer goods. Were Korea to remain disunited, and hence American loans not forthcoming, it seems improbable that the U.S.S.R. would hesitate to go ahead with a program of large-scale capital development, despite the deprivation this would mean in present terms for the people of North Korea. The Soviet Union was in no position to be generous with economic assistance to North Korea. Furthermore, the U.S.S.R.'s years of self-sufficient capital formation would hardly seem to have conditioned it to act otherwise.

Economic planning was a tool which had been given wide application along Soviet lines by the states of Eastern Europe having close relationships with the U.S.S.R. In North Korea a planned economy was an inevitable characteristic of a Soviet administration.

SOCIALIZATION AND OWNERSHIP

As might have been expected, the Soviet-sponsored government met the problem of the status of Japanese-owned prop-

[6] Command 7344, Great Britain Parliament, House of Commons, *Economic Survey for 1948*, p. 38. The gross national product is the total value of all goods produced and services performed in a country during a given period, usually a year. National income, on the other hand, is the net figure obtained by reducing the gross national product to account for such depreciation as had occurred during the period. Gross capital formation is similarly distinguished from net capital formation. It represents the total value of all new capital creation irrespective of capital destroyed or worn out during the period.

erty by a forthright program of confiscation. There are some indications that nationalization may have gone somewhat further. However, the assertion of one writer that "All factories, transportation and communication facilities, mines, power plants, financial institutions, warehouses and granaries were seized outright without compensation" [7] appears to have been an overstatement.

Decision Number 91 of the North Korean Interim People's Committee, dated October 4, 1946,[8] attached very important strictures to any program of nationalization. This decision is quoted in its entirety below:

1. The decisions as to the classification of what constitutes personal property and personal business are to be made by the People's Court but these decisions are subject to review by the North Korean Interim People's Committee. Civic enterprises and similar groups, when claiming ownership, may be ruled incorrect by the People's Committee.

2. Korean-citizen-owned factories, industries, mines, coaling facilities, warehouses, and commercial houses are not to be included in the nationalization program. Claims for recovery of already-confiscated property and enterprises which fall into the above category should be investigated by Provincial People's Committees and errors rectified.

3. As to non-traitor Koreans who own stock in Joint Japanese-Korean companies manufacturing other than war weapons and materials, army clothes, army communications, and army transportation, and who have not yet received remuneration, they are to apply before October 28, 1946, to the North Korean Interim People's Committee to receive proper adjustment. After that date no claims will be recognized.

4. The Departments of Industry, of Commerce, and of Forestry and the Provincial People's Committees are hereby authorized to sell or to make available to Koreans general consumer-goods factories employing less than 50 laborers formerly owned by Japanese.

5. All banks are to allow individual manufacturers and commer-

[7] Henry Chung, *The Russians Came to Korea*, Washington, 1947, pp. 63-64.

[8] A decision of the North Korean Interim People's Committee reproduced in *Report of People's Committee*, pp. 32-34. The translation is not strictly literal; some clauses are in summary form.

cial houses to obtain short-term loans under normal banking regulations.

6. The Departments of Justice and of Industry, for the purpose of encouraging the development of private business enterprises, are to draft laws and plan procedures for the development of commercial activity and submit the results to the NKIPC by October 25.

7. In order to safeguard and assure confidence in savings, the Provincial People's Committees or local organs of authority are not to interfere in banking activity and in privacy of records; the banks are not to allow investigation of accounts other than by authorized persons.

8. The public prosecutor is to ensure the proper enforcement of the above regulations.

On the basis of the text of this decision, a large segment of the economy was to remain in private hands. To be sure, the mining and manufacturing undertakings had been concentrated in Japanese hands but by no means to the complete exclusion of Koreans. In principle, at any rate, this decision did not even prescribe the nationalization of so-called basic industries. All enterprises which had been owned by Koreans who had not lost their citizenship for "traitorous" activities were to remain in private hands. Moreover, Korean citizens were to be compensated for their holdings in former Japanese concerns of other than a military character. It is notable that the terms of the decision even called for an expansion of the Korean privately-owned sector of the economy in some respects.

It must be pointed out that it is not known to what extent the provisions of Decision 91 were fulfilled in practice. It is perhaps not unlikely that a substantial number of Koreans were excluded from claiming property rights under the Decision by virtue of having lost their "citizenship." To have fled south, as did many people of means during the early stages of occupation, was generally interpreted in North Korea as an act of bad faith.

The title of the Decision is noteworthy: Decision Concerning the Protection of Private Ownership in Industrial and Commercial Activity and the Procedure for Encouraging the Development of Private Initiative. Whether it should be taken as a manifestation of the indigenous character of the People's Committee is uncertain. It seems likely, however, that the Decision was the result of a realistic view of the economic situation in North Korea by the Soviets. Although it was probably in the nature of a conciliatory gesture to powerful groups in North Korea, one should not discount that one motive may have been the recognition of the usefulness of the services of these groups. Any program of socialization is faced with critical practical problems which may defeat its ends if it is under the necessity of completely replacing the administration of private operation. The use of groups not in harmony with the objectives of the People's Committee was very possibly necessary in North Korea.

After a year of very low production the People's Committee had ample reason to admit the limitations upon its ability to run the economy by direction. In the Soviet Union expediency rather than doctrinaire implication has often been most important in guiding the socialist order. And during almost its entire life the Soviet regime has attached virtually paramount significance to the maximization of production.

Actually in many instances abrogation of private property rights may have been a usurpation of authority by local People's Committees, as in the case of the banks (see p. 191, below), rather than the result of any policy formulated in the capital. While Decision 91 was perhaps largely the result of the demonstration in terms of production of the impossibility of exercising direct control over the detailed operation of the economy, it by no means suggests that it was an acknowledgement of weakness by the People's Committee. More probably the People's Committee was simply choosing to concentrate its economic authority upon policy-making matters where it could make its will felt. Doubtless it acted with the complete assent of the Soviet command, if not at its direction. Unquestionably the North Korean regime was first of all answerable to its Russian sponsors. Politics were at the most a subtle undercurrent in such decisions.

It is an interesting sidelight that the public stand taken by Dr. Syngman Rhee, the South Korean rightist leader, upon this matter was at least as broad as the policies enunciated by the People's Committee in Decision 91. Dr. Rhee proposed:

> To nationalize all heavy industry, mines, forests, public utilities, railways, water power, fisheries, communication and transportation systems.
>
> To inaugurate state supervision of all commercial and industrial enterprises to insure fair treatment to consumers, traders, and producers alike.[9]

FINANCE

The Banking System under the Japanese

The banking system in North Korea was extremely small relative to the industrial development of the area. By way of analogy the Chosun Bank (in South Korea) pointed out that if the "banking agencies constitute the arteries of a capitalist economic system, such agencies in North Korea were only the capillary vessels of the whole structure in the area." [10]

The credit structure had been much more developed by the Japanese in South Korea where the organs of commerce were centered. Despite the concentration of industry in the north, only 20 per cent of the total of loans and cash holdings in Korea

[9] These proposals were part of a twenty-point program outlined by Dr. Rhee in a radio address in February 1948. See Chung, *op. cit.*, pp. 207-10.

[10] Chosun Bank, "Financial Condition in North Korea," *Monthly Statistical Review*, January 1948, pp. 1-22. The information in the present discussion of North Korean finance is based very largely upon this article. The name Bank of Chosen (based upon the Japanese pronunciation of the name of Korea) is retained when referring to the Bank prior to liberation, whereas Chosun Bank (based upon the Korean pronunciation and transliteration) is used for the Bank when it was taken over by Koreans. Furthermore, the unit of currency is pronounced differently and thus transcribed differently before and after liberation. Under the Japanese it is the *yen*, under the Koreans it is the *won*.

on July 31, 1945, were there. The industrialization of North Korea had been almost entirely financed in Japan.

There had been virtually no direct bank financing of mining and industrial enterprises in North Korea. The extension of credit was limited principally to loans by financial associations to poor farmers, by lottery (*mujin*) companies to petty enterprises, by the Savings, Commercial and Choheung Banks to small merchants, and by the Chosen Industrial Bank on the security of land. North Korean bank deposits, which accounted for only about 30 per cent of the total in Korea, had been, according to the Chosun Bank, "compulsory exactions from the means of living of the poverty-stricken masses," rather than accumulations of idle capital and surpluses.[11] The character of this banking structure is indicated by the fact that 40 per cent of the total bank deposits in North Korea were held by farmers.[12]

Results of the Liberation

In South Korea the Japanese defeat precipitated a run on bank deposits and bank credit with highly inflationary consequences. Its first effect, however, was to seriously undermine the banking system. The six branches of the Bank of Chosen in North Korea were subjected to a particularly great strain. Within a very short time the available cash in these branches, amounting to some 634 million yen, was almost completely withdrawn. Other banking organs, with cash holdings of about 400 million yen, were subjected to a similar demand. Korean depositors were notably unable to withdraw even part of their deposits, while Japanese residents had little difficulty in liquidating their accounts and even in obtaining emergency loans.

In this general atmosphere of confusion a number of factors operated to compel the closing of financial institutions, as the following table on the status of the Bank of Chosen branches shortly after liberation indicates.

[11] *Ibid.*, pp. 1-23.
[12] Chosun Bank, "Financial Conditions in North Korea," *loc. cit.*

TABLE 16

OPERATION OF BANK OF CHOSEN OFFICES FOLLOWING LIBERATION

Use of Japanese Notes Forbidden	*Provinces*	*Cities*	*Soviet Arrival*	*Closed or Suspended*	*Reasons*	*Reopened*	*Cash on Reopening (in 1,000 won)*
	Hamgyŏng North	Rajin	Aug. 11, 1945	Aug. 11, 1945	Damaged in war		
		Chŏngjin	Aug. 13	Aug. 13	Same		
Dec. 10	Hamgyong South	Hamhŭng	Aug. 25	Aug. 29	Taken over by People's Committee	Sept. 1, 1945	30,000
Dec. 8	Same	Wŏnsan	Aug. 22	Aug. 23	Cash confiscated by Soviet Army	Jan. 21, 1945	Nil
Oct. 11	Pyŏngan North	Sinŭiju	Sept. 8	Sept. 30	Due to scarcity of capital	Oct. 20, 1945	5,000
Oct. 11	Pyŏngan South	Pyŏngyang	Aug. 25	Aug. 27	Taken over by People's Committee	Sept. 24, 1945	60,000
Oct. 11	Same	Chinnampo	Aug. 28	Aug. 30	Taken over by People's Committee	Oct. 2, 1945	40,000
Oct. 11	Hwanghae	Haeju	Aug. 22	Sept. 10	Due to scarcity of capital	Oct. 1, 1945	20,000

Source: Chosun Bank, "Financial Condition in North Korea," *loc. cit.*, Table 6, pp. 1-24.

According to the table, an apparently very common reason for suspension of operations was seizure by the local People's Committees acting largely on their own initiative.

Interim Financial Programs

Following a period of suspension after the arrival of the Soviet Army Forces, most banks reopened. They ceased, however, to operate as branches of the principal banking organizations of Korea, and were transformed into independent institutions.

This new status was of brief duration, however. As a result of representations by various Koreans that breaking up the old banking structure was counter to the interests of Korean unity, the Soviet command promulgated Ordinance Number 10 restoring the banks to their original forms. In practice this ordinance had little effect and in large part the banking system remained decentralized and subject to interference by local political bodies.

The principal changes during the first few months after liberation concerned the currency. Withdrawals from old deposits were limited to 3,000 won per month for each family, and Bank of Japan notes and Bank of Chosen notes, which had been issued in October and December 1945, were not to be honored as legal tender. The Soviet Field Bank established on the site of the former Yasuda Bank branch in Pyŏngyang issued military scrip for public use.

Gradually the interference by local People's Committees subsided and the banks resumed more routine courses of operation. Aside from the branches of the Chosun Bank, however, financial institutions suffered from critical shortages of capital. In some instances banks were unable to finance even their own costs of administration. Savings plans, lottery schemes, and compulsory deposit of Japanese-held money were undertaken without much success to strengthen the financial structure.

There was an urgent need for a central bank capable of bringing stability and vigor into the confused financial situation. Accordingly, when the Moscow agreement of December 1945 revealed that the reunification of Korea was probably still somewhat remote, steps were taken to establish a central bank in North Korea. To this end, eighty-five managers of banking organs convened in Pyŏngyang. On February 15, 1946, the establishment of the North Korean Central Bank was announced. This bank was to be directly under the control of the Soviet military and presided over by a Soviet military officer. The Soviet command was to supply the bank's capital of 100 million won. Existing banking organs were to continue operation under their own names and were to be subject only to very general regulations laid down by the Central Bank.

During this period the Central Bank failed rather dismally to accomplish its objectives. The 100 million won capitalization was inadequate in the extreme. The Bank proved unable even to meet its costs of operation, let alone fulfill its role as a central bank. Denied the usual central bank function of note issue, it was deprived of such remaining prestige and strength as it might have had. Its inability to afford capital assistance and the lack of the note-issuing power promoted the extension of instruments of credit by local banking organs against their own limited resources. Moreover, there was widespread resentment of the Central Bank in banking circles where it was regarded as a further obstacle to the unification of the country.

Throughout the greater part of 1946, the North Korean Interim People's Committee did not look with particular favor upon the Central Bank and instead chose to work through the Farmers' Bank which had been created from an amalgamation of a number of other financial institutions. The Farmers' Bank was headed by the director of the Financial Bureau of the People's Committee and treasury accounts were placed with local offices of this organization, rather than with the Central Bank. The Farmers' Bank proved unable to discharge this function satisfactorily, however, and the People's Committee commenced to recant on its opposition to the Central Bank.

The Development of a Comprehensive Program

Steps were taken in late 1946 designed to draw the banking system into closer relations with the financial and economic administration of North Korea. Banking functions were consolidated into two state-managed institutions, the Central Bank and the Farmers' Bank. The banks such as existed before this amalgamation were dissolved and their offices were either incorporated into the central banking system or the property liquidated. Treasury funds were held in the Central Bank.

Individuals and organizations were required by law to deposit all cash in excess of 2,000 won. This and other measures were used with some success in bolstering the assets of the banks. By early June 1947 at least 1,000 million won had been concentrated in the Central Bank. The Farmers' Bank succeeded in collecting in excess of 500 million won through deposit of the prices of taxes paid in kind. As a result the Central Bank was able to extend credits amounting to 900 million won for the economic rehabilitation of North Korea. The Farmers' Bank was in a position to set up a credit of 170 million won against the mutual collateral of farmers for the purpose of supplying fertilizer to over 100,000 North Korean farming families.

This consolidation represented a return to the original objectives of the People's Committee which had called for closer public control over the banking system. Opposition to the changes within the system by banking people was obviated through the widespread replacement of the old banking personnel with persons affiliated with the North Korean Labor Party (Communist Party).

On December 6, 1947, more than a year after the People's Committee acted to strengthen the Central Bank, a comprehensive program of currency reform was announced. In general, this reform sought to reverse the tendency of North Korean goods to move into South Korean markets where the inflation was much higher. The outward flow of goods and the receipt of Chosun Bank notes in exchange exerted a continual inflationary pressure in North Korea. If successfully administered the currency reform would have had the opposite effect.

The reform measure of December 1947 deprived Chosun Bank notes of their legal status and ordered their exchange for newly-created Central Bank notes. The circulating medium of South Korea was thus stripped of any value in exchange in North Korea, in order to halt the undesired movement of goods southward. The redemption and subsequent impounding of Chosun Bank notes at the same time placed in the hands of the political administration of North Korea a tremendous command over South Korean goods.

Evaluation

The North Korean currency program, of course, could be expected to have very disadvantageous consequences for the administration in South Korea. Instead of benefiting from the small unsanctioned trade across the 38th parallel, South Korea was to have the full weight of the supply of Chosun Bank notes available in North Korea levied against its exceedingly small supply of goods. The Chosun Bank in January 1948 observed that the reforms in the north might give rise to a currency reform in the south.

However, the nebulous magnitude which the Chosun Bank note issue had already reached before December 1947 made it unlikely that the North Korean reform would precipitate a volume of trade that would make a similar program for South Korea inevitable. Chosun Bank notes in North Korea at the time of the reform were estimated to amount to only 1,430 million won, probably not more than 5 or 6 per cent of the total amount of money circulating in South Korea. By contrast the note issue in South Korea increased 26.1 per cent in the month of November 1947 alone. In fact, for the two months when the financing of the grain collection program exerted its greatest demand for funds, November and December, the note supply had to be increased by more than 64 per cent.[13] If liquidated gradually in South Korean markets, the North Korean currency fund would hardly have ranked as even a minor cause of inflation.

What was perhaps more significant was that the announcement of this currency program, which carried one step further the division between north and south, was made but a month before the arrival of the United Nations Temporary Commission in Korea, and gave further forewarning that the North Korean regime would not participate in deliberations with that body.

[13] Chosun Bank, "Financial Condition in South Korea," *loc. cit.*, Table 14, pp. 1-11.

Currency and Prices

Information is not available as to the extent of the inflation in North Korea during this period, and evidently AMG officials in the south were completely uninformed about the matter.[14]

One significant factor of course was what happened to the money supply after liberation. The volume of Chosun Bank notes estimated to be in circulation in North Korea immediately prior to December 6, 1947, did not show any appreciable increase since mid-August 1945, whereas in the American zone, Chosun Bank notes outstanding increased more than 1500 per cent in the same period. Chosun Bank notes did not, however, represent the total circulating medium in North Korea. Evidently the military scrip issued by the Soviet command had had some noticeable effect upon the total supply. However, neither the amount of this currency issued nor the rate at which it exchanged for won (from rubles) seems to have been made public.[15]

Presumably the Soviet command acquired Chosun Bank notes both by confiscation during the brief period of military activity and through accession to control over the banking and taxing systems.

Despite a concerted effort to increase the volume of bank deposits, these aggregated only about 1,500 million won in the middle of 1947, or one and one-half times the total of August 15, 1945. By contrast, a similar drive in South Korea, though probably much less intensive, was able to bring bank deposits up to a total at least nine times greater than that for August

[14] *SKIG Activities*, October 1947, p. 139, reported that it had been agreed that South Korea would pay its future electric power bills in goods valued at North Korean prices. However, the prices referred to were evidently 1941 prices. See p. 148 n.

[15] Henry Chung, *op. cit.*, p. 67, states that these "occupation rubles" were used by individual Russian soldiers for the purchase of small items such as fruits and cakes "and for the payment of workers in Russian managed factories." Chung's reporting on North Korean finance is confusing, however. He gives one to believe, for example, that the inflation of the regular currency was fully as great as in the south.

1945. What part privately-issued bills of credit may have played in commercial transactions is not known. The denial of the note-issuing power to the North Korean Central Bank and certain other factors indicate that a deliberate effort was being made to keep the monetary base from expanding. Thus it appears that currency inflation in North Korea since liberation was a good deal less than the increases attributable to the monetization of bank deposits immediately following the Japanese collapse, a circumstance quite contrary to what happened in South Korea.

The very low levels of production, especially during 1946, undoubtedly had a marked inflationary effect. But the fact that these were not accompanied by a rapidly expanding monetary supply, as was the case in South Korea, was of significant importance.

According to Anna Louise Strong, rationed rice in North Korea was selling for five won per kilogram in late 1947.[16] At this time the controlled price of rice in the American zone was somewhat over 16 won a kilo.

Since in both zones rice was a controlled commodity, the reasonable assumption that prices rose much less in North Korea than they did in the south is evidently justified. To infer more from such meager data would, however, be fallacious. A fairly stable price level is of particular benefit, of course, to wage-earning groups whose real income is generally impaired by upward price movements. However, this theoretical benefit may be more than offset by the effects a hard credit policy may have upon the expansion of production. The constricted money supply in North Korea during the first two years after the Russian occupation may very well have hampered new development and hence constituted a drag upon the growth of real income and employment. In fact, it might well have had the net effect of depressing economic activity, let alone restricting its expansion.

It was perhaps just this experience which led to the inclusion

[16] Anna Louise Strong, "Industrial Workers in North Korea," *Soviet Russia Today*, February 1948, p. 27.

in the currency reforms of December 1947 the instruments for an easy money policy, presumably to permit economic expansion. The 1947 economic plan projected widespread investments in new capacity and in the rehabilitation of old facilities. Articles 4 and 5 of Decision Number 30, the currency reform, called for issuing currency to obviate financial inconvenience to public enterprises. The consequences of this policy would, of course, depend upon the extent to which an increase in the real wealth of the area was encouraged thereby. If the easy money policy was followed by a growth in real wealth comparable to the increase in the money supply, price inflation, on balance, would be unimportant.

This monetary policy had been considered some time before its actual adoption, but had been rejected because it was feared that, since the financial system had not been securely established, currency issue might become a principal source for governmental financing. There is always the danger that such a policy may encourage an unwarranted expansion of the essentially nonproductive functions of government.

The disquieting element in the inflation in South Korea was of that sort. The money supply increased by leaps and bounds, while real wealth was no doubt progressively deteriorating. The easy device of deficit financing via overdrafts on the central bank used in South Korea was essentially the same as the mechanism which the reforms in North Korea put at the disposition of the government. Here the parallel might end, however, for planning entailed a certain amount of anticipation which tended to eliminate some measure of injudiciousness from the use of the currency power, and North Korea was sufficiently endowed with basic resources to permit the consideration of largely self-sufficient economic expansion.

CHAPTER ELEVEN

Agriculture, Labor and Industry In the Soviet Zone

AGRICULTURE AND LAND REFORM

Agricultural Production

NORTH KOREA, like the south, was predominantly agricultural, even though the region had had a moderate extent of heavy industrial development. But North Korean agriculture differed in certain basic respects from that in the south. The shorter growing season in North Korea made double-cropping much less prevalent and rice was less predominant, being somewhat eclipsed in importance by that of other cereals—barley, millet, and to a lesser extent maize, buckwheat, oats, and *kaoliang* (sorghum). Vegetable and fruit production was more important than in the south. Also the fishing catch in Korean waters had been particularly concentrated off the northern coast. Diversification, however, was only conspicuous by comparison with the food production of the south. As in the south, rice was the principal crop and cereals accounted for by far the greater part of the diet.

Under the Japanese the food supply in the north had not generally been adequate to meet the food requirements of the whole area. Large surpluses of rice were produced in the western part of North Korea, and in good years these surpluses were sufficient to offset the deficits in the rest of the area which particularly afflicted the two northernmost provinces, North and South Hamgyŏng. However, the large exportation of rice to Japan drained the food surplus areas, jeopardizing the food supply of the deficit areas. Here the "spring hunger" was most severe. It was also in these provinces that the "firefield" cultivators eked out their precarious livelihood.

During the war years North Korean agricultural production suffered a decline similar to that in the south. In 1942 alone the cultivated area decreased by 253,000 *chungbo* (620,000 acres), thus reducing the production of grains and pulses by 400,000 metric tons.[1]

According to Anna Louise Strong, who visited North Korea in late 1947, the area suffered an acute food shortage in 1946 during which the grain ration fell to one pound per capita per day.[2] The flight of refugees to South Korea during this period was in part attributed to this serious contraction in the food supply.

A considerable recovery seems to have taken place during 1947, partially caused by a revival of the chemical fertilizer industry. The grain harvest in 1947 was reported to have yielded two million metric tons, a supply sufficient to provide one and a quarter pounds per person per day. An increase of 17.5 per cent in the area under cultivation over 1945 was reported to have been achieved in the three northernmost provinces (Pyŏngan-Pukto, Hamgyŏng-Namdo, and Hangyŏng-Pukto), whose boundaries were not altered by the rise to political importance of the 38th parallel and hence most directly comparable to pre-occupation conditions.[3]

Thus, in respect to cereal production and expansion of the cultivated area, the agricultural goals of the 1947 economic plan appear to have been largely realized. The plan had called for an increase of 15.5 per cent in the area under cultivation and an

[1] *Report of People's Committee*, p. 85.

[2] Anna Louise Strong, "Land Reform in North Korea," *Soviet Russia Today*, November 1947, p. 42.

[3] *Ibid.*, p. 20.

increase in grain production to 2,150,815 metric tons. The plan may not have been realized, however. The few scattered details concerning agricultural production shown in Table 17 appear to indicate that in general the agricultural goals were only in part achieved.

TABLE 17

PLANNED EXPANSION OF KOREAN AGRICULTURE

	1939	*1946*	*1947 (planned)*	*1948 (planned)*
Cultivated Area (*chungbo*)	2,629,000	1,934,128	2,234,300	2,344,200
Cows (head)	890,000	579,754	801,800	727,191
Horses "	16,800	11,800	12,900	12,597
Hogs "	642,700	216,700	346,900	546,600
Fish (tons)	915,300	209,000	260,000	344,000

Sources: *Report of People's Committee*, pp. 85, 87, 115-17; *Korean Independence*, July 14, 1948, p. 1; USAMGIK sources; fish (1938), *Chosen Nenkan 1941*, pp. 407-09.

The fact that the total cows and horses were to be less numerous in the 1948 plan than in the 1947 plan suggests that the 1947 plan fell short of realization in these respects. On the other hand, the expansion of the hog population and the fishing catch seems to indicate that the 1947 goals for this production had not been unduly ambitious. It is also noteworthy that even if the 1948 objectives were fully attained, production would still be below the 1939 levels.

Land Reform

Considerable importance was ascribed to the program of land reform for the improvements in agricultural production. However, the land reform was unquestionably more important politically than economically. Though tenancy was not so widespread as in South Korea, 58 per cent of the land was in the hands of landlords who comprised but three per cent of the population. Land reform was undoubtedly regarded by the people as the most important innovation in the northern zone. In all probability it was the best propaganda agent of the Russians in the south, especially in view of the American inaction in the same field.

The land reform program in North Korea was announced in a decree issued on March 5, 1946, approximately seven months after the beginning of the Russian occupation.[4]

The first three articles of the decree made clear the purpose and scope of the program:

> *Article I.* The land reform in North Korea arises from historical and economic necessity. The mission of land reform lies in the abolition of Japanese land ownership, land ownership by Korean landlords, and of land tenancy, and bestowing the right to exploit the land on those who cultivate. The agricultural system in North Korea shall be founded on individual ownership by farmers who are not shackled to landlords, and in the management of land.
>
> *Article II.* The land coming into the following categories shall be confiscated and transferred to ownership by farmers: 1) Land owned by the Japanese state, Japanese individuals and organizations; 2) Land owned by traitors to the Korean people, those who have damaged the interests of the Korean people, and who actively participated in the political machinery of Japanese imperialism, and also land owned by those who fled from their own districts at the time of Korean liberation from Japanese oppression.
>
> *Article III.* The land in the following categories shall be confiscated and distributed freely for ownership by farmers: 1) Land owned by Korean landlords in excess of 5 *cho* per family; 2) Land owned by those who did not cultivate but rented land solely for tenancy; 3) All land, regardless of acreage, which is continuously in tenancy; 4) Land owned by shrines, temples, and other religious sects [sic] in excess of 5 *cho.*

The program was to be accomplished by the end of March 1946. All land confiscated was entrusted to the North Korea

[4] For an available text of this decree see Hankum Tralim, "Land Reform in North Korea," *Amerasia*, February 1947, pp. 56-57. This is a translation of an article appearing in *Zenei* (Vanguard), a Japanese periodical, for May 1946. For another translation of the act and administrative orders, see Department of State, Economic Mission, *Land Reform in Korea* (mimeographed), Seoul, September 1947, pp. D1-7. The Korean text may be found in *Report of People's Committee*, pp. 17-20. A careful comparison of the Korean text and the two translations reveals that the *Amerasia* version follows the original more literally and is therefore used below.

People's Committee. This body was to achieve actual redistribution through village committees acting under the District, County and Provincial People's Committees.

An administrative order dated March 8, 1946, elaborated the procedure and scope of the reforms. Village committees of from five to nine members elected at a mass meeting of farm laborers, landless tenants, and tenants short of land were charged with investigating and registering in detail all land, buildings, and equipment liable to confiscation under the land decree, and to prepare a survey of the status of landless and landholding groups. The village committees were to prepare a plan for redistribution of land under the supervision of District People's Committees.

The order, in accordance with Article III of the decree, provided that all land owned by landlords who possessed in excess of five *cho* (12.25 acres) would be confiscated. Where a landowner cultivated part of his land and rented part and the aggregate amounted to more than five *cho*, only that land which he and his family did not cultivate with their own labor would be confiscated. In the case of land held by persons not connected with the agricultural economy (i.e., absentee landlords), all land was to be confiscated.

Land belonging to churches, temples, and other religious institutions, also in accordance with Article III, was to be confiscated when cultivated by hired or tenant labor. Land of religious organizations not utilized "for exploitation of farmers and farm laborers" up to the amount of five *cho* was not to be taken away.

According to Article IV of the decree, land belonging to schools, hospitals, and scientific institutions was not to be confiscated even though the land had been previously rented for continuous tenancy. Future tenancy of such land was, however, prohibited. Schools, it was declared, "should cultivate such land with the labor of their own students and their families, and utilize the crops for school projects." [5] Where schools were

[5] Clause 11, Regulations for Enforcement of Land Decree, *loc. cit.*

not in a position to cultivate land it was to be entrusted to the People's Committees.

Certain other provisions of the decree in general provided that forests should be confiscated and entrusted to the supervision of the North Korea People's Committee. Orchards were regarded in a similar manner. They were not to be divided and Provincial People's Committees were charged with determining appropriate policies for their preservation, cultivation, proper management, and future utilization. Irrigation facilities were permanently entrusted to District People's Committees.

The order stated that "Distribution of land to farm laborers, landless farmers, and farmers short of land shall be executed according to the principle based on the number in the family and the number in said family with labor power." [6] A formula applying this principle was set forth in the order. In distributing land, its quality was to be considered in determining the amount made available to eligible families.[7]

In general, then, the land reform program was a studious application of two cardinal Marxian principles, (1) the implications of the labor theory of value modified by (2) the consideration that reward should also show a relationship to need, representing essentially the current state of Soviet distributive economics.[8] Article IV of the decree and Clause 12 of the order, however, put the property of certain persons beyond the pale of confiscation, taking exception to the strict application of these principles. It excepted the land of those who had been

[6] Clause 15, Regulations for Enforcement of Land Decree, *loc. cit.*

[7] Clause 16, *loc. cit.*

[8] For a commentary upon the precise relationships of the so-called "socialist phase" represented by the contemporary economy of the U.S.S.R. to doctrinaire Marxist concepts see Leo Rogin, "Marx and Engels on Distribution in a Socialist Society," *American Economic Review*, Vol. 35, March 1945, pp. 137-43. The essentials of the land reform program undertaken had been set out twenty-nine years earlier in the first agricultural decree of the Soviet government, issued on the second day of the 1917 Revolution (October 26). For a discussion of this and other Soviet laws relating to the land see Alexander Baykov, *The Development of the Soviet Economic System*, The University Press, Cambridge, 1947, especially pp. 16-24.

outstandingly active in the long independence struggle, persons occupying positions of importance in the building of "a new democratic Korea," including writers, artists, actors, and scientists "who rendered meritorious services for the development of the national culture, science, and art in Korea, as such." By these provisions the new regime rewarded its leaders and the publicists active in its behalf.

Article V of the land decree provided that land was to be transferred without compensation "for permanent ownership." [9] Article VIII provided that lands given to farmers under the decree were to be "exempt from debts and liabilities in general." Article X states that "All lands distributed to farmers under this decree shall not be bought, sold, or rented for tenancy, or mortgaged." One point of criticism of the North Korean land reform centered around these provisions. It made much of the fact that the beneficiaries of the program did not have what amounted to ownership in fee simple.

Under the Japanese, usurious interest rates and depressed crop prices operated like a pincers to squeeze thousands of Korean farm families into tenancy, wage labor, or even out of agriculture altogether. Before Japanese rule, property rights were sometimes subjected to arbitrary impairment [10] and tenancy was an

[9] The State Department translation differs considerably, omitting the "ownership" phrase: "All the land confiscated according to Article 2 and Article 3 will be delivered to the farmers without compensation." *Loc. cit.* p. D1. The Korean original, however, contains the clause, being more accurately translated by the *Amerasia* version. See *Report of People's Committee*, p. 18.

[10] The institutions of "court" and "camp" lands belonging to the royal household represented vast holdings, yet their boundaries were often vague and they were frequently peopled by generations of squatters who had come to assume the land to be theirs. For example, in 1895 the Korean king, exercising his prerogatives as an absolute monarch, granted to an American mining company the "exclusive right of exploitation, even as against the Koreans on the ground" in the Un-san district of northern Korea. This area was already "honey-combed" by native miners who, regarding the land as rightfully theirs, dispatched a letter to the American Minister asking if it was "in accordance with international law that anyone can take away by force the property of another without payment." See Harrington, *God, Mammon and the Japanese*, pp. 156, 163.

institution of age-long standing. The rapid aggravation of the tenancy problem under Japanese rule, however, had profound effects upon the Korean attitude. Writing in 1940, W. J. Ladejinsky noted:

> The Korean tenants were never satisfied with their lot, but until the early twenties customs and traditions regulating the landlord-tenant relations were sufficient to prevent open conflict and insure relative peace in the village. In the past two decades, however, the life and work of Korean tenants has become increasingly conducive to discontent. The growing agricultural distress has brought about a sharp change in the attitude toward landlords. . . . The causes underlying them were numerous, but the principal ones in order of importance were termination of leases, excessive rents, and attempts to raise rents still higher.[11]

The rapid increase in tenancy was spelling "pauperization for the great majority of Korean farmers." [12]

In view of such conditions as these it seems illogical to suppose that redress in their favor, even through confiscation, would be opposed by any appreciable number of the formerly landless farmers who comprised the great bulk of the population of both North and South Korea. Nor is it likely that the strictures placed upon the property lessened by very much the enthusiasm of the North Korean farmer for the program.

Even in South Korea, the land reform proposals advanced by Military Government did not contemplate giving the new landholders unqualified ownership. The "homestead" proposals would have required cultivation of the land by the would-be owner during the entire period in which payments were being made. And since the farmer purchasing the land was not given full title, he obviously could not resell the land. Thus in South Korea it was planned that the state should reserve some stewardship over the land to assure the success of the plan and to assure that the land would not revert to cultivation under a system of tenancy.

[11] W. J. Ladejinsky, "Korean Agricultural Problems," *Foreign Agriculture*, February 1940, p. 114.

[12] *Ibid.*, p. 111.

In actual practice, under the ordinance promulgated in South Korea for the distribution of the formerly Japanese-held agricultural land, the new owner did not gain the right to sell until after the payments had been made and at least ten years had elapsed since he had originally contracted to purchase the land. Such a period of apprenticeship was felt necessary to develop the stability of these new landholders and to forestall any opportunity for debt and intimidation to undo the work of redistribution.

While such limitations upon ownership in the form of an ever-present threat of eviction could be a fierce bludgeon upon the political conscience of individuals in North Korea, reasons similar to those which dictated reservations upon ownership in the land distribution proposals in South Korea were likewise operative. Moreover, there could be no doubt that the reforms in North Korea would put a quietus upon landlordism since Marxian doctrine regards the landlord along with all other *rentiers* as an unequaled parasite. How the North Korean farmer regarded having only rights of permanent possession but not of disposal was very much open to question. That he liked this arrangement better than his tenant status, however, would hardly have seemed disputable.

Another point of criticism of the North Korean land reforms has been that taxes and other levies imposed by the Soviet regime left the farmers in essentially the same position as they had been after paying rent to landlords. If such was the case, it might be expected that in its most favorable terms the Korean reaction would be indifference toward reforms which in fact left conditions essentially unimproved. Upon this matter it is difficult to form anything more than the most general conclusions because it has not been possible to obtain accurate data as to the actual proportion of his crops which the farmer was obliged to give up as taxes or some other public levy. Apparently a basic exaction of 25 per cent in kind was required for taxes in 1947. This was evidently intended to represent the ordinary level of taxation. To this in 1947 was added a "special contribution" about which the information was still more vague. Apparently this latter levy was not imposed uniformly throughout North Korea, nor was its incidence by any means uniform in the areas where it was collected. Technically it was not exactly a tax but a kind of enforced saving to provide capital for the Farmers' Bank, which was financing agricultural rehabilitation including the resumption of operations by chemical fertilizer plants and the production of farm implements. In return the individual farmer was to receive a kind of repayment or dividend in the form of fertilizer and farm tool allocations.

Some estimates fixed this levy as amounting to about 25 per cent or in effect doubling the rate of taxation. Other reports estimated that the tax and the levy together totaled no more than 30 per cent or the maximum legal rental obtainable by landlords in South Korea under the Military Government ordinance. The most extreme report put the total exaction as high as 72 per cent of the crop.[13] Some of the wide variation in figures might possibly be due to varying bases of computation. A legally-fixed exaction of 30 per cent in kind might be a very different burden in reality when quotas were fixed in terms of the crop yields of past years while actual production had plummeted. This was one early difficulty with the crop collection programs in South Korea until the system demonstrated its shortcomings and quotas were overhauled.

It appears probable, nevertheless, that in North Korea during the first year of effective taxation levies were imposed which were inordinately high in many instances inasmuch as agricultural production had fallen precipitously and quotas were out of keeping with the supply. It was also very probable, however, that this situation was later mitigated as production increased and experience caused quotas to be brought within more reasonable limits.

[13] Chung, *The Russians Came to Korea*, pp. 65-66. Clyde Mitchell, the former manager of the southern New Korea Company also reports ("Korean Farm Tenant Purchase Program," *Land Economics*, November 1948, p. 405) that the exaction in North Korea was around 70 per cent.

The fact was that 981,390 *chungbo*, 50 per cent of the farmland in 1946, was distributed among 725,000 farm families under the program.[14] Barring the most gross and unlikely shortcomings, the land reform was undoubtedly an extremely popular measure. Scarcely any act could have had a wider impact.[15] If land reform in North Korea were to press toward collectivization, however, this initial attitude of the Korean peasants might change profoundly. But that stage of Communist planning was still in the future.

LABOR

The Labor Decree

The North Korea land reform decree was shortly followed by a pronouncement relating to the conditions of labor.[16] This labor law decreed an eight-hour day in general employment. For those engaged in hazardous or unhealthful occupations, including specifically mining, work was to be limited to seven hours a day. For minors between 14 and 16 years of age the hours of work were not to exceed six per day. These minor workers were also prohibited from entering hazardous or harmful employment. Labor by minors under 14 was forbidden.

A large portion of the decree initiated measures pertaining to the welfare and security of the workers. Legal holidays and the minimal length of vacation periods were prescribed. The latter

[14] *Report of People's Committee*, p. 85.

[15] In Communist China a land reform virtually identical in principle with the program in North Korea showed great virility as a political device. Like the Korean plan it permitted individual ownership and promised an alleviation of the hardships of the agricultural population. In the opinion of one writer the Communists might eventually gain the support of 90 per cent of the people on the basis of their land reform program alone. See Wang Sze-zee, "Communist Economic Offensive: Equalization of Land," *China Weekly Review*, November 15, 1947, p. 350.

[16] North Korea Labor Ordinance, 25 Articles, promulgated by the North Korea Interim People's Committee, June 24, 1946. Korean text in *Report of People's Committee*, pp. 21-27. An English text of the law appeared in *Amerasia* for May 1947, pp. 156-60, as translated from an article by Kim Doo Yong in *Zenei*, a Japanese periodical, in January 1947.

were graduated upon the same basis as the hours of work. All workers were to receive at least two weeks' regular vacation in every year, minors and workers in harmful or dangerous occupations were to be given at least a month. Wages during the vacation period were to be the average for the previous twelve months. Women workers were to be given vacation periods of 25 days and 42 days before and after childbirth respectively. Special provisions were made for the employment of pregnant women at lighter work and for time out for mothers nursing children under one year of age.

Article XVIII established a comprehensive compulsory social insurance system. It was to afford (1) aid for workers temporarily disabled from work, (2) aid during the period of vacation due to pregnancy and childbirth, (3) aid for funeral expenses, (4) annuities for those disabled for work while on duty or from occupational diseases. A committee was also created to study and prepare provisions for unemployment and annuities. In the summer of 1947, according to one observer, the social insurance agency was operating 85 hostels with 1,400 beds, largely former private Japanese summer villas, and was expected to offer during the season free vacations to 25,000 workers.[17]

In regard to wages two general rules were laid down: (1) equal wages for equal work irrespective of age or sex; (2) one and one-half times the regular rate of payment for all work performed on off-days or legal holidays.

The procedure for wage determination was closely specified. Article VI stated:

> Rates of remuneration shall be prescribed according to occupation, position, and skill of workers. (a) Wages in state enterprises and offices shall be prescribed by the North Korea People's Committee. (b) Wages in privately owned enterprises and offices shall be prescribed by collective or labor contracts.

Article XXII provided that

[17] Anna Louise Strong, "Industrial Workers in North Korea," *Soviet Russia Today*, February 1948, p. 17.

Labor unions and the Finance and Industry Departments shall prepare tables of wage scales and standard wages of workers, and tables of standard salaries for technicians, workers, clerks, and all other occupations in state enterprises, the transportation system, *and all other industrial establishments*. [Italics ours.]

Wage determination, therefore, was placed very definitely within the orbit of state control. For the preponderant share of industry which was operated by the state this was obvious. And while part (b) of Article VI quoted above would appear to leave wage determination in non-nationalized activities to the mutual negotiation of employers and employees, it was apparent by virtue of Article XXII that all wages and salaries in North Korea were to be fixed in accordance with a codified system of rates.

This state control of the wages system was in keeping with the highly centralized economic planning which had been put into effect in North Korea, emulating the Soviet Union. Under such a scheme all payments, wages included, were necessarily subjected to the rationale of the total scheme.

In the matter of labor disputes, the ultimate authority to impose settlements was explicitly vested in the state. According to Article XXIII,

The questions of labor disputes arising between employees and employers shall be settled between employers and labor unions. In the event that an agreement is not reached between employers and labor unions, the final decision concerning such disputes shall be given by the people's courts.

Naturally in a state in which power was supposed to emanate from the workers, the relationship of labor organizations and the government was very close. In North Korea where trade unions had been virtually unknown, the development of labor organizations in effect became a government responsibility. Thus Oh Kisup, the Director of the Department of Labor of the North Korea People's Committee, was active in the organization of the post-liberation labor movement. In all phases of the relationships between worker organization and the state the attitude was deliberately partisan and distinctly in contrast to the judicial and remote role which American Military Government sought to play in South Korea.

Director Oh on occasion acknowledged the affiliation of the North Korean labor movement with organizations in the south. He stated that at first the All-Korean Federation of Trade Unions had operated openly throughout the country. Then, according to Oh, "the American Army began to suppress the trade unions in the South. The chairman of the All-Korean Federation was imprisoned in Seoul. Trade unions grew rapidly in the North, operated quite openly, had collective agreements with all factories, took part in the production plan of the industry and put up candidates for government. In the South they had to work on a semi-legal or completely underground basis. These different policies forced a separation of the trade unions." [18]

At the end of 1947, 380,000 out of a total of 430,000 workers in North Korea belonged to trade unions. This figure included virtually everyone who regularly worked for wages (or salaries). It excluded only such persons as small farmers and fishermen who worked in their off-seasons.[19]

As to unemployment, Director Oh stated that North Korea did not have any. "On the contrary we have a shortage of workers in North Korea because we have so much reconstruction to do and because we are expanding our industry. We need 13,000,000 work-days more than we have just to reconstruct our bridges and roads. This means we could absorb 45,000 more workers just for this reconstruction." [20]

[18] *Ibid.*, p. 26.

[19] *Ibid.* At the end of 1947 the four largest unions and their memberships were as follows:

White collar	100,000
Miners	52,000
Chemical workers	45,000
Transport workers	45,000

[20] *Ibid.*, pp. 26-27.

INDUSTRY

Japanese Destruction and Russian Stripping

It was a matter of some significance that North Korea was overrun by force of arms while South Korea was peacefully occupied after the Japanese surrender. Industrial sabotage by the Japanese was consequently much more widespread against the Russians in August 1945 than was subsequently the case in the American zone. Also, there was much more of a field for spectacular sabotage in the heavy industry of the north.[21]

By the simple process of letting the furnaces cool the largest iron and steel plant in Korea was reduced to uselessness.[22] Sixty-four mines were completely flooded and 178 others flooded to a lesser degree. Nineteen plants were put completely out of use including six of the most important plants: two iron and steel plants at Chŏngjin, two electric steel furnaces in Sŏngjin, and two airplane factories in Pyŏngyang. Damage to 47 other factories was severe.[23]

In his address to the Assembly of People's Committees in January 1947, Kim Ilsung stated that a good start had been made in the reconstruction and rehabilitation of industry. Extensive repairs in 1946 had enabled 822 factories to be in operation on January 1, 1947. Many of these were leading plants such as the Hungnam chemical works; iron and steel mills at Sŏngjin, Kyomipo, and Kangso; metal processing plants at Chinnampo, Haeju, Yongampo, and Munpyong; and mines at Koksan, Sŏnghung, Sunan, Kyomdok, and Tonghi.[24]

Japanese damage was not confined to deliberate sabotage. As

[21] *Ibid.*, p. 17, tells of a struggle which went on at the Hungnam chemical works between the departing Japanese, who planned to blow up the plant with its own explosives, and Korean workers. After a four-hour conflict, runs this account, the Koreans drove out the Japanese and discovered the explosive charge which was set with a time fuse and threw it into the sea.

[22] *Ibid.*, p. 16.

[23] *Report of People's Committee*, p. 75.

[24] *Ibid.*, p. 76.

in the south, severe handicaps were ascribable to the fact that plants had not been properly maintained during the later stages of the war. There were also the difficulties imposed by the lack of industrial integration, inasmuch as many Korean factories were but links in a chain of productive processes carried on outside Korea's borders.

Concerning the question of productive capacity, considerable controversy over possible Russian "stripping" of Korean factories resulted from contradictory reports reaching South Korea early in the occupation. United States Reparations Commissioner Edwin W. Pauley visited North Korea and Manchuria in May and June 1946 at the behest of President Truman with the express intention of learning whether or not these reports were true. Upon completion of his inspection tour Pauley reported that whereas in Manchuria the Russians had removed enough equipment "to wreck the industrial plant," he saw "little if any" evidence of stripping in North Korea.[25]

The validity of Pauley's statements was seriously questioned in American military circles in Seoul, where it was found hard to discount entirely the stream of reports by refugees from North Korea that stripping had occurred. These sources believed that Russian removals were only constrained by considerations of efficiency which dictated using certain plants near their present sources of raw materials, and by transportation difficulties.[26]

In answer to the military men in Seoul, Pauley elaborated upon his previous remarks. He stated that although he had been denied access to two areas he had asked to see, he and his party of nineteen expert observers had seen nothing to indicate large-scale removal of capital goods by the Russians from the remainder of North Korea. Pauley said that "by and large" they saw "an estimated 60 per cent of the heavy industry, speaking in terms of value." [27] He said that "If you will go over the areas carefully you will find that most industry (aside from power

[25] *New York Times*, July 20, 1946, p. 9; December 15, 1946, p. 41.
[26] *New York Times*, June 6, 1946, p. 10.
[27] Dispatch from Seoul, *New York Times*, July 20, 1947, p. 9.

and mining) lies within the three out of five areas we covered." [28] These areas were the Sinŭiju vicinity near the Korean border opposite Antung, Manchuria; Wŏnsan on the east coast; and Chinnampo, the west coast port near Pyŏngyang. Pauley was denied access to Hungnam and Chŏngjin in northeast Korea on the grounds that Russian soldiers were undergoing demobilization at these points. Pauley was also denied access to the oil refinery at Wŏnsan, the Russian general declaring that the area was controlled by the Soviet navy and therefore beyond his jurisdiction. However, Pauley said that from a distance the refinery appeared to be intact and evidently in operation since smoke was rising from its chimneys. This contradicted the widespread belief that the refinery had been dismantled.[29]

Perhaps it was significant, however, that Pauley was not permitted to inspect the Hungnam or Chŏngjin areas. There is almost a complete absence of information in the reports of the North Korea People's Committee on economic planning about Chŏngjin and the iron mines nearby, and Professor Lee Seyoul who visited North Korea in March 1946 makes no mention of visiting plants in any of these places in his report.[30] The People's Committee's reports on economic planning do, however, mention the chemical industry in Hungnam, and reported it as being in operation in January 1947. Moreover, the 1947 plan called for restoring five electric steel furnaces at Sŏngjin to operation during the year, and the rehabilitation of a textile plant in Chŏngjin.[31]

If plants were dismantled at Hungnam, they probably contained specialized equipment for the production of munitions of which there was a large supply in that area. The terms of surrender required the destruction or removal of all such pro-

[28] Dispatch from Seoul, *New York Times*, June 11, 1946, p. 16.

[29] *New York Times*, December 15, 1946, p. 41.

[30] *Amerasia*, February 1947, pp. 61-62, published a summary of the report by Professor Lee of his trip to North Korea. Lee was at that time a member of the faculty of Seoul University.

[31] *Report of People's Committee*, pp. 112-13.

ductive capacity. But the volume of chemical fertilizer production envisaged in the 1947 plan would have been clearly impossible had any major dismantling of the nitrogen fixation facilities in Hungnam taken place. On the other hand, the Soviets possibly removed considerable industrial equipment from the Chŏngjin area, adjacent to Soviet Siberia, where several large industries were located, notably an iron and steel works, and a synthetic fuel plant operated by the Japanese navy. However, the evidence at hand is not conclusive either way. It may be concluded, nevertheless, that the purpose of any withdrawals was not to cripple Korean industry because every effort by the Soviet command appears to have been to rehabilitate rather than destroy the economy of North Korea.[32]

Industrial Production

The 1947 economic plan[33] called for a volume of industrial production having a total value (at 1946 price levels) of 9,900 million won, a 91 per cent increase over 1946 output. The 1948 plan[34] called for a 130 per cent expansion over the 1947 output. (Part of this increase no doubt represents objectives not attained in 1947.) Primary emphasis was placed upon raising coal production and upon improving transportation. The information available concerning the 1948 plan is far too vague to permit a detailed comparison of the objectives of the two plans.

The 1947 plan called for increasing coal production to twice the 1946 output. Ferrous metals production was to be three times greater in 1947 than in 1946. The output of the chemical

[32] See excerpts from Pauley's report, *USAMGIK Summation*, June 1946. He said: "On the whole, the Soviets in the territory were trying to revive the industry. . . ."

[33] The plan is outlined in detail in *Report of People's Committee*, pp. 72-123. Reference to the plan in the following pages is taken from that report.

[34] Details of the 1948 plan have not become available, but meager information is provided from a North Korean news item reproduced in *Korean Independence*, July 14, 1948, p. 1, and *Voice of Korea*, July 16, 1948.

TABLE 18

NORTH KOREAN INDUSTRIAL PRODUCTION PROGRAM FOR 1947

Fuel and Electric Power	
Lignite Coal	1,300,000 tons
Anthracite Coal	1,500,000 "
Bituminous Coal	280,000 "
Electric Power	3,800,000,000 kw. hr.
Chemicals	
Chemical Fertilizer	300,000 tons
Various Acids	210,000 "
Caustic Soda	9,900 "
Carbide	70,000 "
Ferrous Metals	
Pig iron	25,000 tons
Steel Ingots	80,000 "
Rolled Steel, Piping, Etc.	55,000 "
Machines and Tools	
Cast Iron and Steel Equipment	5,600 tons
Motors and Motor Parts	450 pieces
Drilling and Cutting Machines	5,000 "
Miscellaneous Machinery	19,000,000 won value
Farm Machinery (Irrigation Equipment, etc.)	68,000 pieces
Farm Tools (Ploughs, hoes, etc.)	350,000 pieces
Construction Material	
Cement	300,000 tons
General Manufactures	
Textiles	4,000,000 meters
Clothing	12,000,000 pieces
Rubber Shoes	3,500,000 shoes
Paper	1,000 tons
Alcohol 94%	1,800,000 liters

Source: *Report of People's Committee*, pp. 109-11.

industry—primarily chemical fertilizer, sulphuric acid, and carbide—was to be doubled. Five chemical plants were reported to have been rehabilitated during 1946 and six more plants were under construction in 1947, the latter for the production of light chemicals.

In general outline the 1947 plan touched upon every phase of North Korean industry. Commencing with a program for expanding raw materials production—mining activities, the felling of timber, and the production of industrial crops—the plan traced its course through power production, the production of primary goods, the manufacture of capital equipment, the facilities for transportation, the output of consumption goods, and the channels of distribution.

It is difficult to determine in any meaningful terms from the sketchy information available how the levels of production under the plan compared with the realities of previous years. It is clear, however, that while the plan did contemplate an enlargement of output from its 1946 levels, it was principally focused upon reconstruction. Thus the plan aimed for expansion upon the levels of the immediate past, not a net historical increase. For example, about 465,000 metric tons of lignite coal were mined in North Korea in 1946.[35] In 1944 North Korean lignite production had been 2,821,659 metric tons,[36] but the target for 1947 was set at only 1,300,000 metric tons, a figure 2.8 times the 1946 output but less than half the 1944 volume. The same was true of anthracite production. The 1946 output was about 775,000 metric tons. This amount was to be increased by 93 per cent to 1,500,000 metric tons, yet 1944 output had been 3,240,749 tons, or somewhat over twice as much. Cement plant capacity in 1940 was 1,705,480 metric tons,[37] yet planned 1947 output was fixed at only 300,000 tons.

Although evidently little new construction was projected in either the 1947 or 1948 plan, the 1947 plan called for the com-

[35] *Report of People's Committee*, p. 77.
[36] See Table 5, p. 58.
[37] USAMGIK sources.

pletion of a 15,000-spindle rayon mill apparently left unfinished by the Japanese [38] and the 1948 plan included the erection of a new power plant on the Su Gang River.[39] The volume of goods to be handled through the semi-official distributive channels of the cooperatives in 1947 was to increase seven and one-half fold. This expansion was to be fostered by the formation of a large joint-stock company to be owned by local cooperatives.[40] Yet, as in South Korea, there was little likelihood that output of consumer goods would reach prewar levels for some time, let alone attain the prewar supply, since Korean-produced goods constituted but a small share of the prewar supply.

Improvements in rail transportation placed emphasis upon a more intensive use of equipment. The period required for the circulation of freight cars was to be reduced to six days, and cars were to move at an average daily speed of 105 kilometers.[41] There was anticipation of considerable difficulty in the maintenance and replacement of rolling stock. North Korea did not have any shops equipped to manufacture locomotives and the principal repair shops at Chŏngjin were reported to have been destroyed in 1945.[42] The major expansion of communications facilities was the projected construction of 1,734 kilometers of new telephone lines.[43]

The 1948 plan apparently followed the same broad plan as its predecessor, although purportedly it gave a greater share of emphasis to finished goods production than had the 1947 plan. The main emphasis remained, however, upon the production of raw materials, particularly metals and coal.[44]

In general, then, the plans for industry were necessarily directed at reconstruction rather than at any net expansion. Yet

[38] *Report of People's Committee*, p. 113; *Korean Independence*, July 14, 1948, p. 1.
[39] *Korean Independence*, July 14, 1948, p. 1.
[40] *Report of People's Committee*, p. 120.
[41] *Ibid.*, p. 118.
[42] *Ibid.*, p. 89.
[43] *Ibid.*, p. 119.
[44] *Korean Independence*, July 14, 1948, p. 1.

reconstruction alone promised to divert a large part of North Korea's energies in view of the destruction, the disrepair, and the segmented nature of the economy in this outpost of Japanese industry. And despite Kim Ilsung's tribute [45] to the magnitude of Soviet assistance in the task of rehabilitation, this aid, in material terms, was not spectacular. It consisted largely of supplying advisers and technicians, pharmaceuticals and medical assistance, and petroleum, the same sort of minimal assistance given by the Americans in South Korea, except that the Americans were importing food as well.

Yet the plan clearly brought the North Korean economy earnestly to grips with the problems of reconstruction. The seriousness of the North Korean attack upon the matter and its magnitude is conveyed by the fact that capital investments in North Korean industry were to amount to 880 million won [46] in 1947, 55 per cent of the 1,600 million won anticipated value of all 1947 consumer goods production exclusive of food.[47]

[45] *Ibid.*, p. 101-07.

[46] *Ibid.*, p. 111.

[47] *Ibid.*, p. 114. Value was based upon 1946 price levels. Total industrial production was to value 9,900 million won.

CHAPTER TWELVE

Divided Korea [1]

TWO GOVERNMENTS

On V-J Day, August 15, 1948, the people of South Korea heard General Douglas MacArthur acclaim the passing of government from American into Korean hands and Syngman Rhee as the first President accept authority for the new government. As the American flag was lowered in front of the capitol and the standard with the ancient Korean Taeguk on it raised in its place, the great bell of Seoul at Chongno intoned the rebirth of the Republic of Korea.[2] Three weeks later, on September 10, 1948, in Pyŏngyang, Kim Ilsung took office as the premier of the northern Democratic People's Republic of Korea.[3]

Three years of occupation by the United States and the U.S.S.R. had ended in the partitioning of Korea. The country

[1] Portions of this and the following chapter have already appeared in the *Far Eastern Survey* for September 8, 1948, under the title, "The Korean Situation."

[2] Rhee and his followers maintained that the present government originated in the ill-fated provisional government that had been declared twenty-nine years before as part of the independence movement of 1919.

[3] The difference in the Korean names of the two regimes was still more significant than indicated by the official English versions. The southern republic was the Taehan Min'guk, literally the Taehan republic. Taehan was the name used for the Korean "Empire" between 1897 and 1910, when the Korean monarchy discarded the name Chosŏn, long associated with Chinese suzerainty, and used the Han appellation which went back to a classical name used for the Korean people before the time of Christ. The northern

was separated into two states ruled by mutually antagonistic regimes, each claiming sole right to jurisdiction over the entire country. A compromise which would make possible the formation of a single government had not materialized. Instead, two nominally independent regimes faithfully reproduced the points of conflict of the two sponsoring powers.

Almost a year before the establishment of the Republic of Korea, the United States had taken the Korean problem to the General Assembly of the United Nations. At American request, the United Nations established a Temporary Commission on Korea which "observed" elections held in South Korea on May 10, 1948. These elections resulted in the formation of the government headed by Syngman Rhee which the United States, and subsequently the United Nations, accepted as the "Government of Korea."

In North Korea, the Soviet Union boycotted the American plan to bring a government into being through the intercession of the United Nations. Mainly as a countermove, the North Korea regime was strengthened as a nominally independent government: the Democratic People's Republic. On October 13, 1948, the Soviet Union formally recognized the Democratic People's Republic, followed by similar action on the part of other Communist-dominated countries.[4]

KOREA AND THE UNITED NATIONS

In a preceding chapter, the progression of circumstances which was ultimately to culminate in the emergence of two

---

Koreans have taken the name of the Chosŏn Inmin'guk, or literally, the Democratic People's Republic of Chosŏn. Chosŏn is the same name the Japanese used for Korea, transcribed as Chosen, the name used by the Yi dynasty from 1932 on. This name was derived from an ancient legendary name for the peninsula. Curiously enough, the Han name is of southern origin and has always been favored by the conservative literary class whereas Chosŏn is of northern origin and has always been the popular, and vernacular, name.

[4] The texts of the notes exchanged between Kim Ilsung and Stalin concerning recognition of the Democratic People's Republic by the U.S.S.R. are given in Appendix A.

separate governments has been traced through the creation of the Temporary Commission of Korea (UNTCOK) by the General Assembly of the United Nations. The U.S.S.R. and other Eastern bloc countries had opposed the formation of the Commission. The Soviet delegate to the U.N., Andrei Gromyko, had declared that the Soviet Union could not participate in the voting because the resolution creating the Temporary Commission on Korea proposed by the United States was "a result of the ignoring of the interests of the Korean people" and was intended to further the ambitions of the United States in Korea, politically, economically, and as a base for operations against the Soviet Union.[5] These remarks made it clear that the Commission could expect little assistance from the U.S.S.R.

The resolution establishing the Temporary Commission prescribed that membership should consist of representatives from Australia, Canada, China, El Salvador, France, India, the Philippines, Syria, and the Ukrainian Soviet Socialist Republic. At the time of the voting on the resolution, the delegate of the Ukrainian S.S.R. declared that his country could not take part in the Temporary Commission as proposed in the resolution, because no representatives of Korea had been invited to attend the debate. He also said that it would have been better if the Temporary Commission had consisted of neutral persons and not of representatives "obeying government instructions in most cases favorable to United States policy." [6] The Temporary Commission therefore carried out its work without the Ukrainian delegate.

The Temporary Commission convened in Seoul for its first meeting on January 29, 1948. Upon his arrival in Seoul shortly before, the chairman of the Commission, Dr. K. P. S. Menon of India, had informed the respective military commanders that he wished "to pay immediate courtesy calls" upon them.[7] In a

[5] See *Korea, 1945 to 1948, Washington,* U.S. Department of State, 1948, "Address by Andrei Gromyko before the General Assembly . . . ," pp. 51-61, especially pp. 60-61.

[6] United Nations Document A/AC. 19/80, p. 10-11.

[7] United Nations Document A/575, Add.1, p. 6.

reply dispatched by U.N. Headquarters at Lake Success, Mr. Gromyko "reminded" the Commission of the "negative attitude taken by the Soviet Government" toward the establishment of the Commission.[8] Subsequent attempts by the Commission to visit North Korea[9] were unsuccessful. The Soviet objections to the Commission in the Political and Security Committee and on the floor of the General Assembly had made it an almost foregone conclusion that the Commission would not be permitted to function in North Korea.

The failure of the Commission to gain entry to North Korea, or even to establish any contact with the Soviet authorities, raised some doubts within the Commission as to its status in view of the terms of reference laid down in the General Assembly resolutions.[10] Chairman Menon, therefore, left Seoul for United Nations Headquarters in mid-February to consult with the Interim Committee[11] of the General Assembly. The Commission in Seoul was soon advised that the resolutions had been interpreted to mean that the Commission should observe such elections as could take place "in a free atmosphere." Thereupon the Commission declared it would proceed with the observing of elections to be held "in such parts of Korea as were accessible to it not later than 10 May 1948."[12]

This statement was issued mainly to prevent riots and disorder which were expected to occur on Korean Independence Day, March 1.[13] Although the statement was unanimously endorsed by the Commission, the matter was not actually settled. A résumé issued by the Commission on March 12 disclosed that there had subsequently been considerable debate within

[8] *Ibid.*
[9] *Ibid.*, pp. 6-9.
[10] U.N. Document A/AC. 19/80, pp. 69-72.
[11] The Interim Committee, or "Little Assembly," was also boycotted by the U.S.S.R.
[12] U.N. Document A/AC. 19/80, p. 74.
[13] *Ibid.*, p. 74.

the Commission where there was by no means unanimous acceptance of the proposition of separate elections.[14]

The Australian representative held that all parties except those of the extreme right would boycott the election and therefore proposed an alternate plan. He recommended that the Commission withdraw at an early date after having made recommendations to the military authorities, and that it return later to re-examine the situation and then, if advisable, to carry on with its task. The Canadian representative held that the advice of the Interim Committee was unwise and unconstitutional. The Chinese delegate took a strong stand in favor of separate elections. The representatives of El Salvador, France, India, and the Philippine Republic also favored holding separate elections. The Syrian delegate unsuccessfully sought to attach reservations to the resolution to the effect that the Commission should reject any elections it found to be held in an "unfree" and "fettered" atmosphere. Some observers felt that the positions taken by the respective representatives on this issue were largely determined by what they considered to be the interests of their own national states rather than the merits of the case.

Activities of the Commission Before the Elections

Before the decision to conduct separate elections was reached, the Commission had already had an opportunity to hear the views of "representative Koreans" and to consult with Military Government officials.[15] As a result, the Commission made a number of recommendations to the American commander, General Hodge, for ensuring "a freedom of atmosphere" in the elections.

Subsequent to these recommendations, General Hodge issued a Korean Bill of Rights enumerating the "inherent liberties of the Korean people." The Military Governor also freed some

[14] *Ibid.*, pp. 76-79.

[15] See U.N. Document, No. A/575, Add. 2, for a verbatim report of these hearings.

3,000 political prisoners and promulgated an ordinance on criminal procedure which extended such guarantees as requiring warrants for the making of arrests.[16] Some modifications were also made in the election laws.

The Commission, however, was skeptical of the efficacy of these measures alone in view of the complaints received about the conduct of the national police and the so-called "youth organizations." [17] For this reason it decided to observe closely the attitude of the police during the pre-election and election periods.[18] The Commission was particularly wary of the National Youth organization, headed by General Lee Bumsuk, and supported in some measure financially and otherwise by Military Government. The Commission noted that "almost all" of these organizations were "markedly prone to organize bellicose demonstrations against their political opponents, thus giving frequent indications of a dangerous lack of tolerance towards the ideas they did not share," and that "the membership of these youth organizations included a large number of adults." [19]

Attitudes of Korean Groups Toward Separate Elections

Although certain changes had been made in accordance with the Commission's recommendations, the situation in South Korea in the weeks preceding the elections on May 10 was far from satisfactory. Middle-of-the-road and leftist groups both opposed the holding of separate elections on the grounds that adequate efforts had not been made to reach an agreement with the regime in North Korea, and also because they believed that a separate election would permanently divide the country.[20] They

[16] Ordinance 176, dated March 20, 1948.

[17] U.N. Document A/AC. 19/80, p. 114.

[18] *Ibid.*, p. 115.

[19] U.N. Document A/AC. 19/80, p. 115.

[20] The moderate Dr. Kimm Kiusic, then the Chairman of the South Korean Interim Legislative Assembly, told the Temporary Commission that "any Korean who talks about a South Korean unilateral government will go down in history as a 'bad egg' because once that term is used, the Communists in the North under the direction of the Soviet Union will establish what is called a 'People's Republic' or the 'People's Committee.' Then you

also felt that a free atmosphere for conducting elections did not exist in South Korea. These groups were joined by the rightist Kim Koo and his Korean Independence Party who opposed the elections on the ground that they would irreparably divide the country.

Active support of separate elections came only from rightist groups, particularly the organization of Dr. Rhee, the Society for the Rapid Realization of Korean Independence and the Han'guk (Korean) Democratic Party headed by Kim Sŏngsoo. Dr. Rhee had been agitating for many months for separate elections. It was the expressed view of these groups that separate elections were necessary because of the non-cooperation of the North Korean authorities,[21] and maintained that a sufficiently free atmosphere in which to conduct elections did exist in South Korea.[22]

Before registration for the elections took place, the American command launched a large-scale propaganda campaign to persuade the people to participate in the elections despite the opposition of the leftists and the middle-of-the-roaders. Tension mounted as the Communists opened a drive to disrupt the elections by sabotage and terrorism, though the Commission found that reports of such disorders were often "exaggerated" by the police.[23] Fire was used to fight fire, the government going so far as to label all non-rightists Communists. Extreme rightists organized themselves in all sections of the country to

---

will have two unilateral governments in this little space of something over 85,000 square miles. Not only that, but once such a thing occurs in history, it will go down forever, and it will be perpetuated; then you are responsible, and we are responsible for perpetuating the division of Korea into a Northern half and a Southern half. . . ." (U.N. Document A/575, Add. 2, p. 80).

[21] See U.N. Document A/575, Add. 1, p. 64, and the testimony of Dr. Rhee and Mr. Kim Sŏngsoo before the Commission, U.N. Document A/575, Add. 2, pp. 55-66 and pp. 96-102.

[22] In fact Kim Sŏngsoo (Han'guk Democratic Party) expressed the view that there was too much freedom, which permitted Communist activities, such as strikes, riots and assaults (U.N. Document A/575, Add. 1, p. 65).

[23] U.N. Document A/AC. 19/80, p. 115.

insure a favorable vote by legal or other means. Both right and left formed terrorist bands.

Most of the candidates for election to the National Assembly represented either the Han'guk Democratic Party or the Society for the Rapid Realization of Korean Independence, both rightist parties. Other candidates, while for the most part independent of party connections, were, of course, rightist sympathizers.[24] The Commission found that "independent" candidates in some instances were probably members of a major rightist party trying their luck against the official party nominees notwithstanding orders from their party headquarters in Seoul against it, or were actually rightist nominees running as independents because their parties feared that their official nominees "would be prejudiced by the local prevailing political situa tion." [25]

The Elections

To provide for the maintenance of law and order during the election period, the American command authorized the police to deputize large bands of "loyal citizens," called Community Protective Associations.[26] Registration totaled about 80 per cent of the electorate, although in many districts the roll of registrants included involuntary participants.[27]

The expected violence did not occur on election day. Ap-

[24] For a further analysis of the May 10 elections, see Benjamin Weems, "Behind the Korean Elections," *Far Eastern Survey*, June 23, 1948.

[25] U.N. Document A/AC. 19/80, p. 119.

[26] The Associations continued to be active after the elections and soon were violating civil liberties freely with police consent. After their terrorist acts became too obnoxious, the Military Government was obliged on May 22 to issue an order dissolving them. *Seoul Times*, May 26, 1948.

[27] An example of the pressure to which citizens were subjected in this regard noted by the Commission was that in some cases registration was taking place in local administrative offices where rice ration cards were also issued, so "that threatened confiscation of rice cards resulted, in some instances, in compulsory registration," and "that in the background of Japanese rule, the advice given by the police and youth organizations to register was regarded as a form of coercion." (U.N. Document A/AC. 19/80, p. 117.)

proximately 95 per cent of the registrants—or 75 per cent of all eligible voters—were reported to have voted.[28] The American command and the South Korean Interim Government described the elections as a great victory for democracy and a repudiation of Communism.[29] Many unofficial reports were less favorable, some observers maintaining that the elections had been fraudulently conducted in an atmosphere of terrorism. A more moderate view was that the elections were not in fact a free expression of the Korean will. In this connection it is to be noted that actual observation of the elections by the Temporary Commission was necessarily limited. The entire staff—national representatives and secretariat—of the Commission consisted of only about thirty persons, and it was on this group, divided into observation teams, that the Commission had to depend for a direct knowledge of the validity of the elections.[30]

The figures later released by the South Korean Interim Government concerning the casualties which attended the elections indicate that improper pressure had been exerted by officials and terrorist groups. Between March 29 and May 10, 589 persons were killed. They were classified as follows: 63 policemen, 9 members of policemen's families, 37 government officials and candidates for election, 150 civilians (presumably members of the Protective Associations), and 330 "rioters." [31] In addition

[28] *Ibid.*, p. 121.

[29] See "An Official Analysis of the Korean Election," *Far Eastern Survey*, June 23, 1948, p. 147.

[30] In its first hearing, the Temporary Commission discussed the use of U.N. elections observers with Brig. Gen. Wickerling, U.S. liaison officer with the Commission. General Wickerling pointed out that in the Saar plebiscite of 1935 and the Nicaraguan elections of 1930, the ratio of neutral observers to voters was one to 500. He also stated that even if as many as 500 observers were available to the Commission, the ratio would be about "one observer to every 10,000 voters." See U.N. Document A/575, Add. 2, p. 6. (Actually, on the basis of votes cast, the ratio here would have been one observer to every 14,000 voters.) The limited staff of the Commission makes any discussion of ratio as a factor in determining the real situation patently absurd.

[31] Statement by P. O. Chough, Director of National Police, as quoted in *Seoul Times*, June 4, 1948, p. 2.

there was much property destruction and personal injury. A complete list of arrests was not made public but, from the partial figures given out, it appears that upwards of 10,000 "rioters" were processed in police stations.

The Decision of the Commission

Following the elections, the Temporary Commission departed for Shanghai to prepare its report for submission to the General Assembly. In early June the Commission returned to Seoul to consult with the elected Assembly concerning measures for the establishment of a Korean government and the reunification of the country as called for in the U.N. resolution of November 14, 1947. The Commission accepted an invitation to attend a meeting of the Korean National Assembly on June 30. At this meeting, Mr. Miguel A. P. Valle of El Salvador, then Chairman of the Commission, informed the Assemblymen of the Commission's decision "that the results of the ballot of May 10, 1948 were a valid expression of the free will of the electorate in those parts of Korea which were accessible to the Commission." [32]

The Commission did not, however, immediately disclose its attitude toward the claims of the National Assembly to form what would be the national government of all Korea. J. L. Paul-Boncour, the French representative, stated in July that a unanimous report would be presented to the General Assembly of the United Nations when it convened in Paris for its third session in September, but declined to elaborate upon the nature of the report.[33] In effect, however, the Republic of Korea became the real government of Korea without waiting upon the decisions of the Temporary Commission. Under Rhee's leadership, the National Assembly acted with the cooperation of the American command to assume full responsibility for the organization of government in South Korea. On August 12, China extended formal diplomatic recognition to the Republic of Korea,[34] and

[32] U.N. Document A/AC. 19/80, Add. 1, p. 8.

[33] Associated Press dispatch from Seoul, July 21, 1948.

[34] A partial text of this document is given in U.N. Document A/AC. 19/80, Add. 1, p. 24.

on the same day the U.S. Department of State released a statement which amounted to giving *de facto* recognition to the new government.[35] On August 19, the President of the Philippines extended to the Republic of Korea "sincerest wishes . . . for the success of the new State of Korea. . . ." Thus the establishment of a government based upon the elections of May 10 was an accomplished fact well before the General Assembly was scheduled to meet in Paris.

The Commission was not able to adopt a final report until October 8, 1948.[36] This report showed that the Commission favored immediate unification of Korea under a regime stemming from the government which the May 10 elections had established in the southern zone.[37] The Commission then reported its approval of the conduct of the elections in the south, and expressed its criticism of the Soviet-sponsored government in the north.

The Commission took the stand that the Republic of Korea was entitled to its claim over all Korea and the recognition of this claim by the United Nations, because of its adoption of a democratic constitution, and because candidates of the Han'guk Democratic Party and the Society for the Rapid Realization of Independence had in many instances been unsuccessful in the elections, suggesting that a considerable opposition existed. The

[35] The text of this statement appears in *New York Times*, August 1948, p. 1. It named Mr. John J. Muccio, personal representative of the President to the Government of Korea, with the rank of ambassador. In this capacity, Mr. Muccio would assume duties previously performed by Joseph E. Jacobs as political adviser to the commanding general. On August 23, Lieut. Gen. John R. Hodge was succeeded as the Commander of U.S. Army Forces in Korea by Maj. Gen. John B. Coulter, formerly the commanding general of the Seventh Infantry Division in Korea. On January 1, 1949, the U.S. Department of State announced full American diplomatic recognition of the Republic of Korea. On March 21, 1949, President Truman named Mr. Muccio as the first ambassador to the Republic of Korea in accordance with an agreement between the two governments that their respective diplomatic missions should be raised to Embassy rank.

[36] U.N. Document A/AC. 19/80, Add. 1, p. 12.

[37] *Ibid.*, especially pp. 29-31.

Commission pointed out as an example of this fact that members of liberal leanings had been able to exercise influence in the early sessions of the National Assembly.[38]

Action of the General Assembly

The discussion and action within the General Assembly upon the report proceeded to follow much the same course as had the debate of a year before which had concluded in the establishment of the Temporary Commission. On December 6, the Political and Security Committee rejected a resolution offered by Czechoslovakia to invite representatives of the North Korea regime to participate in the discussion of the Korean question. Opponents said this measure was designed to bring about implicit recognition for the northern Democratic People's Republic. Later the same day the Committee adopted a Chinese resolution inviting representatives of the southern Republic of Korea to participate in its deliberations.

On December 7 Australia, China and the United States offered a resolution that was adopted by the Committee the following day by a vote of 41 to 6 and on December 12 accepted by the General Assembly. The resolution[39] declared that "lawful government with its seat at Seoul was established in that region of Korea which is south of the 38th Parallel occupied by the United States forces; and that it is the only such government in Korea." The resolution necessarily left to the United Nations member states to decide whether or not they would recognize the southern government. However, it emphasized that the Republic of Korea was "the only such government in Korea" because it was based upon free elections conducted in accordance with democratic methods. The resolution further urged that the occupying powers withdraw their military forces "as early as practicable," reiterating the attitude taken in Resolution II passed the year before. Implicitly this left to the United

[38] *Ibid.*, pp. 20-21.

[39] For the text of this resolution see Appendix A.

States to decide when it should withdraw its military forces.[40]

The resolution also called for the establishment of a "commission on Korea" to continue the work of the Temporary Commission and to carry out the provisions of the resolution. This Commission was to consist of representatives from the nations that were affiliated with its predecessor body, excepting Canada and the Ukrainian S.S.R. The resolution required the Commission to establish itself in Seoul within thirty days.

Among the duties imposed upon the Commission were a number of clauses which had appeared in the resolution of the year before relating to the use of its "good offices" to bring about the unification of Korea. The Commission was charged with observing "the actual withdrawal of occupying forces" and verifying "the fact of withdrawal when such has occurred." It was also "authorized to travel and consult throughout Korea." Yet it was a remote possibility indeed that the new Commission would be able to fulfill these provisions any better than had the Temporary Commission.

The Eastern bloc representatives in the Political and Security Committee lobbied for abolition of the Commission maintaining that it had not "attained the objectives" for which it was appointed. They charged that the Commission had failed to liquidate Japanese collaborationists, had not furthered the unification of the country, and had obstructed the establishment of conditions favorable to the democratic evolution of the country. It was further stated that the Commission had not contributed to the holding of free elections, but, on the contrary, had countenanced the repressive police measures of the American-sponsored Interim Government in South Korea in setting up a "reactionary government" which would in the end "smash the democratic forces within the Korean nation." [41] In view of the

[40] *New York Times*, December 7, 1948, p. 1.

[41] *New York Times*, December 9, 1948, p. 1. Subsequently, on April 8, 1949, the U.S.S.R. vetoed a resolution to recognize the Republic of Korea placed before the U.N. Security Council by China. The Soviet representative on the Security Council, Deputy Foreign Minister Malik repeated

deliberate Soviet obstruction of the work of the Commission, it could not be said that these criticisms were offered in good faith.

Nevertheless the Political and Security Committee was not an impartial arbiter in the Korean controversy as it had followed very largely the course of action urged upon it by the United States. The other most outspoken nation in favor of the measures adopted was China, who, because of her own internal difficulties with Communism, had reason to be profoundly interested in bolstering strongly anti-Communist regimes such as the rightist government of South Korea.

Thus the approach of the Political and Security Committee to the Korean impasse left little reason to suppose that it could contribute anything to the pacific unification of Korea under a single government. If there had ever been any real possibility of an amicable solution, it had not been developed by the United Nations Assembly. John Foster Dulles, the acting chief United States delegate to the General Assembly, made it clear that the United Nations action on Korea was to be taken as an endorsement of the wider opposition of American foreign policy to Communism. Dulles linked support of the South Korean government to the creation of a common front among U.N. members against "the methods of coercion, terrorism, and violence that are often employed by Communist governments and taught to party members." [42]

By the fall of 1948 there was little chance that either protag-

---

earlier Soviet contentions and declared that the whole subject of South Korea was an illegal and unconstitutional one, since it grew out of authorization of separate elections by the Interim Committee, or "Little Assembly," itself an illegal body, according to Malik. He also contended that the Seoul regime was composed of many former Japanese collaborators and that it did not represent the will of the people. He said that the only regime truly representative of the people in Korea was the Soviet-sponsored "Democratic People's Republic." Earlier the U.N. had rejected a Soviet bloc motion to recognize the North Korean government. See *New York Times*, April 9, 1949.

[42] *New York Times*, December 7, 1948, p. 39.

onist had much interest in any settlement that was not on its own terms. The establishment of separate governments, each recognized by its protagonist, was a strong disclaimer by both the United States and the U.S.S.R. of any further direct jurisdiction. The rigidities in the Korean situation of a year earlier had been institutionalized with the appearance of the Republic of Korea and the Democratic People's Republic of Korea.

THE REPUBLIC OF KOREA

Despite the favorable attitude which the United Nations Temporary Commission on Korea showed toward the Assembly elected in South Korea, it had continued after May 10 to consult several leaders who had boycotted the elections. While the Commission did not undertake these consultations for the purpose of selecting a national government, as orginally instructed by the U.N. General Assembly, Yasim Mughir of Syria, the temporary chairman, suggested that the new government invite the participation of the middle-of-the-road leaders. The elected leaders were outspoken in rejecting this suggestion.[43] The new government was formed, therefore, without reference to the U.N. Commission, and did not become a coalition regime as originally envisaged by UNTCOK.

On May 25, 1948, General Hodge issued a proclamation authorizing the Chairman of the National Election Committee to determine the date for the first meeting of the representatives elected on May 10. Accordingly, these representatives were convened as the National Assembly on May 31. Dr. Syngman Rhee was designated Temporary Chairman and he immediately proceeded to make his appointments, including members of the Constitution-Drafting Committee. The Assembly was obliged to work rapidly, as Military Government had planned a schedule which called for vesting the new government with its powers on August 15. Thus the constitution was adopted after only perfunctory debate on July 12.

[43] *Seoul Times,* May 15, 1948.

The Constitution [44]

The constitution of the new government showed traces of both the principles of responsible parliamentary democracy and of the American concept of an independent executive. In practice, however, the constitutional machinery meshed in a way that was peculiarly its own.

The most significant feature, however, was the power of the presidential office. The constitution specified that the National Assembly elect the president and the vice-president, and that the president in turn select the prime minister with the approval of the National Assembly. But while displaying the outward forms of responsible parliamentary government, it was obvious that the new government did not intend the presidency to be the passive office it is in the French system.

Both the indirectly chosen president and the popularly elected National Assembly were to hold office for four years. At first glance this feature might suggest mutually independent relationship like that of the American president and Congress. On closer inspection, however, it seemed that in the Korean political situation, characterized by the relative importance of individual leaders and the relative unimportance of parties, the government would often necessarily be constituted across party lines. In such a situation, the president really selected the cabinet. The fact that the legislature was a unicameral body also probably made it easier to control. The position of prime minister under the constitution appears to have been "first" minister and nothing more. Like the other ministers his tenure was to be at the pleasure of the president. The president, not the prime minister, was the real head of the government.

Certain other provisions of the constitutional framework also facilitated the concentration of authority. The most explicit of

[44] See also, Paul S. Dull, "South Korean Constitution," *Far Eastern Survey*, September 8, 1948, pp. 205-07. The text of the constitution has been reprinted in a number of places, i.e., in the U.S. Department of State pamphlet, *Korea, 1945 to 1948*, Washington, 1948, Far Eastern Series 28, pp. 77-95, and *Voice of Korea*, August 14, 1948.

these is Article 57 which confers upon the president broad "crisis" powers.[45] One writer has already pointed out the reasonable conclusions concerning this power.

> For the new state to meet the future without some machinery for rapid decisions would be to ignore the realities of the situation. Whether this clause will destroy "democracy" in Korea, only time will tell. It is a strong weapon in the hands of those impatient with democratic processes and dubious of the wisdom of legislative decisions.[46]

Article 803 established a Constitution Committee to consist of the vice-president as Chairman and five justices of the Supreme Court and five members of the National Assembly to rule on the constitutionality of laws. This provision suggests that the risks to the executive and the legislature of constitutional review were much less than under, say, the American and Australian systems. The participation of the legislature in decisions and the provision requiring a two-thirds majority to hold laws unconstitutional would appear to have permitted the constitution to be very loosely interpreted. Since the first president would appoint all of the justices of the Supreme Court, the hostility of judicial members of the Constitution Committee to the executive could be expected to be at a minimum.

[45] This article read:

"When in time of civil war, or in a dangerous situation arising from foreign relations, or in case of a natural calamity, or on account of a grave economic or financial crisis it is necessary to take urgent measures for the maintenance of public order and security, the President shall have the right to issue orders having the effect of law or to make necessary financial dispositions; provided, however, that the President shall exercise such powers exclusively if time is lacking for the convocation of the National Assembly."

The prototype of crisis powers, Article 48 of the Weimar constitution which permitted Hitler to circumvent the Reichstag, permitted the President to invoke it upon only the countersignature of the Chancellor. Article 57, however, hedges on permitting such facile application:

"Such orders or dispositions shall be reported without delay to the National Assembly for confirmation. If confirmation of the National Assembly is not obtained, such orders shall lose their effect, thereupon, and the President shall announce it without delay."

[46] Paul S. Dull, *Far Eastern Survey*, *op. cit.*, p. 206.

Another aspect of the constitutional structure which served to centralize authority were the provisions relating to local government to be found in Chapter VIII of the constitution. Article 96 states that local organizations shall "perform their administration within the framework of laws and orders and shall perform such additional tasks as are delegated to them by law." Thus the Republic of Korea was definitely a unitary form of government with local government existing at the suffrance of the national state.

Organization of the Government

On July 17 Rhee, as Chairman of the Assembly, signed the constitution as adopted by the Assembly. On July 20 he was elected by the Assembly to the presidency of the new government. The Assembly then elected Rhee's choice for vice-president, Lee Siyung, 80-year-old member of the old Korean nobility who defeated a strong, younger candidate representing a less conservative clique. In choosing a cabinet, Rhee ran into stiffer opposition. His first choice for premier, Lee Yoonyung, a young Methodist minister and acting chairman of the Chosun Democratic Party,[47] was emphatically rejected 132 to 59. The leader of the Han'guk Democratic Party, Kim Sŏngsoo, was supported by a large group in the Assembly but Dr. Rhee refused to accept him. A compromise was reached in the selection of General Lee Bumsuk, a former official of the refugee Korean government in China, and the head of the Korean National Youth Movement. Selection of the cabinet was completed by August 4.[48]

Prime Minister and Defense Secretary General Lee graduated from the Whampoa Military Academy and later became a friend of Chiang Kai-shek. Upon his return to Korea in late

[47] This party was composed largely of North Korean refugees residing in South Korea. Its chairman *in absentia* was Cho Mansik, the widely respected Christian leader reportedly held under house arrest in Pyŏngyang.

[48] A short biography of cabinet members is to be found in *Voice of Korea*, August 17, 1948. Also see Hugh Deane, "South Korea's New Premier," *China Weekly Review*, October 2, 1948, p. 113.

1945 he broke his connection with the provisional government and avoided political party ties. He was a forceful leader and an able administrator, although his passion for military order and discipline inclined him toward police-state methods. He was strongly anti-Communist and opposed any sort of compromise with the northern regime. His Youth Movement, created to provide a nucleus for a Korean army, received considerable support from the American Military Government; together with the Korean constabulary, it was part of the military arm being built to offset the Korean Communist army in North Korea.

Foreign Minister Chang Taiksang, a graduate of the University of Edinburgh in economics and political science, had served as a representative to the Paris peace conference of 1919. More recently he had been the chief of the Seoul metropolitan police under the South Korean Interim Government and a strong rightist Han'guk Party leader. Known as "the Tiger," he was efficient, eccentric, and often the object of bitter criticism from liberal and left-wing elements because of the brutal and terroristic methods of his police force.

Commerce Minister Louise Yim, American-educated organizer and leader of the Woman's Democratic Party, "represented" the Korean Democratic Assembly (Dr. Rhee's unofficial body) at the United Nations Assembly in 1947–1948. She was credited in Korea with having obtained U.N. intervention in the Korean question and appears to have been rewarded by the cabinet appointment. Her previous experience had been entirely in social work and education.

Minister of Finance Kim Duyun, also American-educated (Ph.D. in Economics, American University, Washington, D.C.), belonged to the old plutocracy and was a member of the Han'guk Party and previously of the Interim Legislative Assembly.

Minister of Transportation Min Hisik, a graduate of the University of Nevada, was the only carry-over without change of position from the South Korean Interim Government. He belonged to a once-noble family and was reputed to favor an anti-union labor policy and police-state methods of control.

Minister of Justice Lee In, Chief Prosecutor under the South Korean Interim Government, was a Japanese-trained lawyer who practiced in Korea under the Japanese. He was known for his patriotism, nevertheless, having served a jail sentence for his connection with the Korean Language Society.

Minister of Agriculture Cho Pongam was a former Communist who had split with the party leadership in 1946. Though he had renounced Moscow leadership, he had not foresaken his socialist ideas and favored a strong program of agrarian reform aimed at breaking up all landlord holdings. However, he had not had much experience with agriculture.

Minister of Education Ahn Hosang, a graduate of the University of Mannheim in Germany, had long previously been a philosophy professor. He lacked experience in administration or educational techniques, but, after liberation, became influential in party circles because of his vigorous campaigning for the extreme right.

Three other cabinet members, newly elected to the Assembly, were active party politicians. They were Minister of Social Affairs (and Labor) Chun Chinhan, a graduate of Waseda University, Japan, and a leader in the rightist Taehan labor union; Minister of Internal Affairs Yun Chiheung, American-educated in international law and a member of Rhee's Korean commission in Washington before the war; and Minister of Communications Yoon Sukkoo. Yun Chiheung, as Minister of Internal Affairs, succeeded to the control of the national police, formerly responsible to a Director who was under the authority of the Military Governor. This Director, Dr. Chough Pyung Ok, was named a "goodwill ambassador" to Washington and London by Rhee, who reputedly regarded Chough's power in South Korea as a threat to his own.

Appraisal

The Temporary Commission was inclined to believe that some of the opposition President Rhee encountered to his cabinet appointments in the Assembly indicated the existence of a reasonably strong liberal opposition.[49] Subsequent differences of opinion in the Assembly have borne out this observation. Some of this opposition, however, emanated from the extreme right, represented by the Han'guk Party, which sought to place its representatives in important posts in opposition to appointees of President Rhee.

The most important cause of criticism of the South Korean Interim Government had been the activities of the police and the suppression of civil liberties. Chapter II of the Constitution extended the usual civil rights to the people, and the U.N. Temporary Commission remarked with approval upon their inclusion.[50] However, Article 13 virtually gave the government a blank check to abridge these guarantees. It provided that

> Citizenship shall not be subjected to any restrictions on the freedom of speech, press, assembly and association *except as specified by law*. [Italics ours.]

A great impetus was given to the suppression of civil freedom by the Yŏsu rebellion in South Korea, which occurred during the latter part of October and early November 1948.[51] Rebel

[49] U.N. Document A/AC. 19/80, Add. 1, pp. 20-21.

[50] *Ibid.*, pp. 19-20.

[51] This rebellion broke out on the night of October 19, in the port of Yŏsu on the southern coast 200 miles southwest of Seoul, when a regiment of the American-trained constabulary revolted, killed the local police, and pushed on to seize the city of Sunchŏn (population 60,000), 20 miles to the north. Political prisoners were freed and sought revenge. On October 23 Sunchŏn was retaken and five days later loyal troops entered Yŏsu.

According to Republic of Korea sources, the rebellion had begun in a Communist cell of about 40 soldiers who precipitated an insurrection of the Yŏsu garrison, and, under the flag of the North Korean regime, captured Yŏsu and Sunchŏn. These sources said the rebellion was North Korea inspired and owed much of its strength to a Communist-disseminated report that all Korea had fallen. Direct information was, however, unobtainable by the press. It was noted that "While not imposing a direct censorship, the U.S. Army . . . evidenced a reluctance to inform the press on the progress of the fighting, attributing this attitude to lack of information." (Johnston dispatch from Seoul, *New York Times*, October 27, 1948, p. 9. Also see *Newsweek*, November 1, 1948, p. 34, on the same subject.)

forces overpowered local police and killed many. With the collapse of the revolt, the rebels were dealt with ruthlessly. Government forces displayed a brutal vengeance in handling prisoners and suspected dissident elements.[52] While attributing the revolt to Communist leadership and inspiration, informed parties acknowledged privately that police brutality and repression had attracted many civilian followers to the rebels.[53]

Premier and Defense Minister Lee was sharply critical of the methods of American recruitment for the constabulary, declaring that Korean leaders had warned that a lack of close investigation of recruits would make a "Trojan Horse" of the constabulary.[54] Rightist leaders cited, by contrast, the example of the carefully screened national police force of 30,185 men which was completely loyal. The police force was built along Japanese lines and a large part of its complement had served under the Japanese.[55]

After this incident, rumors of impending or actual invasion from the north were frequent. On one occasion North Korean troops dressed as civilians were reported to have crossed the 38th parallel near Chunchon and to have penetrated as far as Yŏngwŏl, a distance of fifty miles from the frontier. The report was without foundation. While some conceivably real threat of invasion from the north existed, there was no doubt that rightist sources lost little opportunity to play up and exaggerate the danger. The threat of invasion and provisions for security became pretexts for exerting pressure on many who were critical of the government.

During the first week in November approximately 700 persons

[52] See Carl Mydans, *Time*, November 8, 1948, pp. 32-33, and *Life*, November 15, 1948, pp. 55-58.

[53] *Life* (*loc. cit.*, p. 58) flippantly reported that the rebels were joined by many Koreans "who traditionally jump at a chance to attack their police and officials."

[54] *New York Times*, October 29, 1948, p. 19.

[55] Dr. P. O. Chough, then Director of National Police, told the U.N. Temporary Commission in February 1948 that 25 per cent of the men and 53 per cent of the officers held police positions under the Japanese. U.N. Document A/575, Add. 2, p. 117.

had been arrested for political reasons, including many prominent figures of very varied political affiliations.[56] A measure regulating press activities which was highly reminiscent of Japanese press regulations was enacted.[57] On December 1 in Seoul the chief of police plastered the city walls and bulletin boards with a proclamation asserting the "North Korea People's Army has already begun its invasion of South Korea" and that persons inciting disturbances would be shot on sight.[58] On December 7, the Minister of Education, Ahn Hosang, ordered the directors of all educational institutions to file detailed personal histories of all teachers. Ahn stated that "teachers who are Communists or inclined to the left or who do not make their beliefs clear will be excluded from any position in the educational field." Student committees were set up in schools to report students who were leftists or did not clearly support President Syngman Rhee's regime.[59]

The Temporary Commission also noted with satisfaction the inclusion of certain provisions in Chapter VI of the Constitution, entitled "Economy," as an indication of the influence of liberal elements.[60] Yet the expressed willingness in the Constitution to use the power of the state in directing the economy cannot be unguardedly accepted as the influence of more liberal political groups. Many of the adherents of the right are confirmed believers in both political and economic statism, and Rhee had expressed himself as being in favor of nationalized ownership

[56] *Voice of Korea*, December 15, 1948.

[57] The text of this law appears in *Voice of Korea*, *loc. cit.*

[58] The proclamation declared: "This is a dangerous agitation; from now on the police will, without hesitation, shoot anybody who scatters handbills or in any way incites people to riot. Citizens are requested not to stand too near these dangerous elements." United Press dispatch, Seoul, December 1, 1948.

[59] United Press dispatch, Seoul, December 7, 1948. One of the announced functions of the Students National Guard organized by Ahn in April 1949 to succeed the previous officially sponsored youth organization was "to investigate the thought trends of students in particular." *Seoul Times*, April 27, 1949, p. 3.

[60] U.N. Document A/AC. 19/80, Add. 1, pp. 20-21.

of many economic activities. Contrary to the opinions of Americans who thought the Rhee government a bulwark of private enterprise, informed observers reported that banking, public utilities, the railways, coal mining, and textile manufacturing, among others, would eventually be nationalized by the existing government. The Constitution left the question of the extent of nationalization to be determined later by law (Article 87).

The Constitution and the government of the Republic of Korea bore the impression of the personality of Syngman Rhee. The office of president seemed designed to fit Rhee's desire to exercise a strong personal rule. For many reasons Rhee could regard the Republic of Korea as his own handiwork. While in exile in the United States, he was elected president of the government formed by the ill-fated Independence Movement of 1919. When his widely reputed friendship with President Wilson failed to win a hearing for Korea at Versailles in 1919, he established a group with headquarters in Hawaii where he continued the agitation for independence, and later in Washington he organized the Korean Commission. When Syngman Rhee returned to Korea in October 1945, he was unquestionably better known among the people than any other leader.

Rhee's long activity on behalf of Korean independence, and his well-known hostility to Soviet Russia, made him the logical favorite of the American Army authorities for heading up a Korean regime. For a number of reasons, however, Rhee was unable to occupy the preferred position immediately. Many Americans objected to his reactionary methods and favored sponsoring Koreans who would be more conciliatory toward the Russians.

In December 1946, Rhee incurred the wrath of General Hodge for bypassing him and going to Washington to lobby for the establishment of a Korean government and the withdrawal of American troops. Rhee later had cause to repent having made this latter request.[61]

[61] During early August 1948 reports of American troop withdrawal, as part of the process of establishing an independent government, appeared

Eventually the heightening tension between the north and south brought the United States into Rhee's camp. Rhee was recognized as the rallying point of a strong regime which would be "safe" against Communist infiltration. Yet while Rhee was a determined leader and a forceful opponent of Communism, he did not succeed in creating a strong government. The U.N. Temporary Commission reported that "There was widespread criticism of the personnel appointed to the Cabinet and the opinion was expressed that the President had failed to utilize fully the best talents available." [62]

The cabinet of the new regime was composed largely of inexperienced political appointees. The strongest members, the Premier and Foreign Ministers, were noted for their dictatorial methods. Criticism was immediately directed against the new cabinet on the score that it was entirely "southern"—that is, drawn from southern families—although many "northern" Koreans then living in the south were available. This was a bitter criticism because it perpetuated an ancient political and social feud between northern and southern Koreans.

The cabinet was weakened by bitter internal controversies, and individual members worked assiduously to develop their own followings. Rhee himself was quick to suppress possible rivalry to his own power. Within three and a half months after the proclaiming of the Republic, Rhee had removed two of his ministers and a third had resigned as the result of a sharp intragovernmental controversy.[63] The Minister of Social Affairs, Chun Chinhan, resigned as the result of a dispute with the Internal Affairs Minister, Yun Chiheung.[64] Rhee removed the latter from office, and also Chang Taiksang, the Minister of

---

in the American press. In view of the threat from the north, President Rhee announced his government would formally request that U.S. forces remain a while longer. Associated Press dispatch, Seoul, August 5, 1948.

[62] U.N. Document A/AC. 19/80, Add. 1, p. 22.

[63] Min Hisik, the Minister of Transportation, had already resigned to accept the post of consul-general at Los Angeles.

[64] *New York Times*, December 25, 1948, p. 2.

Foreign Affairs, evidently because of their independent strength. Yun was given the post of special envoy to Manila, presumably as a ticket out of political life, as in the case of Chough Pyung Ok, the former national police director, who had earlier been named a "goodwill Ambassador" to Washington but refused. Former Foreign Minister Chang refused a similar appointment to London declaring that Rhee had "every means and power" to relieve him of his office but that he had "no right to ostracize" him "from his country." [65]

THE DEMOCRATIC PEOPLE'S REPUBLIC OF KOREA

A new constitution and a new flag purporting to apply to all Korea were announced in the north by the Korean People's Committee on May 1, 1948. In early July the North Korea regime announced that elections would be held on August 25 to a 572-member Supreme People's Assembly. Representatives of the population of South Korea were to occupy 360 seats in this body.[66]

The Soviet-controlled radio in Pyŏngyang subsequently announced that elections to choose these representatives had been held in South Korea "despite bitter South Korean police oppression." It was reported that candidates had been endorsed by 77.6 per cent [67] of the 8,681,745 persons [68] who were claimed to have voted in South Korea. The total vote claimed in South

[65] *Ibid.* Rhee subsequently named Ko Changli, former Vice-Minister of Foreign Affairs, as Minister; Lee Yun, youthful former minister without portfolio, as Minister of Social Affairs; and Shin Seungmo, a former captain in the British merchant marine, as Minister of Internal Affairs.

[66] V. Kudryavtsev, "The Constitution of a Renascent People," *Izvestia*, September 23, 1948, in *Soviet Press Translations*, University of Washington, Seattle, November 15, 1948, p. 615.

[67] Voting was presumably either for or against a single slate of Communist-approved candidates. For one account of the elections held on August 25 in North Korea see *Voice of Korea*, October 15, 1948.

[68] Soviet sources claimed that 85.2 per cent of all persons eligible to vote participated in these elections (*Soviet Press Translations*, November 1, 1948, p. 583, from *Izvestia*, September 23, 1948).

Korea seemed the less credible since it exceeded by 650,000 the number of votes polled in South Korea in the May 10 elections under conditions which gave every legal encouragement, and probably a good deal of illegal encouragement, to a large vote.

Although mass arrests of South Koreans for suspected activities in connection with these elections were reported to have occurred in South Korea,[69] no evidence was available to indicate that the number of persons who actually voted even remotely approached the figure of over 8,600,000 given. What actually did occur was a convention of 1,002 "delegates" purporting to represent the people of South Korea, which met in Haeju, just north of the 38th parallel, on August 22-24, to select 360 of their number to represent South Korea in the Supreme People's Assembly.

On September 3, the new Supreme People's Democratic Assembly ratified the constitution which had been announced by the People's Committee on May 1.[70] This constitution was mainly an embodiment of principles laid down in earlier acts of the People's Committee.[71] It reaffirmed the land reform, guaranteed equal rights to all citizens irrespective of sex, race, religion, education, or profession. It also accorded equal rights irrespective of property status, although many members of the propertied classes had already been excluded automatically by the provision which guaranteed the "final and irrevocable disenfranchisement of Korea's oppressors, whatever the basis of their previous domination." [72] Thus the guarantee did not apply to landlords who fled to South Korea and those who were regarded as Japanese collaborators for one reason or another.

Citizens were also guaranteed freedom of speech, assembly, press, and demonstration. Unfortunately, the practical meaning of these provisions cannot be ascertained, although the

[69] *Voice of Korea*, September 17, 1948.

[70] The length of this first session of the Supreme People's Assembly, September 2-10, 1948, suggests that it was even less a deliberative body than the National Assembly in South Korea.

[71] *Soviet Press Translations*, November 15, 1948.

[72] *Ibid.*, p. 616.

unanimity of governmental action alone suggested that political activity is as rigorously controlled as in other "satellite" countries. The Constitution also embraced provisions of the previous labor decree as to the principles of equal remuneration for equal labor, the right to rest, the right to education, the obligation to work, and the entitlement of the aged to retirement with pensions.

The Constitution confirmed the nationalization of all mineral and other resources of the earth, the forests, the waters, large-scale industry, banks, railroads, water and air transport, natural sources of power, communications, waterworks, all former Japanese property, and the property of all persons who actively collaborated with the Japanese. It also declared that citizens were guaranteed the right to the free development of small and medium-sized industry and commerce.[73]

The Constitution reaffirmed the principle of government at the village, county, and provincial level by people's committees, and established the Supreme People's Assembly as the highest legislative organ. As such the Supreme People's Assembly succeeded the former Assembly of People's Committees of North Korea over which Kim Ilsung had presided as chairman.

Kim assumed the successor post of premier in the new government and on September 10 the Supreme People's Assembly unanimously approved the three vice-premiers and twelve ministers Kim had selected for his cabinet.[74] According to a Pyŏng-

[73] *Ibid.*

[74] The complete membership of the cabinet named by Premier Kim Ilsung was as follows: Pak Heunyŏng, Vice-Premier and Minister of Foreign Affairs; Kim Chaik, Vice-Premier and Minister of Production; Chung Chungtaek, Minister of Planning; Park Ilwoo, Minister of Home Affairs; Chai Yongkim, Minister of Health; Kim Wonbong, Minister of National Defense; Park Moongyu, Minister of Agriculture and Forestry; Chang Chiyu, Minister of Commerce; Chu Yŏngha, Minister of Transportation; Chai Changik, Minister of Finance; Paek Namoon, Minister of Education; Kim Chungyu, Minister of Communications; Lee Syŏngup, Minister of Justice; Hŏ Sŏngtaik, Minister of Labor; Lee Pyŏngnam, Minister of People's Welfare; Lee Yŏng, Minister of City Planning; Lee Kyŏngno, Minister without Portfolio; and Miss Hŏ Chŏngsook, Minister of Culture and Propaganda.

yang broadcast, eight of the twelve ministers selected by Kim represented South Korea.[75] Evidently some of these eight ministers from South Korea had served in the previous People's Committee regime, for at least seven ministers in the new government had occupied similar positions in the earlier body.[76] The most prominent of the South Koreans in the new government was Pak Heunyŏng, who was appointed Vice-Premier and Minister of Foreign Affairs.

Although several other parties affiliated with the Korean National Democratic Front were represented in the cabinet, the great majority of the ministers were members of the Labor (formerly Communist) Party, as had been the case in the People's Committee regime. The chairman of the legislative organ of the new government, the Supreme People's Assembly, was Kim Tubong, the chairman of the Labor Party. Vice-Premier Pak Heunyŏng was the chairman of the South Korea Labor Party and Vice-Premier Kim Chaik was a vice-chairman of the Labor Party in North Korea. Miss Hŏ Chŏngsook, the propaganda minister and the only woman in the cabinet, doubled as the secretary-general of the central committee of the Labor Party. A number of other cabinet members also were Labor Party officials.

It seems reasonable to suppose that the coalition regime was a convenient fiction which involved no real sharing of power by the Labor Party with other political groups and that its main importance was as a device for giving the government a national rather than purely partisan appearance. The other groups in the Korean National Democratic Front were probably entirely tractable to the Labor Party.

The cabinet of the northern Democratic People's Republic differed in more respects than in political orientation from the

[75] *Korean Independence*, September 29, 1948.

[76] The names of the department heads of the People's Committee, together with brief biographical comments, are given in the handbook, *Inmin Winŏn-hoe Taehoe Chungyo Munhŏnjip* (Important Acts of the Assembly of the People's Committees of North Korea) previously cited.

cabinet of the southern Republic of Korea. The cabinet of the latter government drew heavily upon the small group of Western-educated Koreans for its personnel. The members of the northern body were generally much less cosmopolitan in their background. The college- and university-trained members of the northern body had received their education almost exclusively in Japan and Korea. Unlike numerous members of the South Korean cabinet who had resided for long periods in the United States and other Western countries, the members of the North Korean cabinet were generally not widely traveled outside the Far East, although several had visited the Soviet Union. Both governments contained many persons who had served prison terms under the Japanese and had been active against the Japanese regime at one time or another, although the northern government probably contained a larger number of actual revolutionaries.

The northern government was more closely patterned after the governmental structure of the Soviet Union than the southern government paralleled American political forms. Both showed some traces of Japanese institutions, however, though such a survival was much more marked in the southern government.

CHAPTER THIRTEEN

The Future of a Divided Korea

ECONOMIC ASPECTS

South Korea

As early as March 1947, the United States was considering the launching of an economic rehabilitation plan for South Korea alone.[1] This decision was subsequently shelved pending the outcome of the second meeting of the United States-Soviet Joint Commission which convened in Seoul from May until September 1947. An economic rehabilitation program was further delayed many months while the Korean question was being acted upon by the United Nations.

On December 10, 1948, the United States signed an economic aid agreement with the Republic of Korea under the Economic Cooperation program.[2] Under this Aid Agreement, the United States government agreed to assume the responsibility for assisting the Korean government in financing a long-

[1] Associated Press dispatch, Washington, March 20, 1947.

[2] See Economic Cooperation Administration, U.S. Department of State, Press Release 999, December 10, 1948, for the text of this agreement. Prior to the signing of this agreement United States and Korean representatives negotiated an "Initial Financial and Property Settlement" on September 11, 1948, disposing of assets acquired by the Military Government to the Republic of Korea. For text of this settlement see *Korea, 1945 to 1948, op. cit.*, pp. 104-12. For a detailed description of the ECA program for the U.S. fiscal year 1950 see the ECA-State Department publication, *Economic Aid to the Republic of Korea*, Washington, June 1949, 48 pp.

range economic rehabilitation program. Ambassador Muccio [3] also announced at the time the agreement was signed that shipments valued at 126 million dollars were already en route or on order under the previous army program.[4]

Economic assistance provided under army auspices has amounted to over 250 million dollars between September 1945 and August 1948,[5] and the Economic Cooperation Administration is obligated to meet both these requirements as well as to furnish funds for capital development with the amount allotted.

Food production has increased sufficiently to enable South Korea to become self-sufficient in foodstuffs and permit the anticipation of some food exports by 1950. The shortage of power resources is a serious problem. However, both thermal and hydro-electric facilities are in the process of expansion. By the spring of 1949 power production in South Korea had increased by 100 per cent over production of a year before. The sharply increasing coal supply has enabled industrial plants to increase production, with the result that output in March 1949 was the highest since the end of the war. However, power production is only about two-fifths of rated capacity, and further improvements in efficiency are expected to bring substantial additional increases in output.

The generally unfavorable mineral-resource position of South Korea, among other factors, makes an expansion of agricultural production important as a means of gaining exchange to purchase necessary imports. Without an expansion of electric power facilities, the development of a chemical fertilizer industry to replace North Korean sources of supply is not possible and agricultural production cannot be expanded except by the use of costly imported fertilizers.

During 1948 industrial production recovered somewhat from the low of the early post-liberation months, yet it is still far

[3] See p. 231, note 35.
[4] *New York Times*, December 11, 1948, p. 1.
[5] *Korea, 1945 to 1948*, *op. cit.*, p. 39.

below the production of the pre-liberation period. Many industries will require a great deal of new equipment before much use can be made of existing facilities. It will be necessary to spend a large share of the 150 million dollars allotted by ECA during 1950 for items such as petroleum, commercial fertilizer, bituminous coal, raw cotton, raw rubber, and for certain finished consumption goods, including possibly foodstuffs. Even if this were not the case, and all funds which the United States could reasonably be expected to allocate were to be spent upon the rehabilitation of existing mines and factories and the construction of production facilities no longer available because they are in North Korea, it is uncertain that a stable economy could be established permitting a standard of living even fully commensurate with the pre-war period.

To achieve economic stability, South Korea must be able to pay for its essential imports. To do so domestic production must be expanded both to reduce wherever possible the dependence upon foreign sources of supply and to provide exportable surpluses with which to pay for goods that cannot be produced at home.

The gap between South Korea's exports and its most rudimentary requirements for imports appears to be immensely difficult to close. Not only is the area poorly supplied with natural resources, but those resources it does possess are not well-developed. Manufacturing, which was always small, has become smaller since the liberation as equipment has worn out, and industries dependent upon processes carried on outside South Korea have been forced to suspend operations. Moreover, exportable surpluses formerly consisted chiefly of agricultural staples. These surpluses have been absorbed by the great expansion of the population in the last three years, and the resumption of a higher per capita rice consumption than that permitted throughout much of the Japanese period. It is probable, therefore, that South Korea will still be in need of outside economic assistance when the present three-year program expires. In fact, the maintenance of political stability in South Korea may depend upon the continued availability of such assistance.

The Truman Administration repeatedly emphasized the importance of American economic aid to the South Korean government. In urging Congress to pass the proposed $150,000,000 ECA appropriation for the U.S. fiscal year 1950, Secretary of State Acheson stated that the Republic of Korea government would fall "within three months" if economic assistance were not provided. Undersecretary James Webb advised Congress that, "without a continuation for the present of outside assistance . . . , the Korean economy would suffer a rapid and inevitable collapse." The Korean issue received scant attention in the first session of the 81st Congress, however, although there was apparently a prevailing sentiment for a "wait and see" attitude on Korean appropriations in the light of developments elsewhere in the Far East, notably in China. Consequently the ECA Korean appropriation, which was contained in the supplemental appropriation bill passed on the last day of the session (October 19, 1949), reduced the amount originally requested by the Administration down to $30,000,000 for a period ending February 15, 1950. On January 19, 1950, critics of the Administration's Far Eastern policy in the House of Representatives mustered sufficient support to prevent by a narrow margin the passage of a $60,000,000 appropriation for the period after February 15.

Outside Congress, in fact even in the Senate where a bill had previously been passed to extend further economic aid, the House vote was received with dismay. Press criticism of the defeat of the bill was strong, and Republican advocates of cooperation with the Administration in foreign affairs proved unwilling to have their party judged for this first open legislative breach in the bi-partisan foreign policy. The immediate and widespread unfavorable reaction to the defeat assured that the measure would be reconsidered. On February 9, the House of Representatives finally approved a 60-million-dollar ECA appropriation extending economic aid until June 30, 1950. The bill contained the striking proviso that aid should be terminated "in the event of the formation in the Republic of Korea of a coalition government which includes one or more members of the Communist Party or of the party now in control of the government of North Korea."

Some observers felt that Secretary Acheson was unwise when he stated before a Congressional committee that the American line of defense in the Far East extended from Japan through Okinawa and the Philippines and made no mention of Korea. Congressional opponents of further aid were able to infer from this statement that the United States was pouring money down a "rathole" in South Korea, their assumption being that the communist regime in the north would take over the south before long.

Opponents to the Korean aid bill tried to invoke against Korea the same arguments which the Administration had raised against further aid to Formosa. Even if plausible on military grounds, these arguments overlooked the numerous international obligations the United States had assumed toward Korea and the very direct role Americans were playing in that country's affairs. When it had become clear that the terms of the Moscow Declaration could not be carried out, the United States had blown life into the ambitions of these Korean leaders who advocated an independent government in southern Korea alone, if necessary. It was clearly unfair and unrealistic in terms of American self-interest to bring an anti-communist government into being in Korea and then fail to provide it with American moral and material support. Consequently American spokesmen pointed out that the inauguration of the South Korean Republic was not a final step in the execution of American commitments to establish a "free and independent Korea," but would have to be followed by economic assistance of a character which would enable South Korea to become a solvent trading partner in the world economy and to withstand communist ideological penetration from within as well as attack from without.

The United States had unwittingly made Korea the tragic victim of far-reaching international rivalries when it accepted the principle of a joint occupation of the country with the Soviet Union. However, continued American assistance to South Korea was justified on grounds other than atoning for the consequences of an over-optimistic expectation that agreement could be secured with the Soviet Union concerning Korea's future. The United States could not base its support of nations along the perimeter of the communist world entirely upon military estimates of their defensibility (as the erstwhile Congressional foes of economic aid to Korea appeared to advocate) if it was to prevent continuing communist expansion. These nations would certainly be chary of close cooperation with the United States if American support of their independence of action were to depend solely upon Washington's confidence in their powers of self-defense.

Nonetheless the difficulties which the Truman Administration experienced in securing the passage of the Korean ECA appropriation was a warning to the Republic of Korea that its anti-communism alone did not constitute a valid claim against the United States Treasury. It was evident that the South Korean government had not discharged its responsibilities in a manner that enabled Secretary Acheson and his aides to compensate for its military weakness by praise for its other achievements when asking for Congressional approval of further appropriations.

Only a few days before the aid bill was voted down by the House of Representatives in January, Dr. Philip C. Jessup, United States Ambassador-at-Large, had visited southern Korea in the course of a two-month survey of the Far East. Dr. Jessup had answered the criticism of Korean officials that United States aid to South Korea and other anti-communist states was "rather weak and scattered" and that the United States was only pursuing a "negative" policy in the Far East with some quite pointed criticism of the South Korean government. His replies to these attacks on American policy reflected the feeling among

U.S. experts in Korea that the South Korean government had been lax in its promotion of economic recovery and indicated American dissatisfaction with the severe restraints the government had recently imposed upon civil rights. Addressing the National Assembly, where observers noted that many opposition deputies were either in jail or out on bail, Dr. Jessup quoted from President Truman's Annual Message to Congress delivered on January 4, as follows: "Strength is not simply a matter of arms and force. It is a matter of economic growth and social health and vigorous institutions, public and private. We can achieve peace only if we maintain our democratic freedom and our firm belief in individual freedom." Dr. Jessup said that this applied not only to the United States but "elsewhere," as well. And while he noted that "extraordinary" progress had been made in some directions, he said, "there are certain other things which are within your power to accomplish which you have not done."

One publication, the *Voice of Korea*, published in Washington, declared on January 27, 1950, that the difficulties in passing the aid bill should remind the South Korean government that it did not have the United States "over a barrel," as some of its leaders seemed to believe, and that it could not survive as a "beggar" nation since continued American aid would be very temporary and uncertain. Ambassador Jessup had already sounded a similar warning when he said, "the problems of the Far East certainly will not be settled if you and other Far East nations sit back and hope the United States will cope with the situation alone."

The Future Role of Japan

It is a matter of great importance for South Korea that Japan has been quicker to resume normal patterns of economic activity than has any other Far Eastern area and that much of the impetus to a revival of Far Eastern trade will probably come from Japan. This is sufficient reason for apprehension that South Korea may be unable to prevent the re-establishment with Japan of close economic relationships in many ways similar to those of the colonial period.

Very favorable changes in the economic situation facing Korea internally and abroad are necessary to prevent the reappearance of the economic dependence upon Japan, and no such changes have occurred. Internal conditions obviously have not been favorable. Moreover, the recovery of other areas of the Far East besides Japan, which is necessary if Korea is to establish new external economic relationships, has been generally forestalled by shortages of capital and political uncertainty and civil conflict in many areas.

At the end of the war Allied policy favored reducing the industrial predominance of Japan in the Far East. Heavy reparations were planned which would have reduced the Japanese economy to a level of activity comparable with that for the years 1930–1934. More recently, however, this policy has been gradually abandoned and increasing emphasis has been laid on encouraging the industrial recovery of Japan, a decision which has caused no small amount of apprehension in other Far Eastern countries.

Korea, especially a weak Korea, has particular cause to fear an economically strong Japan. Korea, with an economy in no respect stronger than before the war, is vulnerable to renewed exploitation by Japan. The inference of further parallels of this sort between the past and the reasonably possible future offer ample cause for Korean fears since the loss of Korea's independence in 1905 was a direct result of Japan's economic penetration of the peninsula.

North Korea

North Korea is probably somewhat less dependent upon external economic considerations than South Korea. To be sure, North Korea is by no means self-sufficient and its maintenance of even a semi-modern economy depends upon its ability to import a great many types of goods, but the area will probably be less dependent upon foreign capital than South Korea.

Two features, one physical and one peculiar to the political regime in North Korea, are responsible for this apparently greater independence. In the first place, North Korea, by virtue of its superior resource position and greater heavy industrial development, can probably become a substantial exporter of industrial raw materials with much less further effort than will be required in South Korea. At the outset, then, North Korea appears to have more to offer an industrial producer country such as Japan, for example, and is not under such great need to pledge its future to foreign sources of capital.[6]

In the second place is the fact that the Communist regime is not likely to show hesitation in practicing economic autarky when that is necessary. As a matter of principle it cannot encourage non-Soviet capital development, and as a matter of practice it could not attract such capital. Also as a matter of practice the North Korea regime cannot expect much assistance from areas friendly to it. Its orientation toward the Soviet Union, Manchuria, and perhaps eventually China draws it into an association whose other members are also in urgent need of capital.[7] Therefore, whatever the cost in terms of retarded development and low living standards, North Korea will probably be

[6] It is of course possible that North Korea is liable to exploitation by the Soviet Union, perhaps even through such crude devices as the compelled surrender of stock in North Korean enterprises to the U.S.S.R. that has been recurrently rumored. There is no definite action either to substantiate or refute such reports, and if they have any foundation in fact, it is to be supposed that the information is a closely guarded secret.

[7] This is not to overlook the fact that there might be definite economic benefits which would facilitate North Korean development to be derived from association with these areas, particularly the rapidly developing Soviet East.

On March 17, 1949, the U.S.S.R. signed an agreement with the North Korean Democratic People's Republic by which it agreed to loan the latter 212 million rubles (about 40 million dollars at the over-valued official exchange rate) for the period July 1, 1949, to July 1, 1951. Interest is to accrue at the rate of two per cent per year, and the loan is to be repaid over a three-year period commencing in 1956. (See *Voice of Korea*, May 16, 1949.) This small sum cannot be expected to make much impression upon economic conditions in North Korea.

obliged to pay its way to a much greater extent than South Korea.

It is apparent that if the North Korean economy is obliged to conform to strict conditions of self-help, the standard of living in the area will be at a very low level for a long time to come. The fact that production in North Korea compares more favorably with pre-war levels than that in South Korea does not modify this conclusion, since consumer goods production is concentrated in South Korea. Furthermore, the flow of refugees into South Korea from the north testifies as much to the seriousness of the agricultural situation as to political dissatisfaction. Many parts of North Korea are deficit rice-producing areas and hence even a reattainment of pre-war levels of agricultural production is insufficient.

The Economic Future of Both Areas

Both North and South Korea are each in vital need of the goods produced in the other. North Korea needs to exchange its heavy industrial goods for the consumer goods and food which can be produced in the south. South Korea needs the producers' goods and the artificial fertilizer manufactured in the north to operate its consumer goods industries and to expand agricultural production. Nothing can contribute so directly to improving economic conditions in both areas as unrestrained economic relations between them, and no extreme of political or ideological differences can make sense out of permitting the 38th parallel to become a more complete barrier to commerce than are actual national frontiers when this action is so detrimental to both areas.

Unfortunately, purely political considerations have obscured the benefits of such trade. In the early occupation period, the political disagreement between the north and the south was allowed to determine the economic relations of the two areas with the result that there was no legalized trade between them. A regulated trade in South Korean supplies of raw rubber, raw cotton, and other raw materials in exchange for North

Korean wood pulp, fertilizer, and calcium carbide was permitted after December 1947. The persistent clamor of public opinion for open trade relations and a growing secret border trade encouraged the southern Department of Commerce to legalize all trade with the north on August 2, 1948. The transfer of governmental authority from SKIG to the Republic of Korea precipitated another crisis, and on September 27, 1948, the South Korean Minister of Commerce announced that the border was closed to all trade.[8] After about a month trade was resumed on a restricted basis until April 2, 1949, when it was terminated by the South Korean government. On April 23, 1949, a trade agreement was signed with Japan despite previous denials that such a pact was being considered and in the face of widespread opposition to it.[9]

Comparative Positions of the Two Areas

While the greater accessibility of South Korea to new capital may give the south a greater apparent prosperity for some time to come, the judicious use of this capital is jeopardized by the present dangerous preoccupation with short-run speculative profits at the expense of an interest in earnings based upon production. The government will have to show much greater vigor in opposing inflation and promoting stability if it is to combat this danger. Although the Economic Cooperation Administration is charged with supervising the use of aid it furnishes,[10] the actual determination of whether these expenditures

[8] *Seoul Union Democrat*, October 10, 1948, p. 1.

[9] For a further discussion of north-south commercial relations, see *Voice of Korea*, April 15, 1949.

North-south disagreement has permitted Hongkong traders to occupy a highly lucrative position as intermediaries in the exchange of northern and southern goods. Profits to these traders as high as one hundred per cent have been reported on South Korean goods brought to Hongkong and then transported in ships to the North Korean coast to be bartered for North Korean goods (Chicago Daily News Service dispatch from Hongkong, December 2, 1948).

[10] Economic Cooperation Administration Press Release 999, Korea-Aid Agreement, Article 3.

will inject real vitality into the economy of South Korea will depend upon the Koreans themselves. It remains to be seen if the government's present plans to control the use of foreign capital, as required by the Aid Agreement,[11] actually indicate adoption of a program of "austerity" to promote the greatest possible use of the limited amounts of resources obtainable from abroad and an equitable distribution of the burden of this privation. There has been a considerable feeling among South Koreans that the Rhee government is not attaching sufficient importance to capital development.[12] Should the division of the country be prolonged indefinitely, the strong measures being taken by the North Korean government to promote capital development and the generally more favorable resource position of the north may eventually make North Korea the more economically stable of the two areas.

POLITICAL ASPECTS

The Coalition Conference[13]

As early as December 1947 certain South Korean political groups were seriously considering convening a joint conference of northern and southern leaders to discuss the reunification of the country.[14] Dr. Kimm Kiusic, Mr. Kim Koo, and Mr. Lyuh

[11] *Ibid.*, Article 3, par. 6, and *Voice of Korea*, November 30, 1948.

[12] There was some sharp criticism of the appointment of Miss Louise Yim as Minister of Commerce and Industry. Miss Yim's appointment despite her lack of business experience was interpreted as a sign that the government was failing to attach proper importance to economic development. Miss Yim was subsequently accused of nepotism in the appointment of her subordinates and formally charged with accepting bribes. Public indignation over her conduct compelled President Rhee to remove her from office in April 1949.

[13] For information concerning the Coalition Conference see numerous news dispatches from Korea and especially the *Seoul Times*, April and May 1948. See also *Korean Independence*, May 5, 12, and 19, and June 16 and 30, 1948, and U.N. Documents A/AC. 19/80, pp. 55-59, and A/AC. 19/80, Add. 1, pp. 25-27.

[14] U.N. Document A/575, Add. 2, p. 83.

Woonhŏng became actively engaged in promoting such a plan. After the U.N. Temporary Commission agreed to observe elections in South Korea, the North Korea People's Committee invited many of the political leaders in South Korea (not including Dr. Rhee) to attend a coalition conference in Pyŏngyang to discuss the formation of a government. This invitation immediately drew the fire of the American command and of most of the southern rightist elements, who denounced it as a Soviet attempt to seize countrywide power.

Despite such opposition, more than fifty political leaders in South Korea attended the conference. The most distinguished of these were Dr. Kimm, the liberal chairman of the Korean Interim Legislative Assembly and leader of the Nationalist Independence Federation; Kim Koo, rightist former president of the Korean Provisional Government in Chungking, and head of the Korean Independence Party; Choi Tongo, rightist vice-chairman of the Interim Assembly; Hong Myungki, liberal head of the Democratic Independence Party; Lyuh Woonhŏng, liberal chief of the Socialist Democratic Party and brother of the famous patriot Lyuh Woonhyung, who had been assassinated the year before. The great common ambition of these men was to reunite their country.

The Coalition Conference met on April 22 and 23, and was attended by 545 delegates from both North and South Korea. South Korea was represented by 240 persons. The Conference passed a resolution calling for the formation of a unified Korean government, the rejection of dictatorship and "monopolistic capitalism," the immediate withdrawal of American and Soviet occupation troops, and voiced opposition to the establishment of foreign military bases on Korean soil. This conference was followed by a meeting of top-ranking leaders, notably Kim Il-sung, chairman of the North Korea People's Committee, Kim Tubong, North Korea party chief, Kimm Kiusic, and Kim Koo, who issued a statement on April 30, demanding the immediate withdrawal of foreign armies, opposing civil war, proposing the formation of a coalition government and the holding of a national election, and denouncing the forthcoming elections in South Korea.

Upon their return in late April and early May the South Korean delegates, who were outspoken in approval of what they referred to as the moderate views and unquestionable patriotism of the North Korean leaders, reported favorably on conditions in North Korea. However, General Hodge, the American commander, warned the people of South Korea against heeding the counsel of these men and suggested that they were "blind men" who had been "baited by the Communists." Under the circumstances, the unity efforts of the North and South Korean leaders proved abortive. Kim Koo, Kimm Kiusic, and their associates held a series of meetings after the May 10 elections in the south to formulate a course of action, and decided that, since the American command and the U.N. Temporary Commission so vigorously opposed further consultative steps between leaders of North and South Korea, any direct action should be postponed. In late June North Korean leaders convened a second coalition conference in Pyŏngyang to establish the Democratic People's Republic of Korea. Many of the South Korean leaders who had participated in the first conference in April declined to attend and issued a declaration denouncing this second conference as illegal and contrary to promises of North Korean leaders that they would not set up a separate government.

On the eve of the inauguration of the Republic of Korea, one final attempt was made by a South Korean group to promote joint north-south efforts at unification. On August 3, eighteen members of the newly-elected National Assembly introduced a motion urging the establishment of a North and South Special Unification Committee to explore all the possibilities for achieving the unification of the country. The motion was not carried.[15]

[15] U.N. Document A/AC. 19/80, Add. 1, p. 27.

Political Polarization

The materialization of separate governments on each side of the 38th parallel, each strongly supported by one of the occupying powers, put an effective end to organized unification efforts. This situation was the direct outcome of more than two years of disagreement between the two occupying powers and the result of the Korean demand for greater autonomy. Owing to the circumstances of the Japanese surrender, recounted in detail in earlier chapters, the division of Korea became inevitable. The final steps in that direction were taken under the guidance of the United Nations after the United States presented the problem to it for action.

That each regime was anathema to the other was abundantly clear. The North Korea radio delivered an endless stream of invective against the Republic of Korea in the south. Northern propaganda derided the southern government as the "reactionary" puppet of American capitalists who sought to make Korea the "springboard" of American "imperialism." In the south the leaders of the northern regime were labeled as traitors who had sold out their country for the Soviet Union.[16]

There was a widespread feeling among Americans in Korea that the open allusions to conflict coming over the radio from Pyŏngyang were not idle threats and that invasion was imminent. Such a feeling was not new, although there was markedly greater tension. Since the beginning of the occupation there had been some apprehension throughout the American command as to Soviet intentions. Unquestionably there was an equally strong suspicion in North Korea of American intentions. However, in spite of rival claims to sovereignty over the peninsula and in spite of the poor prospects for amicable settlement, open conflict did not seem to be an immediate prospect.

[16] For example, see the statement regarding North Korea in President Rhee's inaugural address. Reproduced in *Korea, 1945 to 1948, op. cit.*, p. 97.

Military Strength

In a military sense the North Korea regime was undoubtedly the stronger at the outset, but it was rapidly being overtaken by the South Korean government. Estimates vary as to the North Korean army, but a reasonable figure is 150,000 men.[17] This army had been organized, equipped, and trained by the Soviets and was reported to be in excellent fighting condition.[18] North Korea was also reputed to have a military alliance with the Communist government of Manchuria.

In South Korea, the nucleus of an army was formed by the American command in what was called the Korean constabulary. Before the assumption of administration by the Republic of Korea, the reported size of this army was 26,000 men. However, it was rapidly enlarged. The enlistment program, begun May 1, 1948, was to continue until the "quota" was reached. In addition to the constabulary, several young men's organizations, such as General Lee's Youth Movement and the Daidong Youth Corps of General Lee Chungchun, have provided military training for rightist youth. In October 1948 the former organization was reported to have a membership of one and a quarter million.[19]

At first the Republic of Korea depended heavily upon American military support for its defense. Reports from South Korea in late 1948, however, indicated that a stronger force was being developed. The loyalty of the police in the Yŏsu rebellion was cited by rightist leaders as an example of the effectiveness of Korean methods of organization and discipline. Increased confidence in South Korea's military strength was apparent in

[17] James Stewart, Chief of Civilian Information of Military Government in South Korea, was quoted in an Associated Press dispatch, Washington, D.C., July 26, 1948, as setting the total at 125,000 although some persons have estimated as high as 500,000.

[18] People's Army, Home Guard and Peace Preservation Corps units made up the bulk of the northern forces. The People's Army received superior training and equipment from the Russians.

[19] *New York Times*, October 10, 1948, p. 19.

the greater boldness with which southern officials spoke of the northern regime.[20]

Troop Withdrawal

A recurrent issue between the United States and the U.S.S.R. was the proposal first made by the Soviet Union just prior to the introduction of the Korean problem into the United Nations that the two occupying powers make a simultaneous withdrawal of their troops. In the United Nations discussion on Korea in 1947, the U.S.S.R. reiterated this proposal, suggesting the withdrawal of foreign troops before the end of the year. The General Assembly resolution rejected the Soviet proposal and approached the issue more circumspectly, proposing that troops be withdrawn "as soon as practicable." On September 20, 1948, the Soviet Foreign Ministry announced that the withdrawal of all U.S.S.R. forces from Korea would be accomplished by January 1, 1949, and invited the United States to do likewise.[21] The proposal was received with some surprise in American quarters but interpreted to mean that Moscow believed that the North Korea regime now had sufficient military strength to stand independently.[22] President Rhee declared that he believed the United States would not be lured into the "Soviet game" and would not agree to any Russian proposals concerning Korea.[23] The United States continued to adhere to the position set forth in the General Assembly resolution of 1947, which was in substance repeated in the 1948 resolution. On December 30, 1948, the Soviet government announced it had completely withdrawn its troops from North Korea.[24] On July 8, 1949, the

[20] Foreign Minister Chang declared that the South Korea government would not hesitate to go into action against traitors in the north to recover "lost territory." He also stated that Koreans in the north "will be dealt with" if they continue to support the Communist-dominated government of North Korea. United Press dispatch, Seoul, December 18, 1948.

[21] The text of this note and that of the United States reply are given in *Korea, 1945 to 1948, op. cit.*, pp. 114-16.

[22] *New York Times*, September 20, 1948, p. 1.

[23] *Ibid.*

[24] Troop withdrawal was reported to have been completed on December 24, 1948. *New York Times*, December 31, 1947, p. 4.

U.S. Ambassador to Korea informed the U.N. Commission "that the withdrawal of the U.S. military forces in Korea was completed on June 29, 1949, and the U.S. military occupation organization, known as 'USAFIK,' was deactivated as of midnight, June 30, 1949." [25]

Joint Occupation in Retrospect

Developments within the two zones during the occupation placed great difficulties in the way of unification then and in the future and led Korea almost inexorably into perpetuating the American-Soviet conflict in its own affairs. In the north a Soviet prototype Korean regime was established very early in the occupation, which lost no time in initiating social revolution.

In many respects the Korean economy, suffering from a feudal agriculture and Japanese exploitive colonialism, demanded severe measures. The larger part of Korean industry, developed by the dispossessed Japanese, made a neat package for nationalization. Agriculture, carried on by innumerable small units under conditions of primitive back-breaking labor, did not make such a neat package. Evidently agriculture was not considered "ripe" for collectivization, which in the Soviet experience followed the introduction of tractor and machine technology to agricultural operations, and, instead, North Korea's leaders were content with less ambitious, but probably more popular, agrarian reforms. In evaluating the North Korean regime this accomplishment must be discounted against the lack of true political freedom and democratic self-expression inherent in the essentially one-party bureaucratic system of government that has been established.

Although developments followed a less steadfast course in the

[25] U.N. Document A/936, Add. 1, Volume II, Annexes, p. 36. As of June 30, 1949, the only U.S. troops remaining in Korea were 50 Air Force personnel required to operate Kimpo Airport in Seoul until civilian administration could be instituted and the Korean Military Advisory Group under the command of Brig. Gen. W. L. Roberts with an authorized strength of 500 officers and men. These and other advisory groups and the U.S. Embassy comprised the American Mission in Korea (AMIK).

American zone than in the north, they must nevertheless be accepted as substantially representing the character of the occupation. But while the American occupation is to be generally held accountable for the course of political developments in the south, the regime which came to power was not notably amenable to American ideals.

Aside from an expressed intention to further the establishment of a Korean government, there seemed to be little underlying continuity in American policy during the three-year period. Developments were much slower to crystallize in the south, and even the objective of constituting a Korean administration was realized much later than in the north. This was in part due to an unwillingness openly to favor any particular political group and prejudice public opinion and to a reluctance to establish a regime which might complicate attempts to unify the country. It was also attributable to the almost impromptu way in which the occupation was undertaken with very little prior preparation for the immense problems that were to confront the United States in Korea. The production of a viable democracy in a country which had been politically dead for thirty-five years demanded more positive encouragement than the occupying force was prepared to give. In the absence of uninterrupted and definitive guidance upon matters of policy by Washington, the occupation authorities were often so uncertain and cautious about inaugurating definite policies as to appear dominated by the situation.

As a consequence of these factors there was a great deal of inconsistency in such policies as did materialize. The otherwise commendable objective of sponsoring the South Korean Interim Government as a moderate regime was simultaneously undermined by the failure to curb certain rightist activities which were certainly not conducive to free political development. This inconsistency was, moreover, not entirely the result of weakness but, at times, also of a conscious pursuit of cross-purposes such as the direct support that Military Government gave the National Youth Movement which many persons have felt was an implied endorsement of strong-arm political action. Such strange contrasts in the policies pursued were not so much the bland cynicism they may have seemed as military caution reacting to the indecisiveness of the general situation at the expense of political objectives. Increasingly occupation policy seemed to acquiesce in favor of the extreme rightist groups, which appeared to offer greater security by virtue of their superior organization and their openly hostile attitude toward the Communists.

The importance of economic reform for the development of political democracy in a country such as Korea did not seem to be adequately reflected in occupation policies. Between the two landmarks of reform in the occupation period, the reduction of tenants' rents very early in the occupation and the distribution of former Japanese agricultural lands to tenants near the close of the period, very little progress was made. The United States stood ready to be generous about supplying Korea with financial assistance once the country had an established government, but it was apparently unwilling to make material changes in the existing social-economic pattern which could help to free the people from political manipulation through the feudal agricultural system. The general absence of any positive economic policies was evidently as much due to the extent to which certain highly-placed occupation officials were captivated by the passive philosophy of government as it was to indecisiveness.

The Prospects for Unification

Future developments in Korea will depend in large measure upon the extent to which the two regimes move toward reconciliation or into deeper antagonism. The former course is not impossible in view of the tremendous power of patriotism among all Koreans. It is, however, not only beset by the deep distrust and hostility with which both the northern and southern governments regard each other. The situation continues to be immensely complicated by the conflicting positions of the United States and the U.S.S.R., even though the establishment of legally independent governments has removed these two powers from the role of direct protagonists in the Korean problem.

It is also, of course, quite conceivable that an improvement in U.S.-Soviet relations may take place which could probably still produce the unity of Korea. In this connection it is also possible that an improvement in U.S.-Soviet relations could commence in Korea. The fact that the "cold war" has reached an advanced form in Korea with the establishment of separate fully recognized governments does lend some logic to looking toward Korea for signs of a turning point in international relations.

Moreover, the United Nations Commission on Korea might actually be able to induce the use of its good offices for the mediation of the Korean problem. There is little optimism for this prospect alone, however, since the Commission has almost no chance of becoming an instrument of negotiation unless a great and unforeseeable change occurs in Soviet policy within the United Nations toward the Commission.[26]

Furthermore, except for recurrent speculation from unofficial sources that the Far East will be the place to watch for new developments in world affairs, there is little to suggest that Korea might be in the vanguard of either rapprochement or further tension in the United States-U.S.S.R. relations. Unless such a material shift of the Far East into a position of uppermost importance for the United States and the Soviet Union

[26] In the conclusion to its report published in August 1949, the Commission noted that, "The world-wide antagonism between the Union of Soviet Socialist Republics and the United States of America continues to be . . . one of the basic factors underlying the present difficulties. Without a new effort by those powers to reach agreement on the question of Korea, no substantial progress towards the achievement of unification on the basis of the principles approved by the General Assembly can be made. . . . The present Commission, like its predecessor, must place on record an acknowledgement that the situation in Korea is now no better than it was at the beginning, and that it has not been able to facilitate the achievement of the objectives set by the General Assembly." See Appendix A for the full text of the conclusions of the Commission.

should occur, it is not probable that the Korean problem will do more than continue to tag along in the general trend of international developments.

The international situation and the conflicting ideologies involved made a paradox of the liberation of Korea. At one and the same time liberation extended the promise of the freedom for which the country had sought so long, and created the division of the country which has become its despair. The great majority approached each new crisis of the occupation period hoping some new solution could be found which would refute the ironic conclusion that national independence was only to be had at the price of the country's dismemberment. Both for reasons of patriotism and because their personal welfare critically depends upon it, Koreans will never cease to hope for their country's unity, although the present prospect is of prolonged and deepening antagonism.

APPENDICES

Appendix A

SELECTED DOCUMENTS RELATING TO KOREAN FOREIGN RELATIONS

DOCUMENT NO. 1

Extract Relating to Korea from the Moscow Agreement, December 27, 1945[1]

III. KOREA

1. With a view to the re-establishment of Korea as an independent state, the creation of conditions for developing the country on democratic principles and the earliest possible liquidation of the disastrous results of the protracted Japanese domination in Korea, there shall be set up a provisional Korean democratic government which shall take all the necessary steps for developing the industry, transport and agriculture of Korea and the national culture of the Korean people.

2. In order to assist the formation of a provisional Korean government and with a view to the preliminary elaboration of the appropriate measures, there shall be established a Joint Commission consisting of representatives of the United States command in southern Korea and the Soviet command in northern Korea. In preparing their proposals the Commission shall consult with the Korean democratic parties and social organizations. The recommendations worked out by the Commission

[1] Department of State Bulletin, December 30, 1945, p. 1030.

shall be presented for the consideration of the Governments of the Union of Soviet Socialist Republics, China, the United Kingdom and the United States prior to final decision by the two Governments represented on the Joint Commission.

3. It shall be the task of the Joint Commission, with the participation of the provisional Korean democratic government and of the Korean democratic organizations to work out measures also for helping and assisting (trusteeship) the political, economic and social progress of the Korean people, the development of democratic self-government and the establishment of the national independence of Korea.

The proposals of the Joint Commission shall be submitted, following consultation with the provisional Korean Government for the joint consideration of the Governments of the United States, Union of Soviet Socialist Republics, United Kingdom and China for the working out of an agreement concerning a four-power trusteeship of Korea for a period of up to five years.

4. For the consideration of urgent problems affecting both southern and northern Korea and for the elaboration of measures establishing permanent coordination in administrative-economic matters between the United States command in southern Korea and the Soviet command in northern Korea, a conference of the representatives of the United States and Soviet commands in Korea shall be convened within a period of two weeks.

DOCUMENT NO. 2

Aims of the United States Delegation; Statement by Lt. Gen. John R. Hodge, Head of the U.S. Delegation, Joint American-Soviet Commission, March 11, 1946 [2]

On the eve of the convening of the Joint Commission, it is considered appropriate to state the aims of the U.S. delegation in the Joint Soviet-American Commission and the steps taken thus far by the American Command to prepare for the achievement of these aims.

First and foremost, it has been the object of the American

[2] *Voice of Korea*, April 6, 1946, Washington, D.C.

Forces to establish and perpetuate the freedoms of speech, assembly, religion and press in Korea. These freedoms are not mere words to be used to gain political favor. They represent principles on which any genuine democracy must be based and are as old as democracy itself. Furthermore, they are absolute and not relative or subject to exceptions. They apply to all democratic persons, all democratic schools of thought, all democratic parties, no matter how small their following or whether or not their programs may correspond to the ideas of the existing authorities. Thus in South Korea it has been the American policy to permit all democratic groups, whether moderates or extremists, capitalist or communist to establish their own parties, hold their own meetings, broadcast their own speeches, propagate their own ideas and philosophies and publish their own newspapers without censorship, restriction or special privilege. These freedoms are basic in the American idea of democracy. They are also what we believe the vast majority of the Korean people want, and it is what the American delegation of the Joint Commission wants to help the Koreans to attain throughout their entire country.

The purpose of the Joint Commission as stated in the Moscow Communiqué is to assist the formation of a provisional Korean government and to undertake the preliminary elaboration of appropriate measures to that end. It is also the task of the Joint Commission, with the participation of the provisional Korean democratic government and of the Korean democratic organizations, to work out measures for assisting the political, economic, and social progress of the Korean people, the development of democratic self-government and the establishment of the national independence of Korea. The Communiqué specifies that in preparing their proposals the Commission shall consult with the Korean democratic political parties and social organizations.

It is of course impossible to say at this time the precise manner in which the details will be worked out, since this is a matter to be determined by the Joint Commission and approved by the four great powers. However, it is the view of the American delegation that one of the primary requisites for accomplishing the Commission's tasks is the early unification of

Korea both economically and politically. Until the economic entity of the country has been restored and the effects of the 38° parallel eliminated in the internal functions of Korea and until all democratic elements of the country have freedom to hold meetings, to confer among themselves, to propagate their ideas by speeches, by radio and by the press, and to organize parties, recruit members, and carry on political activities not only in North and South Korea separately, but between the two areas, it is not considered possible to form a genuinely representative democratic government. In the carrying out of its function as part of the Commission it is the intention of the American delegation to travel throughout the country and to confer freely with representatives of democratic political and social organizations. It is the American view that Korean political leaders of all democratic parties both in the north and in the south should enjoy the same opportunities.

In its efforts to assist in forming a provisional government for Korea, it is not the purpose of the American delegation to bring about a government of any particular group or wing. It is their purpose to see that a government that corresponds to the views of the majority is established. The programs thus far published by the political parties in Southern Korea differ considerably from those of the leading parties in America, but these programs have not been opposed nor will they be opposed by the American authorities so long as they represent the views held by most of the truly democratic Koreans. At the same time it is the earnest intention of the American delegation to prevent the domination of Korea by small minorities, no matter how vocal and well organized they are or how energetic they may be in their political activities.

This statement is to present the attitude of the American members of the Joint Commission in solving the problems of Korea. The Soviet members of the Commission represent another great nation that fought for liberation of Korea from the Japanese, was a signatory to the Moscow Agreement and is greatly interested in making Korea an independent democratic nation. Therefore, it is safe to assume that the two delegations will work together harmoniously and in a truly cooperative effort to accomplish the aims expressed in that agreement.

DOCUMENT NO. 3

Aims of the Soviet Delegation; Statement by Col. Gen. T. F. Shtikov, Head of the Soviet Delegation, Joint American-Soviet Commission, March 20, 1946 [3]

General Hodge, gentlemen, our Joint Commission representing the American and Soviet Commands is called upon to carry out the historic decisions of the Moscow Conference of the Foreign Ministers of the Soviet Union, the United States of America and the United Kingdom pertaining to Korea. These decisions express the good will and the wishes of the Great Allied Powers to assist by all means in the rehabilitation of an independent Korea, and in the creation of conditions for the development of this country on a democratic basis.

The great armies of the United States of America and the Soviet Union, having crushed the Japanese Imperialists, have forever eliminated Japanese domination in Korea and liberated the Korean people.

Korea has entered a new stage of her development—a stage of national rebirth and re-establishment of state independency.

Gentlemen, the people of Korea with their ancient culture, vividly expressed national self-consciousness, year after year suffering hardships and the humiliation of colonial slavery. This people deserves the best future possible. With their blood and innumerable sufferings, the Korean people earned the right for independence and a free way of life.

The Soviet people warmly supported this right of the Korean people. The Soviet Union has always championed and will always champion their self-determination and free existence of any nation, without exception.

As all of us are convinced, the people of Korea are bent upon and have already shown their determination to create, with the help of the Allied Powers, a free democratic Korean government, friendly to all the freedom-loving nations.

The great aims of creating a democratic independent Korean state have brought to life wide political activity of the whole of the people of Korea.

[3] *Ibid.*

The Korean people have formed their democratic parties, public organizations, people's committees as organs of democratic self-government.

However, in the way of gradual democratization of the whole of the internal life of the Korean people, there stand serious difficulties, brought about by the furious resistance of reactionary and anti-democratic groups and certain elements whose object is to undermine the work of creating and firmly establishing a democratic system in Korea.

The task of the United States-Soviet Commission is to help the Korean people to create a provisional Korean democratic government capable of fulfilling the tasks arising from the democratization and reconstruction of the country.

The future provisional Korean democratic government must be created on a basis of wide unification of all the democratic parties and organizations, supporting the decisions of the Moscow Conference of the Ministers of Foreign Affairs.

Only such a government will be able to abolish entirely the remnants of the former Japanese domination in the political and economic life of Korea, to launch a decisive battle with reactionary anti-democratic elements inside the country, to carry out radical measures in the rehabilitation of economic life, to give political liberties to the Koreans and to fight for peace in the Far East.

The Soviet Union has a keen interest in Korea being a true democratic and independent country, friendly to the Soviet Union, so that in the future it will not become a base for an attack on the Soviet Union.

The task of the Joint United States-Soviet Commission deriving from the decision of the conference of the three ministers concerning Korea consists also in working out, with the participation of the provisional Korean democratic government and assistance of Korean democratic organizations, the measures of aid and assistance with respect to trusteeship in political, economic and social progress of the Korean people and the development of democratic self-government and in establishing the sovereign independence of Korea. Such temporary trusteeship corresponds with the fundamental interests of the Korean people, inasmuch as it assures the condition of a most rapid national reconstruction and a revival of independence on a democratic basis.

General Hodge, concluding my speech, I wish on behalf of the Soviet delegation, to extend my sincere greetings to you and your distinguished delegates, and to express my deep gratification that we shall work together with the representatives of the American command in the interests and for the good of the Korean people.

I am fully assured that our joint work will proceed in a spirit of mutual understanding and friendship and that we shall successfully and honorably fulfill the will of our governments, expressed in the decisions of the Moscow Conference of the Foreign Ministers concerning Korea.

DOCUMENT NO. 4

Secretary of State Marshall to Foreign Minister Molotov, April 8, 1947 [4]

I wish to call your attention to the situation in Korea. The representatives of the Soviet Union and the United States on the Joint U.S.-U.S.S.R. Commission in Korea have been unable to make progress toward the establishment of a Korean Provisional Government. It has been nineteen months since the Japanese surrender, yet Korea has profited little. The country is divided into two zones. The Soviet Commander in Northern Korea has refused to permit freedom of movement and free economic exchange between these zones. This has precluded freely chosen political amalgamation of the Korean people and has resulted in grave economic distress.

The policy of the United States toward Korea has the following basic objectives:

(1) To assist in the establishment as soon as practicable of a self-governing sovereign Korea, independent of foreign control and eligible for membership in the United Nations.

(2) To insure that the national government so established shall be representative of the freely expressed will of the Korean people.

[4] *Department of State Bulletin,* April 20, 1947, pp. 716-17.

(3) To aid the Koreans in building a sound economy as an essential basis for their independent and democratic state.

The United States, in the Cairo Declaration of December 1, 1943, declared its determination that in due course Korea should become free and independent. The United Kingdom and the Republic of China were parties to the same declaration. The Cairo Declaration was specifically reaffirmed by the Three Powers in the Potsdam Declaration, which defined terms for the Japanese surrender. The U.S.S.R. in its declaration of war on Japan on August 8, 1945, declared its adherence to these declarations.

Upon the surrender of Japan, United States and Soviet forces accepted the surrender of Japanese forces in Korea in the areas respectively south and north of a line arbitrarily assigned for this purpose, the thirty-eighth degree parallel. This line of demarcation became in effect a boundary between zones of occupation. At the conference of the Foreign Ministers of the U.S., the U.K. and the U.S.S.R. in Moscow in December, 1945, the serious consequences of the bizonal division of Korea were discussed and an agreement regarding Korea was reached and published in part three of the communiqué of the conference. The Republic of China subsequently subscribed to this agreement.

On March 20, 1946, the Joint U.S.-U.S.S.R. Commission appointed under the terms of the Moscow Agreement met and began its task, as outlined in the agreement, of assisting in the formation of a provisional Korean democratic government as a first step in assuring the establishment of an independent and sovereign Korean nation.

It was the hope of the Government of the United States that speedy action would be taken by the Joint Commission, a provisional Korean government would rapidly be established, the unfortunate results of the line of demarcation between the United States and the Soviet forces would be overcome and Korea could be started on the way to attaining an independent and democratic government.

Unfortunately the work of the Joint Commission became stalemated after a short time through the failure to agree on the definition of the word "democratic" as it pertained to the representatives of the parties and social organizations mentioned in the Moscow Agreement to be consulted by the Joint Commission in its task of assisting in the formation of a provisional government. As it became evident that no agreement could be reached at the time, the Joint Commission adjourned *sine die* on May 8, 1946.

The United States Commander in Korea has several times suggested to the Soviet Commander that the Commission reconvene and get on with its work.

However, the Soviet Commander has insisted on a formula which would result in eliminating the majority of representative Korean leaders from consultation as representatives of Korean democratic parties and social organizations, and has reiterated this position in a letter to the American Commander as recently as February 28, 1947. It has therefore been impossible to agree upon a basis for reconvening the Commission.

Now in April 1947, almost sixteen months since the agreement pertaining to Korea was reached in Moscow, there has still been no real progress made toward the implementation of that agreement.

In fulfillment of the intent of the Agreement and Declaration made at Moscow in December 1945, the Government of the United States desires to further the work of establishing a free and independent Korea without additional delay.

To this end I ask that our Governments agree to instruct our respective Commanders in Korea to reconvene the Joint Commission as soon as possible and charge it with expediting its work under the terms of the Moscow Agreement on a basis of respect for the democratic right of freedom of opinion. I further suggest that a mutually acceptable date during the summer of 1947 be fixed for a review by the two Governments of the progress made to that date by the Joint Commission. In the meantime, the United States, mindful of its obligations under the Moscow Agreement, sees no alternative to taking without further delay such steps in its zone as will advance the purposes of that agreement.

I am furnishing copies of this letter to the British and Chinese Governments.

DOCUMENT NO. 5

Foreign Minister Molotov to Secretary of State Marshall, April 19, 1947 [5]

DEAR MR. MARSHALL:

In reply to your letter of April 8 on the question of Korea, I am communicating the following:

At the Moscow meeting of the Foreign Ministers of the Soviet Union, the United States of America and the United Kingdom in December 1945, an agreement was reached which determined the policy of the three powers with respect to Korea. A basis for this agreement were the proposals of the Soviet Government, to which the Government of the U.S.A. also agreed, having consequently abandoned its first intention not to establish a National Korean Government in Korea. The Moscow Agreement held the establishment of a provisional democratic Korean Government which could take all the necessary measures for the development of Korean industry, transport, agriculture and the national culture of the Korean people, to be a problem of primary importance.

Having made these proposals, the Soviet Government deemed that the unification of Korea under the leadership of the Korean National Government was the most important prerequisite for the restoration of Korea as an independent state and the establishment of bases for the development of the country on democratic principles.

The Soviet Government continues to adhere to this point of view and insists on a steadfast implementation of the Moscow Agreement on Korea, being certain that, on the basis of the execution of this agreement Korea would be successfully developed along democratic principles and would become an independent and prosperous state and an equal member of the United Nations.

However, the legislative program provided for Korea by the Moscow Agreement has not yet been carried out. A provisional democratic Korean Government has not been established. The work of the Joint Soviet-American Commission, established for

[5] *Ibid.*, May 4, 1947, pp. 812-13.

the purpose of collaborating in the establishment of a provisional democratic Korean Government was suspended as a result of the fact that the American delegation on this Commission took a stand contrary to the Moscow Agreement on Korea. Furthermore, the American Command in southern Korea did not agree to a serious consideration of the proposals by the Soviet Command in northern Korea on the question of an economic exchange between the two zones, which made it impossible to reach an agreement on this question.

In the course of the work of the Joint Soviet-American Commission during the period from March to May, 1946, the Soviet delegation made every effort to effect the execution of the aforementioned agreement on Korea and, first of all, provide for a prompt establishment of a provisional democratic Korean Government and for the unification of Korea under its leadership. However, the Soviet delegation met not only with difficulties in this connection, but also with direct counter-action on the part of the American delegation. Basing itself on the agreement on Korea, which provides that the Joint Commission, in formulating its proposals, should consult Korean democratic parties and social organizations, the Soviet delegation insisted on a wide-scale attraction of such parties and organizations to consultation with the Commission. The American delegation excluded participation by a whole series of large democratic organizations in southern Korea and insisted on consultation with groups which had taken a stand in opposition to the Moscow Agreement, consultation with which, naturally could not facilitate the execution of this agreement. The American delegation included in the list of parties and organizations submitted by it for consultation with the Joint Commission, seventeen political parties and social groups of southern Korea which took a stand against the Moscow Agreement, and only three democratic parties which supported the agreement. The American delegation excluded such large democratic parties and social organizations as the All-Korean Labor Confederation, the All-Korean Peasant Union, the Korean National Revolutionary Party, the All-Korean Youth Union, etc., from participation in consultation. Deeming it impossible to agree to this position of the American delegation, the Soviet delegation nevertheless did its utmost to find a way to reach an agreed decision. This, however, appeared impossible and the work of the Commission, on the suggestion of the American delegation, was curtailed.

The intolerance of the resulting situation is evident. As a result of this, as you know, it was necessary to take new measures in endeavoring to find a way out of such a situation.

The Soviet Commander in his relations with the American Commander endeavored to find a basis for the renewal of the work of the Joint Commission. As a result of an exchange of letters, there has been a considerable *rapprochement* of the points of view of both sides, which fact was noted by both commanders. It was expected that an agreement would soon be reached and the Joint Commission would begin its work very shortly. However, no reply has been received to date from the American Commander to the last letter of February 28 from the Soviet Commander and the proposed agreement was not reached. Disagreement of action was a serious obstacle for the opportune fulfillment of the program of measures proposed in the Moscow Agreement of Korea as a whole.

In connection with northern Korea, during the period beginning with the capitulation of Japan, considerable progress was made in the field of democratization, and also with respect to the restoration of national economy and culture. Wide democratic reforms have been made which guarantee political freedom and raise the standard of living of the population. I have in mind, first of all, the introduction of an over-all electoral right; a law on equal rights for women; the establishment of local authority agencies and the People's Committee of Northern Korea on the basis of free democratic elections; land reform as a result of which 725,000 landless peasant farmers and those having little land received more than 1 million hectares of free land, which formerly belonged to Japanese colonists and their accomplices in Korea; the nationalization of former Japanese industries, the 8 hour work-day, safeguarding of labor and social insurance; public educational reform, as a result of which the Korean language has been re-established, the network of schools was increased and the number of students was increased, etc. However, such wide democratic reforms have been carried out only in northern Korea, where there is only two fifths of the population of Korea.

The Soviet Government, closely adhering in their policy toward Korea to the program planned in the Moscow Agreement, believes the following to be points of primary importance:

1. The establishment of a provisional democratic Korean Government on the basis of a wide-scale participation of Korean democratic parties and social organizations, in order to expedite the political and economic unification of Korea as a self-supporting state independent of foreign interference which would do away with the division of the country into two zones.

2. The establishment of democratic authority agencies throughout Korea by means of free elections on the basis of a general and equal electoral right.

3. The aiding of Korean people in the restoration of Korea as an independent democratic state and in the development of its national economy and national culture.

In conformity with the steadfast aspiration on the part of the Soviet Government for the prompt restoration of Korea as a united sovereign state and elimination of difficulties arising from the fact that Korea to date has not been unified and does not have a national government, I propose that the Joint Soviet-American Commission resume its work on May 20 of the current year in the city of Seoul, on the basis of an exact execution of the Moscow Agreement on Korea, and that the Commission present the result of its work on the elaboration of recommendations with respect to the establishment of a provisional democratic Korean Government for consideration by the two governments in July and August 1947.

I am sending copies of the present letter to Mr. Bevin and to the Chinese Ambassador in Moscow.

I beg you [etc.]

V. MOLOTOV

DOCUMENT NO. 6

Acting Secretary Lovett to Foreign Minister Molotov, August 26, 1947[6]

DEAR MR. MOLOTOV:

In your letter of August 23, 1947 to Secretary Marshall the position of the Soviet Delegation to the Joint Commission has been set forth in terms which corroborate a recent report received by this Government from the United States Delegation to the Joint Commission. The report of the United States Delegation was in compliance with the desire of Secretary Marshall as set forth in his letter to you of August 12 that a report from the Joint Commission should be submitted by August 21 in order that our governments might immediately consider what further steps may be useful to achieve the long-delayed unification and independence of Korea. The report of the United States Delegation makes it clear that the Joint Commission has been unable to reach agreement regarding the basis on which representatives of democratic Korean parties and social organizations shall be consulted by the Joint Commission. The United States Delegation also reports that it has been unable to obtain the agreement of the Soviet Delegation to any alternative method of completing the task of the Joint Commission.

As pointed out in your letter it was agreed in the interchange of correspondence in May of this year that "the Joint Commission should consult with those democratic parties and social organizations which fully support the Moscow Decision on Korea." You will, however, recall that in your letter of May 7 you expressly agreed to the interpretation of the above phrase as proposed by the United States Commander in Korea that "signing the declaration in Communiqué No. 5 will be accepted as declaration of good faith with respect to upholding fully the Moscow Decision and will make the signatory party or organization eligible for initial consultation." The parties and organizations mentioned by you as belonging to the Anti-Trusteeship Committee did sign Communiqué No. 5 and are,

[6] *Department of State Bulletin*, September 7, 1948, pp. 473-75.

in the opinion of the United States Government, eligible for initial consultation. Your letter of May 7 also provided that any decision excluding individuals, parties and social organizations for active opposition to the work of the Joint Commission "shall be by agreement of the Joint Commission." Accordingly, the United States Delegation has repeatedly, but without success, attempted to obtain from the Soviet Delegation agreement to criteria for consultation with Korean parties and social organizations applying for such consultation in accordance with the terms embodied in your letter. The Soviet Delegation has insisted on the unilateral right to exclude parties which have expressed distaste for "trusteeship," even though such parties have declared and reiterated their intention fully to support the Joint Commission and have in fact, since signing the declaration not instigated active opposition to the work of the Commission. The Soviet position is not only contrary to the specific terms of the agreement between you and Secretary Marshall, it is also contrary to the democratic principle of freedom of opinion.

In Secretary Marshall's letter to you of August 11, 1947, reference was made to the fact that the United States Delegation has several times offered to limit oral consultations to parties and organizations with membership in excess of one thousand, or any other reasonable figure proposed by the Soviet Delegation. The United States Delegation reports, however, that when the Soviet Delegation proposed limiting consultation to parties of 10,000 or more, the Soviet Delegation submitted a list which omitted 24 such parties which claimed total membership of 15,200,000 and refused to consider any other list or alternative proposal.

The United States Government denies categorically that there has been oppression or persecution of Korean parties or individuals in the United States zone as charged in your letter. The arrests which you mention have been necessary to control subversive activities aimed at the destruction of constituted government and law and order in the American zone. United States forces are charged with the responsibility for maintaining law and order in south Korea without interference with democratic rights. That they have done so successfully is amply proven by the freedom with which all shades of political opinion are expressed and respected in the United States zone.

It is noted that you have no objection to the proposal that the Joint Commission furnish an agreed report to our two governments. The United States Delegation has accordingly been instructed to take immediate steps to reach agreement on a joint report of the status of the deliberations of the Joint Commission. In view of the position set forth in your letter and the report already rendered by the United States Delegation, however, it is apparent that a joint report can accomplish little other than a formal delineation of the issues which have prevented the fulfillment of the Moscow Agreement.

For almost two years the Government of the United States has devoted its utmost efforts to carrying out the terms of the Moscow Agreement on Korea. The present stalemate in the Joint Commission negotiations and the failure of that Commission to accomplish even the first task of its mission have made it abundantly clear to all that bilateral negotiations on the subject of consultation with Korean political parties and organizations will only serve to delay the implementation of this agreement and defeat its announced purpose of bringing about early independence for Korea. The United States Government cannot in good conscience be a party to any such delay in the fulfillment of its commitment to Korean independence and proposes that the four powers adhering to the Moscow Agreement meet to consider how that agreement may be speedily carried out.

The United States Government therefore submits for the consideration of your government the enclosed outline of proposals designed to achieve the aims of the Moscow Agreement on Korea. The United States Government proposes that these suggestions be considered at an early date by the powers adhering to that Agreement. It is therefore hoped that the Soviet Chargé d'Affaires at Washington or an authorized deputy may be designated to participate in four-power conversations on this problem at Washington beginning on September 8, 1947.

It is believed that the Joint Commission's report on the status of its deliberations might be helpful in consideration of the United States proposals during these four-power conversations. The United States Delegation has accordingly been instructed to endeavor to reach agreement with the Soviet Delegation on a joint report to be submitted not later than September 5, 1947.

Copies of this letter are being transmitted to the Foreign Ministers of the United Kingdom and China together with invitations to participate in the four-power conversations referred to above.

Please accept [etc.]

ROBERT A. LOVETT

United States Proposals Regarding Korea

1. In both the U.S.S.R. and U.S. zones of Korea there shall be held early elections to choose wholly representative provisional legislatures for each zone. Voting shall be by secret, multi-party ballot on a basis of universal suffrage and elections shall be held in accordance with the laws adopted by the present Korean legislatures in each zone.

2. These provisional zonal legislatures shall choose representatives in numbers which reflect the proportion between the populations of the two zones, these representatives to constitute a national provisional legislature. This legislature shall meet at Seoul to establish a provisional government for a united Korea.

3. The resulting Provisional Government of a united Korea shall meet in Korea with representatives of the four Powers adhering to the Moscow Agreement on Korea to discuss with them what aid and assistance is needed in order to place Korean independence on a firm economic and political foundation and on what terms this aid and assistance is to be given.

4. During all the above stages the United Nations shall be invited to have observers present so that the world and the Korean people may be assured of the wholly representative and completely independent character of the actions taken.

5. The Korean Provisional Government and the Powers concerned shall agree upon a date by which all occupation forces in Korea will be withdrawn.

6. The provisional legislatures in each zone shall be encouraged to draft provisional constitutions which can later be used

as a basis for the adoption by the national provisional legislature of a constitution for all of Korea.

7. Until such time as a united, independent Korea is established, public and private Korean agencies in each zone shall be brought into contact with international agencies established by or under the United Nations and the presence of Korean observers at official international conferences shall be encouraged in appropriate cases.

DOCUMENT NO. 7

Foreign Minister Molotov to Secretary of State Marshall, September 4, 1947 [7]

DEAR MR. MARSHALL:

In acknowledging receipt of Mr. Lovett's letter of August 26, 1947, I consider it necessary to draw to your attention that the preliminary elaboration of measures to assist the formation of a provisional Korean democratic government, in accordance with the decision of the Moscow Conference of the three Ministers for Foreign Affairs, is to be carried out by the Joint Commission consisting of representatives of the Soviet Command in northern Korea and of the United States Command in southern Korea. For the consideration of the four Governments, including the British and Chinese Governments, according to the Moscow decision, there should be submitted the recommendations worked out by the Joint Commission prior to adoption of a final decision. Furthermore, the Governments of Great Britain and China will take part, together with the Governments of the U.S.S.R. and the U.S.A., in the consideration of the proposals worked out by the Joint Soviet-American Commission concerning measures for helping and assisting (trusteeship) the political, economic, and social progress of the Korean people, the development of democratic self-government, and the establishment of the national independence of Korea, in order to work out an agreement concerning a four-power trusteeship with relation to Korea.

[7] *Korea, 1945 to 1948*, pp. 45-47, Department of State Publication 3305, Far Eastern Series 28, U.S. Department of State, Washington, D.C.

The task of the Joint Soviet-American Commission, as is known, is to render assistance in the formation of a single provisional democratic government for all Korea.

The Joint Commission has still, in fact, done little in this direction, but this situation is primarily the result of the position adopted by the American delegation on the question of consultation of the Commission with Korean democratic parties and social organizations, as was pointed out in my last letter to you. If the American delegation had shown the necessary desire to render assistance in the creation of a really democratic government in Korea, the work of the Joint Commission would have been more successful, the task laid upon it would have been fulfilled, and there would not be that stagnant situation in the work of the Joint Commission which in Mr. Lovett's letter is called an *impasse*.

As you know, the Soviet delegation, wishing to resolve the situation which had been created in the Joint Commission and seeking to expedite the work of creating a provisional Korean democratic government, agreed with the proposal of the American delegation not to carry on oral consultations with Korean democratic parties and social organizations, and on August 26, 1947 introduced a new proposal for the establishment of a consultative organ—the provisional general Korean people's assembly of representatives of democratic parties and social organizations of all Korea. This proposal in our opinion should meet no objection on the part of the American delegation in as much as it might remove the difficulties which the Joint Commission has encountered.

I consider it necessary to add to the above that the successful realization of the measure set forth in the proposal of the Soviet delegation is possible only on the basis of free and unfettered activity of the democratic parties and organizations, representatives of which at the present time in southern Korea are subjected to arrests and other repressions, which is incompatible with the principles of democracy and legality and also with the obligations which the Governments of the U.S.A. and the U.S.S.R. took upon themselves with respect to Korea.

In connection with the assertions contained in Mr. Lovett's letter concerning the position of the Soviet delegation to the

Joint Commission, the sense of which is that the Soviet delegation does not display sufficient understanding of the proposals of the American delegation, I see no necessity for stopping on these assertions in view of their obvious unsoundness.

At the same time I cannot fail to express regret concerning unilateral acts undertaken by you such as the despatch of an invitation to the Governments of Great Britain and China to take part in the discussion of this question, fixing the place and date for the conference.

The Soviet Government considers inexpedient your proposal to submit the question of the establishment of a provisional Korean democratic government to the consideration of the Governments of the four countries in as much as the Joint Commission is still far from exhausting all its possibilities for working out agreed recommendations, which is entirely possible. The "United States proposals concerning Korea" set forth in Mr. Lovett's letter are also unacceptable.

These proposals cannot fail to entail the further division of Korea in as much as they envisage the establishment of separate provisional legislative assemblies in the south and in the north of Korea (in the Soviet and American zones) whereas the vital task is to achieve as rapidly as possible the establishment of a single, even though provisional, organ of authority—the General Korean Provisional Democratic Government. The American proposal does not correct the situation now existing in Korea—the division of the country into two zones, to the liquidation of which all efforts should be directed—but on the contrary consolidates this abnormal situation.

Having in mind that the proposal for the consideration of the question of Korea in a joint conference of the representatives of the four powers does not stem from the Moscow decision of the three Ministers for Foreign Affairs concerning Korea, and taking into consideration the views set forth above, the Soviet Government sees no possibility of accepting the proposals advanced in Mr. Lovett's letter.

Copies of this letter are being sent by me to the Governments of Great Britain and China.

Please accept [etc.]

V. M. Molotov

DOCUMENT NO. 8

Acting Secretary Lovett to Foreign Minister Molotov, September 17, 1947 [8]

MY DEAR MR. MOLOTOV:

The decision of the Soviet Government as conveyed in your letter of September 4, not to participate in Four Power discussions of proposals of the United States Government designed to achieve the speedy realization of the aims of the Moscow Agreement on Korea is deeply regretted. For almost two years the United States Government has been faithfully endeavoring to reach agreement with the Soviet Government to carry out the terms of the Moscow Agreement but with no appreciable success. It has even proved impossible for the Soviet and United States Delegations on the Joint Commission in Korea to agree upon a joint report of the status of their deliberations up to the present. There is no sign of the early setting up of a Korean Provisional Government. Korea remains divided and her promised independence unrealized.

The United States Government believes that this situation must not be permitted to continue indefinitely. In view of the fact that bilateral negotiations have not advanced Korean independence and that the Soviet Government does not agree to discussions among the powers adhering to the Moscow Agreement, there is but one course remaining. It is the intention, therefore, of my Government to refer the problem of Korean independence to the forthcoming session of the General Assembly of the United Nations. It is suggested that the members of the Joint Commission hold themselves in readiness to give such aid and assistance to the General Assembly as may be required during the Assembly's consideration of this problem.

It is the hope of my Government that consideration of this problem by the General Assembly may result in bringing about the early restoration of freedom and independence to the long suffering people of Korea.

Copies of this letter have been furnished to the Governments of the United Kingdom and China.

Accept [etc.] ROBERT A. LOVETT

[8] *Department of State Bulletin,* September 28, 1947, p. 624.

DOCUMENT NO. 9

Foreign Minister Molotov to Secretary Marshall, October 9, 1947 [9]

DEAR MR. MARSHALL:

The position taken by the U.S. Delegation in the Joint Soviet-American Commission at Seoul provides evidence that the U.S.A. Delegation does not wish to continue the work of the Joint Commission with a view to reaching, on the basis of an exact observance of the Moscow Agreement on Korea, agreed decisions on questions connected with the establishment of a provisional Korean democratic government.

In violation of the Moscow Agreement on Korea and the understanding reached between the Governments of the U.S.S.R. and the U.S.A. in May 1947 concerning the conditions for resuming the work of the Joint Commission, the U.S.A. Delegation insists that not only democratic parties and groups in northern and southern Korea which have signed the declaration of support for the aims of the Moscow Agreement and are loyally carrying out the conditions of this declaration, but also such reactionary groups which, having signed this agreement, are carrying on a struggle against the Moscow Agreement and are continuing to comprise the so-called "Anti-trusteeship Committee," which contradicts the above-mentioned understanding between the Governments of the U.S.S.R. and the U.S.A., shall take part in the formation of the Korean Government. The Soviet Delegation, consistently defending the principles of the Moscow Agreement, obviously cannot agree with this.

The position of the U.S.A. Delegation has made impossible the formation of a provisional Korean democratic government in accordance with the Moscow Agreement, which hinders the re-establishment of Korea as a united democratic state.

In view of the situation which had been created the Government of the U.S.S.R. instructed the Soviet Delegation to introduce in the Joint Commission at Seoul a new proposal, namely: To give to the Koreans the possibility of forming a government themselves, without aid and participation on the part of the

[9] *Korea, 1945 to 1948*, pp. 48-49.

United States of America and the Soviet Union, on condition that American and Soviet troops be withdrawn from Korea. If the Government of the U.S.A. should agree to the proposal for the withdrawal from Korea of all foreign troops at the beginning of 1948, the Soviet troops would be ready to leave Korea simultaneously with the American troops.

Notwithstanding the fact that this proposal was introduced by the Soviet Delegation at the session of the Joint Commission on September 26, the U.S.A. Delegation has unfortunately not replied to date, which cannot fail to delay the solution of the Korean question.

With reference to the consideration of the Korean question at the session of the General Assembly of the United Nations Organization, which was proposed in Mr. Lovett's letter of September 17, the position of the Soviet Government on this question, as you know, has already been set forth by the Soviet Delegation to the General Assembly.

Copies of this letter are being sent by me to the Governments of Great Britain and China.

Please accept [etc.]

V. Molotov

DOCUMENT NO. 10

Acting Secretary Lovett to Foreign Minister Molotov, October 18, 1947 [10]

Dear Mr. Molotov:

In your letter of October 9, 1947, you state that the position taken by the United States Delegation in the Joint Soviet-American Commission at Seoul has delayed a decision on the Korean question and you refer to the proposal made by the Soviet Delegation in Seoul on September 26, 1947, for the immediate simultaneous withdrawal of the United States-Soviet occupation forces to which you state no reply has been received.

The Secretary of State announced on September 17 that the problem of setting up an independent Government for a unified

[10] *Ibid.*, pp. 50-51.

Korea would be presented to the General Assembly of the United Nations and on September 23 the General Assembly voted to place this question on its agenda. In the opinion of the United States Government the question of withdrawal of occupation forces from Korea must be considered an integral part of the solution of that problem.

The United States Delegation to the General Assembly meeting in New York City has now had circulated to the various delegations for their consideration a proposed resolution which is designed to bring about the early establishment of an independent Korean Government representative of the will of the Korean people, and the consequent speedy withdrawal of all occupation forces. In submitting this proposal to the Secretary General, specific attention was called to the Soviet proposal for the simultaneous withdrawal of troops with the statement of the United States' hope that having both proposals before it the General Assembly would be able to recommend a solution of the problem. A copy of the United States proposals was delivered to the Soviet Delegation in New York prior to its being communicated to the Secretary General of the United Nations for transmission to the other delegations.

In view of the continued inability of the Soviet and United States Delegations in the Joint Commission to agree on how to proceed with their work and the refusal of the Soviet Government to participate in discussions on this problem with the other Governments adhering to the Moscow Agreement on Korea, the United States Government considers it is obligated to seek the assistance of the United Nations in order that, as the Secretary of State said on September 17, "the inability of two powers to reach agreement" should not further delay the early establishment of an independent, united Korea.

Copies of this letter have been furnished to the Governments of the United Kingdom and China.

Accept [etc.]

ROBERT A. LOVETT

DOCUMENT NO. 11

United Nations Resolution on Korea, Adopted by the General Assembly November 14, 1947[11]

A

INASMUCH AS the Korean question which is before the General Assembly is primarily a matter for the Korean people itself and concerns its freedom and independence, and

RECOGNIZING that this question cannot be correctly and fairly resolved without the participation of representatives of the indigenous population,

The General Assembly

1. *Resolves* that elected representatives of the Korean people be invited to take part in the consideration of the question;

2. *Further resolves* that in order to facilitate and expedite such participation and to observe that the Korean representatives are in fact duly elected by the Korean people and not mere appointees by military authorities in Korea, there be forthwith established a United Nations Temporary Commission on Korea, to be present in Korea, with right to travel, observe and consult throughout Korea.

B

The General Assembly,

RECOGNIZING the urgent and rightful claims to independence of the people of Korea;

BELIEVING that the national independence of Korea should be re-established and all occupying forces then withdrawn at the earliest practicable date;

RECALLING its previous conclusion that the freedom and independence of the Korean people cannot be correctly or fairly resolved without the participation of representatives of the Korean people, and its decision to establish a United Nations Temporary Commission on Korea (hereinafter called the "Commission") for the purpose of facilitating and expediting such participation by elected representatives of the Korean people,

[11] U.N. Doc. A/447, November 6, 1947. *Korea, 1945 to 1948*, pp. 66-67.

1. *Decides* that the Commission shall consist of representatives of Australia, Canada, China, El Salvador, France, India, Philippines, Syria, Ukrainian Soviet Socialist Republic;

2. *Recommends* that the elections be held not later than 31 March 1948 on the basis of adult suffrage and by secret ballot to choose representatives with whom the Commission may consult regarding the prompt attainment of the freedom and independence of the Korean people and which representatives, constituting a National Assembly, may establish a National Government of Korea. The number of representatives from each voting area or zone should be proportionate to the population, and the elections should be under the observation of the Commission;

3. *Further recommends* that as soon as possible after the elections, the National Assembly should convene and form a National Government and notify the Commission of its formation;

4. *Further recommends* that immediately upon the establishment of a National Government, that Government should, in consultation with the Commission: (*a*) constitute its own national security forces and dissolve all military or semi-military formations not included therein, (*b*) take over the functions of government from the military commands and civilian authorities of north and south Korea, and (*c*) arrange with the occupying Powers for the complete withdrawal from Korea of their armed forces as early as practicable and if possible within ninety days;

5. *Resolves* that the Commission shall facilitate and expedite the fulfillment of the foregoing programme for the attainment of the national independence of Korea and withdrawal of occupying forces, taking into account its observations and consultations in Korea. The Commission shall report, with its conclusions, to the General Assembly and may consult with the Interim Committee (if one be established) with respect to the application of this resolution in the light of developments;

6. *Calls upon* the Member States concerned to afford every assistance and facility to the Commission in the fulfillment of its responsibilities;

7. *Calls upon* all Members of the United Nations to refrain from interfering in the affairs of the Korean people during the

interim period preparatory to the establishment of Korean independence, except in pursuance of the decisions of the General Assembly; and thereafter, to refrain completely from any and all acts derogatory to the independence and sovereignty of Korea.

DOCUMENT NO. 12

Resolution of the United Nations Interim Committee, February 26, 1948 [12]

Whereas the Chairman of the United Nations Temporary Commission on Korea, accompanied by the Assistant-Secretary-General, consulted the Interim Committee on the following questions:

"1. Is it open to or incumbent upon the Commission, under the terms of the General Assembly resolutions of 14 November 1947, and in the light of developments in the situation with respect to Korea since that date, to implement the programme as outlined in resolution II in that part of Korea which is occupied by the armed forces of the United States of America?

"2. If not,

(a) Should the Commission observe the election of Korean representatives to take part in the consideration of the Korean question, as outlined in resolution I of 14 November 1947, provided that it has determined that elections can be held in a free atmosphere? and

(b) Should the Commission consider such other measures as may be possible and advisable with a view to the attainment of its objectives?"

The Interim Committee,

Bearing in mind the views expressed by the Chairman of the United Nations Temporary Commission on Korea;

Deeming it necessary that the programme set forth in the General Assembly resolutions of 14 November 1947 be carried out and as a necessary step therein that the United Nations

[12] *Department of State Bulletin*, March 7, 1948, pp. 297-98. U.N. Doc. A/AC. 18/31.

Temporary Commission on Korea proceed with the observance of elections in all Korea, and if that is impossible, in as much of Korea as is accessible to it; and

Considering it important that the elections be held to choose representatives of the Korean people with whom the United Nations Temporary Commission on Korea may consult regarding the prompt attainment of freedom and independence of the Korean people, which representatives, constituting a National Assembly, may establish a National Government of Korea;

Resolves

That in its view it is incumbent upon the United Nations Temporary Commission on Korea, under the terms of the General Assembly resolution of 14 November 1947, and in the light of developments in the situation with respect to Korea since that date, to implement the programme as outlined in Resolution II, in such parts of Korea as are accessible to the Commission.

DOCUMENT NO. 13

United States Policy Toward New Korean Government, August 12, 1948 [13]

In the Joint Declaration issued at Cairo on December 1, 1943, the three subscribing powers—the United States, China, and Great Britain—expressed their determination "that in due course Korea shall become free and independent." This determination was reaffirmed in the Potsdam Declaration of July 26, 1945, with which the Soviet Union associated itself upon its declaration of war against Japan on August 8 of that year. On December 27, 1945, in Moscow the Foreign Ministers of the Soviet Union, the United States, and Great Britain concluded an agreement, later adhered to by the Government of China, designed to re-establish Korea as an independent state.

Although the annexation of Korea by Japan was effectively terminated with the occupation of that country by the armed

[13] Department of State Press Release 647, August 12, 1948. *Korea, 1945 to 1948*, pp. 100-01.

forces of the Soviet Union and the United States in August and September 1945, the freedom and independence of Korea so solemnly pledged by the Four Powers have proved slow of realization. After nearly two years of painstaking but unavailing effort to give effect to those pledges through negotiations with the other occupying power, the United States Government, on September 17, 1947, laid the problem of Korean independence before the General Assembly of the United Nations. The will of an overwhelming majority of that body was expressed in two resolutions adopted by it on November 14, 1947, the purpose of which was to make it possible for the Korean people to attain their long-sought freedom and independence through the holding of free and democratic elections and the establishment, on the basis thereof, of a national government.

In pursuance of those resolutions, elections were held in Korea on May 10 of this year, under the observation of the United Nations Temporary Commission on Korea, for the purpose of electing representatives to a National Assembly which might in turn form a national government. The National Assembly so elected convened on May 31 and has proceeded to form a government—a government in which it is hoped that the people of north Korea, who were prevented from participating in the May 10 elections by the refusal of the Soviet Union to permit the implementation of the General Assembly resolutions in its zone of occupation, will be free in due course to assume their rightful role. Notification of the formation of the new government was communicated to the United Nations Temporary Commission on Korea on August 6, 1948.

It is the view of the United States Government that the Korean Government so established is entitled to be regarded as the Government of Korea envisaged by the General Assembly resolution of November 14, 1947. Pending consideration by the General Assembly at its forthcoming Third Session of the report of the United Nations Temporary Commission on Korea, the United States, pursuant to its responsibility as occupying power, is sending to Seoul a special representative who will be authorized to carry on negotiations with that Government, in consultation with the United Nations Temporary Commission on Korea, concerning the implementation of the further provisions set forth in paragraph 4 of the second of the General Assembly resolutions of November 14, 1947. As such special representative the President has named John J. Muccio of Rhode Island, who will have the personal rank of Ambassador.

DOCUMENT NO. 14

The Establishment of Diplomatic Relations Between the Soviet Union and the Korean People's Democratic Republic [14]

To Mr. Joseph Vissarionovitch Stalin, Chairman of the Council of Ministers of the U.S.S.R.:

On behalf of the government of the Korean People's Democratic Republic, I have the honor to address you, most esteemed Mr. Chairman, in the present letter, and to convey to you the following desire of my government:

During the three years that have elapsed since the liberation of Korea from long years of colonial oppression by Japanese imperialism, profound changes, which have tremendous significance for the history of our country, have occurred in the lives of the Korean people. Nation-wide elections have been held throughout Korea to the sole, nation-wide, legislative organ—the Supreme People's Assembly of Korea. As a result of the elections a government of the People's Democratic Republic was formed, which consists of representatives from all social strata of the population from the north of Korea to the south, and which has elicited the warm approval and unanimous support of the entire Korean people. The government of the Korean People's Democratic Republic has undertaken to fulfill its obligations and has begun to work for the welfare of the Korean people.

Expressing the unanimous aspiration of the entire Korean people, I, in behalf of the government, address myself to you and, in your person, to the government of the U.S.S.R., with the request to establish diplomatic relations with the Korean People's Democratic Republic and to exchange ambassadors.

[14] *Soviet Press Translations*, Far Eastern Institute, University of Washington, Seattle, December 1, 1948.

Along with the establishment of diplomatic relations, I likewise beseech the government of the U.S.S.R. to establish close economic relations between the two states for the common welfare of our peoples.

I am profoundly convinced that the establishment of diplomatic relations between the Korean People's Democratic Republic and the U.S.S.R. will help to strengthen friendly relations between our peoples and will serve the cause of peace and security in the Far East.

Very respectfully yours,

KIM IL-SENG
Chairman of the Cabinet of
Ministers of the Korean
People's Democratic Republic

Pyŏngyang, Korea, October 8, 1948

To Mr. Kim Il-seng, Chairman of the Cabinet of Ministers of the Korean People's Democratic Republic, Pyŏngyang:

I acknowledge receipt of your letter of October 8, in which you inform me that the government of the Korean People's Democratic Republic has undertaken to fulfill its obligations, and in which you propose the establishment of diplomatic relations with the U.S.S.R., the exchange of ambassadors, and also the establishment of corresponding economic relations between the two states.

The Soviet government, which invariably defends the right of the Korean people to create its own united, independent state, welcomes the formation of the Korean government and wishes it success in its work for the national rebirth and democratic development of Korea. The Soviet government expresses its readiness to establish diplomatic relations between the U.S.S.R. and the Korean People's Democratic Republic, and to exchange ambassadors, and along with this to establish corresponding economic relations.

J. STALIN
Chairman of the Council of
Ministers of the U.S.S.R.

October 12, 1948

Pravda, October 13, 1948

DOCUMENT NO. 15

United Nations Resolution on Korea, Adopted by the General Assembly, December 12, 1948 [15]

The General Assembly

Having regard to its resolution No. 112 of November 14, 1947, concerning the problem of the independence of Korea:

Having considered the report of the United Nations Temporary Commission on Korea (hereinafter referred to as the "Temporary Commission"), and the report of the Interim Committee regarding its consultation with the Temporary Commission;

Mindful of the fact that due to difficulties referred to in the report of the Temporary Commission, the objectives set forth in the resolution of November 14, 1947 have not been fully accomplished; and in particular that unification in Korea has not yet been achieved;

(1) Approves the conclusions of the reports of the Temporary Commission;

(2) Declares that there has been established a lawful government (the Government of the Republic of Korea), having effective control and jurisdiction over that part of Korea where the Temporary Commission was able to observe and consult and in which the great majority of the people of all Korea reside; that this Government is based on elections which were a valid expression of the free will of the electorate of that part of Korea and which were observed by the Temporary Commission; and that this is the only such Government in Korea;

(3) Recommends that the occupying powers withdraw their occupation forces from Korea as early as practicable;

(4) Resolves that, as a means to the full accomplishment of the objectives set forth in the resolution of November 14, 1947, a commission on Korea consisting of Australia, China, El Salvador, France, India, Philippine Republic and Syria, be established to continue the work of the Temporary Commission and carry out the provisions of the present resolution, having in

[15] *Voice of Korea*, December 15, 1948.

mind the status of the Government of the Republic of Korea as herein defined, and in particular to;

a. Lend its good offices to bring about the unification of Korea and the integration of all Korean security forces in accordance with the principles laid down by the General Assembly in the Resolution of November 14, 1947;

b. Seek to facilitate the removal of barriers to economic, social, and other friendly intercourse caused by the division of Korea;

c. Be available for observation and consultation in the further development of representative government based on the freely expressed will of the people;

d. Observe the actual withdrawal of the occupying forces and verify the fact of withdrawal when such has occurred; and for this purpose, if it so desires, request the assistance of military experts of the two occupying powers;

(5) Decides that the Commission:

a. Shall, within thirty days of the adoption of this resolution, proceed to Korea, where it shall maintain its seat;

b. Shall be regarded as having superseded the Temporary Commission established by the resolution of November 14, 1947;

c. Is authorized to travel, consult and observe throughout Korea;

d. Shall determine its own procedures;

e. May consult with the Interim Committee with respect to the discharge of its duties in the light of developments and within the terms of this resolution;

f. Shall render a report to the next Regular Session of the General Assembly and to any prior Special Session which might be called to consider the subject matter of this resolution, and shall render such interim reports as it may deem appropriate to the Secretary-General for distribution to members;

(6) Requests that the Secretary-General provide the Commission with adequate staff and facilities, including technical

advisers as required; and authorizes the Secretary-General to pay the expenses and per diem of a representative and an alternate from each of the states members of the commission;

(7) Calls upon member states concerned, the Government of the Republic of Korea, and all Koreans to afford every assistance and facility to the Commission in the fulfillment of its responsibilities;

(8) Calls upon member states to refrain from any acts derogatory to the results achieved and to be achieved by the U.N. in bringing about the complete independence and unity of Korea;

(9) Recommends that member states and other nations, in establishing their relations with the Government of Korea, take into consideration the facts set out in paragraph (2) of this resolution.

DOCUMENT NO. 16

Conclusions of the United Nations Commission on Korea[16]

The people of Korea are remarkably homogeneous. Ethnically and culturally they are one. They have a passionate longing for unity and independence and have a profound desire for the peaceful unification of their country.

The division of Korea has resulted in adverse economic consequences in the south, the only part of Korea to which the Commission has had access. The aftermath of the Second World War would have made the need for outside aid urgent in any case. But if the country were united, the south would not require such aid in the same degree and would be able to stabilize its economy more easily and at a higher level.

The division of Korea has caused bitterness, frustration and mutual distrust among its people. The frequent raids along the 38th parallel have further accentuated these feelings. The division of Korea was caused by the exigencies of the Second World

[16] General Assembly Official Records, Fourth Session, Supplement No. 9, Report of the United Nations Commission on Korea, Lake Success, 1949, Volume I, Document A/936, Part D, "Conclusions," p. 34.

War. There is no justification for the continued separation of the two parts of the country.

The Republic of Korea looks to the United Nations for the solution of many of its problems, for it feels that the Republic is in some sense a creation of the United Nations. In the opinion of the Government, as evidenced by its request that the stay of the Commission in Korea be prolonged for another year, the presence of the Commission has been a stabilizing factor in the situation.

Bearing in mind these fundamental considerations underlying the Korean problem, the United Nations Commission on Korea has reached the following conclusions:

(1) The embittered propaganda and hostile activities which now mark the relations between the two parts of Korea render the prospect of unification more and more remote.

(2) As long as the opposition of the Union of Soviet Socialist Republics to the efforts of the United Nations Commission to achieve the objectives of the General Assembly resolution of 12 December 1948 continues, neither a relaxation of hostile propaganda nor any other measure can facilitate to a substantial degree the achievement of unification.

(3) The world-wide antagonism between the Union of Soviet Socialist Republics and the United States of America continues to be, as it was when the Temporary Commission was in Korea, one of the basic factors underlying the present difficulties. Without a new effort by those Powers to reach agreement on the question of Korea, no substantial progress toward the achievement of unification on the basis of the principles approved by the General Assembly can be made.

(4) From its very inception, the newly formed Republic of Korea has been confronted with many difficulties. It faced insurgent uprisings from within and was menaced by continuous clashes on the 38th parallel. While making due allowance for these factors, the Commission believes that a broadening of the Government's political base would allow it to meet these difficulties more successfully and so enable it to play a more effective part in achieving unification.

(5) The present Commission, like its predecessor, must place on record an acknowledgment that the situation in Korea

is now no better than it was at the beginning, and that it has not been able to facilitate the achievement of the objectives set by the General Assembly.

DOCUMENT NO. 17

Extract Relating to Korea from the Report of the House Committee on Foreign Affairs, *Economic Assistance to Certain Areas in the Far East*, February 1, 1950[17]

The Record of United States Assistance

The first-year segment of a 3-year program of economic assistance, as contemplated in H.R. 5330, was never carried out. Instead, the Congress legislated the program, if it might be called a program in view of the circumstances, a piece at a time. The Korean aid program was snarled in part by the lack of statutory authorization and in part by the general impasse regarding appropriations.

First, on June 30, 1949, there was enacted Public Law 154. This enabled the Korean program to be carried along on the basis of operations in the fiscal year 1949. Then, on August 1, 1949, Public Law 196 was enacted. It continued the above formula for an additional 15 days. Under these two provisions, the sum of $17,500,000 was made available for the South Korean program. No further appropriations were made for the Korea program for almost 2 months—until October 10, 1949. Then Public Law 349 was enacted, making $30,000,000 available for the period July 1 to October 15, 1949. This provided that the funds appropriated by Public Law 154 and Public Law 196 should be charged to this appropriation. Finally, on October 28, 1949, another $30,000,000 was appropriated by Public Law 430 for use during the period October 15, 1949, to February 15, 1950.

[17] *Economic Assistance to Certain Areas in the Far East.* Report of the Committee on Foreign Affairs. 81st Congress, 2d Session, House Report No. 1571, February 1, 1950, Washington, D.C., p. 13 ff.

The program for South Korea has received a total of $60,000,000 for 7½ months, rather than the contemplated $93,750,000 which would have been the share if the original program had been put into effect. Moreover, the money was made available in small and irregular portions. This added to the difficulties of the capital-installation program. Actually the program received $17,500,000 for 6 weeks; then nothing for 6 weeks; then $12,500,000 for 6 weeks; then nothing for 10 weeks; then $30,000,000 for the 10 fallow weeks and for the next 9 weeks.

In pointing out that the assistance program in South Korea has not been carried on at the scale contemplated when H. R. 5330 was reported last July, it is well to stress that the difference has not been simply one of scope. It has been one of nature as well. A recovery program pared down too drastically becomes a relief program. It palliates the symptoms. It does not cure the ills.

The Economic Cooperation Administration asserts that this fiscal stringency has been met by a program of "preparatory deferment." It has gone ahead with recovery projects that it could afford. It has accomplished the preengineering planning of those projects which it was most reluctantly compelled to defer.

The Korean program has been delayed in time. Moreover, the effect of this delay has fallen on recovery portions of the projected program. These recovery projects are the key to the Korean problem. They are the chief means whereby Korean imports can be reduced, Korean exports increased, and the Korean balance-of-payments problem resolved.

Present Status of the Korean Economy

The new nation has had to assume primary responsibility for its own defense. It has been able to do so—though at the cost of some strain to its economy. It has not yet achieved that degree of national security necessary to the inducement of private investment from abroad. State-owned factories, mines, and other vested property have remained in limited production or virtual nonproduction—a factor soon to be alleviated if the hopes behind the recent legislation providing for sale of such property are borne out. Finally, the fundamental political obstacle to trade between the northern and southern portions of the peninsula remains unmoved. In the words of the report of last August of the United Nations Commission for Korea:

> . . . The Commission must report that until now it has met opposition from the Government of the Republic to suggestions for a renewal of economic exchange, while it has never been given an opportunity of making proposals to that end to the north. . . .

That circumstance remains unchanged.

Notwithstanding the above difficulties the Koreans have more than met their targets in industrial production, according to Economic Cooperation Administration headquarters. Economic Cooperation Administration reports that the objectives with regard to Korean exports have been fulfilled. It reports that South Korea has gone twice as far as planned in its railway-building program and that South Korea has more than met the projections for coal production to date. . . .

As to negative aspects of the South Korean economy in its present phase, a *New York Times* dispatch of January 13, 1950, makes note of

> the Korean financial situation, which United States experts describe as "deteriorating" in the face of unchecked deficit spending.

The dispatch continues:

> During the first 8 months of the fiscal year 1949–50, deficit expenditures of the Government exceeded the entire budget for the year. The chief spenders were the Ministry of National Defense and the Home Ministry. The latter pays for a police force of army proportions. The office of the Prime Minister spent more than three times its entire budget on intelligence activities alone.
>
> Most of the deficit money was obtained either from printing presses or overdrafts on the Bank of Korea. The abrupt rise of currency in circulation during the last few months, despite a slight reduction in 1949, is shown by the following figures: December 31, 1948, 43,000,000,000 won; March 31, 1949, 38,000,000,000 won; January 7, 1950, 74,000,000,000 won.
>
> The present situation, in the opinion of United States financial experts here, has arisen because of uncontrolled spending not only by agencies concerned with hunting down Communists but by other departments, inadequate tax collections, and failure to absorb United States aid matériel. . . .

According to information given to the committee by the Economic Cooperation Administration, the situation concerning absorption of aid material is satisfactory. They report that approximately 92 per cent of landed goods has been distributed, judging by the ratio of billings to deposits in the counterpart fund. In general, however, Economic Cooperation Administration officials confirm the reports of economic difficulties.

In recognition of these difficulties, the Department of State has sent instructions to Ambassador John J. Muccio to make it abundantly clear to President Rhee of the Republic of Korea that the Korean Government must put its financial house in order if it expects continued United States assistance. Concurrently, the Economic Cooperation Administration has presented to the Government of South Korea an eight-point program summarized as follows:

In order to increase the income of the Korean Government, the prices of ECA supplies should be raised so that the money deposited in the counterpart fund is more nearly equal to the value of these goods in won at a realistic rate of foreign exchange.

The second method of increasing the Government revenue is to raise the prices of all public utilities and Government services where these prices are much below the cost of production.

A third method of increasing Government income is to increase the effectiveness of tax collections so that a larger percentage of the taxes assessed are collected.

Another method of bringing balance between the expenditures and the revenue is to cut all nonessential expenditures to a minimum.

A further method of increasing Government revenue would be to sell to private Korean individuals or corporations as rapidly as possible all the vested properties which the Korean people do not wish to nationalize.

In order to assist in the sale of vested properties and in order to satisfy the desires of tenant farmers, the Land Reform Act could be put into operation immediately so that much of the land can be sold to the farm operators this fall and winter.

A further action which would be beneficial to the whole economy would be a rapid distribution of the large amounts of ECA goods at present held in warehouses because of difficulties in distribution.

Another action which could be taken by the Korean Government to offset inflation would be for the Foreign Exchange Bank and the Government to offer for sale at the exchange auction sufficiently large quantities of dollars so that those persons having import licenses for essential commodities could purchase dollars freely at a reasonable rate of exchange.

The Economic Cooperation Administration is presently seeking to recruit two outstanding authorities on public finance to work out with the Koreans a precise plan of expenditure control, and show them precisely how the tax system can be made more efficient and productive. According to information from Economic Cooperation Administration headquarters, reforms along the following lines are in progress: Prices of goods furnished by the Economic Cooperation Administration are being steadily advanced to more realistic levels; counterpart deposits are being increased in rate; transportation rates have been markedly increased; electric rates were doubled as of January 1, 1950; 10,000,000,000 won of short-term bonds are being sold to Korean purchasers; more rigid controls are being imposed on bank loans; plans for the reorganization of the Bank of Chosun are being completed; the Korean Legislature has passed, and President Rhee has signed, a law which will make possible the sale of vested property.

In recent days, moreover, there have been immediate signs of an improvement in the economic situation.

The New York Times for January 17, for example, contains a dispatch from Seoul, reading as follows:

> . . . The Government began dumping rice on the city markets here today and as a result the price of that basic commodity dropped appreciably for the first time in many weeks of constant soaring. The price dropped about 15 per cent from Saturday's all-time high. It is too early, however, to tell whether the inflationary spiral of the past month has been broken.

The Economic Cooperation Administration headquarters in Washington received on January 17, a cable from Korea confirming that the Korean Government has made final arrangements for the export of 100,000 metric tons of rice to Japan. It is estimated that this will add an extra $14,000,000 to the Korean self-generated exchange.

The Program for the Rest of the Fiscal Year 1950

The Economic Cooperation Administration is seeking a total authorization of $120,000,000 for the fiscal year 1950. This contrasts with the $150,000,000 originally contemplated. It will involve an additional authorization of $60,000,000 for the remaining 4½ months of the fiscal year as compared with a like amount appropriated for the first 7½ months of the fiscal year.

The reduction from $150,000,000 to $120,000,000 is not because the $150,000,000 was not needed at the time it was requested. To use the whole of the $150,000,000 in fiscal year 1950 at this late date would mean the spending of $90,000,000 over a 4- to 5-month period. Such a rate of spending would result in gorging the Korean economy with materials and supplies in excess of its assimilative capacity. On the other hand, in the words of the Economic Cooperation Administration:

> The $60,000,000 now requested will permit the recovery program for Korea to go forward for the remainder of fiscal year 1950 with the vigor and soundness that was envisaged initially in the use of the $150,000,000 for the entire fiscal year 1950.

It is contemplated that approximately one-third of the sum sought for the balance of the fiscal year will be devoted to strictly recovery items. The apportionment among various types of recovery functions is illustrated in an accompanying chart.

The Economic Cooperation Administration further explains the reduction as resulting from the following factors developed in a reappraisal of Korean resources and supplies. This new national inventory, taken last November, revealed the following information: (*a*) fertilizer supplies (to which Economic Cooperation Administration had given procurement priority) were larger than had been expected; (*b*) raw cotton inventories were much smaller than had been believed; (*c*) petroleum requirements had been seriously underestimated; (*d*) certain savings which had not been anticipated could be made in lumber; a portion of the essential materials for railway construction were available in Korean inventories. (Against these savings, however, must be placed certain deficiencies now very clearly revealed: Manila fiber stocks are virtually exhausted, and some 6 months will be required to restore basic inventories; sulfide pulp is in short supply; cement stocks have been exhausted, both for general use and for recovery projects; creosote stocks are exhausted at the very moment when the building of railway extensions calls for supplies to treat the new ties that are being laid.)

According to the explanations given by the Economic Cooperation Administration, the 1950 program has been reduced from the original request of $150,000,000 to $120,000,000 for the following additional reasons: An unprecedented drought increased the production of salt so that all salt imports for fiscal year 1950 could be eliminated; nitrogen requirements, originally calculated at 110,000 metric tons, were reduced to 106,000 as a result of a careful screening of Korean requests based on careful experiments in the capacity of dense paddy land to hold nitrogen longer than is normally the case; curtailed consumption resulting from more stringent controls allowed a programed cut-back of petroleum; delay in reopening the Samwha iron works (from lack of funds for rehabilitation) made possible the elimination of coking coal in fiscal year 1950; certain industrial chemicals programed in finished form, are now scheduled in crude form because of the improved situation in the Korean chemical industry; the circumstantial availability of safe-haven cotton (from China) has made possible the elimination of certain marine textiles; unavailability of funds for fishing boats has resulted in a cut-back in total lumber requirements; ropes and nets programed originally in finished form are now programed as materials with a substantial saving.

The details of the revised recovery program for the current fiscal year appear in an adjoining table.

The Outlook for Subsequent Years

While the reduction in the current program from $150,000,000 to $120,000,000 has been accomplished at the expense of many recovery items originally contemplated, at the same time it should be noted that it is not planned to make compensating enlargements of the program in the subsequent years. An accompanying table summarizes the estimated needs, year by year, in terms of current account deficits of the economy of the Republic of Korea. A comparison of this table with that presented on page 28 of the report accompanying H. R. 5330 (H.

REVISED FINANCIAL ESTIMATE BY PROJECTS FOR ECONOMIC ASSISTANCE TO THE REPUBLIC OF KOREA, FISCAL YEAR 1950

Projects	*Total estimate, fiscal year 1950*	*Appropriated (first period), July 1, 1949-Feb. 15, 1950*	*Supplemental estimate (second period), Feb. 16-June 30, 1950*
Food	$202,000	$202,000	None
Fertilizer	38,071,000	23,500,000	$14,571,000
Petroleum products	10,000,000	5,770,000	4,200,000
Medical supplies	508,000	424,000	84,000
Raw materials	34,268,000	11,614,000	22,654,000
Industrial equipment	3,206,000	580.000	2,626,000
Recovery projects	19,988,000	7,862,000	12,126,000
Surveys and contracts	1,593,000	561,000	1,032,000
Kimpo airport	630,000	350,000	280,000
Technical assistance	3,572,000	1,875,000	1,697,000
Administration	1,700,000	1,050,000	650,000
Ocean freight	*6,162,000	6,162,000	None
Transportation on relief packages	100,000	50,000	50,000
Total	120,000,000	60,000,000	60,000,000

* For transportation costs incurred for commodities procured but not shipped in the fiscal year 1949 by the Department of Army.

Rept. 942, 81st Cong., 1st Sess.) shows the same diminution of the volume of assistance in the fiscal years 1951 and 1952 to $115,000,000 and $85,000,000, respectively. Moreover, present estimates show the current account deficit for the fiscal year 1953 at $20,400,000 instead of the $35,000,000 originally predicted. . . .

During the recent House debate on H. R. 5330 some Members expressed the belief that the program represented it as a $385,000,000 undertaking covering four fiscal years. The bill (H. R. 5330) presented a contemplated 3-year program envisaging expenditures of $350,000,000, at the conclusion of which the calculated trade deficit of the Republic of Korea would be $35,000,000—a figure believed to be readily susceptible of handling by private financing. Thanks to extra-stringent management and to a level of endeavor among the Koreans even higher than expected, the program has now evolved into one contemplating the expenditure of $320,000,000 (of which

ESTIMATED BALANCE OF PAYMENTS FOR REPUBLIC OF KOREA, FISCAL YEARS 1950–53

	1950	*1951*	*1952*	*1953*
Current accounts:				
In-payments:				
Commodity exports	$26,400,000	$50,600,000	$51,200,000	$59,500,000
Invisibles	1,000,000	1,200,000	1,300,000	1,400,000
Total in-payments	27,400,000	51,800,000	52,500,000	60,900,000
Out-payments:				
Commodity imports:				
Korean funding	22,600,000	42,500,000	42,700,000	66,600,000
United States funding	81,400,000	86,000,000	63,200,000	None
Total	104,000,000	128,500,000	105,900,000	66,600,000
Invisibles:				
Korean funding	3,800,000	9,300,000	9,800,000	14,700,000
United States funding	39,600,000	29,000,000	21,800,000	None
Total	43,400,000	38,300,000	31,600,000	14,700,000
Total out-payments	147,400,000	166,800,000	137,500,000	81,300,000
Current account deficit	120,000,000	115,000,000	85,000,000	20,400,000
United States aid:				
Commodity imports	81,400,000	86,000,000	63,200,000	None
Invisible items	39,600,000	29,000,000	21,800,000	None
Total aid	120,000,000	115,000,000	85,000,000	None

$60,000,000 has already been spent), in 3 years, with an even more manageable deficit of a little over $20,000,000 as its sequel.

The reduction in current account deficit is the end objective of the recovery aspects of the program now in being in the Republic of Korea and contemplated for an additional 2 years beyond the present fiscal year. The export development program upon which the hopes of the whole recovery effort are based is indicated in an adjoining table. . . . The figures behind this program appear to be conservative. For example, the calculation of earnings through rice exports for the fiscal year 1951 is based on an assumption of a price of $125 per ton, and for the fiscal years 1952–54 on an assumption of a price of $100 per ton. These assumed prices compare with the current price of $140 per ton.

ESTIMATED EXPORTS FROM REPUBLIC OF KOREA

Category	*Fiscal year*				
	1950	*1951*	*1952*	*1953*	*1954*
Rice	$12,500,000	$31,000,000	$30,000,000	$35,000,000	$40,000,000
Other agricultural	1,298,000	2,713,000	3,035,000	3,200,000	3,800,000
Marine products	8,773,000	10,998,000	12,000,000	13,000,000	14,000,000
Minerals—metals	2,578,000	4,087,000	4,200,000	5,500,000	7,000,000
Manufactured and semimanufactured goods	1,250,000	1,775,000	2,000,000	2,800,000	3,500,000
Total	26,399,000	50,573,000	51,235,000	59,500,000	68,300,000
Miscellaneous and invisibles	1,000,000	1,200,000	1,300,000	1,400,000	1,500,000
Total	27,399,000	51,773,000	52,535,000	60,900,000	69,800,000

It should be emphasized, moreover, that the rate of spending in the contemplated 3-year recovery program will not represent an advance over the previous period, when South Korea was under United States Army occupation, and the primary emphasis was, at least in the first part, on relief. United States forces entered Korea more than 2 months after the beginning of that fiscal year, and still more months elapsed before an appreciable civil program was organized; $6,000,000 were spent on the purpose by the end of the fiscal year. In the fiscal year 1947, the rate rose to $93,000,000; in the fiscal year 1948, to $113,000,000; in the fiscal year 1949, to $144,000,000. Thus in the most recent three fiscal years the rate has been $118,666,000; in the fiscal year 1950 and the ensuing two fiscal years the rate is predicted as $106,666,000.

Requirement for Subsequent Approval by Congress

In the discussion above, the program for establishing a self-sustaining economic basis for the Republic of Korea has been referred to as a 3-year program extending through the fiscal year 1952. It should be made completely clear that the program is not being undertaken as a matter of obligation upon this Government. A 3-year program is contemplated, but its extension will be subject to congressional scrutiny and approval each year, not only by the Committees on Appropriations but also by the committees having substantive jurisdiction—in the House the Committee on Foreign Affairs. It is anticipated that further legislation enabling the Congress to have a second look at the policy questions involved will be acted upon later in this session. . . .

Appendix B

A NOTE ON KOREAN DEMOGRAPHY[1]

Accurate demographic data can, of course, be an important source of insight into the structure of a national community. While much of the information on Korea in this field is of a fragmentary character and of dubious accuracy, some rather significant information exists for the period after 1925. In fact, during the latter years of the Japanese regime, Korean population statistics had been far more thoroughly recorded than those of most other areas in Asia. However, many tentative conclusions which might have been drawn from this information have become less valuable since 1945. The Japanese collapse precipitated wholesale population movements which distorted the pattern in many respects. For example, many long self-exiled Koreans poured back into the homeland. Simultaneously Japanese residents were compelled to leave the country. The Korean immigration, however, more than offset this latter movement. The population movements ultimately were mainly into the southern zone. Together with the flow of refugees from the north, this migration caused the population of southern Korea to increase enormously,[2] while the north possibly experienced a net decline.

[1] For a survey of Korean population factors, see Irene B. Taeuber, "The Population Potential of Postwar Korea," *Far Eastern Quarterly*, May 1946, pp. 289-307. A more limited analysis concerned primarily with the Japanese period was made by Andrew J. Grajdanzev, in *Modern Korea*, pp. 72-83.

[2] For a statistical summary of postwar population movements, see Table 9, p. 335. For a further analysis of the causes of this population growth

The end of Japanese rule in Korea terminated political and economic relationships upon which many factors determining Korean demographic patterns had been predicated. Koreans who had taken residence in Manchuria, in Japan, in China, and elsewhere for a mixture of reasons greeted the Japanese surrender as the signal to return home. This movement originated largely in the general conviction that the Japanese defeat negated the causes of political persecution and abject hardship which had obliged the emigrants to leave Korea. Thus it was principally a short-run phenomenon essentially unrelated to the basic forces which would determine future population changes.

In the postwar period the probable course of Korea's future economic development was quite uncertain, even after the establishment of some measure of political stability separately in the north and in the south. Thus the eventual population trends were obscure. Certain available facts concerning the years of Japanese rule, however, were not immediately irrelevant. Despite the defects of Japanese statistics on births and mortality the general picture of the prewar years can be fairly adequately gauged. During the period of Japanese domination the population grew very rapidly, from about 15 million in 1910 to nearly 26 million in 1944. According to Korean taxation records during the monarchy, the population actually decreased between 1717 and 1904,[3] while in the thirty-five year period after annexation it increased by perhaps more than 70 per cent.

In the absence of actual censuses, the Japanese prepared annual estimates of the population during the first years of their regime. In these estimates the Japanese seem to have underestimated the number of inhabitants of their new colony. Continually revised upward from year to year, these estimates, when

---

see *Population of South Korea by Geographical Divisions and Sex*, Department of Public Health and Welfare, USAMGIK, Seoul, September 1946, Introduction, pp. 6-7.

[3] The method of census-taking seems to have produced figures which were only about half the true number. Thus the 1904 figure was 5,952,093, whereas the true number was probably about 12,000,000. The ancient Korean figures are: 1717, 6,846,568; 1753, 7,304,232; 1807, 7,566,406 and 1852, 6,918,826. See Hoon K. Lee, *Land Utilization and Rural Economy in Korea*, pp. 40-41.

studied in sequence, indicated a spectacular rate of growth. The conclusion has been reached, however, that the Japanese erred initially by underestimating the population in 1909 by perhaps two million.[4]

Plans for an actual census in 1920 were disrupted by the independence disturbances in 1919. This census was postponed until 1925, when the first of several quinquennial enumerations was made. The size of the population as reported by these censuses was as follows: in 1925, 19,522,000; in 1930, 21,058,000; in 1935, 22,899,000; in 1940, 24,326,000; and in 1944, 25,900,000.

Although the population of Korea evidenced a rapid rate of growth in the Japanese period, it is perhaps somewhat misleading to describe this trend as the product of a so-called "oriental" birth rate and an "occidental" death rate. While it is true that Japanese administration in Korea was accompanied by some reduction in the incidence of epidemic disease and a regularization of the food supply, the available figures indicate that the accomplishments in these fields were of very limited scope. Privately conducted surveys covering the period from 1926 to 1935 revealed that official mortality tables grossly underestimated the death rate. According to Taeuber, only 60 per cent of the males and 63 per cent of the females survived to reach age six. Only 55 per cent of the males and 58 per cent of the females lived to attain age fifteen, half the males were dead by age 27 and half the females by age 31.[5]

> The expectation of life at birth for Koreans in Korea in the decade between 1926 and 1935 was lower than that in the majority of countries of Western Europe in the middle of the nineteenth century and only slightly above that in the European territory of Russia in 1896–97. . . . Judged even by the achievements in mortality control elsewhere in the Japanese Empire . . . the vaunted achievements in Korea seemed pitiably small.[6]

Yet even if the Japanese achievements failed to live up to their publicity, they were sufficient, in the absence of a decline in the birth rate, to produce a rapid rise in population. That the birth rate remained at a high level during these years is, how-

[4] Official figures fixed the population in 1909 at 13,091,000 persons. See Grajdanzev, *op. cit.*, p. 73.

[5] Taeuber, *loc. cit.*, p. 293.

[6] *Ibid.*, pp. 293-94.

ever, a facet of Korea's population problems which displayed the influences of an exploitative colonialism. A declining birth rate has had its chief and first incidence in Western countries in the cities. Principally control over fertility has been an urban phenomenon—the product of a growing material culture. Only considerably later has this set of values become diffused through the countryside.

The impact of a high birth rate[7] and something less than a moderate death rate gave Korea a population pattern sharply in contrast with the preponderantly "older" population of the United States and even substantially "younger" than that for the Japanese Empire as a whole, as shown in Table 1.

TABLE 1

PERCENTAGE DISTRIBUTION AMONG AGE GROUPS OF THE POPULATIONS OF KOREA, THE JAPANESE EMPIRE, AND THE UNITED STATES, IN SPECIFIED YEARS

Age Groups	*Korea* * *1935*	*Japanese Empire* † *1935*	*United States* ‡ *1870*	*United States* ‡ *1930*
Under 9 years	29.3	26.8	26.8	19.6
10 to 19 years	20.8	20.7	22.9	19.2
20 to 29 years	16.1	16.5	17.7	16.9
30 to 39 years	11.8	12.4	12.6	14.9
40 to 49 years	9.5	9.4	9.1	12.2
50 to 59 years	6.6	7.4	5.8	8.7
60 to 69 years	3.9	4.4	3.3	5.4
70 years and over	2.0	2.4	1.7	3.2

* Computed from official census figures, *The Japan Yearbook*, 1943–44, pp. 30-31.

† *Ibid.*, pp. 896-97.

‡ Percentages are as reported in the *Sixteenth Decennial Census of the United States, Population*, Volume II, "Characteristics of the Population," Part 1, p. 26, Table 8. Neither column totals exactly 100 per cent.

[7] Japanese census records showed an annual natural increase of 1.7 per cent in the early 1940's. In the study previously cited, Irene Taeuber expressed the opinion that the inadequacy of vital statistics reporting caused the rate of increase to be underestimated. Military Government employed the 1.7 per cent rate of increase in its calculations until May 1948, when a revised estimate of 1.8 per cent was adopted for official computations.

Since industrialization made only slight inroads in Korea, urbanization had very little attractive power. Actually the general tide of population movements away from rural areas favored emigration rather than settlement in cities. Such urban development as occurred was much more the province of the Japanese than of the Koreans.[8] Following the war, the influx of Koreans entering South Korea from the north and from abroad contributed to a great expansion of the population resident in cities. Thus the urban population increased 72.7 per cent, as against an increase of 26.5 per cent in the agricultural population, in the seven and one-third year period from October 1940 to January 1948. Even so, in absolute numbers these figures did not indicate any relief for South Korea's already overpopulated agriculture. In this seven and one-third year period, the urban population increased from about 2,200,000 to 3,800,000, the rural population from 12,000,000 to 16,200,000.[9]

The infiltration of Western material culture could be expected in time to make telling assaults upon the high Korean birth rate, despite the strong "primitive" emphasis upon fertility. But before such a trend set in, there might be a period during which an extension of medical improvements and the regularization of the diet at normative levels would more than offset the downward slope of the birth rates.

If Korea were to become more industrialized, the former geographical distribution of the population might be materially changed. The continued industrialization of the north might substantially reverse the prewar distribution between north and south.[10] This would, of course, be in contrast with the movements of the occupation period. The ultimate results, if Korea were united, might be quite different from the distribution which would be furthered by the political division of the country. While the relative prosperity of the north and south would manifest much authority over population flows in any event,

[8] In 1938, 71 per cent of the Japanese population of Korea was urban, while only 11.5 per cent of Koreans resided in cities. In all communities, however, the Japanese were a minority of the population. See, Grajdanzev, *op. cit.*, p. 80.

[9] *SKIG Activities*, May 1948, p. 6.

[10] In 1944, about 15,900,000 people were living south of the 38th parallel and about 10 million persons resided in the north.

the character of the prosperity would probably be significantly different under the respective circumstances of unity and division. Essentially the same primary factors that would eventually determine the geographic distribution of the population would fix the future arrangement of the population into occupational categories, namely the future course of industrialization.

An interesting characteristic of the Korean population was its relative homogeneity. After the expulsion of the Japanese, who had numbered 708,000 in the 1944 census, some 75,000 Chinese constituted the largest foreign group. Only about ten thousand of this number resided south of the 38th parallel, the principal concentration of Chinese being in the Manchurian border area. European residents, before the war consisting chiefly of the representatives of governments and commercial interests, missionaries, and émigré Russians, aggregated but a handful. The European community, never consequential in size, underwent a progressive decline, largely as a result of the growing pressure exerted upon foreigners by the Japanese.

In the future, Korea might well attract a great deal of immigration from even less fortunate areas of Asia. For some time to come, however, it seemed unlikely that Japanese would be given much opportunity for entry. The presence of foreigners in Korea has had considerable political significance in the past. Anti-foreign feeling, however, has been more an expression of resentment against threatened foreign domination than an expression of racism. There has been little opportunity in recent times for Korea to demonstrate its capacity for assimilation. Thus the matter of how hospitably the country would receive any large immigration has been largely a matter of conjecture.

A number of population tables derived from the Japanese censuses, the Military Government census of South Korea taken in September 1946, and various Military Government tabulations and estimates, which supplement the above text, are included in the following pages.

Table 2

POPULATION IN SOUTH KOREA BY PROVINCES, 1940–1948*
(In thousands)

	1940 October 1	*1944 May 1*	*1946 September 1*	*1948 January 1* †	*1940–48 Percentage Increase*
Kyongsang-namdo	2,148	2,318	3,186	3,287	53
Kyongsang-pukto	2,428	2,561	3,179	3,247	34
Cholla-namdo	2,381 ‡	2,486 ‡	2,945	3,046	28
Kyonggi-do	2,080	2,264	2,486	2,565	23
Cholla-pukto	1,564	1,639	2,016	2,084	33
Chungchong-namdo	1,548	1,647	1,909	1,984	28
Seoul City	775 §	826	1,142	1,243	60
Kangwon-do	898	947	1,117	1,162	29
Chungchong-pukto	935	971	1,113	1,142	22
Cheju-do	212	220	276	281	33
South Korea, Total	14,969	15,879	19,369	20,041	34

* Korean population only. Data for 1940 and 1944 have been adjusted: (1) to exclude Japanese and other non-Koreans, and (2) for boundary changes at the 38th parallel in Kyonggi-do and Kangwon-do.

† Estimates by Committee on Population and Census Statistics.

‡ Adjusted to separate the population of Cheju-do from Cholla-namdo.

§ The concentration in Seoul of the Japanese in Korea at the time, and their exclusion from this data, make the downward adjustment for Seoul more pronounced than for the rest of South Korea.

Source: Committee on Population and Census Statistics.

Table 3

POPULATION OF THE PRINCIPAL CITIES OF SOUTH KOREA, AUGUST 25, 1946

City	Population	City	Population
Seoul	1,141,766	Kaesong	87,962
Pusan	400,156	Chinju	86,852
Taegu	269,113	Chonju	83,333
Inchon	215,784	Masan	82,175
Mopko	103,081	Gunsan	66,715
Kwangju	100,451	Chungju	51,522
Taejon	96,207	Chunchon	46,089

Source: Vital Statistics Section, Department of Public Health and Welfare, USAMGIK, *Population of South Korea by Geographical Divisions and Sex*, Seoul, September 1946.

TABLE 4

POPULATION OF KOREAN NATIONALS BOTH WITHIN AND OUTSIDE KOREA, 1925–1947 * (In thousands)

	1925	*1930*	*1935*	*1940*	*1944*	*1947*
Within Korea						
TOTALS..........	19,020	20,438	22,208	23,547	25,120	28,059
Male	9,726	10,399	11,271	11,839	12,599	14,030
Female	9,294	10,039	10,937	11,708	12,521	14,029
Outside Korea						
TOTALS..........	720	1,234	1,579	2,326	3,292	† 1,636
In Japan	40	419	600	950	1,550	400
In China, mainly Manchuria	500	620	774	1,162	1,500	1,000
In Siberia	160	170	175	180	185	215
Elsewhere	20	25	30	34	57	21
TOTAL KOREANS throughout the world.	19,740	21,672	23,787	25,873	28,412	29,695

* Population statistics for Koreans within Korea, 1925–1944, are from official Japanese census reports: 1947 Korean population is estimated. Figures for Koreans abroad are taken from a wide variety of sources, mainly official Japanese census reports; 1947 Korean population is estimated. Estimates for Korean population in Siberia are on the basis of 1939 official Soviet census, which stated that there were 180,412 Koreans in the U.S.S.R. at that time, and from other unofficial reports. There was a heavy movement of Koreans into Soviet Far Eastern areas at the end of the war, which exceeded by at least 40,000 the movement of Soviet Koreans into northern Korea.

† Between the end of the war and April 1946, Koreans known to have entered southern Korea numbered: from Japan, 1,103,000; from China (mainly from Manchuria), 375,000; other areas, 33,000. An estimated 125,000 Koreans entered northern Korea from China (mainly from Manchuria), and a few thousands entered from Siberia.

Source: Korea Economic Mission, Dept. of State, June 1947.

TABLE 5

TRENDS IN OCCUPATIONAL COMPOSITION OF THE POPULATION IN KOREA, 1926–1944 * (In thousands)

A. Numbers of the Total Population Dependent upon Various Occupations

Year	*Agriculture* Number	%	*Industry and Mining* Number	%	*Commerce and Communications* Number	%	*Public and Professional Services* Number	%
1926	15,513	81.2	468	2.4	1,306	6.8	567	3.0
1930	15,912	78.6	532	2.6	1,432	7.1	706	3.5
1934	16,175	76.6	570	2.7	1,529	7.2	858	4.1
1938	16,660	73.6	972	4.3	1,820	8.0	892	3.9
1944	17,944	69.8	3,230	12.4	2,348	8.6	960	3.8

B. Numbers of Koreans Dependent upon Various Occupations

Year	*Agriculture* Number	%	*Industry and Mining* Number	%	*Commerce and Communications* Number	%	*Public and Professional Services* Number	%
1926	15,464	83.1	415	2.2	1,143	6.1	420	2.3
1930	15,853	80.5	449	2.3	1,254	6.4	523	2.6
1934	16,127	78.6	483	2.4	1,340	6.5	629	3.1
1938	16,616	75.6	843	3.9	1,619	7.4	646	2.9
1944	17,917	71.1	3,000	11.7	2,142	8.5	700	2.9

C. Numbers of Japanese Dependent upon Various Occupations

Year	*Agriculture* Number	%	*Industry and Mining* Number	%	*Commerce and Communications* Number	%	*Public and Professional Services* Number	%
1926	41	9.2	65	14.5	139	30.6	146	33.5
1930	42	8.4	72	14.4	147	29.4	177	35.2
1934	38	6.8	77	13.7	167	30.0	225	40.1
1938	34	5.4	120	23.0	185	29.1	241	38.0
1944	24	3.4	210	30.0	200	28.0	260	37.0

* These statistics do not include a variety of other miscellaneous occupations or the unemployed, which together include from six to twelve per cent of the total. Therefore the percentages for any given year will total less than 100 per cent. Compiled from tables in *Chosen Sotokufu Tokei Nempo*, 1936, pp. 22-23, 32-39, and from *Nihon Takumu Daijin Kambo Bunsho-ku (Showa junen) Takuku Tokei*, pp. 9-13. Figures for 1944 are compiled from *Chosen Government-General Census*, 1944.

Source: Same as Table 5.

Table 6A

POPULATION AND EMPLOYMENT OF KOREANS, 1944

	Managerial		Clerks & White Collar Workers		Professional & Technical		Laborers		Public Servants & Small Businessmen		Unemployed		
Age	*Men*	*Women*	*Men*	*Women*	*Men*	*Women*	*Men*	*Women*	*Men*	*Women*	*Men*	*Women*	*Totals*
under 12 yrs.	—	—	9	2	—	—	71,688	82,302	46	71	4,555,661	4,412,022	9,121,801
12–15	2	2	1,853	1,393	88	6	450,661	330,485	1,154	469	713,977	756,503	2,256,588
16–20	68	8	30,569	6,221	2,658	51	870,451	519,133	18,132	4,808	170,221	695,837	2,218,151
21–25	371	23	43,495	1,166	6,892	115	741,559	444,552	30,150	1,866	33,607	499,569	1,803,365
26–30	845	44	33,750	564	6,303	77	727,009	417,833	23,668	946	21,508	432,861	1,665,408
31–35	1,248	64	25,013	323	4,763	44	687,177	403,234	18,074	747	17,391	376,078	1,534,156
36–40	1,252	64	17,097	223	3,012	223	591,319	345,823	12,854	546	15,159	299,047	1,284,435
41–45	1,097	42	9,753	124	1,581	124	543,229	305,124	7,355	406	16,153	258,453	1,143,330
46–50	878	53	5,895	58	979	58	498,997	264,537	4,624	336	19,511	242,344	1,038,221
51–55	594	36	2,921	27	623	27	412,062	216,495	2,670	289	27,353	234,210	897,284
56–60	367	8	1,236	23	367	4	294,598	136,737	1,549	228	43,512	216,568	695,202
over 60	429	21	831	42	635	4	403,949	160,653	1,854	561	264,812	626,431	1,460,222
TOTALS	7,151	365	172,422	10,166	27,901	366	6,292,704	3,626,908	122,130	11,273	5,898,865	8,949,923	25,120,174

Source: Results of 1944 Census (in Japanese), Chosen Government-General, May 1944.

Table 6B

POPULATION AND EMPLOYMENT OF JAPANESE IN KOREA, 1944

Age	*Managerial*		*Clerks & White Collar Workers*		*Professional & Technical*		*Laborers*		*Public Servants & Small Businessmen*		*Unemployed*		
	Men	*Women*	*Men*	*Women*	*Men*	*Women*	*Men*	*Women*	*Men*	*Women*	*Men*	*Women*	*Totals*
under 12 yrs.	—	—	—	2	—	—	28	35	—	4	113,161	110,409	223,639
12–15	—	2	330	564	17	3	4,509	1,410	169	69	23,995	24,720	55,787
16–20	11	4	7,638	8,485	1,449	83	14,617	8,539	1,707	3,074	12,527	14,899	73,033
21–25	14	1	3,795	2,609	1,033	67	4,793	5,472	3,565	1,450	1,550	28,391	52,740
26–30	87	20	6,884	882	2,121	55	7,586	3,274	8,199	663	670	31,107	61,548
31–35	257	24	6,694	504	2,463	44	7,349	3,008	7,066	606	397	27,194	55,606
36–40	380	26	6,461	434	2,373	33	7,083	2,527	5,923	366	282	19,106	44,994
41–45	585	33	7,233	295	2,080	27	7,412	2,839	4,448	231	348	15,223	40,754
46–50	570	37	5,507	206	1,333	13	6,280	2,456	3,056	191	346	10,849	30,844
51–55	566	37	4,304	161	874	11	5,304	2,148	1,975	158	472	8,612	24,622
56–60	477	36	2,670	96	495	10	4,516	1,473	1,198	113	1,060	6,381	18,525
over 60	465	33	1,841	106	248	6	5,087	1,442	935	141	4,308	11,744	26,356
TOTALS	3,412	253	53,357	14,344	14,486	352	74,564	34,623	38,240	7,066	159,116	308,635	708,448

Source: Results of 1944 Census (in Japanese), Chosen Government-General, May 1944.

TABLE 7

INDUSTRIAL EMPLOYMENT STATISTICS FOR ALL KOREA, 1943

A. All Industry

Category	Laborers				Technicians & Engineers		
	Total	*Japanese*	*Koreans*	*Others*	*Total*	*Japanese*	*Koreans*
TOTAL for *All Industry*	549,751	26,966	512,907	9,878	9,852	7,993	1,859
Male workers	456,925	24,042	423,087	9,796	9,821	7,973	1,848
Female workers	92,826	2,924	89,820	82	31	20	11
Metals (645 concerns)							
Male workers	39,860	4,742	34,682	256	1,422	1,273	149
Female workers	1,824	340	1,479	5	1	1	—
Machine Tools (1,345 concerns)							
Male workers	46,367	3,789	42,399	179	1,572	1,212	360
Female workers	1,454	196	1,258	—	1	1	—
Chemicals (927 concerns)							
Male workers	50,695	7,441	42,879	375	2,316	2,089	227
Female workers	13,023	1,212	11,811	—	16	7	9
Gas, Electric, Water (123 concerns)							
Male workers	6,676	903	5,772	1	1,027	788	239
Female workers	245	146	99	—	1	1	—
Ceramics & Cement (1,818 concerns)							
Male workers	32,775	685	31,870	2	263	215	48
Female workers	4,145	54	4,091	—	1	1	—
Textiles (2,605 concerns)							
Male workers	26,858	759	25,913	186	604	458	146
Female workers	52,905	615	52,227	13	2	1	1
Lumber (2,005 concerns)							
Male workers	26,809	511	25,281	1,017	104	77	27
Female workers	1,608	32	1,560	16	—	—	—
Food Processing (2,202 concerns)							
Male workers	24,247	845	23,202	200	370	263	107
Female workers	7,511	117	7,393	1	—	—	—
Printing (606 concerns)							
Male workers	9,377	175	9,187	15	1	1	—
Female workers	676	30	645	1	—	—	—

TABLE 7 (*cont.*)

INDUSTRIAL EMPLOYMENT STATISTICS FOR ALL KOREA, 1943

A. All Industry

Category	Laborers				Technicians & Engineers		
	Total	Japanese	Koreans	Others	Total	Japanese	Koreans
Engineering & Construction (1,700 concerns)							
Male workers	183,157	3,954	172,131	7,072	2,036	1,496	540
Female workers	3,641	133	3,507	1	—	—	—
All others (871 concerns)							
Male workers	10,284	238	9,771	275	105	100	5
Female workers	5,794	49	5,700	45	9	8	1
B. All Mining (1,239 mines)							
TOTAL for *All Mining*	183,358	1,935	178,881	2,542	3,468	2,145	1,323
Male workers	170,075	1,660	165,875	2,540	3,465	2,144	1,321
Female workers	13,283	275	13,006	2	3	1	2
Coal & Metal (1,044 mines)							
Male workers	159,767	1,558	155,782	2,427	3,414	2,001	1,313
Female workers	12,594	271	12,321	2	3	1	2
1) *Metal* (594 mines)							
Male workers	84,168	1,089	82,320	759	1,818	1,250	568
Female workers	6,473	203	6,270	—	2	—	2
2) *Coal* (82 mines)							
Male workers	54,902	323	52,915	1,664	1,306	680	626
Female workers	2,394	61	2,331	2	1	1	—
3) *Others* (368 mines)							
Male workers	20,697	14	20,547	4	291	171	120
Female workers	3,727	7	3,720	—	—	—	—
Sand (28 mines)							
Male workers	2,621	15	2,606	—	26	23	3
Female workers	6	1	5	—	—	—	—
Excavating (167 mines)							
Male workers	7,687	87	7,487	113	25	20	5
Female workers	683	3	680	—	—	—	—
C. Transportation (excluding Government Railroads)							
TOTAL	85,589	4,791	80,128	670	1,125	1,003	122
Male workers	79,235	3,405	75,162	668	1,125	1,003	122
Female workers	6,354	1,386	4,966	2	—	—	—
D. Business Offices, Commercial Stores, Other Business Enterprises							
TOTAL	24,419	3,675	20,545	199	3,934	1,343	2,591
Male workers	19,565	1,747	17,621	197	3,932	1,342	2,590
Female workers	4,854	1,928	2,924	2	2	1	1

Source: Report on 1943 Census of Laborers and Technicians in Korea (written in Japanese), Chosen Government-General, 1943.

TABLE 8

STATUS OF EDUCATION OF POPULATION IN KOREA, 1944

	Koreans		*Japanese*			*Japanese Percentage of Total*
	Male	*Female*	*Male*	*Female*	*All Korea Totals* *	
Graduate Students (on university level)	7,272	102	7,147	83	14,604	50.0
Graduates College, Normal and Technical Schools	18,555	3,509	14,921	4,324	41,309	47.0
Graduates Middle School	162,111	37,531	68,366	86,868	354,876	44.0
Preparatory School (equivalent of Jr. High School—at least two yrs. Middle School)	40,702	9,240	76,848	65,582	192,372	74.0
Graduates of National Primary Schools	1,281,490	355,552	52,543	75,367	1,764,952	7.0
Attendants of National Primary Schools	190,250	64,555	2,141	5,573	262,519	3.0
"Literate" without a formal education (self-taught)	864,308	115,814	—	—	980,122	.0
Uneducated, no formal schooling or class instruction	8,430,940	11,211,835	75,578	82,762	19,801,115	.8
TOTALS	10,995,628	11,798,138	297,544	320,559	23,411,869	

* Information available only on number of persons listed here.

Source: Results of 1944 Census, Chosen Government-General, May 1944.

Table 9

MOVEMENT OF POPULATION IN AND OUT OF SOUTH KOREA, OCTOBER 1945–APRIL 1948 *

Nationalities	*Cumulative Totals*	
	Outbound	*Inbound*
Japanese, Military	179,273	
Japanese, Civilian	704,613	
Chinese	1,940	
Formosan	103	
Okinawan	274	
Japanese from North Korea		288,516
Koreans from North Korea		829,886
Koreans from Manchuria		58,836
Koreans from Japan		1,111,971
Koreans from China		58,143
Koreans from other Pacific Areas		37,201
TOTAL	886,203	2,384,553

* These figures are believed to minimize actual entries into South Korea. Persons are known to have entered South Korea from the north at points other than those where refugee entry stations were established.

Source: *SKIG Activities*, April 1948, p. 5.

Appendix C

TABLE I

NOTE CIRCULATION OF CHOSUN BANK, 1937–JULY 1949 *

(In million won)

Month	Year	Amount	Month	Year	Amount
	1937	280	Apr.	1947	17,240
	1938	322	May	1947	17,418
	1939	444	June	1947	18,036
	1940	581	July	1947	18,638
	1941	742	Aug.	1947	19,497
	1942	909	Sept.	1947	20,445
	1943	1,467	Oct.	1947	21,873
	1944	3,136	Nov.	1947	31,012
July	1945	4,698	Dec.	1947	33,388†
Aug.	1945	7,988	Jan.	1948	31,600
Sept.	1945	8,680	Feb.	1948	30,900
Oct.	1945	8,798	Mar.	1948	29,300
Nov.	1945	8,626	Apr.	1948	28,200
Dec.	1945	8,763	May	1948	28,600
Jan.	1946	8,905	June	1948	30,000
Feb.	1946	8,884	July	1948	30,500
Mar.	1946	9,080	Aug.	1948	30,000
Apr.	1946	9,196	Sept.	1948	30,900
May	1946	9,221	Oct.	1948	32,500
June	1946	9,422	Nov.	1948	40,300
July	1946	10,333	Dec.	1948	43,400
Aug.	1946	10,962	Jan.	1949	42,600
Sept.	1946	11,341	Feb.	1949	40,800
Oct.	1946	12,198	Mar.	1949	37,800
Nov.	1946	14,881	Apr.	1949	37,900
Dec.	1946	17,711	May	1949	38,600
Jan.	1947	18,278	June	1949	40,800
Feb.	1947	17,689	July	1949	45,400
Mar.	1947	17,199			

* Includes notes in circulation in North Korea before September 1945. Before September 1945 Bank of Japan notes were also circulated as legal tender.

† Figures reported after January 1948 are only to the nearest tenth of a billion won.

Source: Chosun Bank, *Monthly Statistical Review*, January 1948, pp. 11-43; *Republic of Korea, Statistical Summation*, August 1949, p. 71.

TABLE 2

GOVERNMENT DEPOSITS IN AND WITHDRAWALS FROM CHOSUN BANK, OCTOBER 1945–JULY 1949

Period	*Revenue Deposits* *	*Withdrawals*	*Excess Withdrawals*	*Cumulative Excess Withdrawals*
1945				
Oct.				21
1946				
Jan.	45	452	407	590
Apr.	107	666	559	1,584
July	185	1,398	1,213	3,665
Oct.	440	936	496	5,219
1947				
Jan.	539	1,282	743	8,466
Mar.	679	1,279	600	9,763
Apr.	616	2,242	1,626	11,389
Jul.	622	2,021	1,399	17,228
Oct.	1,358	2,795	1,437	19,859
1948				
Jan.	1,264	1,805	541	21,710
Apr.	1,555	2,340	785	22,005
July	1,739	1,283	456†	21,573
Oct.	3,014	3,892	878	38,400
1949				
Jan.	2,841	3,780	939	40,732
Apr.	3,525	4,460	935	45,128
July	689	5,960	5,271	61,305

* Revenue from the Department of Transportation is not included.
† Excess deposit.

Source: Chosun Bank.

TABLE 3

RETAIL PRICES OF 26 MAJOR COMMODITIES USED IN FAMILY LIVING, AT SELECTED PERIODS, AUGUST 1945–MAY 1948
(In won)

Commodity	*Unit* *	*Aug. 1945*	*May 1946*	*May 1947*	*Jan. 1948*	*May 1948*
Cleaned rice	mal	220	500	1,000	1,500	1,460
Soy beans	mal	45	300	750	1,100	1,200
Red beans	mal	140	580	960	1,300	1,540
Wheat flour	22 kg.	130	1,100	1,400	1,800	2,250
Cleaned barley	mal	60	200	330	500	600
Cleaned millet	mal	66	340	520	700	670
Beef	600 gram	16	70	180	250	300
Pork	600 gram	20	75	180	250	280
Dried myungtai	20 fish	12	75	140	350	320
Chinese cabbage	3.75 kg.	8	10	70	250	140
Korean turnip	3.75 kg.	5	20	80	120	150
Red pepper powder	doi	80	120	250	280	450
Sesame oil	doi	60	300	1,000	1,900	2,000
Sugar	600 gram	15	180	300	550	200
Salt	doi	10	40	90	130	120
Cotton sheeting	yard	7	60	210	520	430
Cotton shirting	yard	13	100	350	600	750
Korean silk	pill	130	500	2,000	4,500	3,900
Rubber shoes	pair	40	80	200	270	210
Leather shoes	pair	250	650	2,100	3,000	3,500
Work shoes	pair	35	85	300	350	370
Fire wood	2.3 cu.m.	350	650	3,100	6,000	4,500
Charcoal	22.5 kg.	45	60	250	650	500
Briquettes	1,000 kg.	350	1,400	3,700	8,500	8,500
Matches	10 small boxes	9	50	70	70	65
Laundry soap	piece	4	25	130	240	220

* 1 mal = 4.76 gallons = 14.6 kilograms.
1 doi = 2 liters.
1 pill = about 30 yards.

Source: Chosun Bank.

TABLE 4

PRICES OF CONTROLLED COMMODITIES PRODUCED IN SOUTH KOREA, 1947 AND 1948

Item	*Unit*	*Controlled Price March 1948 in won*	*Effective date*
Food			
Rice, cleaned, 2nd grade	large mal	280	Jan. 20, 1948
Soy beans, yellow, 2nd grade	60 kg.	680	Nov. 1, 1946
Red beans, 2nd grade	60 kg.	760	Nov. 1, 1946
Barley, cleaned 1st grade	1 kg.	15.60	Sept. 15, 1947
Wheat, cleaned	1 kg.	15.85	Sept. 15, 1947
Millet, cleaned	1 kg.	10.37	Nov. 1, 1946
Wheat flour	22 kg.	462	Sept. 15, 1947
Salt, refined	60 kg.	855	July 15, 1946
Textiles			
Cotton cloth, sheeting	yard	56	Aug. 1, 1947
Cotton cloth, shirting	yard	91	Aug. 1, 1947
Undershirt	each	190	Feb. 29, 1948
Footwear			
Shoes, rubber, women's	pair	110	Aug. 1, 1947
Shoes, rubber, work	pair	100	Aug. 1, 1947
Shoes, calf leather	pair	1,660	Apr. 3, 1948
Fuel			
Anthracite, lump	metric ton	3,500	Mar. 5, 1948
Anthracite, dust	metric ton	2,700	Mar. 5, 1948
Lignite	metric ton	2,500	Mar. 5, 1948
Coke	metric ton	5,200	Jan. 1, 1948
Miscellaneous			
Tires, truck	each	16,000	Oct. 20, 1947
Tires, automobile	each	6,700	Oct. 20, 1947
Tubes, truck	each	1,450	Oct. 20, 1947
Tubes, automobile	each	960	Oct. 20, 1947
Tires (26 in.), bicycle	each	580	Dec. 10, 1947
Tires (28 in.), bicycle	each	630	Dec. 10, 1947
Tubes (26 in.), bicycle	each	195	Dec. 10, 1947
Tubes (28 in.), bicycle	each	200	Dec. 10, 1947
Paper (Senhwa)	pound	55	Dec. 1, 1947
Printing paper	pound	63	Dec. 1, 1947
Rice bran oil	16.5 kg.	1,090	Jan. 15, 1948
Nails (2 in.)	60 kg.	5,300	Jan. 29, 1948
Matches	10 boxes	35	Aug. 1, 1947
Soap, laundry	piece	32	Aug. 1, 1947

Source: SKIG Activities, April 1948, p. 37.

TABLE 5

WEIGHTED INDEX OF WHOLESALE PRICES IN SOUTH KOREA *

(1947 = 100)

Month	*1945*	*1946*	*1947*	*1948*	*1949*
January		17	86	158	195
February		22	91	158	191
March		32	90	157	194
April		34	84	157	205
May		33	85	157	213
June		35	89	166	218
July		43	96	171	240
August	19	51	98	185	264
September	13	56	105	187	
October	11	57	112	177	
November	11	59	121	179	
December	14	74	143	196	

* For a consideration of the assumptions made in the construction of this index see *SKIG Activities*, June 1948, pp. 31-46.

Source: National Price Administration and Bank of Korea.

TABLE 6

EMPLOYMENT AND WAGES ON RAILROADS IN SOUTH KOREA, APRIL 1946 TO JUNE 1948

Period	*Number of Employees*	*Total Wages Paid (thousands of won)*	*Average Monthly Wages per Employee (won)*
Fiscal year 1946–47 monthly average	35,366	61,114	1,728
Fiscal year 1947–48			
Apr.	32,575	86,495	2,655
May	32,442	84,738	2,612
June	32,724	84,969	2,596
July	34,033	92,042	2,704
Aug.	33,957	196,659 *	5,850
Sept.	33,635	111,933	3,327
Oct.	33,561	115,723	3,448
Nov.	33,464	128,582	3,842
Dec.	33,281	152,982	4,596
Jan.	33,099	128,979	4,105
Feb.	32,998	117,659	3,566
Mar.	32,832	147,054	4,479
Apr.	33,609	115,361	3,432
May	33,719	150,830	4,467
June	33,036	122,279	3,701

* Includes retroactive wages back to April 1947.

Source: *SKIG Activities*, April 1948, p. 103, and June 1948, p. 101.

TABLE 7

PER-CAPITA DISAPPEARANCE OF FOODSTUFFS, INCLUDING AND EXCLUDING IMPORTS UNDER EMERGENCY CIVILIAN SUPPLY PROGRAM, MAY 1946–APRIL 1947

	Per Capita Disappearance, Pounds		
		May 1946–April 1947	
Commodity	*1932–36 Average* *	*Domestic Production Only* †	*Total Available (incl. imports)*
Rice	145	206	211
Wheat	31	7	33
Flour			5
Barley	102	47	53
Millet	95	10	10
Rye	Neg.	2	2
Other grains	28	6	7
Soy beans	45	10	10
Other beans	12	1	1
All other legumes	3	Neg.	Neg.
Potatoes	80	43	43
Vegetables	146	75	75
Fruits & nuts	11	7	7
Sugar	3	0	Neg.
Candy	0	0	.5
Fish	48	34	34
Meat	6	6	6
Eggs (number)	10	5	5
Other canned goods	—	—	1
TOTAL	768	459	490.5

* *Civil Affairs Handbook, Korea*, p. 91.

† USAMGIK, *Present Agricultural Position of South Korea*, Seoul, April 1947, *passim*.

Neg.: negligible.

Source: Compiled from USAMGIK reports.

TABLE 8

FOODSTUFFS IMPORTED UNDER EMERGENCY CIVILIAN SUPPLY PROGRAM TO SOUTH KOREA, MAY 1946–MAY 1948

Commodity	*Amount (metric tons)*
1. From Army stocks:	
Rice	155
Beans, dry	100
Sugar	411
Case goods	10,370
2. From other U.S. sources: *	
Wheat	366,689
Flour, wheat	106,014
Flour, soya	8,147
Barley	167,184
Corn	24,940
Oats	906
Rice	56,678
Beans	1,463
Peas, dry	1,102
Sugar	43,872
Milk, dehydrated	3,444
Candy	9,204
Case goods	15,255

* Includes imports from U.S. sources in Burma, Siam, the Philippines, and Red Sea area, as well as directly from the United States.

Source: *SKIG Activities*, May 1948, p. 82.

TABLE 9

LIVESTOCK POPULATION OF SOUTH KOREA, 1937–JANUARY 1, 1948

Kinds of Livestock	*1937*	*1940*	*1941*	*1942*	*1943*	*1944*	*1946*	*January 1, 1948*
Dairy cattle	948	1,130	1,121	1,263	2,420	NIA	1,127	1,339
Work or beef cattle	925,030	935,739	1,074,206	961,403	963,751	886,842	556,220	640,572
Horses, racing	92	111	140	181	NIA	NIA	235	
Horses, work	31,936	29,354	32,010	48,465	34,958	"	24,760	
Ponies	1,947	3,559	5,335	5,962	NIA	"	8,715	35,663
Mules	264	110	71	54	"	"	35	
Donkeys	496	147	80	78	"	"	54	
Hogs	931,412	677,885	703,264	603,730	345,174	"	181,331	373,882
Goats, native	40,766	51,370	49,381	45,880	NIA	"	25,043	41,814
Goats, milk	NIA	NIA	2,172	1,938	"	"	821	
Sheep	1,756	11,862	14,088	13,057	11,188	"	4,317	3,226
Chickens	3,970,721	3,478,549	3,171,584	2,789,074	2,260,308	"	1,516,389	2,050,789
Ducks	6,380	4,643	3,308	3,291	NIA	"	1,748	
Rabbits	14,568	170,200	161,002	96,448	50,051	"	12,356	31,164

Source: USAMGIK, *Present Agricultural Position of South Korea*, pp. 14-15, and *SKIG Activities*, April 1948, p. 20. "NIA" indicates no information available.

Table 10

MARINE PRODUCTS LANDINGS BY GROUPS, SOUTH KOREA, 1932–1948

(Thousands of metric tons)

Year	*Fresh Fish*	*Shell Fish*	*Sea-weed*	*Sea Animals*	*Total*
1932	574	68	34	—	676
1933	427	50	25	24	526
1934	462	55	28	36	581
1935	720	23	71	42	856
1936	514	14	37	43	608
1937	538	16	29	55	637
1938	525	17	40	46	629
1939	499	10	41	49	600
1940	455	11	35	45	545
1941	364	15	33	52	463
1942	288	28	28	33	377
1943	282	14	33	45	373
1944	229	7	30	30	296
1945	150	10	23	19	202
1946	251	10	15	23	299
1947	264	5	8	25	302
1948	226	40	6	13	285

Source: Voice of Korea, October 1, 1948, for the years 1932–47; Republic of Korea Statistical Summation, May 1949, p. 14 for 1948.

TABLE 11

ELECTRIC POWER DELIVERED IN SOUTH KOREA FROM ALL SOURCES, 1946 TO AUGUST 1949

(In millions of kilowatts)

Month	*Total*	*From North of 38°*	*From South of 38°*
1946:			
Total	666.0	442.0	224.0
Mo. average	55.4	36.8	18.6
1947:			
January	69.7	53.5	16.2
February	66.1	46.7	19.4
March	73.6	54.8	18.8
April	62.6	33.5	29.1
May	63.6	40.5	23.1
June	62.7	42.7	20.0
July	64.2	31.6	32.6
August	61.2	39.0	22.2
September	64.4	31.0	33.4
October	79.6	54.6	25.0
November	80.5	62.9	17.6
December	68.6	51.8	16.8
Total	816.8	542.6	274.2
Mo. average	68.7	45.2	22.9
1948:			
January	74.3	53.1	21.2
February	71.6	47.5	24.1
March	80.7	47.6	33.1
April	75.9	42.2	33.7
May	56.5	15.1*	41.4
June	41.1		41.1
July	56.1		56.1
August	55.6		55.6
September	45.6		45.6

* North Korean power cut off on May 14, 1948. All power subsequently delivered generated within South Korea.

TABLE 11 (*cont.*)

ELECTRIC POWER DELIVERED IN SOUTH KOREA FROM ALL SOURCES, 1946 TO AUGUST 1949

(In millions of kilowatts)

Month	*Total*	*From North of 38°*	*From South of 38°*
1948:			
October	46.1		46.1
November	47.8		47.8
December	44.2		44.2
Total	693.8	204.8	489.0
Mo. average	57.8	45.5	40.7
1949:			
January	44.5		
February	45.2		
March	58.6		
April	59.3		
May	59.3		
June	54.2		
July	52.2		
August	58.8		

Source: *SKIG Activities*, April 1948, p. 116; *Republic of Korea Statistical Summation*, May 1949, p. 16, August 1949, p. 22.

TABLE 12

REQUIREMENTS * FOR AND PRODUCTION † OF LOGS IN SOUTH KOREA (Unit = koku) ‡

Item	*Requirements*	*1946 Production*	*1946 Stock*	*Deficit*
Ship timbers	187,552	34,976	36,280	116,296
Const. logs	372,174	69,405	326,520	23,751
Lumber	885,012	165,043	72,300	647,669
R. R. sleepers	325,000	40,440	73,500	211,060
Mine props	190,483	35,522	36,000	118,961
Poles	49,819	9,253	3,900	36,666
Wagon stock	67,403	12,569	—	54,834
Box board	316,494	59,022	—	257,472
Pulpwood	295,980	55,196	500	240,284
Veneer log	146,525	27,325	1,000	118,200
Others	202,201	37,708	—	164,493
TOTAL	3,038,643	546,500	550,000	1,942,143

* Requirements based on average of amounts used in 1932–1933.

† Estimated production—S. of latitude 38° N. from April 1, 1945, to March 31, 1946.

‡ 1 koku equals 80 board feet.

Source: Report of Natural Resources Section, SCAP, original data from Department of Forestry, Korea.

TABLE 13

COTTON YARN AND COTTON CLOTH PRODUCTION IN MAJOR PLANTS IN SOUTH KOREA, 1946–1948

	Cotton Yarn (kg.)			*Cotton Cloth (meters)* *		
Period	*1946*	*1947*	*1948*	*1946*	*1947*	*1948*
Jan.	70	498	367	383	2,485	1,621
Feb.	87	459	406	536	2,215	1,812
Mar.	156	492	522	825	2,549	2,286
Apr.	235	541	604	1,293	2,665	2,668
May	279	636	569	1,580	2,884	2,379
June	295	605	411	1,730	3,028	1,724
July	344	502	502	2,024	2,833	2,311
Aug.	403	433	564	2,259	2,537	2,426
Sept.	476	359	495	2,560	2,136	1,985
Oct.	551	427	539	2,775	2,329	2,063
Nov.	632	370	501	2,991	1,964	1,936
Dec.	437	266	439	2,136	1,377	2,083
Total	3,965	5,588	5,919	21,092	29,002	25,293
Mo. av.	330	466	493	1,758	2,417	2,108

* Average width of cloth is 36 inches.

Source: Republic of Korea Statistical Summation, August 1949, p. 34.

Bibliography

I. BIBLIOGRAPHICAL WORKS

Chosen Sotokufu (Government-General of Chosen), *Chosen Tosho Kaidai* (Bibliography of the Korean Royal Library, in Japanese), Seoul, 1919; second edition, 1931.

Courant, Maurice, *Bibliographie coréenne . . .*, critical bibliography of works published before 1890, Paris, E. Leroux, 1894–1896, 3 vols.

Supplément à la Bibliographie coréenne, Paris, Leroux, 1901, x + 122 pp.

Kerner, Robert J., *Northeastern Asia, A Selected Bibliography*, "Korea," pp. 230-270, Vol. II, Berkeley, University of California Press, 1939.

McCune, Shannon, *Western Language Materials on Korea*, New York, Institute of Pacific Relations, 1950, 13 pp.

Trollope, Mark N. "Corean Books and Their Authors," *Transactions of the Korea Branch of the Royal Asiatic Society*, Vol. XXI (1932), pp. 1-104.

Underwood, Horace H., "A Partial Bibliography of Occidental Literature on Korea from Early Times to 1930," *Transactions of the Korea Branch of the Royal Asiatic Society*, Vol. XX (1931), pp. 1-198.

———, "Supplement to a Partial Bibliography of Occidental Literature on Korea from Early Times to 1930," *Transactions of the Korea Branch of the Royal Asiatic Society*, Vol. XXIV (1935), pp. 23-48.

II. BACKGROUND BIBLIOGRAPHY FOR THE PERIOD BEFORE 1945

Periodicals

Transactions of the Royal Asiatic Society of Great Britain and Ireland, Korea Branch, Seoul, 1900–1940.

The *Korea Review* (monthly), Seoul, Methodist Publishing House, 1901–1906.

Korea Review, Philadelphia, Korean Information Bureau, 1919–1922.

The *Korean Repository* (monthly), Seoul, Trilingual Press, 1891–1898.

Korean-American Cultural Association, *The Culture of Korea*, 1945–46, 334 pp. This work is a collection of articles that appeared before 1946.

Before 1905

a. KOREAN AND JAPANESE SOURCES

Chong, Changsun (compiler), *Tongmun Hwigo* (Documents of Foreign Relations, in Korean), 129 books in 60 volumes. Compiled at the request of King Chongjo (1777–1800), 1789. Two volumes of a projected edition of 12 volumes published by Keijo Imperial University, 1938.

Chosen Shi Gakukai (Korean Historical Association), *Chosen Shi Taikei* (Outline History of Korea, in Japanese), Seoul, 1937, 5 volumes.

Chosen Sotokufu (Government-General of Chosen), *Chosen Shi* (History of Korea, in Japanese), Seoul, 1931–1938, 35 volumes.

Kim, Kyongmun (compiler, 1720), *Tongmun Guanji* (Records of the Office of Interpreters, or Foreign Office, in Korean), Seoul, 1881, 12 books in 6 volumes. Abridged edition published by the Council on Korean History, Government-General of Chosen, 1913, 1 volume.

Kukcho Pogam (National History of Korea, in Korean), Seoul, 1908, 90 books in 28 volumes.

Oda Sensei Shoju Kinen Chosen Ronshu (Collection of Essays

Concerning Korea, Commemorating Professor Oda, in Japanese), Seoul, 1934.

Tongguk Munhon Pigo (Official Korean Encyclopedia, in Korean), compiled in compliance with the request of King Yongjo (1725–1777). Revised and enlarged edition published at the request of King Kojong, 1864–1907, 250 books in 50 volumes.

Yijo Sillok (The Yi Dynasty Annals, in Korean), 1392–1864. Reproduced by photo-offset by the Government-General of Chosen and Keijo (Seoul) Imperial University, 1930–1934, 864 volumes. Also see G. M. McCune, "The Yi Dynasty Annals of Korea," *Transactions of the Korea Branch of the Royal Asiatic Society*, Seoul, 1938.

b. ENGLISH LANGUAGE COMMENTARIES

Allen, Horace N., *Things Korean*, New York, Revell, 1908, 256 pp.

———, *A Chronological Index: Some of the Chief Events in the Foreign Intercourse of Korea from the Beginning of the Christian Era to the Twentieth Century*; Supplement for 1901–1902, Seoul, 1901.

Bishop, Isabella L. (Bird) *Korea and Her Neighbors*, London, J. Murray, 1898, 2 vols.

Carles, W. R., *Life in Korea*, London-New York, Macmillan, 1888, 317 pp.

Carnegie Endowment for International Peace, *Korea: Treaties and Agreements*, Washington, 1921, viii + 68 pp.

Curzon, George N. (Marquis), *Problems of the Far East: Japan, Korea, China*, London, Constable, 1896. Pages 80-165 relate to Korea.

Gale, James S., *Korean Sketches*, New York, Revell, 1898, 256 pp.

Griffis, William E., *Corea: The Hermit Nation*, New York, Scribner's, 1907, 8th edition, 512 pp.

Hamilton, Angus, *Korea*, London, Heinemann, 1904, 315 pp.; 2nd revised edition, Boston-Tokyo, J. B. Millet, 1910, xvi + 326 pp.

Harrington, Fred, *God, Mammon and the Japanese*, Madison, University of Wisconsin Press, 1944, x + 362 pp.

Hulbert, Homer B., *The History of Korea*, Seoul, 1905, 2 volumes.

———, *The Passing of Korea*, New York, Doubleday, Page, 1906, xii + 473 pp.

Longford, J. H., *The Story of Korea*, London, Fisher Unwinn, 1911, vii + 400 pp.

Lowell, Percival, *Chosen: The Land of the Morning Calm*, Boston, Ticknar, 1888, x + 412 pp.

McCune, Geo. M., "The Exchange of Envoys between Korea and Japan during the Tokugawa Period," *Far Eastern Quarterly*, May 1946, pp. 308-25.

Nelson, M. Frederick, *Korea and the Old Orders in Eastern Asia*, Baton Rouge, Louisiana State University Press, 1946, xvi + 326 pp.

Oppert, Ernst, *A Forbidden Land*, London, Sampson Low, Marston, 1880, 349 pp.

Rockhill, William W., *China's Intercourse with Korea from the XVth Century to 1895*, London, Luzac, 1905, 60 pp.

Sands, William Franklin, *Undiplomatic Memories*, New York, Whittlesey House, McGraw-Hill, 1930, 5 + 328 pp.

Underwood, H. G., *The Call of Korea*, New York, Revell, 1908, 204 pp.

Whigham, H. J., *Manchuria and Korea*, London, Isbister, 1904. Pages 176-206 relate to Korea.

Wilkinson, Sir William Henry, *The Corean Government: Constitutional Changes, July 1894 to October 1895, With an Appendix on Subsequent Enactments to 30th June 1896*, Shanghai, 1897, xi + 192 pp.

Japanese Accession to Control

Brown, Arthur Judson, *The Mastery of the Far East: The Story of Korea's Transformation and Japan's Rise to Supremacy in the Far East*, New York, Scribner's, 1919, lx + 671 pp.

Gale, James S., *Korea in Transition*, New York, Eaton and Mains, 1909, 270 pp.

Kassei, Yoshihisa, *Nichi-Kan Gappo Hishi* (The Secret History of the Annexation of Korea, in Japanese), Tokyo, Kokuryukai, 1931, 2 vols.

"Kennan and Korea," *Korea Review*, Vol. 6 (1906), pp. 203-217.

Kennan, George, "The Japanese in Korea," "Korea: a Degenerated State," "The Korean People: the Product of a Decayed Civilization," "What Japan Has Done in Korea," 4 articles, *Outlook*, Vol. 81 (1905), pp. 307-315, 409-416, 609-616, 669-673.

Kida, Sadakichi, *Kankoku no Heigo to Kokushi* (The Annexation of Korea and Its History, in Japanese), Tokyo, Sanshodo, 1910, 182 pp.

McKenzie, F. A., *The Tragedy of Korea*, London, Hodder and Stoughton, 1908, xii + 312 pp.

The Japanese Period

a. OFFICIAL PUBLICATIONS

Chosen Sotokufu (Government-General of Chosen), *Chosen Tetsudoshi* (History of the Railways in Korea, in Japanese), Seoul, 1915.

Residency General in Korea, *Annual Report for 1907 on Reforms and Progress in Korea*, Seoul, 1908, viii + 140 pp.

———, *The Material Progress of Korea for the Last Five Years* (1905–1910), 1910, iv + iii + 52 pp.

———, The Second Annual Report on Reforms and Progress in Korea, Seoul, 1909, vii + 215 pp.

Government-General of Chosen, *Annual Reports on Reforms and Progress in Chosen*, Keijo (Seoul), 1910–1922, and *Annual Reports on the Administration of Chosen*, 1923–1936.

———, *The New Administration of Chosen*, 1921, iv + 26 + xxx pp.

———, *Results of Three Years Administration of Chosen Since Annexation*, January 1914, 66 + 95 pp.

———, *Thriving Chosen*, Keijo (Seoul), 1935, 94 pp.

b. OTHER

Bank of Chosen, *Economic History of Chosen*, Seoul, 1920, 266 pp.

Chosen Keizai Nempo (Korea's Economic Annual, in Japanese), Tokyo, Kaizosha, 1939 and 1940.

Chosen Nenkan (Korea Yearbook, in Japanese), 1941, Seoul, Keijo Nipponsha, October 1940, 734 pp.

Drake, Henry B., *Korea of the Japanese*, London, John Lane, 1930, 225 pp.

Economic Development of Korea and Manchuria, Tokyo-Osaka, Japan Times Publishing Co., 1923, 319 pp.

Fujimoto, Jitsuya, *Sen-Man Oyobi Kita Shina no Sangyo* (Industry in Korea, Manchuria, and North China, in Japanese), 1926.

Grajdanzev, Andrew J., *Modern Korea*, New York, Institute of Pacific Relations and John Day, 1944, x + 330 pp.

Japan and Manchoukuo, 1935–36, Tokyo, Japan Publishing Company, 1936.

Japan-Manchoukuo Yearbook, Tokyo, Japan-Manchoukuo Yearbook Co., 1933–1940.

Japan Yearbook, published by the Foreign Affairs Association of Japan, Tokyo, 1933–1943/44.

Keijo (Seoul) Chamber of Commerce and Industry, *Tokei Nempo* (The Annual Statistical Report, in Japanese), Seoul, 1937, 173 pp.

Keijo Imperial University, *Chosen Keizai no Kenkyu* (Study of Korean Economy, in Japanese) Tokyo, Toko Shoin, 1932, 773 pp.

Kojima, Seiichi, *Sen-man-shi Shinko Keizai* (Rising Economy of Korea, Manchuria, and China, in Japanese), Tokyo, Shunshusha, February 1938, 4 + 400 pp.

Ladd, Geo. Trumbull, *In Korea with Marquis Ito*, New York, Scribner's, 1908, xiii + 477 pp.

Lee, Hoon K., *Land Utilization and Rural Economy in Korea*, Shanghai, Kelly and Walsh Ltd. (Chicago, University of Chicago Press), 1936, xii + 289 pp.

Nasu, Shiroshi, *Aspects of Japanese Agriculture*, New York, Institute of Pacific Relations, 1941 (mimeographed), ix + 168 pp.

Nippon Gakujutsu Shinkokai (Japanese Society for the Advancement of Science), *Chosen Beikoku Keizairon* (Economics of Korean Rice, in Japanese), Tokyo, Iwanami Co., 1937, 147 pp.

Sunoo, Hagwon, "A Study of the Development and Technique of Japanese Imperialism in Korea, 1904–1910," *Korean Review*, Seattle, Korean-American Cultural Association, June 1948, pp. 27-51.

Takahashi, K., *Gendai Chosen Keizairon* (Contemporary Korean Economy, in Japanese), Tokyo, Chigura Co., April 1935, 12 + 593 pp.

U.S. Department of Agriculture (for Army Service Forces), *Civil Affairs Handbook, Korea, Section 7: Agriculture* (no others published), Washington, Army Service Forces, 1944.

The National Independence Movement

Baird, Annie L., *Daybreak in Korea: A Tale of Transformation in the Far East,* New York, Revell Co., 1909, 124 pp.

Brown, Arthur Judson, *The Korean Conspiracy Case,* New York, 1912, 27 pp.

Chung, Henry, *The Case of Korea,* New York, Revell, 1921, 367 pp.

Cynn, Hugh Heung-wo, *The Rebirth of Korea,* New York, Abingdon Press, 1920, 272 pp.

Federal Council of Churches of Christ in America, *The Korean Situation: Authentic Accounts of Recent Events by Eye Witnesses,* New York, 1919?, 125 pp.

Japan Chronicle, *The Korean Conspiracy Trial: Full Report* . . . , Kobe, Japan, 1913, 309 pp.

Kim, San (pseud.) and Nym Wales, *Song of Ariran: the Life Story of a Korean Rebel,* New York, John Day, 1941, xxvi + 258 pp.

Korean-American Council, *Korean Liberty Conference* (collection of addresses), Washington, 1942, 103 pp.

McKenzie, F. A., *Korea's Fight for Freedom,* London, Simpkin, Marshall Co., 1920, 320 pp.

Oliver, Robert T., *Korea: Forgotten Nation,* with an introduction by Syngman Rhee, Washington, Public Affairs Press, 1944, 138 pp.

Pak, Unsik, *Han'guk Tongnip Undong-sa* (History of the Korean Independence Movement, in Korean), Shanghai, Sonusa, 1922, 236 pp.

Wales, Nym, "Rebel Korea," *Pacific Affairs,* March 1942, pp. 25-43. Reprinted in, Korean-American Cultural Association, *The Culture of Korea,* pp. 235-254.

III. PUBLICATIONS SINCE 1945

Official Publications *

a. NORTH KOREAN PEOPLE'S COMMITTEE

Propaganda Department, *Inmin Winŏn-hoe Taehoe Chungyo Munhŏnjip* (Important Acts of the Assembly of the People's Committee of North Korea), Pyŏngyang, Korea, April 1947.

b. SOVIET UNION

Ministry of Foreign Affairs, *The Soviet Union and the Korean Question*, Moscow, 1948, 84 pp.

c. UNITED NATIONS

Department of Information, *United Nations Bulletin:*
"Assembly Endorses Korean Government," January 1, 1949, pp. 46-48;
"Committee Approves Korean Commission," November 11, 1947, pp. 635-638;
"Divided Korea: a Grim Reality," November 15, 1948, pp. 921-922;
"The Mission to Korea," August 1, 1948, pp. 613-615.

General Assembly Official Records, Third Session, Supplement No. 9, *First Report of the United Nations Temporary Commission on Korea*, Lake Success, 1948, Volume I, Document A/575, 47 pp. (same mimeographed as Document A/AC. 19/80, 66 pp.); Volume II, Document A/575, Add. 1, Annexes I-VIII, 99 pp.; Volume III, Document A/575, Add. 2, Annexes IX-XII, 304 pp.

———, *Second Part of the Report . . .*, Paris, 1948, Volume I, Document A/575/Add. 3, 14 pp. (same mimeographed as Document A/AC.18/80/Add. 1, 31 pp.); Volume II, Document A/575/Add. 4, Annexes I-VII, 38 pp.

———, Fourth Session, Supplement No. 9, *Report of the United Nations Commission on Korea*, Lake Success, 1949, Volume

* For further documentary references see Appendix A.

I, Document A/936, 34 pp.; Volume II, Annexes, Document A/936/, Add. 1, 62 pp.

d. UNITED STATES

Department of the Army, *Report on the Economic Position of Japan and Korea and the Measures Required to Improve Them*, April 1948 (mimeographed), 22 pp. The "Johnston Committee" report.

Department of State, *Korea, 1945 to 1948*, Far Eastern Series 28, October 1948, 124 pp.

———, *Korea's Independence*, Far Eastern Series 18, October 1947, 60 pp.

———, *Korea's Independence: Current Developments*, March 1948, 13 pp.

———, *Foreign Affairs Background Summary on Korea*, August 1947, 44 pp.

———, *Problems of Greece, Korea, and Palestine*, International Organization Series III, 26, February 1949, 65 pp.

——— and the Economic Cooperation Administration, *Economic Aid to the Republic of Korea, ECA Recovery Program for Fiscal Year 1950*, June 1949, 48 pp.

———, and the Economic Cooperation Administration, *The Economy of South Korea: Basic Survey*, May 1949, 44 pp.

———, *Joint ECA-State Department Semi-Annual Report on Korea, January-June 1949*, prepared by the American Mission in Korea, Seoul, September 7, 1949 (mimeographed), 31 pp.

Department of State Bulletin:

Acheson, Acting Secy. Dean, "U.S. Policy in Korea," October 13, 1946, p. 670. Statement to the press.

Cassidy, Velma Hastings, "American Policy in Occupied Areas," August 18, 1946, pp. 291-296, *passim*.

Dulles, John Foster, "United States Urges Continuation of Temporary Commission on Korea," December 19, 1948, pp. 756-760. Statement before the United Nations.

Hildring, Asst. Secy. of State John H., "Korea: House Divided," March 23, 1947, pp. 544-547. Address delivered before the Economics Club of Detroit.

"Korea and the Far East," January 28, 1946. NBC broadcast of January 19, 1946; participants: John Carter Vincent, Edwin M. Martin, and Col. Brainard E. Prescott.

Pauley, Ambassador Edwin W., "Survey of Resources in Manchuria and Korea . . . ," August 4, 1946, p. 233.

"U.S. Objectives in Policy toward Korea," September 8, 1946, p. 462.

Department of State, Korean Economic Mission, *Land Reform in Korea,* Seoul, September 13, 1947 (mimeographed).

Department of the Army, Civil Affairs Division, *Educator's Guide to Korea,* by Richard Werth, 1948 (mimeographed), 18 pp.

———, *The Impact of the War and Japanese Imperialism upon the Economic and Political Rehabilitation of Korea,* by Nels W. Stalheim and J. T. Suagee, January 1947 (mimeographed), 44 pp.

———, *Report of the Educational and Informational Survey Mission to Korea,* 1947 (mimeographed).

e. UNITED STATES ARMY MILITARY GOVERNMENT IN KOREA AND REPUBLIC OF KOREA

Department of Agriculture, *Agricultural Production Goals for 1947,* March 1947.

———, *Present Agricultural Position of South Korea,* April 1947, 34 pp.

Department of Public Health and Welfare, Bureau of Vital Statistics, *Population of South Korea by Geographical Divisions and Sex,* September 1946, 70 pp.

Department of Public Information, *Chukan Digest,* weekly gazette published in Seoul; Korean language with English translation; October 18, 1945.

National Economic Board, *Price Developments in South Korea,* September 1947 (mimeographed), 96 pp.

———, *Selected Economic Statistics for South Korea,* April 1947 (mimeographed), 40 pp.

———, *Summation of United States Army Military Government Activities in Korea,* issued monthly, November 1945 through March 1946 issues appended to SCAP (Japan) Summaries. After August 1947 called *South Korean Interim Gov-*

ernment Activities. Published as *Republic of Korea Economic Summation* since September 1948.

———, *Survey of Grain Collection in South Korea*, April 1, 1947 (mimeographed).

Office of the Military Governor, *Ordinances* (numbered), English and Korean texts.

Books

Chung, Henry, *The Russians Came to Korea*, Washington, D.C., and Seoul, 1947, 212 pp.

Friedrichs, Carl J., and associates, *American Experience in Military Government in World War II*, New York, Rinehart, 1948. Chapter XVI by Philip H. Taylor and Donald S. MacDonald deals with South Korea.

Gayn, Mark, *Japan Diary*, New York, Sloan, 1948, 517 pp. Pages 347-443, 490-491, and 505-510 deal with Korea.

Isaacs, Harold R., *No Peace for Asia*, New York, Macmillan, 1947, 295 pp. See especially pp. 81-102.

Lauterbach, Richard E., *Danger from the East*, New York, Harper, 1947, 430 pp. See especially pp. 183-250.

Periodicals

Korean Economic Digest, New York and Los Angeles, Korea Economic Society, ten issues per annum, June 1944–February 1946. Superseded by *Korea Digest*, a publication of the Korean Chamber of Commerce in America, Los Angeles, May 1946–July 1946.

Korean Commerce and Industry replaced the above publication, November 1946. Succeeded by *Korean Chamber of Commerce Bulletin*, an undated commercial newssheet.

Korean Independence, weekly newspaper published in Los Angeles, Calif. Represents the left-wing Korean groups in America and on its English language page prints translations from left-wing groups in Korea.

Korean Review. Published semi-annually by the Korean-American Cultural Association, Wash., D.C., June 1948—.

Monthly Statistical Review, Seoul, Chosun Bank, articles in Korean and English.

The New Korea, weekly newspaper published by the Korean

National Association, Los Angeles, Calif. English language page was discontinued in January 1947.

Seoul Times, English language daily published in Seoul.

Seoul Union Democrat, English language daily published in Seoul.

The Voice of Korea, bi-weekly publication of the Korean Affairs Institute, Washington, D.C. Contains numerous signed articles and reproduces much of the official documentation on Korean affairs.

Articles

a. GENERAL ARTICLES

Bailey, Sidney D., "Korea: Cockpit of the Far East," *London Quarterly of World Affairs*, July 1946, pp. 142-155.

Baldwin, Roger N., "Blunder in Korea," *Nation*, August 2, 1947, pp. 119-121.

Bertsch, Leonard M., "Korean Partition Prevents Economic Recovery," *Foreign Policy Bulletin*, January 28, 1949.

Borton, Hugh, "Occupation Policies in Japan and Korea," *Annals of the American Academy of Political and Social Science*, January 1948, pp. 146-155.

Brinton, J. P., III, "Small Korea Is a Big Test," *New Republic*, March 14, 1949, pp. 19-21.

Bristol, Horace, and Martin, Robert P., "Korea: The Country Nobody Knows," *'48*, April 1948, pp. 42-56.

Butler, Sir Paul, "A Korean Survey," *International Affairs*, July 1946, pp. 361-375.

Deane, Hugh, "Economic Deterioration in South Korea," *China Weekly Review*, October 30, 1948, p. 233.

———, 'South Korea's New Premier," *China Weekly Review*, October 2, 1948, p. 113.

Dull, Paul S., "South Korean Constitution," *Far Eastern Survey*, September 8, 1948, pp. 205-207.

Fisher, J. Earnest, "Korea Today," *Far Eastern Quarterly*, May 1946, pp. 261-271.

Gayn, Mark, "Cold War: Two Police States in Korea," *New Republic*, September 15, 1948, pp. 15-16.

Grajdanzev, Andrew J., "Korea Divided," *Far Eastern Survey*, October 10, 1945, pp. 281-283.

Guins, George C., "Korean Plans of Russian Imperialism," *The American Journal of Economics and Sociology*, October 1946, pp. 71-86.

Gull, E. M., "Chinese Views on Japan and Korea," *The Asiatic Review*, January 1948, pp. 101-106.

Hamlin, Will (pseud.), "Korea: An American Tragedy," *Nation*, March 1, 1947, pp. 245-247.

Henning, Charles N., "Korea's Foreign Trade," *Foreign Commerce Weekly*, Washington, U.S. Department of Commerce, November 17, 1945, pp. 7-9.

Hodge, Lt. Gen. John R., "With the U.S. Army in Korea," *National Geographic Magazine*, June 1947, pp. 829-840.

Kang, Yonghill, "How It Feels to be a Korean in Korea," *United Nations World*, May 1948, pp. 18-21.

Kaukinen, J. L., "The South Korean Wage Earner Since Liberation," *Monthly Labor Review*, April 1949, pp. 401-406.

Kehoe, Monica, "Higher Education in Korea," *Far Eastern Quarterly*, February 1949, pp. 184-186.

———, Monica, "Report from Korea," *Common Ground*, Winter 1949, pp. 10-16.

Kim, Yongjeung, "The Cold War: The Korean Elections," *Far Eastern Survey*, May 5, 1948, pp. 101-102.

———, "Korea in Crisis," *Eastern World*, December 1947, pp. 14-15.

"Korea: The U.S. Gets to Work," *Fortune*, June 1947, pp. 98-103.

Lauterbach, Richard E., "Hodge's Korea," *Virginia Quarterly Review*, June 1947, pp. 349-368.

Lerch, Maj. Gen. Archer L., "Expediency Decision to Divide Korea Created 90% of Troubles," *Commonwealth* (Club), San Francisco, August 18, 1947, p. 162.

Liem, Channing, "United States Rule in Korea," *Far Eastern Survey*, April 6, 1949, pp. 77-80.

Limb, Ben C., "The U.N. in Korea," *China Monthly*, March 1948, pp. 81-83.

McCune, George M., "The Essential Unity of the Korean Economy," *Korean Economic Digest*, January 1946, pp. 3-8.

———, "Korea: The First Year of Liberation," *Pacific Affairs*, March 1947, pp. 3-17.

———, "The Korean Situation," *Far Eastern Survey*, September 8, 1948, pp. 197-202.

———, *Korea's Postwar Political Problems*, New York, Institute of Pacific Relations, Tenth Conference Secretariat Paper No. 2, September 1947 (mimeographed), 56 pp.

———, "The Occupation of Korea," *Foreign Policy Reports*, October 15, 1947, pp. 186-196.

———, "Occupation Politics in Korea," *Far Eastern Survey*, February 13, 1946, pp. 33-37.

———, "Postwar Government and Politics of Korea," *Journal of Politics*, November 1947, pp. 605-623.

McCune, Shannon, "Land Reform in Korea," *Far Eastern Survey*, January 28, 1948, pp. 13-18; further notes, *loc. cit.*, June 2, 1948, p. 132.

———, "Physical Basis for Korean Boundaries," *Far Eastern Quarterly*, May 1946, pp. 272-278.

———, "The Thirty-Eighth Parallel in Korea," *World Politics*, January 1949, pp. 223-232.

Mitchell, Clyde, "Korean Farm Tenant Purchase Program," *Land Economics*, November 1948, p. 105.

———, "Land Reform in South Korea," *Pacific Affairs*, June 1949, pp. 144-154.

Noble, Glenn A., "Science Education in Korea," *Science*, January 9, 1948, pp. 31-32.

Noble, Harold J., "Our Most Dangerous Boundary," *Saturday Evening Post*, August 31, 1946, pp. 20-21 *et seq.*

Oliver, Robert T., "Korea's President," *Eastern World*, June–July 1948, pp. 7-8.

———, "The Korean Election," *Far Eastern Survey*, June 2, 1948, pp. 131-132.

———, "The Republic of Korea Looks Ahead," *Current History*, September and October 1948, pp. 156-161, 218-221.

———, "The Tragedy of Korea," *World Affairs*, Spring 1947, pp. 27-34.

Olmsted, D. L., "Korea: Experiment in Hypocrisy," *Korean Independence*, serially, July 17 to September 4, 1946, six installments.

Ray, J. Franklin, Jr., "Unfinished Business in Korea," *The Educational Record*, January 1948, pp. 36-49.

Rosinger, Lawrence K., "Future of Korea Hinges on U.S.-

Soviet Relations," *Foreign Policy Bulletin*, November 16, 1945.

Sarafan, Bertram D., *Far Eastern* Survey, November 20, 1946, pp. 349-352.

Shoemaker, James, *Notes on Korea's Postwar Economic Position*, New York, Institute of Pacific Relations, Tenth Conference, Secretariat Paper No. 4, September 1947 (mimeographed), 29 pp.

Snow, Edgar, "We Meet Russia in Korea," *Saturday Evening Post*, pp. 18-19 *et seq.*

"Southern Korea under U.S. Military Government," *Foreign Commerce Weekly*, March 9, 1946, pp. 6-9.

Strong, Anna Louise, "Korea: The Two Zones," *Soviet Russia Today*, December 1948, p. 14 *et seq.*

———, "First Report from North Korea," "Land Reform in North Korea," "Industrial Workers in North Korea," *Soviet Russia Today*, October and November 1947, February 1948, pp. 8-9 *et seq.*, 20-21 *et seq.*, 16-17 *et seq.*

———, "North Korea," *The New Statesman and The Nation*, London, January 17, 1948, p. 47.

Sugg, Harold, "Watch Korea," *Harper's*, January 1947, pp. 38-44.

Sunoo, Hagwon, and Angus, William N., "American Policy in Korea: Two Views," *Far Eastern Survey*, July 31, 1946, pp. 228-231.

Taeuber, Irene B., "The Population Potential of Postwar Korea," *Far Eastern Quarterly*, May 1946, pp. 289-307.

Washburn, John N., "Russia Looks at Northern Korea," *Pacific Affairs*, June 1947, pp. 152-160.

———, "The Soviet Press Views North Korea," *Pacific Affairs*, March 1949, pp. 53-59.

Weems, Benjamin, "Behind the Korean Elections," *Far Eastern Survey*, June 23, 1948, pp. 142-146.

Williams, John Z., "Reorientation of Korea," *Far Eastern Advertiser*, March 1947, pp. 36-39.

b. ARTICLES FROM RUSSIAN SOURCES AND ARTICLES DEALING WITH NORTH KOREA

"The American Democrats Reveal Their True Colors in Korea," *Izvestia*, October 2, 1947. Translation in *Soviet*

Press Translations, Seattle, Far Eastern Institute, University of Washington, December 15, 1947, pp. 290-291.

"Appeal of the Korean Supreme People's Assembly to the Governments of the U.S.A. and the Soviet Union," *Pravda,* September 14, 1948. Translation in *Soviet Press Translations,* November 1, 1948, pp. 581-582.

"Appeal to the Korean People by the United Democratic National Front of North Korea," *Pravda,* February 23, 1948. Translation in *Soviet Press Translations,* April 15, 1948, pp. 229-232.

"Conditions in Northern and Southern Korea," *Trud,* April 8, 1947. Translation in *Soviet Press Translations,* June 14, 1947, p. 37.

"Election Results for the People's Committees of Northern Korea," Tass dispatch, *Izvestia,* November 16, 1946. Translation in *Soviet Press Translations,* December 14, 1946, p. 21.

"Financial Condition in North Korea," *Monthly Statistical Review,* Seoul, Chosun Bank, January 1948, I: 22-33.

Gitovitch, A., "Korean Acquaintances," *Literaturna Gazeta,* February 1947. Translation in *Soviet Press Translations,* May 5, 1947, pp. 9-12.

Goette, John, "Red Yin, Blue Yang," *China Monthly,* November 1946, pp. 1-4.

Ivanov, P., "Elections in Northern Korea," *Pravda,* November 2, 1946. Translation in *Soviet Press Translations,* December 14, 1946, pp. 18-20.

"K Voprosu o Vozobnovlenii Raboty Sovmestnoi Sovetsko-Amerikanskoi Komissii po Koree" (On the Question of Renewing the Joint Soviet-American Commission on Korea), *Pravda,* October 31, 1946.

Kim, Duyong, "Labor Legislation in North Korea," *Amerasia,* May 1947, pp. 156-160. (Translated from the Japaneses periodical *Zenei* of May 1946.)

"The Korean People Welcome the Soviet Government's Decision," *Izvestia,* September 25, 1948. Translation in *Soviet Press Translations,* November 1, 1948, pp. 584-585.

Kovyzhenko, V., "Upswing of the National Economy of Northern Korea," *Izvestia,* January 11, 1949. Translation in *Soviet Press Translations,* February 1, 1949, pp. 68-69.

Lee, Seyoul, "A Picture of North Korea's Industry," *Amerasia*, February 1947, pp. 61-62.

Markov, M., "The Soviet Union and the Korean Question," *New Times* (published by *Trud*, Moscow), December 15, 1948, pp. 7-10.

Moran, R., "The Position of the Korean Pretender," *Izvestia*, December 24, 1946. Translation in *Soviet Press Translations*, March 31, 1947, p. 23.

Noble, Harold J., "North Korean Democracy: Russian Style," *The New Leader*, May 1947, Section 2, pp. 2-12.

Osipenko, N., "American Policy in Korea," *New Times*, May 1, 1947, pp. 27-29.

Perlin, V., "On Both Sides of the Thirty-Eighth Parallel," *Trud*, August 20, 1947. Translation in *Soviet Press Translations*, November 1, 1947, pp. 191-193.

Protsenko, N., "Letter from Phyongyang," *New Times*, August 6, 1947, pp. 15-18.

"Resolution Passed by the Joint Conference of Representatives of Northern and Southern Korea Concerning the Political Situation in Korea," *Pravda*, April 28, 1948. Translation in *Soviet Press Translations*, June 1, 1948, pp. 346-347.

"Results of the Convention of People's Committees of Northern Korea," Tass dispatch, *Izvestia*, March 5, 1947. Translation in *Soviet Press Translations*, May 15, 1947, pp. 13-14.

"Session of the Supreme People's Assembly of Korea," *Pravda*, February 5, 1949. Translation in *Soviet Press Translations*, April 1, 1949, pp. 203-205.

"A Significant Event in the History of the Korean People," *Izvestia*, September 25, 1948. Translation in *Soviet Press Translations*, November 1, 1948, pp. 582-584.

Smolensky, V., "The Situation in Korea," *Pravda*, November 16, 1946. Translation in *Soviet Press Translations*, March 15, 1947, pp. 8-11.

"The Soviet Union and Korea," *New Times*, October 20, 1948, pp. 4-5.

Tralim, Hankum, "Land Reform in North Korea," *Amerasia*, February 1947, pp. 55-60. (Translated from the Japanese periodical *Zenei* of May 1946.)

Viktorov, Y., "The Situation in the Joint Soviet-American

Commission on Korea," *Pravda*, September 1, 1947. Translation in *Soviet Press Translations*, October 1, 1947, pp. 123-127.
Volochayevsky, A., "In South Korea, Travel Notes," *New Times*, August 18, 1948, pp. 18-22.

Index

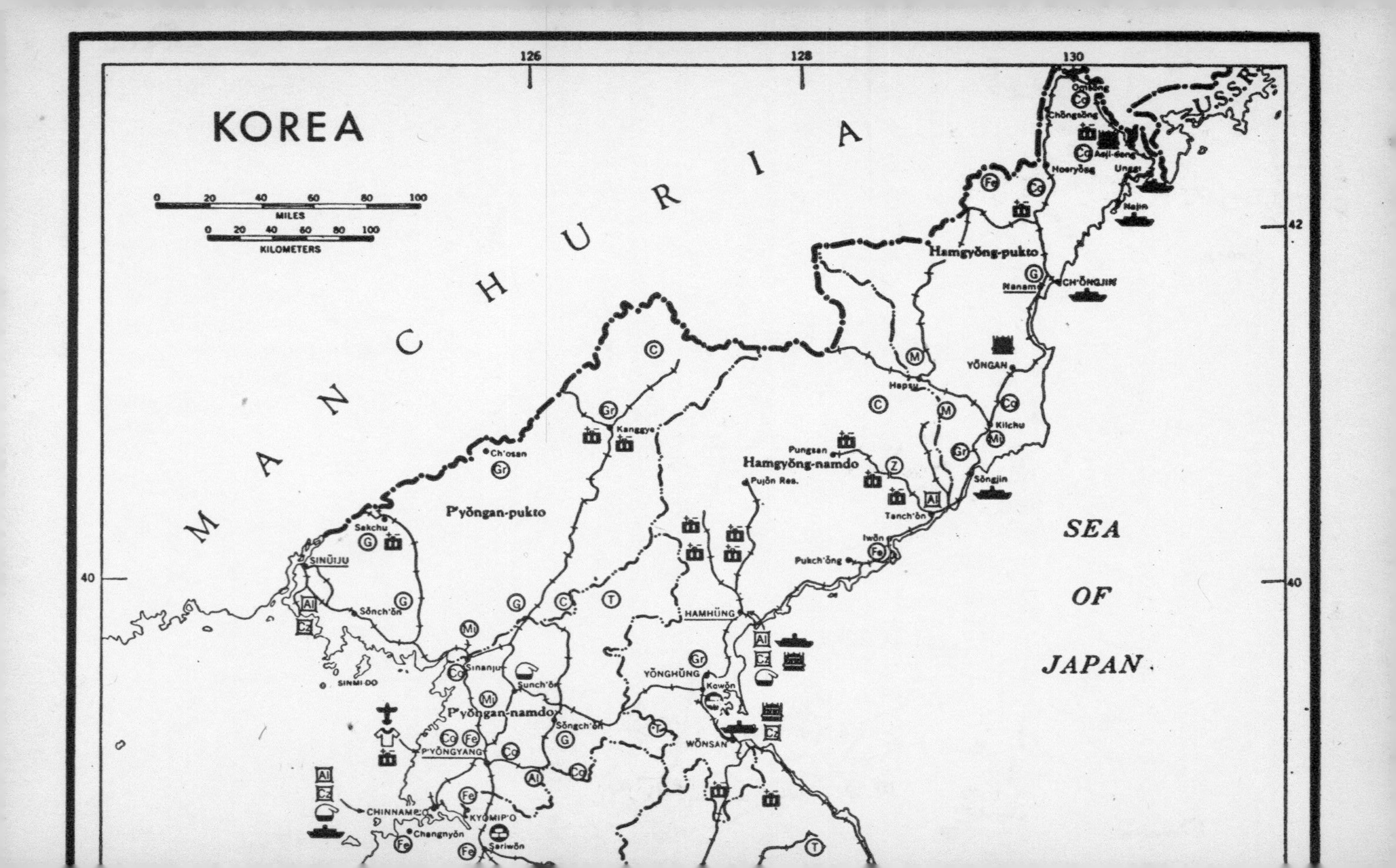
KOREA
MILES
0 20 40 60 80 100
KILOMETERS
0 20 40 60 80 100
126
128
130
42
40
MANCHURIA
U.S.S.R.
SEA OF JAPAN
Hamgyŏng-pukto
Hamgyŏng-namdo
P'yŏngan-pukto
P'yŏngan-namdo
Chŏngsŏng
Hoeryŏng
Unggi
Najin
CH'ŎNGJIN
Nanam
YŎNGAN
Hapsu
Kilchu
Sŏngjin
Pungsan
Pujŏn Res.
Tanch'ŏn
Iwŏn
Pukch'ŏng
Kanggye
Ch'osan
Sakchu
SINŬIJU
Sŏnch'ŏn
SINMI-DO
Sinanju
Sunch'ŏn
Sŏngch'ŏn
HAMHŬNG
YŎNGHŬNG
Kowŏn
WŎNSAN
P'YŎNGYANG
CHINNAMP'O
KYŎMIP'O
Chaeryŏng
Sariwŏn